IRELAND AND THE IRISH

The New French Revolution (The New France)
A Tale of Five Cities
France in the 1980s
Rural France
The South of France
Germany and the Germans
France Today
Writers' France
The Shell Guide to Germany
Cultural Atlas of France

IRELAND
AND THE IRISH

Portrait of a Changing Society

John Ardagh

HAMISH HAMILTON · LONDON

HAMISH HAMILTON LTD
Published by the Penguin Group
Penguin Books Ltd, 27 Wrights Lane, London W8 5TZ, England
Penguin Books USA Inc., 375 Hudson Street, New York, New York 10014, USA
Penguin Books Australia Ltd, Ringwood, Victoria, Australia
Penguin Books Canada Ltd, 10 Alcorn Avenue, Toronto, Ontario, Canada M4V 3B2
Penguin Books (NZ) Ltd, 182–190 Wairau Road, Auckland 10, New Zealand

Penguin Books Ltd, Registered Offices: Harmondsworth, Middlesex, England

First published 1994
3 5 7 9 10 8 6 4 2

Typeset by Datix International Limited, Bungay, Suffolk
Printed in the United States of America
Filmset in 12/14 pt Monophoto Bembo

A CIP catalogue record for this book is available from the British Library

ISBN 0–241–13275–4

To my beloved wife, Katinka

CONTENTS

Contents

MAPS

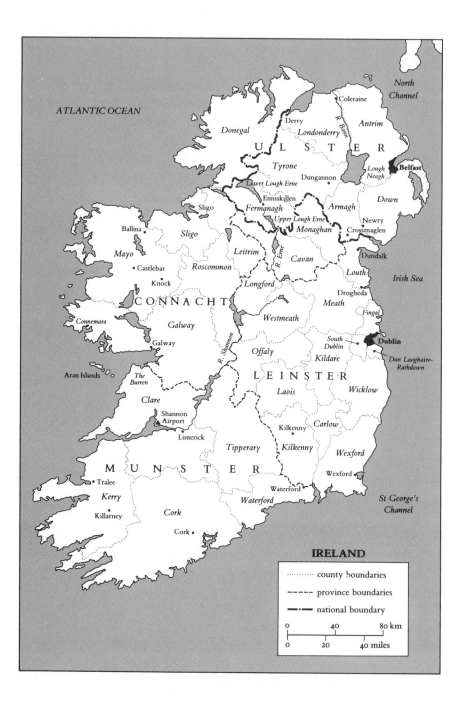

ATLANTIC OCEAN

North
Channel

Coleraine

Derry

Londonderry

Antrim

U L S T E R

R. Bann

Donegal

Tyrone

Dungannon

Lough
Neagh

Belfast

Lower Lough Erne

Enniskillen

Fermanagh

Armagh

Down

Sligo

Upper Lough Erne

Monaghan

Newry

Crossmaglen

Ballina

Sligo

Leitrim

R. Erne

Cavan

Dundalk

Mayo

Roscommon

Louth

Irish Sea

Castlebar

Longford

Drogheda

Knock

C O N N A C H T

Westmeath

Meath

Fingal

Connemara

Galway

R. Shannon

Offaly

South
Dublin

Dublin

Galway

Kildare

Dun Laoghaire-
Rathdown

Aran Islands

The
Burren

L E I N S T E R

Clare

Laois

Wicklow

Shannon
Airport

Kilkenny

Carlow

Limerick

Tipperary

Kilkenny

Wexford

M U N S T E R

Wexford

Tralee

Waterford

Kerry

Waterford

St George's
Channel

Killarney

Cork

Cork

IRELAND

.... county boundaries

– – – – province boundaries

–·–·– national boundary

| 0 | 40 | 80 km |
| 0 | 20 | 40 miles |

PREFACE

Like my Penguin books *France Today* and *Germany and the Germans*, this one is primarily a study of society – of the remarkable social, economic and cultural changes that have swept over the Republic of Ireland in the past fifty years.

Let me say what this book is not. It is not a work of history, though Chapter 2 does include a brief scene-setting historical survey. It is not a study of the Irish character, though the vexed question of the Irish identity does recur, as in so many an Irish conversation. It is not a book about foreign policy; nor is politics its main focus, though I do briefly analyse the political system and culture. And although there is one long chapter on life amid the Troubles in the North, my book is foremost a study of the Republic – not of the political issue of the North's constitutional future.

For my field research, I spent much time in Ireland in 1991–3, and I went almost everywhere – from the small farms of Mayo to the slums of North Dublin, from the peaceful mansions of the Anglo-Irish gentry (such as remain) to the less peaceful 'peace lines' of West Belfast. Using the techniques of the journalist, I interviewed hundreds high and low, including President Mary Robinson, Gay Byrne, the king of Irish television, and Dr Éamonn Casey, ex-Bishop of Galway, whom I met soon before the scandal that drove him into exile. Everywhere I encountered the familiar Irish warmth, wit, helpfulness and volubility. My acknowledgements are on page 450.

I was happy to explore a country where, as my name implies, my roots lie – on my father's side: his father emigrated from Co.

Waterford in the 1880s, as a young doctor, and settled in England. But although I am thus a product of the great Irish diaspora, I am English born and bred, and this book is written from an English perspective. I am frankly critical of many aspects of modern Ireland and the Irish persona: but these are much the same as the criticisms that many liberal-minded Irish make themselves, such as the columnists of the *Irish Times* – the Irish can be extremely harsh about their own country, while still feeling a proud and loving loyalty. Like them, I criticize with empathy. As the French say, *qui aime bien châtie bien.*

As for the North, despite the Troubles I liked the place much more than I had expected. I warmed to its friendly, resilient, down-to-earth people, of both communities. I even enjoyed their nasally melodic accent – 'Och, man, it's the Twailfth!' – which John Cole of the BBC made so familiar to British viewers. And believe it or not, in many ways I preferred Belfast to Dublin, and I met other non-Irish who felt the same way. Dublin's laid-back charms I found somewhat overrated; Belfast may be no beauty, but it has character and culture, and a terrific robustness and energy, in part a response to the challenge it faces. My chapter on the North seeks to give some picture of how its people have tried to continue normal daily life under the abnormality of the Troubles, and of the constant efforts by individuals and by the Government to bring the two sides closer: but I have dealt little with the political negotiations for a solution.

In the Republic, I was struck by how little the struggle in the North impinges on people's lives, and how little they talk about it, though of course they feel disturbed by it. Most southern Irish may vaguely desire a united Ireland, but they are in no hurry for it. So here lies the paradox. Ireland is really one country, in my view, and it is in the logic of history that it will be reunited one day; but in the meantime, there is surprisingly little contact between its two parts, except maybe in border areas and in some intellectual circles. At present, South and North are two separate entities, and that is how this book treats them.

★

Europe – what's in a name? Quite a lot, for it can cause confusion. It was originally called the European Economic Community (EEC); 'Common Market' was never more than a nickname, generally used pejoratively. It was then called the European Community (EC), but since the ratification of the Maastricht Treaty in November 1993 it has become the European Union (EU). In this book, I use the term EU when referring to the present, EC when referring to the past.

The money figures given in £s are in Irish punts (pounds), not in sterling. In summer 1994 the punt was roughly at parity with the £ sterling and Ir£0·67 to the US dollar.

1

INTRODUCTION

Ireland has always been a special case. This green and beautiful island, with its talented, eloquent and wayward people, has frequently aroused strong feelings among foreigners – of romantic affection or plain exasperation. And the Irish themselves have always felt an exceptional patriotism. Like the Jews, they have a huge diaspora. And apart from the Jews there are few other peoples in the West with so strong a sense of their own identity, even uniqueness. Yet the Jews have much more ethnic and religious justification for feeling so special: in the case of the Irish, they are one among several Celtic nations and many Catholic ones. So why feel so unique?

The detached island location, out against the wild Atlantic, certainly explains a lot. Or it may be some mystic streak in the Celtic genes. But above all, across eight centuries the Irish have felt the need to protect their culture and identity against a far more powerful colonizing neighbour, who brought some civilizing benefits but also oppressed them horribly. Even today, after seventy-plus years of freedom, the colonial complex has not yet been entirely digested.

Ireland was for long a very poor country, from which millions emigrated to survive. This gave the Irish special worldwide links with the United States, Canada and Australia, as well as Britain: yet in many ways it remained till recently a curiously enclosed and self-absorbed society. It was still locked in its own internal heroics and wrangles, related to the struggle for freedom, and it expected outsiders to take them as seriously. This drove some Irish émigré writers to scorn. Bernard Shaw was one. Another, Louis

MacNeice, admittedly a Belfast Protestant not typically Irish, kept a wry affection for 'Ireland, my Ireland', and in 1938 he wrote of it memorably: 'I hate your grandiose airs, / Your sob-stuff, your laugh and your swagger, / Your assumption that everyone cares / Who is king of your castle.'

Then in the 1950s the Irish began to modernize their economy, and to change their attitudes; in 1973 they joined the European Community, which has brought a new range of outside links and commitments. Horizons have broadened, prosperity has risen, self-confidence has greatly increased. Today the Irish think of themselves as truly European, and much more than the British they want to be fully part of a Europe that has already given them so much. The old insular self-absorption has declined, all agree: but it is still there, often an irritation for the visitor. These New Europeans are much preoccupied with their Irishness and with what many of them see as the special Irish values, possibly under threat from the modern world they have now entered.

'Over the past forty years, society in Ireland has changed more than in any other country that I know,' says the writer William Trevor. The first big turning-point came in 1959, when that ageing old-fashioned idealist, Éamon de Valera, was replaced as Taoiseach (prime minister) by the modern-minded Seán Lemass: he introduced a policy of economic growth and foreign investment, normal in many other countries but novel for Ireland. After this, prosperity increased rapidly; and though Ireland today is still poorer than the EU average, much of the old back-breaking poverty has gone. New modern industries have arrived, in a country hitherto almost entirely agricultural. On the far Mayo coast where Synge's Playboy impressed the simple farm girls, their great-granddaughters are now working for German or Japanese hi-tech firms. The old romantic West is less isolated than it used to be, and less poor, as the EU pays for new highways, and even priests build international airports. But the West is now being forced to seek a new vocation, through industry, forestry, tourism, for although many small farms have modernized, many are doomed, as Europe's farming faces new changes. Thousands of people have drifted from the rural areas to the towns, and from the West to the East, where Dublin sprawls with new suburbs.

The economic transformation, and the opening out to the modern world, have brought big changes in lifestyles and, more important, in social, moral and family attitudes; it is the same trend as in many other countries, but it has come later, and the impact has been especially dramatic in an Ireland hitherto so enclosed and rigid. Under the de Valera family ethos, women's place was firmly in the home. But more women have now been getting jobs (one is even President), and they have demanded and won the same rights as in other countries – until 1977, a woman on marriage had to resign from a civil service job, but EC membership changed that. In a society so tightly supervised by the Catholic Church, there was till recently no public debate on moral matters such as marital breakdown, incest or suicide, nor on the role of the Church, nor even on the sacred cow of nationalism. All awkward issues were tucked out of sight. But then the impact of television, and other factors, gradually broke these taboos; and today there is a vast non-stop national debate, frank and critical, about all such topics, notably abortion. Steadily the Government has been pushed by liberal public opinion into legalizing birth control, decriminalizing homosexuality, slightly loosening the anti-abortion laws. Now divorce, too, may be finally on the way. The Church has fought a rearguard action against these changes, but its hold over Irish society has been waning steadily; even its control of school education is now losing ground heavily to secular influences. It is true that regular Mass attendance, some 80 per cent, is still uniquely high in Europe. But many churchgoers have in practice ceased to follow the Church's stricter moral dogmas: the stealthy spread of contraception since the 1970s is one reason for the sharp decline in the birth rate, as younger couples abandon the old Irish practice of large families.

The Irish today are torn. Of course, they want to enjoy the fruits of modern material progress. And many of them also want the full personal rights of a modern liberal society; but many others are still warily conservative. Nearly everyone remains against abortion on demand; and at least 40 per cent, perhaps

3

more, are still hostile to the legalizing of divorce, so that by summer 1994 the outcome of the referendum on this, planned for early 1995, was far from sure. These are symptoms of an ongoing struggle between an old Ireland and a new, and between two sets of values – the one upheld by a Church still quite powerful, the other promoted by a liberal lobby that has gained ground in the towns but still represents only a small part of the old rural Ireland. In town and country alike, the Irish have not been finding it easy to adapt to a new kind of society, with new values. Many express the fear that modernism and modern mores are already spoiling something of the old, precious Ireland – certain values that they see as essentially Irish and admired by visitors, too.

And the old Ireland of the tourist brochures? In most ways it is still there for real, for tourists to enjoy. An Ireland of horses galloping along empty beaches, where majestic mountains slope to the sea. A rural Ireland of quiet lakes, green valleys, romantic ruins and not too many people, where the tempo of life is slow and everyone has time for a chat. An Ireland of friendly, unsophisticated people, witty anecdotes, old legends, and music in the pubs; an Ireland where the work ethic does not dominate and the regulations are few, or not rigidly enforced; an Ireland ideal for those who like country life, and especially popular with Germans of a Greenish hue who settle here to escape all they dislike about their own country.

But on top of this idyll a new, different Ireland has been arising – an efficient world of modern industry, and go-getting modern business in the cities. This is fully needed, if Ireland is to prosper in today's world, and if the Irish are ever to move closer to the living standards of their richer neighbours. And the economy itself has been doing rather well, despite recession. But there are black spots; and this former peasant society has been finding it harder than many to come to terms with the special urban problems of the late twentieth century. Unemployment, for several complex reasons, is alarmingly high, over 22 per cent; and with it, petty crime and drugs have increased sharply in some poorer parts of Dublin, among ex-peasant emigrants alienated by the transition from their strict but safe rural world. 'Dublin in the 1980s took to the twentieth century as an aborigine takes to whiskey, as teenagers moved in one hop from lollipops to heroin,' says the young writer Dermot Bolger, who has depicted this world in his epic novel *The Journey Home*. And although the easygoing approach to rule-enforcement may have its charms, for German refugees and others, the obverse is a weak, *laissez-faire*, Irish style of government: Georgian Dublin, for example, suffered fearfully from official planning neglect and the ravages of crude office development, until a conservationist lobby recently managed to rally public opinion and get the damage stopped. Across the lovely countryside, too, there are some new eyesores, for officialdom has been lax in checking the spread of 'bungalow blight', the rash of graceless little white villas built by local farmers and others. Great singers and talkers, the Irish have rather less visual sense, or sense of tidiness.

So has the Irish character been changing, under the impact of social change? One old image that certainly needs to be revised, if indeed it was ever valid, is that of the Irish as violent drunkards. They are now drinking less, and many pubs are doing quite badly; alcohol has risen sharply in price, the Irish are now better educated, and they have other things to do. Similarly, brawling, violence and wife-bashing have diminished; apart from petty crime, this is now a rather gentle country, and the political violence across the border is something else. Relations between the sexes, too, have been changing for the better. Countless Irish writers (mostly men, to their credit, such as William Trevor and Seán O'Faoláin) have described the sad lot of Irishwomen quite recently, nobly enduring the weakness, brutality or emotional inadequacy of Irishmen, those immature mummy's boys. Today relations are more equal, women have gone out and got their rights, even Irish husbands are improving.

Exit, unlamented, the stage Irishman? Not entirely, for behind the clichés various true classic traits persist, many of them highly attractive. The Irish, if one is to generalize, remain superb talkers, funny, literary, musical, great 'crack' (good company) – I have heard it suggested that Irish eloquence was the product of poverty, for words cost nothing and that was the way to woo, impress, get what you want, Synge's Playboy being the archetype. The Irish today remain gregarious, gossipy, often inquisitive, in this small country made up of intense little local units where everyone knows everyone's business. Family life, and social life, still keep a remarkably cosy, intimate quality – even if Ireland is widely said to be a less caring society than it once was. It is a bitchy, yet in its way very tolerant society, in the sense that people of totally opposing views can be quite chummy together and accept each other: in a Dublin suburb, a friend of mine who is keenly 'pro-choice' on the abortion issue introduced me to a neighbour with whom she is on perfectly friendly terms, a leader of the main 'pro-life' movement. Rather as in Italy, there's an obvious charm to this easygoing other side of the coin of Catholic strictness: but it can also embrace a turn-a-blind-eye tolerance of corruption, and that is less pleasant.

'With our temperament and society, we are the Latins of the North – why have we been put up here on this damp island, when we ought to be in the sunny South?' said someone I met. Yet the Irish are not just Italian-style extroverts: they are at the same time moody introverts. As is so often said, their jokey joviality, their love of gregarious fun ('the crack'), may be a cover for a degree of torment and self-doubt, and for the melancholy that is so constant a theme of Irish writing. Their well-known boastfulness, a kind of defence, is waning now that they have more self-confidence and actually more to boast about. But Irish love of hyperbole can still come out endearingly, when they need to assure themselves and you that their small country has the biggest and the mostest. I was told confidently, by serious people: 'Galway is the fastest-growing town in Europe', 'Dublin is the drugs capital of Europe', 'Killybegs, Donegal, is the AIDS capital of Europe', 'the Shannon and Erne, linked by a new canal, form Europe's longest waterway' (the Danube, for a start, is over three times as long), and 'Irish food is Europe's best' (I blinked, but my informant, a leading restaurateur, meant the farm produce, not the cooking). It is the trait that I noted above: the Irish are keen to be part of Europe, but their gaze is mainly at themselves. They know what they think, and they don't want to be confused by the facts.

If the Irish do still have a complex, even sometimes an inferiority one, it is directed essentially at their former colonizers – and understandably so. Personal relations between these two peoples, whether they meet in Ireland or England, are today pretty good. But the Irish do often find the English patronizing – maybe with reason, for it's a common English fault. They are ever on the alert against signs of this, and it can make them touchy. Especially they dislike the tendency of the British media to 'appropriate' Irish success-figures when it suits them, rather as the French do with the Belgians. When the Irishman Richard Harris was named Best Actor at Cannes, the London press rejoiced, 'British actor wins award'; when he got drunk a month later, the headlines ran, 'Irish actor arrested in bar'. This is typical. And the same with Bob Geldof: when he was not yet a big star, the British called him 'the Irish rock singer', but after his Band Aid triumph they called him 'British' – and Mrs Thatcher even said publicly that this Dubliner had 'true British grit'. The Irish were livid. They can also resent what they see as the English tendency to look on Irishness as some amusing parlour trick. When I suggested to the writer Jennifer Johnston, a Dublin-born Protestant who feels very Irish, that maybe the Irish were too obsessed with their Irishness, she said: 'But it's not *our* fault, it's foreigners who play up to it. When I'm at a party in London, people say, "Oh, you're *Irish*, how *fascinating!*" – and then I'm expected to behave like some peforming bear. It's *you* who won't leave our Irishness alone.' I said I was not so sure.

One old saying is, 'The Irish and British get on better with each other than either with anyone else, but they'd both rather die than admit it.' I doubt this is quite true either, but certainly relations have much improved from the old days. The large Irish community in Britain is now much better accepted and respected (see pp. 312–16); and British tourists and residents in Ireland are well liked, even found comically amusing (so long as they do not patronize). However, there is a major distinction to be drawn between friendly Irish feelings towards the British as individuals, and continuing Irish reservations about Britain itself, still coloured by the past. Heinrich Böll, the most anti-Nazi of writers, described in his *Irische Tagebuch* how, when touring Ireland in the 1950s, he was alarmed to find that many Irish felt quite indulgent towards Hitler, with whom they had shared a common enemy. He had to explain that, cruelly though the British had once treated them, Hitler's was a far worse tyranny – something not always realized, he said. Today, forty years later, attitudes have mellowed. But there is still widespread suspicion, even dislike, of British foreign policy, British government (well, we all might agree on that), British officialdom and authority. Hence the Queen could not visit Ireland; and there are many places where even the British Ambassador, ex officio, does not get invited. All this relates less to current events in Ulster (though it's true that the British Army is much hated by nationalists of both North and South) than to the legacy of earlier British rule and the bloodshed of the 1916–21 period. But even here the old passions are now cooling.

It has often been said that the Irish live the present in terms of the past, that elephant-wise they never forget. If this applies to great tragedies such as the Famine or Cromwell's near-genocide, then why should they forget? But the trait seems less noble when it relates to the minor heroics of the period just before independence, and to the farce of the civil war that followed. Yet these events have inspired the so-called national myths that till recently have coloured public life – the glorification of the patriots of the 1916 Easter Rising, and the issue of who fought on which side, and why, in the civil war. The two main political parties were born of these myths and nationalist ideals, which up till the end of the de Valera era in the late 1950s seemed so often to be pulling the Irish away from focusing on the present and the future. But since then even older people have begun to weary of them, while the concerns of the young are elsewhere. In 1966, the fiftieth anniversary of the Rising was still the occasion for proud official celebrations: the seventy-fifth, in 1991, was marked only by a muted, minor ceremony. The shift was due in part to the Troubles in the North, which had begun in 1969: in 1991 it was felt that to honour the patriot gunmen of the Rising might seem like condoning the IRA. But the change was due also to a decline in public enthusiasm. Younger intellectuals, writing in 1991 about their views on Easter 1916, were mostly dismissive: Philip Casey (born 1950) called it 'an act of monumental foolishness', Fintan O'Toole (born 1958) of the *Irish Times* said it had created a befuddling cult of failure.

As for Irish unity and the civil-war myth, it is true that some older Fianna Fáil voters still feel strongly that partition was a wicked betrayal – and this has made it hard for the Reynolds Government to modify the Constitution's claim to rightful owner-ship of the North. It is an example of how the stubborn old myths can endure, as enemies of political realism. And yet, their force is fading. The big parties now depend on them less for their ideo-logies, such as they are. Even in the 1960s, while officialdom was still honouring Pearse's doomed Rising, the real public mood was already changing, as Seán O'Faoláin observed in his book *The Irish* in 1969: 'Time was when common words on every lip in every Irish pub were Partition, The Civil War, The Republic, The Gun. The vocabulary of the mid-fifties and sixties was very different – the Common Market, Planning, Growth Rates, Strikes, Jobs, Educational Opportunities, or why this factory failed or that one flourished.' That is still so. True, there is again plenty of talk nowadays about Partition and The Gun, inevitably. But for most nationalists in the South, the drama in the North is today little more than a tragic irritant, as it is for British opinion; and their prime focus is elsewhere. They are ceasing to live in the past – of which the Troubles are a last, unresolved hangover.

This is not to say that the Irish are ceasing to be patriots. They are as proud as ever to be Irish, and very consciously so. But their patriotism is taking new forms – with less looking backwards, and more looking to contribute their culture and talents to a new outside world, a new future. For many of them, this future is spelt Europe. In fact, 'Europe' has emerged as a new myth to rival the old nationalist ones. Some people proclaim a faith in Europe that recalls France in the heyday of Monnetism – a belief that through European Union the Irish can find their true weight and identity, escaping from the devils of the past and the British bear-hug.

There may be an element here of fantasy and wishful thinking, for in practice nearly all Irish remain strikingly ignorant of other European countries, and culturally they are still heavily focused on the English-speaking world, and on themselves. Yet it may be this sudden new encounter with Europe, this self-reappraisal in face of a new world of which they know little, that is causing their renewed concern with their identity. For some, the challenge is frightening, so they draw inwards. But for others it is exciting. The Irish know that as individuals they are highly popular on the Continent; and that they are gaining a lot from the EU, not only in terms of the annual £1·2 billion of special aid, but through the chance to put relations with Britain on a more equal basis.

Long after gaining independence in 1921, Ireland remained hugely dependent on Britain, which in the 1960s was still taking over 70 per cent of its exports; Britain had bequeathed to the free Ireland its civil-service and legal systems, and much of its culture; and the inevitable emigration still relied chiefly on the British labour market. Many Irish thus felt that the ties were still too unhealthily close, both psychologically and economically. But joining the EC, and other factors, have brought some remedy: Britain's share of the export trade, for instance, has fallen to 34 per cent, while with the rest of the EU it has risen from 7 to 39 per cent. In many ways, Irish reliance on its big neighbour is at its lowest since the twelfth century.

However, at about the same time as EC entry, or earlier, another danger was arising as some Irish saw it – a cultural one, a kind of neocolonialism by the back door. Anglo-American commercial popular culture was spreading, the Irish in their mass were watching either the British TV networks or American soap material – and the sharing of a language with these big nations made Ireland especially vulnerable, compared with, say, a nation like Denmark. Some Irish had no objection to these trends. The young writer Ferdia Mac Anna told me that he was proud of his Irish culture but also deeply fascinated and influenced by American pop culture, and he found the two compatible, indeed complementary. But others have not been so sure. The historian F.S.L. Lyons wrote warningly in 1979: 'Both parts of the island are now so exposed to the dominant Anglo-American culture . . . It could very easily and quickly happen that Anglo-Americanism could extinguish what remains of our local and regional identities.'

Hence the concern of the Irish to preserve their identity by strengthening their own specific Irish culture – even exporting it. Much of the old folk culture has inevitably gone, as the *seanchaí* (storyteller) gives way to television. But Irish traditional music, which in the 1950s seemed in danger of dying out, has since enjoyed an enormous popular revival, as the Irish re-explore their rich heritage. The renewal has even helped to inspire the new wave of Irish rock, pop and folk groups, and singers, who have made such an impact around the world, led by the searing rhythms of U2. It is this worldwide musical triumph, together with the successes abroad of new novels, plays and films (*Dancing at Lughnasa, My Left Foot*, etc.), that has done more than anything to increase Irish cultural confidence. The fears expressed in the 1970s, by Lyons and others, are now heard less often. Of course, Anglo-American pressures remain great: but the Irish now have more faith that they are not merely passive consumers of this fodder, but can also contribute their own culture on the world stage. In proportion to Ireland's size, this contribution is immense.

In other areas of culture, the unique Irish games of hurling and Gaelic football remain hugely popular; but here again there is a 'foreign' challenge, coming from the increasing vogue for soccer (Association football), in which Ireland's own team is now doing remarkably well in world matches. As for the Irish language, that vital component of Irishness, it continues to die out in the remote rural areas of the 'Gaeltacht' (Gaelic entity), but in the cities it is making a modest comeback, as State-backed Irish-language schools become more popular, and as it even becomes chic to talk Irish in some educated circles. But sceptics ask whether it is at all realistic to try to revive this lovely but little-used Celtic tongue, in a modern EU context where the Irish should be doing more to learn foreign languages. The debate is coloured by nationalism. The primacy of the Irish language, written into the Constitution, is one of the key national myths: but does it make sense? The challenge for the Irish today, and this is fundamental to their politics and society, is how to translate an old-style, nostalgic, narrow nationalism into a modern, legitimate pride in their own Irish culture and identity, within a wider European framework. Certainly they are making progress. My own view is that the Irish did great damage to themselves, in the seventeenth to nineteenth centuries, in conniving at the virtual extermination of their own language by the British. Today they would feel more at ease in their Irishness if they still had their own first daily language to protect and champion them, like other small countries from Greece to Finland. But it is too late.

The writer Tim Pat Coogan has spoken provocatively of Ireland having suffered for so long from 'two forms of colonialism' – that of London, and that of Rome. London's is now largely digested and a matter of the past. Rome's is still quite strong, in the sense that the Catholic Church in Ireland is ultra-ultramontane in its subservience to a Vatican that appoints all its senior bishops, taking care to pick orthodox conservatives: Pope John Paul is said to regard Ireland as his last firm bastion in Europe, as much as his native Poland, at a time when in many countries the faith has been receding. He notes that regular Irish attendance at Mass, though gently falling, remains at the uniquely high figure of 82 per cent, in a land where 95 per cent of people are baptized Catholic. And of course a huge number of Irish do still support their Church and derive from it spiritual support and guidance. But others have become more wary. They may still be believing Christians, hence churchgoers: but they have grown critical of a Church that they see as too authoritarian and secretive, too centred on the moral sexual issues. And in their private lives very many young people, older ones too, no longer follow its moral teachings. Hence the obsessive national debate on these issues, as abortion remains outlawed but birth control and homosexual practice are now finally legalized, despite Church opposition. Basic changes in society and the family have fuelled these trends, and with them has come a decline in Church influence over the State. The bishops today interfere in politics much less than forty years ago; and even in education, though religious bodies still own and run most schools, their crucial power base is being eroded as a new secularism gains ground. So Rome's 'colonialism', too, a mixture of loving benevolence and love of power, is in retreat.

These and other changes underlie the much-debated moral crisis in Ireland today. On the positive side, the gains have included huge advances in personal freedom, a breaking of the old taboos of silence, a new openness of public debate, and the end of the puritanical censorship of literature. The changes have exposed much hypocrisy, but are accompanied by a greater moral tolerance: for example, divorce remains illegal, but it is now quite widely accepted socially that someone from a broken marriage can cohabit openly, if 'illicitly', with a new partner (and to end this anomaly, divorce may now be finally on its way).

However, the decline of Church authority has also led to what some commentators today describe as a 'moral vacuum' in society. The Church, although stern and narrow in some of its teachings, did provide a clear moral ethic whose family-based values offered a sense of security to many people. Now there is little to take its place. For as the Church enjoyed a moral monopoly, Ireland has never really developed the alternative found in many other countries, of a liberal, humanist or socialist ethic of civic-cum-personal responsibility. It missed out on the Enlightenment, and in many ways on the influence of the French Revolution (except for the 1798 uprising); the Protestant ethic of the colonizers was never widely accepted and it then departed with them. Thus many Irish today feel bereft, confused.

The Church might not like to hear it, but I find strong parallels with the current situation in Eastern Europe, where the Communists in their way did also provide an ethic, a sense of justice and discipline, and without it people there today feel adrift amid Western consumerism and excess freedom. One difference is that the Communist ethic (widely rejected) was above all collective, while the Catholic ethos centres on individual spiritual salvation. Or rather, the Church has also had a community ethic in Ireland, locally: in the parish, among family and neighbours, there was always a strong sense of local solidarity in rural Ireland. But this has not been properly transplanted to a wider modern secular level. Hence, I suggest, the lack of a dynamic sense of civic responsibility – one reason for the malaise of Ireland today.

Disillusioned Decades: Ireland 1966–87 was the title of the book by Coogan from which I quoted above, while another pundit, Desmond Fennell, wrote in 1983 of a national mood of 'punch-drunk mental confusion'. Indeed, in the past ten or fifteen years it has been fashionable among media folk and intellectuals to bemoan modern Ireland and to detect a malaise in the country. Some of this talk may be exaggerated, an aspect of the volatile Irish tendency to swing from chirpy confidence to depression. Yet the crisis is in many ways real. It has something in common with the crises of late-Thatcherite or Majorite Britain, or indeed of much of Western Europe today; but other causes are more specifically Irish. And while some are moral, linked to the waning of the Church's role, others are socio-economic. The buoyant growth and change of the Lemass era of the 1960s had created a new confidence that spawned the politicians' famous catchphrase 'the rising tide that will lift all boats' – and this mood lasted well into the 1970s. But not all boats have risen. It became clear that economic and social progress did not solve all the old problems, and created new ones. The economy mostly still did well, but erratically; and the 1980s saw renewed high emigration, fast-rising unemployment, and new urban stresses marked by the rise of crime.

What is more, a new consumerist ethos and quick business profits seemed to be germinating a new kind of brash, materialistic, go-getting society, untypical of Ireland. From the 1970s, this was the era of the so-called 'men in the mohair suits' (another clever Coogan phrase) – bright entrepreneurs epitomized by the rise of Charlie Haughey and the Fianna Fáil new wave. In the 1980s, idealism seemed to be giving way to a certain cynicism in public life, amid much talk of the rise of corruption, with much-publicized scandals in 1991. And the successes of the new *nouveau riche* class fuelled the jealousy of the nonentities and the have-nots – the notorious age-old Irish spirit of begrudgery ('The Irish carry from their mother's womb not so much a fanatic heart as a begrudger one,' that expert on the subject, Professor Jo Lee, has written).

The ineffectual political system could be blamed for some of Ireland's problems, and here a contrast could be pointed with France. The Irish in the past years have been following along much the same path of economic, social and moral change as the French, but a decade or two later, and on a more modest scale: sudden industrialization, the exodus from the farms, regional development, town planning, freer speech in the media, the advent of birth control, and much else. One difference is that in France much of the impetus for change, not only economic, came from dynamic State technocrats or government leaders with coherent ideas for reform. In Ireland, with a few exceptions such as the Lemass policy, change has happened piecemeal, under pressure of events or of public opinion, without much real government lead or inspiration. Reform, even when decided on, tends to be painfully slow in application, as if following the familiar slow Irish tempo of life. And often change will happen only when the authorities have finally been pushed and goaded into action by some progressive lobby, as in the efforts to end the desecration of historic Dublin buildings. The ineffectualness and lethargy of government can in part be explained by the lack of clear party platforms; by a clientelist tradition that mortgages politicians to petty local interests; and by over-centralization, for the weakness of town and county councils stultifies local initiative. And why has there never been more pressure for reform of the whole system? Emigration may be a factor, for it has long tended to be the brighter or more enterprising who leave; if they agitate for change they are told, 'If you don't like it here, why not go?' – and the duller or more conservative are left. That always used to be the pattern, but it may now be changing.

Terence Brown has written of the transformations since the late 1950s: 'A small protected agricultural economy opened its markets to the forces of international capitalism, producing three decades of rapid and sometimes bewildering change. A settled, conservative, inward-looking, patriarchal, highly structured society found itself confronted by challenges in almost all spheres – to its sense of uniqueness as life became more and more modelled on the consumerist ideals of the commercially advanced societies around it; to its moral code as consumerism made the pursuit of status and pleasure a kind of national imperative; to its family values, as social disruption and a changing ethos about the role of women in advanced societies placed strains on what were deemed traditional mores.' Or as the Irish film-maker Neil Jordan, now in his forties, put it to me more sharply: 'My parents had a certain idealism, that of the de Valera generation – rather admirable ideals, but their values are not viable any more, they don't apply. We have lost a sense of coherent idealism.' Yet many do still adhere to these old ideals. So Ireland is torn between traditional and modern values, and thus between town and country: the lifestyles and mores of Dublin, at all social levels, tend to be very different from those of the rural West. For example, a poll in 1993 showed that 57 per cent of large farmers were still opposed to divorce reform, but only 28 per cent of urban voters.

De Valera's moral vision was at first built on a certain national consensus, in the 1930s. By the 1950s it was losing its appeal, for economically it had been such a disaster. But what ideal has come next? Politicians such as Lemass have fostered the vision of modern economic progress: but others who have tried to promote a new moral vision – notably Garret FitzGerald with his ideal of pluralism – have generally failed to find the needed consensus, for the country is morally so divided. Yet a growing body of younger people are now looking for a new, modern, liberal Ireland with a coherent ethos, and are seeking a new kind of leadership. They have not yet found much answer from the political parties, trapped in the old political system.

But they did find an important answer outside party politics, when in November 1990 they helped to elect Mary Robinson as Irish President – the first woman to hold that post, the first youngish, modern-minded liberal, and the first President not from Fianna Fáil. It was quite a breakthrough. Robinson, formerly of the Labour Party, was already well known as a radical barrister and senator crusading for human rights. Today as President she has no direct political power: but she serves as a rallying-point and an inspiration for the forces of the new Ireland, and she discreetly encourages them. Her victory was due in part to her opponents' faults: but her final 52 per cent share of the vote was also an indication of how much the Irish mood was changing. It is still too soon to assess the real effect of her election, but it may come to be seen as a turning-point in Irish affairs. A majority of Robinson's voters were women, and very many were young – that impressive new Irish generation, so full of talent, vitality and concern, so impatient with the old myths.

In fact the Irish think of themselves as 'a young country', which today indeed they are: at the 1991 census, 44 per cent of people were under twenty-five, much the highest proportion in the EU. But this figure is declining, owing to a sharp fall in the formerly very high birth rate. This fall is welcomed in economic terms, for in due course it could well alleviate two of the gravest Irish problems, high unemployment and involuntary emigration. But it could also turn Ireland into not so young a country, like almost all others in Europe. The plummeting birth rate, linked to a decline in the number of marriages, marks a major psychological change in society, and is the latest twist in the remarkable saga of Irish demography over the past 150 years.

At the start of the Famine in the 1840s, the island of Ireland, with over eight million people, was one of the most densely populated countries in Europe: today it is the opposite. The Famine deaths, followed by steady emigration ever since, thinned out the population, notably in the South, at a time when in most other countries it was growing fast. Today the Republic is *the* most sparsely inhabited nation of the EU by far: 51 inhabitants per km², Greece coming next with 76. The island's 1841 population of 8·2 million had dropped by 1961 to some 4·3 million, of which 2·8 million were in the Republic – its rock-bottom figure. After this, owing to decreased emigration and a still high birth rate, the population rose again, to reach 3,506,000 at the 1986 census. But now it has levelled off: in the 1986–91 period it even fell again by 17,000, as the declining number of births failed to keep pace with continuing emigration.

The fall in the birth rate seems to have been due above all to the spread of contraception; but also to changing lifestyles and the shift to the towns, as urban dwellers are less dependent on large families than the old peasant ones; and to a growing reluctance to bring up children to face the prospect of emigration or the dole. The downturn began in the late 1960s with the arrival of the pill; it was not much affected by the Pope's *Humanae Vitae* encyclical of 1967, forbidding all birth control; and it continued in the 1970s. After 1979, when the sale of contraceptives became more or less legal, the trend gathered pace, as Ireland followed the pattern of other Catholic countries in Europe, some ten or fifteen years later, and then moved even faster. From 74,388 live births in 1980, the total fell to 51,659 by 1989, but has since bottomed off. The Irish natality rate is now down to just about zero growth, which puts it still slightly above the west European average, for in some countries such as Italy there are now more deaths than births. But for Ireland the change is huge. The percentage of under-25s in the population has already dropped since 1980 from 48 to under 44 per cent. With the under-15s, the Irish figure of 28 per cent remains well above the EU average (18 per cent), but it too is falling quite fast.

And so finally a poorish Catholic nation which cannot find the jobs for its own people has rebelled against the ethic of large families, which for so long has imposed upon so many of them the anguish of emigration. At the same time, marriages have become fewer. The post-Famine phenomenon of widespread celibacy and very late marriage persisted until about the 1950s; then it changed, as Ireland moved towards the European norms of earlier marriage. But since the early 1970s the old Irish practice has reappeared, in a new guise: people now are again marrying later, no longer from economic necessity but of free choice, or they simply cohabit unwed as in other countries. And this affects the birth rate, for most couples delay starting a family until they do decide to marry. The annual tally of marriages has fallen by nearly 40 per cent since 1973 – disturbing to the upholders of Catholic family values.

However, the fall in the birth rate itself is not viewed with the same alarm as in, say, Germany. Economists and others would like the present natality level to move back above zero, but not too far: if the old high birth rate had stayed, the effect on a country with 22 per cent unemployment, and hence on emigration, could have been socially and psychologically disastrous. As it is, the big drop in births since 1980 will soon begin to ease pressures on the labour market – and this is one of the brightest aspects of the long-term economic outlook today.

The Republic of Ireland has come such a very long way in the past fifty years. It is now, in so many ways, a modern society. Apart from unemployment, the economy is quite strongly placed, though it may still take many decades for Ireland to narrow the gap with her richer EU neighbours. It will also take time for the nation to absorb the great social and moral changes that still have it in confused turmoil. And, as society changes further, might it not be in danger of losing what many Irish see as the unique Irish values? The young are less worried by this: they want a modern Ireland, an open Ireland, not an Ireland of the old myths. But even they are torn. So is Ireland to remain a 'special case'? Or, for better or worse, is it finally to enter 'into the great general stream of European culture' (in Seán O'Faoláin's words) after all its long and tormented history?

2

HISTORY AND POLITICS: FROM COLONIALISM TO CLIENTELISM

The old obsessive myths of nationalism may be losing their appeal for a younger generation, yet the Irish today remain more involved with their history than most peoples – witness the large sections devoted to it in the bookshops, and the popularity of plays on Irish historical subjects. Maybe this relates to the Irish concern with their identity, and to their pride in a long saga of resilience and survival, despite the confusion and sometimes absurd heroics.

That pride can date back to the sixth century BC, when Ireland became a Celtic nation with the arrival from Central Europe of the first Celtic settlers. This Celtic Ireland was a cultural entity of its own, with its own language, legal code and social structure, long before the Norman and English colonizers came.

When Europe was smothered by the Dark Ages, the Irish experienced what today they like to call the Golden Age of their history – in the sixth to eighth centuries, when this remote 'island of saints and scholars' had some re-civilizing influence on Continental countries. Unlike them, it was spared the barbarian invasions, and thus was able to build up major Christian monasteries, such as Glendalough in Co. Wicklow, whose remains survive today. They became key centres of culture and learning; and from them monks went out across Europe, St Kilian to Würzburg in Germany, St Columbanus to Bobbio in Italy, and others, helping to rekindle a civilization that was in danger of extinction. This paved the way for the Carolingian intellectual renaissance in France in the ninth century. At the same time, the artists of the Irish monasteries were producing ornate illuminated manuscripts, such as the Book of Kells, now in the library of Trinity College,

Dublin, and elaborate jewellery and ornaments, such as the Ardagh Chalice, now in the National Museum, Dublin. This prowess in the visual arts the Irish have never equalled since. Nor have they ever again made the same remarkable impact on Continental Europe. But today, as the Irish finally draw back closer to it, through the European Union, and ponder on their role in the new Europe, a few intellectuals consider it not too fanciful to suggest that they could still take that Golden Age as their inspiration.

Between these two eras lay some 750 years of Norman and then English colonization. The Normans first arrived in the 1160s, with Henry II of England as their overlord; they dominated much of the country, intermarried with the Irish and established the English system of law and administration. The next centuries were marked by a series of more-or-less brutal assertions of English rule, still alive in the Irish collective mind today. The Tudor monarchs waged military campaigns against the Irish, and began the process of trying to implant Protestantism; but this was never widely successful except in Ulster, where in the seventeenth century land was massively confiscated from the Irish to make way for settlers implanted from Scotland and England, thus sowing the seeds of today's conflict in the North. In the 1640s an Irish rebellion was ruthlessly crushed by Cromwell ('To us, he is like Hitler,' one Irishman told me), and hundreds of thousands died. The Irish attempted a comeback under the Catholic King James II, but in 1690 he was defeated by William of Orange at the battle of the river Boyne, near Drogheda, and this completed the ascendancy of the Protestant minority. Penal laws were enacted against the Catholics: they lost their civic rights and were excluded from public office and many professions, and their Church was outlawed. Some fled to the Continent. These laws were gradually repealed in the years up to 1829, under pressure from the Catholic political leader Daniel O'Connell, still much revered in Ireland today.

There then occurred the worst disaster in Irish history, the Great Famine of 1845–8. At the time, Belfast was flourishing as a fast-growing industrial centre, but Dublin was in decay, and in the rest of Ireland the peasantry lived in poverty. They depended on the potato for their staple diet, but this crop was blighted four years running. Out of a population of over eight million, about one million died of starvation and epidemics of typhus and cholera, and in the next ten years some two million others emigrated in desperation, nearly all to Britain and North America. Ireland was changed, radically. The record of the British Government in coping with this tragedy has been much debated. It imported Indian corn meal, it set up soup kitchens and instituted some relief works, but did not do much else. Cecil Woodham-Smith, whose brilliant book *The Great Hunger* (1962) is a key work on the subject, has written that in the first two years of the famine, 'the Government behaved with considerable generosity ... Not enough was done, considering the size of the catastrophe, but it is doubtful if any Government in Europe, at that time, would have done more.' However, the author charges the Government with cruel *laissez-faire* policies in the latter period of the Famine and afterwards: it 'threw the hordes of wretched destitute on their local Poor [Law] rates, refusing assistance when the second total failure of the potato occurred ... Neither during the famine nor for decades afterwards were any measures of reconstruction or agricultural improvement attempted, and this neglect condemned Ireland to decline.' Many individual landlords also behaved callously, evicting their starving tenants (just a few of them did act more generously). It could be argued that the peasantry were themselves partly to blame, for relying so heavily on the potato, but they had too little experience of how to cultivate other crops.

The Famine left a profound mark on the Irish psychology, discernible to this day. Some analysts say that it produced a kind of inner melancholy and fatalism, different from the earlier, more light-hearted spirit of even the poorest Irish. It may even have had some debilitating effect on a people today seldom known for their energy or enterprise inside Ireland. Above all, it created the tradition of mass emigration which has affected Ireland so deeply. And it intensified the old sense of bitterness against the English. Some of the emigrants even talked of 'genocide', believing that the English had deliberately provoked the Famine. This not true: it was *laissez-faire*, not genocide. And even the *laissez-faire* was not as intentionally callous as it might seem: its proponents feared that interference would simply make matters worse. But as Woodham-Smith has written, 'Between Ireland and England the memory of what was done and endured has lain like a sword.' Today the Irish still talk about the Famine, more than about any other event in their history before 1916.

The later nineteenth century saw the rise of political nationalism and the campaign for independence. It also brought pressures for an agrarian reform that would give some basic rights at last to the small tenant farmers – and here the British Government did respond with concessions. It passed the Land Acts of 1882–1909 (see p. 96) that transferred much ownership of land from the big landlords to the people who worked it. But the Irish fight for Home Rule, led by Charles Stewart Parnell, was not so easily won. Gladstone, then Prime Minister, was sympathetic, accepting that autonomy for Ireland was sooner or later inevitable. But in 1886 and again in 1893 his attempts to push a Home Rule Bill through the British Parliament were defeated by the Conservatives, strongly backed by the alarmed Unionists in Ulster. This served to intensify Irish militant nationalism, and in 1899 Arthur Griffith launched a new party, Sinn Féin ('We ourselves'), which planned to boycott Westminster and set up an independent Irish parliament. On a cultural level, too, nationalism was advancing: in 1884 the Gaelic Athletic Association had been founded to promote the Irish sports of hurling and Gaelic football (see p. 287), and in 1893 the Gaelic League was created to promote the Irish language (see p. 291), while W. B. Yeats, Lady Gregory and others were promoting the national cause through the literary revival. Before long, the Home Rule issue was revived in London. After the Liberals returned to power, the House of Commons in 1912 finally passed a Home Rule Bill, and the loyalists under Sir Edward Carson retorted by threatening to take over Ulster if it were enacted. It was due to come into force in 1914, but on the outbreak of the First World War it was shelved for the duration.

And so the long English occupation of Ireland drew to a close. It had not been a glorious story. England's rule had of course brought some benefits to Ireland, as to other British colonies around the world: among them, the English legal system and methods of civil service, still in place today. But few efforts were made to develop the economy, except in the industrial area around Belfast. The Anglo-Irish landed gentry was allowed to grow rich on the backs of the peasantry. The anti-Catholic penal laws were an outrage. And the rebellions of the unruly, provocative Irish were repaid with excessive brutality. London may have seen the strategic need to guard its back door against incursions by Spanish, French, German or other enemies. But this did not justify the failure to allow a decent autonomy much sooner to Britain's small but proud neighbour.

It could be said that modern Irish history was born at the General Post Office, O'Connell Street, Dublin, on Easter Monday, 1916. On that day, ironically at a time when many Irish soldiers, Catholics included, were away fighting *with* the British in France, an armed uprising was staged against the British, with the aim of forcing their hand on independence. It was the work of two small military groups, the Republican Brotherhood led by Pádraic Pearse, a poet and teacher, and the Citizens' Army led by James Connolly. They seized several key points including the post office, from whose steps Pearse dramatically proclaimed Irish independence. But the revolt was badly planned and carried out, and when the British Army brought in superior fire-power, it was quickly crushed; some 60 rebels, 130 British troops and 300 civilians died in the fighting.

This highly controversial putsch has ever since been officially celebrated in free Ireland as a glorious step on the road to freedom; and in all schoolbooks and a million speeches, Pearse and Connolly have been honoured as great patriots and martyrs. Maybe they were, in a sense, but there was more to it than that. These small autonomous groups were not mandated by the Irish people, and the initial public reaction to them, after the bloodshed, was rather hostile. However, the British then played into their hands by creating martyrs. Martial law was applied, some 2,000 Irish were taken to Britain and interned, and fifteen of the leaders of the revolt, including Pearse and Connolly, were executed after secret courts-martial. This swung the public mood towards them quite dramatically, creating the 'terrible beauty' of which Yeats later wrote. Sinn Féin, which itself had played no part in the revolt, was able to capitalize on this new climate, and in the Westminster general election of December 1918 it won 73 of the 105 Irish seats, eclipsing John Redmond's more moderate Home Rule party. The Sinn Féin MPs rapidly constituted themselves as a national assembly (the Dáil Éireann), in Dublin with the rising star Éamon de Valera as their 'prime minister', and they endorsed Pearse's Proclamation of the Republic.

It could thus be argued that the 1916 uprising, though it failed at the time, did bring the reality of Home Rule closer (as Robert Kee has written in *The Green Flag*). On the other hand, some historians claim that, as Home Rule was about to be granted anyway, the uprising was pointless: together with the Sinn Féin victory, it simply served to envenom British–Irish negotiations, and this led to war. In 1919, with London seemingly dragging its feet over Home Rule, the Irish Republican Army was created from the old Irish Volunteers, and in alliance with Sinn Féin it began guerrilla warfare against the forces of the Crown. The Government responded by banning Sinn Féin as a political body. But IRA violence escalated, and in 1920 Britain brought in the notorious Black and Tan volunteers, who carried out savage reprisals. By late 1920 Ireland was in a virtual state of war, with killings everywhere. For example, on 21 November the IRA murdered twelve officers in their beds, and the British replied by firing into a crowd at a Gaelic football match, killing twelve civilians. In July 1921 a truce was finally agreed. By now London had improved on its original Home Rule offer, and the prime minister, David Lloyd George, knew that the time had come to get rid of the mainly Catholic South more-or-less completely. In talks with Sinn Féin, a Treaty was worked out whereby the 'Twenty-six Counties' of the South would get full dominion status within the Commonwealth, but still remain under allegiance to the Crown. The 'Six Counties' of the North, largely Protestant and loyalist, already had their separate parliament and would remain within the United Kingdom (but possibly with changed boundaries). Neither community in Ireland was entirely happy with this Solomon-like solution, least of all the nationalists, to many of whom partition was anathema. But the Treaty was ratified, and the Irish Free State was born. The issue of partition, and whether it could have been avoided by different tactics, has bedevilled opinion in the South ever since. But at least it seemed clear to many that the Sinn Féin/IRA strategy of violent confrontation had paid off. Southern Ireland was free at last.

Almost immediately, however, civil war broke out: no sooner had the Irish won their independence than they started fighting each other. At stake were two issues of principle: partition, and more especially the decision to keep the oath of allegiance to the Crown. De Valera and many others in Sinn Féin felt strongly that these terms should never have been accepted by those, led by Arthur Griffith and Michael Collins, who had signed the Treaty with Britain. So when the Dáil narrowly ratified the Treaty, de Valera resigned and Griffith took his place. Sinn Féin and the IRA both split down the middle, with many of the more violent hardline IRA elements taking the anti-Treaty side. In June 1922 Ireland held its own first election, which produced a large majority in the Dáil in favour of the Treaty, thus giving Collins and Griffith a democratic sanction. But although they and indeed de Valera himself were anxious to avoid civil war, it seemed inevitable as the IRA grouped into two opposing camps. Heavy fighting began in Dublin and spread across the country, as de Valera joined the anti-Treaty forces in the south-west. Collins was killed in an ambush, Griffith also died suddenly but of natural causes, and William Cosgrave took over as Government leader. But despite these losses, gradually the anti-Treaty republicans were defeated, and in May 1923 de Valera ordered them to lay down arms, which they did. Some 13,000 were taken prisoner, and 77 others had by now been executed by Government forces. It was not a happy start for the new State, and the reasons for the conflict may today seem absurd. But, as many historians have argued, it was not solely a matter of the two issues of partition and the oath to the Crown. Professor Joseph Lee has written in his masterly work, *Ireland 1912–1985*:

'The civil war was fought ostensibly over the Treaty, and particularly the oath. But the Treaty was merely the occasion, not the cause, of the war. The cause was the basic conflict in nationalist doctrine between majority right and divine right. The issue was whether the Irish people had the right to choose their own government ... The clash might have been evaded but for the Treaty, but once the issue surfaced the choice lay between democracy and dictatorship ... In the event the aspiring military dictators were crushed. The mere Irish were not to exchange one jackboot for another. If the civil war illustrated with a vengeance the potential for autocracy lurking in Irish political culture, it illustrated even more emphatically the potential for democracy.' Lee went on to refer to the 'poisonous legacy' bequeathed by the civil war. It was to mark Irish life for many years to come, locking the nation in an outdated quarrel, diverting attention from more urgent modern issues. It has even coloured the philosophies of Ireland's two main political parties: the de Valera faction which has become Fianna Fáil (see pp. 42–3); and the pro-Treaty faction which has become Fine Gael, but in the 1920s under Cosgrave was called Cumann na nGaedheal.

Cosgrave's Government, in the decade after independence, managed to obtain stability after a troubled period, and to curb the violence that was still latent. This was its main achievement. It took over the public administration left by the British, and ran it quite efficiently. But on the entire social and economic front, its record was disappointing. Whereas many new post-colonial governments in the world have embarked on radical policies, sometimes too much so, in Ireland there was virtually no attempt to help the very poor, to develop industry, or to modernize a still backward and inward-looking society. It was as if the nationalist leaders, whether pro- or anti-Treaty, had pushed all their ideals and energies into the struggle for freedom, and had come through without any real social vision for the future, exhausted by two wars.

But matters were not entirely their own fault. British rule had bequeathed them a stagnant rural economy (modern industry was nearly all in the North), and then the sluggish world economy of the 1920s hardly produced the right background for progress. The business class in the South had been largely Protestant, and much of this departed in the Anglo-Irish exodus of the 1920s (see p. 176). Ireland was left with a predominantly rural society of peasant proprietors (in 1926, 61 per cent of people lived outside towns or villages), not exactly the kind to be tempted by liberal or socialist ideas of reform. Over everything there loomed the vast shadow of the Catholic Church, which had won kudos from its role in backing the nationalist cause, and thereby had added to its huge influence over the new Government. The ethos of the country was highly traditionalist, Catholic and rural, with virtually no political opposition to this. Cosgrave and most of his ministers were conservatives, and with Church blessing they pushed through some repressive legislation, strengthening the ban on divorce and installing a puritan censorship (see p. 238). One of their few positive innovations, the bid to revive the Irish language, was inspired by nationalism. And even this failed (see p. 291).

Meanwhile Éamon de Valera, the major Irish political figure of this century (but by no means the best), had been waiting in opposition since his débâcle in the civil war. In 1923–4, although a member of the Dáil, he was held prisoner for a year. His hatred of the oath to the Crown then led him to boycott the Dáil, but in 1927 he took his seat, in order to fight for its abolition. In that year he also left Sinn Féin and launched his own party, Fianna Fáil ('Soldiers of Destiny'), which replaced Sinn Féin as the main opposition. It was more strongly republican than Cumann na nGaedheal (Fine Gael), but less so than Sinn Féin, which later turned its main attention to the North (see p. 357). Fianna Fáil was a curious catch-all of a party (see p. 42), in many ways highly traditionalist yet with a stronger social policy than Cosgrave's party, at least in those early days (de Valera himself, of humble origins, had a true fellow-feeling for the poor). After it won power in the elections of 1932, with de Valera as Taoiseach, Fianna Fáil enacted some social measures that in their Irish context were quite impressive. A modest health-insurance scheme was set up, helping the poor; pensions were introduced for widows and orphans; new low-cost housing was provided, in a country that badly needed it.

On the economy itself, however, de Valera's impact was damaging. This egregious leader was born in New York to an Irish emigrant mother, and a Spanish father whom he never knew; he was then brought up in poverty by his uncle, a farm labourer, in a cottage at Bruree, Co. Limerick. This today is open to visitors; and the village school that he attended is full of mementoes of this tall, patriarchal, de-Gaulle-like figure. For his role in national life, he has sometimes been compared to de Gaulle: but his vision was far narrower. He pursued the arcadian ideal of a self-sufficient rural Ireland, 'satisfied with frugal comfort'; this led to policies that were anti-industrial and highly protectionist (see pp. 69–70), driving Ireland deeper into its backwardness and isolation. De Valera's brand of semi-mystical nationalism proved to be the enemy of modern progress, as Professor Terence Brown of Trinity College has stressed in his brilliant book, *Ireland: A Social and Cultural History 1922–1985*: 'At its most positive the urge towards self-sufficiency reflected a belief in Irish life, in its dignity and potential and in the value of a secure self-confident national identity. That such idealism could only be maintained by ignoring the dismal facts of emigration, economic stagnation, individual inhibition and lack of fulfilling opportunity, was its crippling flaw . . .'

In 1937 de Valera produced a new Constitution, which was passed by referendum; and it remains in force today, along with some later amendments. It reflected de Valera's own values, and those of the Church. It stressed the primacy of the family, it made blasphemy a crime, and it reiterated the ban on divorce. It emphasized the 'special position' of the Catholic Church (see p. 160), but it also recognized the rights of other Churches and religious bodies in Ireland, including 'the Jewish congregations' – an honourable gesture in the Europe of 1937. As to relations with the North and with Britain, its notorious Articles 2 and 3, so much at issue nowadays (see p. 441), formally restated the nationalist doctrine on partition: Dublin had a duty to seek Irish unification, and a right to rule over the whole of Ireland. The new Constitution did away with the oath of allegiance to the Crown; and it created the post of President of Ireland, to which Douglas Hyde, founder of the Gaelic League, was elected. But although it reduced the role of the monarchy in the Free State, it did not yet turn it into a republic. That was to come.

First however came the Second World War, which urgently posed the question of Irish neutrality (again a live issue today, see p. 343). In 1938 Britain had given up its rights under the 1921 Treaty to use two naval bases in the Free State in time of war. This concession was welcomed; and in return de Valera indicated that Ireland would try to stay neutral and not help the Germans. In view of partition, and of earlier history, there was of course little question of Ireland entering the war on the side of its old enemy, as other Commonwealth countries did. What is more, in 1940 Irish leaders reckoned that as Britain seemed likely to be defeated, to join in on her side would be, to say the least, unwise. So it was a mixture of principle and expediency that kept Ireland out. Yet, whatever the dislike of British rule, most Irish recognized that Nazism was something far worse. And after their American friends joined the war, and the Allies' victory grew more probable, so Ireland assisted them in various discreet ways. But the Irish, although spared bombing and invasion, did not have a totally easy time in the war: cut off from most of the outside world, they had to face food shortages and other hardships, during the years of what euphemistically they named 'the Emergency' (they did not like to call it 'the war', for it was not their war). Then in 1949 the first Fine Gael-led Government finally made Ireland into a republic, and took her out of the Commonwealth, too.

The first post-war decade was a bleak period for Ireland. Under an ageing de Valera, Fianna Fáil was growing more conservative, losing even its impetus for social improvement. Isolated from the burgeoning revival elsewhere in the world, the economy continued to stagnate; rural life was poor and archaic; emigration was high; gloom was general. But already beneath the surface, among some farmers, intellectuals, civil servants and others, there were stirrings of demands for change, for a different, more forward-looking policy than de Valera's. And fortunately a new leader was rising up within Fianna Fáil: Seán Lemass. As Taoiseach in 1959–66, he set in train a whole series of events, and did more than anyone else in this century to bring Ireland into the modern world. The Irish in 1921 had gained their political freedom. It was not until the late 1950s that they began to gain other important freedoms – from isolation, poverty, inadequate education, puritan morality. Yet even these advances have not made Ireland a very happy society today.

Today's era: Lemass the innovator, Garret the 'Good', Charlie the 'Bad', and now the Spring tide

Seán Lemass had excellent patriotic credentials. At the age of sixteen he fought in the Easter Rising, then in the civil war on the anti-Treaty side, and was jailed several times. Loyal to de Valera, he held various portfolios, notably as minister of industry, in his Governments between 1932 and 1959. But he was not at all de Valera's brand of nostalgic idealist: he differed from him on industry and economics, of which the old diehard understood little. Lemass was an open-minded man, a pragmatist, described as 'a warm, fatherly figure who smoked a pipe and did not seem to be in love with power'. He was the first Irish leader since 1921 to give old-style nationalism new clothes, recognizing that Ireland's success as a free nation required that it open out to the modern world. In the later 1950s he began listening to the advice of a new wave of civil servants, notably Kenneth Whitaker, who proposed a radical change of policy (see p. 70). This Lemass began to put into practice as Taoiseach after 1959, when de Valera, aged seventy-seven, resigned and was elected President of Ireland, a largely non-political role. A system of *laissez-faire* gave way to one of planned growth; massive foreign investment was encouraged for the first time; protectionism was phased out; and an application was made to join the EC. The results soon became evident, as the economy picked up sharply, and politicians grew euphoric.

Other trends too in the next few years, some spontaneous, some prompted by official action, helped to pull Ireland out of its seclusion and move it closer to West European norms. British television had for some years been viewable in many areas, including Dublin; then in 1962 Ireland's own TV service was created, opening new horizons. Free secondary education for all was introduced in 1967. In the same year the censorship of literature was eased. And in 1973 Ireland was finally able to enter the European Community. This not only created new foreign links, new attitudes, but it greatly reduced Ireland's economic over-dependence on Britain, which in the 1960s was still taking over 70 per cent of its exports (see p. 87).

Lemass retired for health reasons in 1966, and was succeeded as Taoiseach by Jack Lynch, a less inspiring figure; Lynch did however continue Lemass's policies, and it was he who secured Ireland's EC entry, holding a referendum that produced an 83 per cent vote in favour (see p. 327). During the next two decades, Fianna Fáil-led and Fine Gael-led Governments alternated quite frequently; many were coalitions with smaller parties. Fine Gael ('Tribe of Gael') had been formed in 1933 from a merger between Cumann na nGaedheal and a small centre group: it is a party less nationalistic than Fianna Fáil, more middle-class in its appeal, and since the Lemass era it has tended to be the more reform-minded of the two, at least under Garret FitzGerald (see pp. 34 and 43).

After Lynch's Government was defeated in the elections of 1973, a Fine Gael/Labour Party coalition held office for four years, under William Cosgrave's son Liam. It was notable for the emergence of Garret FitzGerald, who performed powerfully as foreign minister, building a very positive role for Ireland in the EC. Then in 1977 Lynch came back to power: but two years later he was ousted from the Fianna Fáil leadership in a coup led by his arch enemy and rival, a certain Charles Haughey, who became Taoiseach in his place. Haughey had already been making a name for himself ever since 1961, as a gifted and forceful minister of justice, agriculture, finance and health. He was anything but an old-style conservative, for in 1979 as minister of health he took the first steps towards legalizing birth control in Ireland (see p. 182), and as minister of finance he introduced the scheme whereby creative artists and writers could live in Ireland tax-free (see p. 237). He was seen as the prototype in Irish politics of a new breed of clever self-made man, ambitious and entrepreneurial. Yet even in his two first short terms as Taoiseach, in 1979–82, his style and methods were soon generating an aura of scandal and intrigue. This was just one of the factors behind the sense of malaise that developed in Ireland at that time and continued through the 1980s – a sense that the promise of the Lemass era had not been fulfilled, and that although the economy continued to do quite well, new, unattractive features were emerging in society.

Like other leaders in that period, Haughey was responsible for serious Government over-spending. Through most of the 1970s and on into the 1980s, this was a fault of both main parties when in power (see p. 72). They were lured by the seductive image of the rising tide, lifting all boats, into supposing that growth would of itself solve all problems; and they were impelled by a populist need to woo voters by pouring money into welfare and social services. So they ran up big public debts. Liam Cosgrave and Lynch were the first to indulge in this spending spree, but others followed. Garret FitzGerald, who became Taoiseach in 1982 after defeating Haughey, was a serious economist who saw the dangers, and at first he made big cut-backs. But even he was later drawn into heavier public spending than he knew was wise.

From late 1982 until early 1987, FitzGerald ruled over a Fine Gael/Labour Party coalition Government, with the young Dick Spring of Labour as his Tánaiste (deputy premier). Known as 'Garret the Good', FitzGerald is one of the most liked and personally admired of modern Irish politicians. He was born in 1926 to a Northern Protestant mother and a father who was foreign minister in Cosgrave's nationalist government – a nice mixture, which fuels his ardent concern that all Ireland should bury its warring tribal past and become an open, pluralist society. He began his career working for Aer Lingus (hence his freaky schoolboyish passion for air timetables), then became an economics lecturer at University College, Dublin, before entering the Dáil in 1969. Tall and curly-headed, he is a true academic, fast-talking and charmingly

33

absent-minded, with an urbane, affable manner, and a breadth of international feeling and knowledge (he speaks perfect French) that is not so common in Dublin politics. Nor, you might say, is his patent political integrity. But as a political tactician, he proved not quite such a paragon.

He and his coalition came to power determined on social reform. They did manage to carry out a few modestly useful measures, such as new housing loans for the poor, and tax allowances for elderly tenants. But there was no major new deal. FitzGerald devoted much effort to the North, negotiating and signing with Margaret Thatcher the important Anglo-Irish Agreement of 1985 (see p. 351). But at home he mishandled two crucial referendums on divorce and abortion (see pp. 196 and 188). And the gaffe of putting VAT on children's shoes and clothing caused such a furore that it helped to bring down his Government. Despite his other qualities, he was not a man with the political flair of Haughey, nor was he a good administrator of his own party. His lack of wheeler-dealing panache, which helped endear him to the public, was his handicap in the tough world of politics. Perhaps history's verdict on him will be that he pointed the Irish down the path, but failed to take them very far along it.

Fianna Fáil then returned to power, for what was to be Haughey's major term as Taoiseach, 1987–92. This was the climax of the Haughey era, warts and all. The two leaders, 'Garret the Good' and 'Charlie the Bad' (or 'The Great National Bastard' as some called him), had a strong mutual antipathy, which lessened only after FitzGerald gave up the Fine Gael leadership in 1987. And they were in total contrast: the liberal bourgeois city intellectual versus the crafty provincial adventurer. One Dublin joke was that if either found a banknote in the street, Haughey would pocket it, whereas FitzGerald would lose it.

Haughey was born in 1925 in Co. Mayo, son of a prominent IRA officer; he studied law at University College, Dublin, and aged twenty-six he married Lemass's daughter. An impeccable Fianna Fáil pedigree! He rose up fast in the party, and as Taoiseach he dominated Irish politics as no one else has done since de Valera. 'The Boss' (another nickname) was an autocrat with great ability to charm, a clever manipulator who commanded strong loyalties, and he divided the Irish for and against him: even his enemies usually found him fascinating.

Haughey's style and ethos may have done harm to Ireland. But on the economic front his actual record in office after 1987 was impressive, and left the economy in fairly strong shape, apart from unemployment. After his damaging over-spending in the early 1980s, this time he changed tune and made some hefty budget cuts, reducing the public debt. Yet he also pushed up growth; and he contained inflation, with the help of wage-restraint agreements worked out with the unions. With his direct man-of-the people approach, he won the confidence of organized labour better than the more élitist FitzGerald had done (see p. 85). Apart from his populism, and his lip-service to nationalism, he carried little ideological baggage but was an astute pragmatist, a tacker-to-the-wind. His policies were often inconsistent, but just as often they succeeded – to the puzzlement of his many critics.

His personal life and values were also a puzzle. He posed as a defender of working-class simplicity, yet he had substantial private wealth, including a Georgian mansion amid 200 acres and a whole island off the Kerry coast: the money was thought to have come from property deals, but he would never explain it. This leader of a Catholic party was publicly known in Dublin to have a regular mistress, a gossip columnist who would slyly hint at their liaison in her articles. Haughey had potent charisma and could be exceedingly generous; he could also be tetchy, abusive and foul-mouthed towards juniors. As for his political style, he was a past master of cronyism and clientelism, Irish-style (see pp. 46–8); and he was clever at cutting corners, hiding his traces by doing deals on the phone with nothing in writing. Some have described him as a typical Mafia boss.

The succession of public scandals that dogged him had begun early in his career. In 1970 he went on trial for gun-running for the IRA in the North: he was acquitted, but some of the mud stuck. In 1982 came the phone-tapping affair: it was alleged that the telephones of two leading liberal journalists had been bugged by Fianna Fáil. Haughey denied any involvement, but his minister for justice was forced to resign. This affair led to strong demands within the party for Haughey to resign as its leader, but he refused. However, in the autumn of 1991 a whole series of potentially more serious scandals emerged, involving several of Haughey's wealthy business friends – Dermot Desmond, Larry Goodman, a baron of the meat trade, and others (see p. 53). Again Haughey denied involvement, and today it is still not clear what his role might have been. But the whole Government seemed implicated, and a nasty whiff of corruption was in the air.

Fianna Fáil were by now very restive, as a growing number of its TDs★ came to regard Haughey as a liability more than an asset. Many of them realized that Mary Robinson's presidential victory, the year before, was a warning that a new national mood was emerging, very different from what Haughey's brand of politics represented. Already there had been several party attempts to oust him: but 'The Great Survivor' (another nickname) had always managed to rally enough support to hold on. Now his position grew worse. On top of the business scandals, in January 1992 the phone-tapping drama resurfaced, when Seán Doherty took his revenge for his earlier dismissal by claiming that The Boss had in fact known all about the tappings all along. The Progressive Democrats (see below), Fianna Fáil's partners in a fragile coalition, now threatened to bring down the Government unless Haughey resigned. So under intense pressure he finally did so. The media got very excited and there was plenty of hype. One mesmerized critic, John Waters, the provocative young *Irish Times* columnist (see p. 62), wrote with tongue only slightly in cheek of the man who turned Irish politics into a soap opera: 'For 25 years the Irish people have been gradually drawn into the personality of Charles J. Haughey, to the point where today – personal relationships apart – we have practically no other means of relating to one another. In the public arena, all life radiated from him . . . Just as *Dallas* would be inconceivable without JR, the drama of modern Ireland is unimaginable without Charles Haughey.'

★ A TD (Teachta Dála) is a deputy of the Dáil, the lower house of the Irish Parliament.

It has to be asked why the Irish allowed themselves to be dominated and enthralled by such a figure, and what this reveals about their public life. They do sometimes show a soft spot for a charming, eloquent rogue, witness *The Playboy of the Western World*; and in Irish politics, personalities tend to matter more than ideas, even principles. But money also matters: electors knew that Haughey was managing the economy efficiently, and for this maybe they forgave him the methods that in other respects were less beneficial. He raised to new heights the intriguing and in-fighting within Fianna Fáil, knocking off his rivals when he chose. More serious, his undercover links with the world of big business revealed a new and disturbing trend in Irish life: the corrosive influence of new money on politics, in the new-rich upper bracket of society. This had never been de Valera's problem, nor even Lemass's. And after the 1991 scandals broke, it added greatly to the malaise already present in Irish society, and to public cynicism about politicians.

One of those who played Cassius towards the end, voting against Haughey in a crucial parliamentary party meeting, was his own finance minister, Albert Reynolds. Haughey sacked him for his treachery, along with other 'rebel' ministers. So, after the fall of The Boss, Reynolds became the popular Fianna Fáil choice for leading the way into a new, cleaner era; and he took over as Taoiseach in February 1992. He too came from a simple provincial background, reared on a small farm in Co. Roscommon; and he too had amassed wealth, first opening a chain of local dance-halls, then building up a highly lucrative pet-food company. But he made no secret of where his money had come from; and he had none of Haughey's flamboyance. He was a decent, pragmatic, business-like conservative, a bit boring. As finance minister since 1989, he had played a large part in improving the economy. And many Irish now turned to him with some relief, as the man who might restore greater integrity to public life, make corruption scandals a thing of the past, and keep the economy on the right track. He started, with an element of vengefulness, by dismissing eight of Haughey's ministers.

His first months in office were marked by some strange events.

In February came the great abortion crisis over the 'Miss X' affair (see p. 190), which dragged on into the early summer. It even intruded into the June debate on the Maastricht Treaty referendum, when the Irish again voted 'yes' to Europe (see p. 329), though less wholeheartedly than in 1972. In between, in May, there was the drama of the resignation of Bishop Casey of Galway, after admitting to a love affair and a love-child (see p. 169). Later, public life settled back into a more routine phase, with unemployment again the main concern. But by the autumn Reynolds's initial popularity was waning. He was regarded by many as a nice man but too uninspiring, a less powerful and effective manager than his predecessor, and possibly not quite up to the top job: in fact, he was widely compared to John Major.

Within his coalition, tensions were growing with the small Progressive Democrats party, under Des O'Malley. This had been created in 1985 by a group of Fianna Fáil TDs who left in protest against Haughey's autocratic style. So they were uneasy partners: but Fianna Fáil needed them to secure a majority in the Dáil, and in 1989 Haughey had reluctantly brought them into his Government. They stayed there, under Reynolds. But the forceful, abrasive O'Malley, one of Ireland's few top-rate politicians, was no lover of Reynolds either; and when in November 1992 the Taoiseach unwisely accused him in public of being 'dishonest' and talking 'crap, pure crap', in a matter concerning the Goodman beef-tribunal hearings, the sparks fairly flew. The PDs demanded an 'abject' withdrawal of the remarks. Reynolds refused. So, on that all-too-Irish note, his Government fell when the PDs voted against him in a confidence debate in the Dáil.

In the general election of 25 November, Fianna Fáil did badly, as was to be expected: but so did Fine Gael, while the Labour Party was the great beneficiary. The seats in the new Dáil, compared with those in the previous one, are listed on page 39.

These were considerable swings by the standards of Irish politics, where party voting loyalties are usually strong and the system of proportional representation (see p. 44) tends to limit changes in seats. Fianna Fáil's vote was the lowest since the party was formed

	Outgoing Dáil	New Dáil	Change
Fianna Fáil	77	68	− 9
Fine Gael	55	45	− 10
Labour Party	16	33	+ 17
Progressive Democrats	6	10	+ 4
Workers' Party (see p. 43)	1	—	− 1
Democratic Left	6	4	− 2
Independents	4	5	+ 1
Greens	1	1	—

in 1927, and Fine Gael's the lowest since 1948; Labour's score, 19 per cent of the total vote, was its best ever. The unemployment situation, plus the sour taste left by the Haughey era, and then Reynolds's lack of charisma, all induced voters to desert Fianna Fáil; but nor were they enticed by Fine Gael, victim of mediocre leadership since FitzGerald's departure. So Labour's advance was in part a protest vote against the larger parties, and in part a vote for change; but not altogether a shift to the left in the usual European sense, for Irish politics are not quite like that − see p. 44.

It also had quite a lot to do with the popularity of Labour's leader, Dick Spring, who in recent years had rejuvenated the party on modern social-democratic lines. This tall, slim Kerryman is a Trinity graduate and former rugby international, and has an American wife whom he met while working as a barman in New York. He performed well as Tánaiste (deputy prime minister) in the mid-1980s; in 1990 it was he who nominated Mary Robinson, formerly of the Labour Party, as presidential candidate; and in the Dáil in 1991 he robustly led the attack on Haughey over the scandals. In short, for those wanting change in politics, he had a most appealing track record; born in 1950, he was of a newer generation than the old guard of Garret, Charlie and Albert. Some observers saw Labour's success as a confirmation of the pro-Robinson vote in 1990, and the headline-writers were quick to proclaim that the much-quoted 'Robinson factor' was now the 'Spring tide'.

He was now kingmaker, for the seat numbers showed that neither larger party could govern without Labour. The option most desired by the electors, according to opinion polls, was for a so-called 'rainbow coalition' of Fine Gael, Labour and the PDs. But plans for this broke down, since the economic philosophies of Labour and the PDs were clearly irreconcilable. So Spring turned instead to Fianna Fáil, and after lengthy negotiations an agreement was pieced together. As Reynolds's party was very keen to stay in power, Labour could demand its price. Thus it managed to secure six of the fifteen cabinet seats, including several major ones, with Spring becoming Tánaiste and foreign minister. And the Joint Programme for government was based essentially on Labour's social and reformist policies. That Fianna Fáil should have felt ready to go along with this was not as strange as might seem; it is not really a party of the Right but pragmatic and populist, and has always been something of a chameleon (witness its shift from de Valera's ideas to Lemass's). Lacking clear policies of its own, it was thus prepared to accept Labour's.

The Joint Programme was a persuasive document. It included various proposals for reducing the gap between rich and poor, for preventing abuses in public life, and so on. Its centrepiece was a National Plan for the economy. This contained no dramatic new remedies for the main problems – hardly to be expected – but it was well argued and presented. So, with Reynolds still Taoiseach, the new Government began work amid a fairly hopeful public mood.

Some new measures came quite rapidly. Dick Spring, as foreign minister, came up with a fresh and resolute new approach to the North's problems (see p. 440). Labour's Mervyn Taylor set to work in the newly created post of minister for equality and law reform, dealing with discrimination of all kinds; homosexuality was finally decriminalized; and a new divorce referendum was planned (see pp. 196 and 200). However, the majority of the social and structural measures proposed in the Joint Programme were slow to materialize – plans for better housing, higher child benefits, fairer taxation, and so forth. An Ethics in Government bill had been promised for an early date, with the aim of 'improving public accountability, transparency and trust' – a clear reference to the recent scandals (one paper called it 'the ethical cleansing of Fianna Fáil'). But by early 1994 it had amounted to no more than a bill for a register of TDs' and senior civil servants' financial interests. And this was being strongly contested as an invasion of privacy.

By early 1994 the 'Spring tide' was no longer at the full, it seemed. The rugby star himself was still scoring high in the opinion polls: but the Government's own rating had fallen, amid the general view that during a year in office it had not done very much. Many liberals who had voted Labour so hopefully now felt a disappointment that so little had yet been achieved for social change. As usual in Ireland, the process of putting reform plans into action was proving agonizingly slow. This time, there was at least a strong and coherent Government programme; but once again it seemed that its execution was faltering in Ireland's creaking and outdated political system.

A creaking political system – but a fine new woman President

Irish politics since Independence have shown considerable stability. And at least since the late 1940s there has been a healthy democratic alternation of power between parties, albeit with Fianna Fáil predominating. Yet, as most experts agree, the political system has seldom thrown up dynamic or creative government. Needed reforms are postponed indefinitely, or are too slowly applied, or turn out to be largely cosmetic; rhetoric too often takes the place of action; national policy-making is subordinated to minor local issues that might win or lose local votes. All this may be true of many countries, but especially of Ireland. Is it due to the nature of the political parties? Or to the electoral system, as is often said? Or to Ireland's political culture, with its close clientelist links between TD and voter? Or to a centralized structure that allows local government very little initiative? Or to all these factors, and maybe others?

Or is it the product of history? It is sometimes said that Fianna Fáil and Fine Gael are still fighting the battles of the civil war, still stuck in that myth. But I think this is misleading. It is true that old loyalties die hard and some older people still vote instinctively according to the side that their parents or grandparents took in 1921, pro- or anti-Treaty. But the civil war itself is no longer an election issue; the only remaining relevant factor, that of partition and the North, today figures way down the list of voters' priorities, as all the polls show (see p. 442). Jobs, grants, welfare, the moral issues and local personalities are all far more important. It *is,* however, true that the two big parties, being born of the civil war, are still coloured by it in the sense that neither has since developed any other ideological base or clear modern policy image. Both are described as 'catch-all' parties, aiming to appeal across much the same broad electoral base, each concerned more with trying to do the other down than with presenting an attractive programme of its own.

Especially this applies to Fianna Fáil, which is a very curious party. Although more conservative on the moral issues than Fine Gael, and more wary of change, it is not in any normal economic or class sense a right-wing party. The bedrock of its support comes from small farmers, local tradespeople and urban workers; it sees itself as the champion of the less privileged (as de Valera did), and it favours generous social spending by the State. Yet it is not averse to having close contacts with big business. In Lemass's time, it showed that under a strong leader it could adapt to real change. But nowadays it tacks to the wind pragmatically, seeking cosmetic solutions that bring votes, trying to be all things to all Irish people. Its clearest ideal remains nationalism, and it regards itself as the rightful protector of the nation: the revival of the Irish language, support for Irish morality and traditions, for Irish unity, are all written into its charter. And it cultivates this patriotic image with a lofty rhetoric, as when Haughey said of its members that 'in their faith and devotion to their country there resides what one can call the Spirit of the Nation'.

Fine Gael also has broad support, but is a little more middle-class, attracting the bigger farmers, professional and business people. Under Costello and FitzGerald it moved away from its extreme conservatism and piety of the 1920s and towards modern social democracy: but it remains less interventionist than Fianna Fáil. It is also less nationalist, more open to the Unionists in the North, and more European. But although it is less of a rag-bag of a party than its rival, and a little more reform-minded, it fails to put itself across to the public with the same clear emotional image. Maybe, too, its clientelism is less resolute. And its recent leadership has not been inspired.

As for the smaller parties, the Progressive Democrats are usually seen as right-wing, but the real picture is more complex. This breakaway group from Fianna Fáil does have an economic policy that is strongly anti-State and pro-private enterprise, but on many social matters, and on the big moral issues, it is reformist. 'We get called Thatcherite, but that's unfair: we are in the European liberal tradition, like Germany's FDP, or Giscard's party in France,' I was told by the tough, brilliant and outspoken Desmond O'Malley, who was scathing to me about the myths and anachronisms still dominating Fianna Fáil. In 1993 he handed on the PDs' party leadership to Mary Harney.

The Labour Party is Ireland's oldest party, founded in 1912 to 'establish a workers' republic founded on socialist principles'. Today it is less militant and doctrinaire than that might imply. Its electoral base is just as much rural as urban; and while it puts a high stress on social justice, and on State direction of the economy, it is closer to modern social democracy than to the old-style European socialist model. Like its sister parties in Europe, it has evolved. The more radical Left is small and has split several times. It is today represented in the Dáil by the Democratic Left, created in 1992 by former members of the Workers' Party, which had been formed earlier from the 'official' section of Sinn Féin after its own split in 1969 with the pro-IRA 'Provos' (see p. 358). Sinn Féin itself now hardly exists in the Republic.

The Left's total share of the vote is usually not more than about 20 to 23 per cent, in a country with no strong Left-wing tradition. Until now its industrial working class has been small, and the Marxist revolutionary ideals of the Continent largely passed it by: moreover, in the independence period the two main parties were too concerned with other issues to establish the usual Left–Right class-based divide. And this legacy remains. The virtual absence of class politics may have brought advantages, for Ireland was little touched by the extremist ideologies of the fascist and communist periods, and it also escaped the kind of Labour/Tory economic-policy reversals that did harm to Britain's economy. To this extent, the Irish political pattern may have its assets. Yet the lack of any dominant ideology except nationalism and Catholicism may also have impeded the larger parties from developing their own constructive policies, and thwarted the growth of real debate on economic and social choices. The recent rise of Labour and the PDs, with their contrasting economic ideas, has now brought a welcome new thrust of argument to the political scene. Yet the two larger parties, notably Fianna Fáil, are still caught in an Irish bog of clientelist vote-catching, fudged policies and personality politics at the expense of real ideas. It is this that hampers effective government.

TDs plead that much of the blame lies with the pressures imposed on them by the electoral system. This is based on proportional representation, written into the original Free State Constitution under a promise made to Britain that the Protestant minority would be protected. Like any PR system, it enables small parties to win seats on their own; and without it there would today probably be no PDs or Democratic Left in the Dáil. It is at least more democratic than Britain's iniquitous first-past-the-post system. But it does cause problems. For the 166-seat Dáil, Ireland is divided into 41 constituencies of three, four or five seats each, and these are allotted under a complex procedure of the single trans-ferable vote. TDs endlessly complain that this pushes them into wasteful and invidious competition with members of their own party in the same area, and obliges them to spend too much time nursing their constituencies. Voices have been raised asking for the system be altered. In 1959 and 1968, attempts by Fianna Fáil to change it to something like the British system were defeated by referendum – wisely. However, today the Irish are at last starting to look more closely at some foreign models – at France's double round of voting in single seats, which has something of the effect of PR; and especially at the excellent German compromise whereby an elector casts one vote for an individual on a first-past-the-post basis as in Britain, another for a party list on a PR basis. But the question is whether the Irish, lovers of the personal, would accept to have half of their TDs elected from an anonymous list.

It is this need for constant constituency-nursing, compounded with the Irish practice of clientelism, that makes life hard for TDs and ministers. Most of those I met complained about it, and none more forcibly than Gemma Hussey of Fine Gael, a former TD and minister of education:* 'Sir Keith Joseph told me that he visited his Leeds constituency once a month. I said that I went to mine in Wicklow, admittedly much nearer the capital, three times a week! And I hated the constant rivalry with the other Fine Gael candidates. TDs fear that if they don't endlessly woo their constituents, they will lose votes, even their seats – and this has sometimes happened. You simply must be seen at all the local functions, the cross-roads dances, the funerals – so important in Ireland – and must ensure that your photo is regularly in the local paper. I pity especially the TDs and ministers from the far west, who go there for the weekends, then have to drive back to Dublin through the night, so they come sleepless into cabinet meetings without having had time to prepare their briefs – and they make wrong decisions. All this explains why I left politics.' I said that I admired the French system, whereby a minister is replaced by a substitute for his or her constituency duties, for the period he or she is in office. The strength of the Irish system is that it does keep a TD close to the grass roots, aware of local feelings. But it puts him too much at their mercy. It trivializes real national policy-making.

* See also her interesting recent book, *Ireland Today* (Town House/Viking, 1993).

However, it is by no means just the electoral system that causes this situation. It derives from the whole political culture of a society which is more fascinated by people than by ideas or policies, and where local factors and personal contacts are of supreme importance. In a pub or round a dinner table, discussion of a political issue will soon turn to spicy gossip about the politicians concerned – more than in most countries. And more than in most, TDs' local roots may go very deep. Some 20 per cent of them are closely related to the TD who held the same seat previously: in the case of one Fianna Fáil dynasty, the Lenihans, Mary O'Rourke (*née* Lenihan), a senior minister under Haughey, 'inherited' her Longford/Westmeath seat from her father, while her brother Brian is another key figure in the party. The elections themselves are fair, but the process of selecting the candidates is often nepotistic. It shows the strength of personal influence and tradition.

This relates to the clientelist system, which dominates Irish politics at least as powerfully as in a Mediterranean country such as Italy. A TD is above all the purveyor of services to his constituents, the agent who takes their little individual problems to the Government and gets them fixed. He or she is expected to hold regular local 'clinics' at the weekends, in pubs or offices, where voters come with their grievances or seeking favours. They might say, for instance, 'Will you ask your friend the minister of industry to arrange a grant for my new little firm?', or, 'Will you ask your friend the minister of health to see that our hospital gets its roof repaired?', or, 'Will you ask your friend the minister of the environment to ensure that traffic lights are installed at the end of my road, because the bureaucrats in Dublin just don't answer our letters?', or, 'Would you ask your friend the minister of education to help find a job for my nephew?' – and so on. Each week, hundreds of begging letters of this kind are passed on by TDs to ministers' offices, where staff spend much of their time dealing with them, to the detriment of real government.

Ireland is such a centralized country that many such minor matters cannot be dealt with locally, but must be sent up to Dublin. And more than in many countries the State bureaucrats are unresponsive, fearfully slow, so that local people feel impelled to ask their TD to intervene – 'As in Italy,' said one wit, 'the TD is a kind of secular priest, interceding to the earthly powers as the priest intercedes to God.' Certainly the practice cuts red tape, speeds things up. But it can verge on corruption, for those who donate to party funds are often the ones best served: 'My neighbour in rural Kerry,' said a friend of mine, 'got the road up to his house resurfaced, as a Fianna Fáil subscriber. I'm still waiting for mine to be done.' And a TD or minister may feel obliged to put local interests even ahead of party policy. In one case, when the Government was preaching economic realism and the need to close down inefficient, outdated services, in Limerick there was such a local outcry against plans to close one old hospital that the TD, Des O'Malley, then minister for industry, took to the streets with his constituents and got the closure averted – yet this clearly contradicted his party's stated principles.

Since most TDs see themselves as local agents more than national legislators, this affects the quality of parliamentary government. Discussions in the Dáil tend to be taken up with parish-pump issues; and often these are debated more keenly than the national ones, for few TDs are much interested in reform or policy-making, as compared with their constituency matters. This climate helps to explain why the ablest and most enterprising people in Ireland today usually avoid going into politics but stick to business or the professions (if they do not emigrate). And so the average quality of TDs is low – something of a vicious circle, for there are not enough enterprising ones to challenge and change the situation. Ireland has some excellent politicians, but they are exceptions. Just a few good young TDs are now entering the Dáil, with more modern attitudes than the older time-servers; but many are soon frustrated to find that the Dáil is little more than a rubber stamp with little serious policy influence on government. For all the Irish gift of eloquence, its debates are seldom sparkling.

TDs may blame the multi-seat PR electoral system, but much more it is their own connivance at outworn political practices that renders government in Ireland so immobile. It is this that makes reform so hard, and so slow, for all has to be subordinated to local needs and pressure-groups. Even on a relatively minor matter such as building a new trunk road (see p. 90), if funds are tight it gets built in little random sections here and there, over a long period, so as to satisfy local TDs and their voters. For the larger matters, short-term cosmetic solutions tend to be preferred, while there is endless foot-dragging over really difficult reforms, repeatedly promised and postponed.

The public readily makes use of clientelism, yet despises the politicians who purvey its favours. They are seen as useful but devious creatures; very few are blatantly to be suborned, so it is felt, but they can generally be wheedled, pressured. The TDs for their part complain ceaselessly about the strains of clientelism, and the need to change it; but they are its accomplices, flattered by the local power and publicity it gives them. And add to this the handicaps of the catch-all party structure. About the whole system many political analysts feel strongly. Joseph Lee has written (op. cit.): 'Stability apart, the Irish have been nearly as sterile in government as they have been creative in politics. The party system has not adapted to the changing role of the State.' But if party structures and clientelism are both to blame, so are over-centralization and the lack of effective local government.

Ireland is the most centralized country in the EU: of all public spending, only 10 per cent is in local rather than national hands, compared with an EU average of over 30 per cent. It is not an issue that greatly excites the average voter: but many experts believe that it is harmful to democracy as well as to local economic initiative. 'How we resent it that all key decisions are taken in Dublin, and we must continually travel there to lobby,' was a view I heard from a businessman in Cork; 'if this city had more control over its own destiny, it could be run far more dynamically.'

Whereas some EU countries have now been decentralizing, Irish centralism tended to grow stronger in the decades after independence. The Free State took over the British system of county and city councils, but Governments then tended to chip away at their powers and transfer them to Dublin – ostensibly with the aim of better controlling public finances and checking corruption, but also with an eye to empire-building, at which the civil servants were expert. The climax came in 1977 when a Fianna Fáil Government, with electoralist motives, did away with the domestic rate, the main local source of council finances; next the local tax on farmland was also abolished, after farmers won a court case that declared it unconstitutional. So today councils are left with a tax on business premises as their only local direct source of revenue, plus services charges (for water, refuse collection, etc.) which not all of them impose. The larger part of their budget comes from government grants, which today account for 65 per cent of local public spending, against 40 per cent before 1977. For any major project such as a new main road or public building, a council is dependent on cash help from the Government, which can thus veto its scheme or even impose its own. And as council budgets are always tight, there is little money to spare for 'non-essentials' such as culture, hence the poor state of funding for the arts in the provinces (see p. 262).

Local authorities also have a restricted range of responsibilities. Unlike in Britain, they do not deal at all with education, health or the police, all of which are run nationally. Apart from operating some basic services such as water supply and garbage disposal, their main task is to look after town planning, roads and urban renewal. These are important matters: but in practice they are in the hands not so much of the elected councillors as of the city or county's non-elected full-time manager, who is the real boss of an Irish local authority. By comparison, a town's mayor is a mere ceremonial figurehead, whose function rotates annually among the councillors, as in Britain. The manager not only runs the executive but has the legal right to overrule the council's decisions in many areas (except in some planning matters, where councillors can propel their own schemes, not always to the best public good). In practice, manager and council often work well together; and some managers are much more dynamic, experienced and far-sighted than the ill-paid part-time councillors. So this technocratic system can bring dividends. It has worked well recently in Cork – but a great deal less well in Dublin (see pp. 137 and 126–7).

A further democratic deficit of the whole set-up lies at local rural level. Ireland has 29 county councils (Tipperary is split in two, and Dublin County into three since 1993), plus 7 borough councils or corporations for the larger towns, and 79 other town councils, but there are no village or rural district councils, so a village or very small town has nothing over it but the county council, which might be up to sixty miles away. This can add to the sense of remoteness from decision-making. 'This weakness of the local government tissue helps to explain why our regional economy is not more dynamic,' says Dr Tom Barrington, the retired senior civil servant who is Ireland's most impassioned anti-centralist; 'people feel isolated, cut off from the forces that might help them.'

Dr Barrington has been leading a campaign to urge the Government to decentralize. Besides arguing for new councils at very local level, his lobby wants increased direct revenue for local authorities; if politically it might not be feasible to reintroduce the domestic rate, then other forms of income should be found. The Barrington lobby also wants Ireland to regionalize, as several other EU countries have been doing, notably France and Spain. Of the twenty-six counties, many are far too tiny to make sense as economic units (Leitrim has 27,000 people, Longford 31,000), and all could be grouped into six or eight regions. It is true that these ancient counties inspire a strong local patriotism, especially for sporting events such as the Gaelic Games, when fervent crowds with waving flags invade the stadium for any big match; and it would be unthinkable politically to abolish them. But they could be grouped into regions while still retaining their identity in other ways, as has happened with the French *départements*. The EU Commission, too, has been urging Ireland to regionalize, for its policy is to give structural aid direct to regions, not to nations. However, a strong centralist lobby in Dublin argues, with some logic, that Ireland *in toto* is much smaller than several of the Spanish regions or German *Länder* and so it hardly needs to regionalize. Dublin's real concern, however, is that it wants to keep control itself of how EU aid is shared out (see p. 89); nor does it want to see its cosy hegemony challenged by new, upstart regions.

None the less, the Government has now accepted that some modest degree of decentralization is necessary. As in Britain and France there has been some shifting of central State services *en bloc* to the provinces: for example, parts of the tax office have been moved to Limerick. But while this is useful deconcentration that creates local jobs, it is not devolution. Then in 1992 the Reynolds Government began to tinker with reform, by proposing eight regional entities with an economic consultative role. The Fianna Fáil/Labour coalition took this a stage further: these new bodies, indirectly elected, were duly set up and were given some role in the local application of the EU structural funds. County enterprise boards were also created. The new Government promised that it would devolve some extra functions to local authorities, as Barrington had recommended; and that it would study the question of setting up district councils at sub-county level. The anti-centralists saw these as modest steps forward but stopping far short of effective regionalization. Fianna Fáil remains Jacobin, reluctant to cede any central power; and it is strongly abetted by a civil service that feels likewise. The argument sometimes put forward is that local councillors are irresponsible and do not know how to take important decisions. But if they are never given the chance, how can they learn? Devolution will always involve some risks, but that is no reason for not trying it – a remedy that centralist France has finally begun to apply.

Irish Governments have been able to hide behind the fact that there is no great grassroots pressure for devolution, never a major election issue. For historical reasons, there is no strong class of provincial *notables* who might use their weight to press for it as Gaston Defferre did in France; TDs may have deep local roots, but their career loyalties are in Dublin, and few of them really wish to alter the power structure. So the Government is able to treat local councils with cavalier highhandedness. Twice recently, fearing defeat, it has actually postponed the council elections for a year or so – as it can do without infringing the Constitution. In many countries this would cause an outcry: but the Irish public resignedly accepted the move as the kind of machination they would expect from their politicians, and they made few protests.

It could say something about the state of democratic involvement in Ireland.

Even so, pressure for change has been growing amongst an alert minority. They feel that regionalization is in the logic of the EU and is bound to come eventually, even in small Ireland. They argue that the present situation deters good people from going into local politics, which is a vicious circle; it widens the gulf between rulers and ruled, and it fuels the resentment of Dublin among provincials who feel powerless to improve their own lot. 'The declining West of Ireland could do far more to help itself, if it had more funds and powers of its own, and thus more self-confidence,' said one local bishop; 'as it is, people just depend passively on largesse from the State.' And Tom Barrington suggested to me: 'The present centralized system has choked the dynamics within our society. Democracy suffers, but so does the economy. A good strong local democracy can stimulate all kinds of local economic activities which otherwise find no expression. Look at Denmark, or Switzerland, countries not so much larger than Ireland. Why are they so much more dynamic? In part, because they are so much less centralized.'

Ireland's civil-service system, like its legal system, was inherited from the British and has since been modified very little. So after 1921 the administration continued much as before, giving rise to the quip that 'at independence, not much changed in Ireland, save that the pillar-boxes were painted green'. Today, civil servants have considerable power; and just a few of them, like T. K. Whitaker, have been forceful individuals with new ideas and a readiness to innovate. The vast majority are of course more cautious, as in any country; and the over-centralized structure limits their direct links with local life. But at least the English tradition of civil-service integrity has been followed, with few exceptions.

In fact there had been few known important cases of corruption in Irish public life before the autumn of 1991, when several curious scandals emerged more-or-less simultaneously. They related to a group of wealthy businessmen friendly with Charles

Haughey, then still Taoiseach. The industrialist Michael Smurfit was suspected of unfair property dealing over a site in Dublin bought by the State telephone company Telecom Éireann, to whose chairmanship he had been appointed by Haughey. His name was later cleared. But his friend Dermot Desmond, a leading stockbroker who handled a number of big Government contracts, was alleged to have made a personal profit from the Telecom deal. Desmond was also thought to have leaked secret information about an Aer Lingus helicopter subsidiary to a rival firm owned by Haughey's son, Ciaran; and to have engaged in insider dealing over the sugar concern Greencore, recently privatized. Under pressure, both Smurfit and Desmond resigned from all their official posts. Public enquiries were held, and Smurfit was declared innocent. But early in 1994 the enquiries over Desmond's role were still continuing.

More serious was the affair involving Ireland's leading meat exporter, Larry Goodman. His firm was alleged to have misused Irish State export-credit insurance and EC intervention funding, to the tune of up to £200 million, in order to sell frozen beef on a massive scale to Iraq and some other countries. In this case some officials at the department of agriculture were thought to have been involved, thus blotting the civil service's usual clean copybook of integrity. It was rumoured that Haughey and some other ministers had known about the dealings, and that Goodman had even given money to Fianna Fáil funds. A public tribunal was set up, at which ministers gave endless conflicting evidence in 1992–3: the hearings went on for well over a year, and by early summer 1994 the presiding judge had still not given his findings.

Nearly all countries have their insider dealers and embezzlers, and there is little reason to suppose that the Irish record is worse than most. Some discreet small-scale local corruption has long existed; if it has recently become more blatant and larger-scale, maybe this is because there is now more money around, so the opportunities are bigger, and a new kind of big-business world has arisen in Dublin. But what especially disturbed Irish opinion in 1991 was the apparent link between that world and government.

Smurfit, Desmond and Goodman all belonged to a so-called 'golden circle' of top financiers and businessmen whom Haughey admired for the new dynamic lead they were giving to the economy, and whom he had helped and encouraged during his years as Taoiseach. His exact role in their alleged activities has never been made clear; if money changed hands, it probably went into party rather than personal funds. And allowance has to be made for the element of gossip and rumour, and the anti-Haughey bias of the liberal media. But the scandals hastened his own downfall, and they left a sour taste. Surely this was cronyism and clientelism writ large, at government level, and it strengthened the case for a change in the Irish political culture.

The Irish legal system, concerning fraud, has also been found to be in serious need of updating, so as to take account of modern business conditions. Before the Goodman affair, much the worst Irish business scandal was that of the Gallaghers in the 1980s. They were members of a farming family from Co. Sligo who did well in the building trade, developed a large and lucrative construction company, and became involved in property speculation in Dublin, while also forming close links with Fianna Fáil. Then in 1982, having seriously overstretched itself, the Gallagher group went bankrupt, owing £30 million to the banks and to small private investors. The legal authorities did nothing. Patrick Gallagher, leader of the group, disappeared to London, where he started again in the British property market – and in 1988 he was arrested, convicted and imprisoned in Northern Ireland, for fraud offences in Belfast. Questions were raised in Dublin about his earlier activities there, and Dick Spring and others tried to force a debate in the Dáil; but Haughey's minister of finance refused. Then to its credit RTE, the State television, screened a powerful and well-researched documentary showing that the fraud squad of the Garda (Irish Police) had been following Gallagher for years, but the Director of Public Prosecutions had refused to make a charge. When RTE gave details of Gallagher's alleged illegal banking activities in Dublin, the DPP said there was insufficient evidence. The basic problem was that, whereas the British had been regularly updating their fraud laws in line with changing business practice,

Irish laws had remained the same since the 1920s. So the DPP had little basis for making a charge.

Finally in 1990 Des O'Malley, as minister of industry and commerce, was instrumental in getting company law amended so as to make it a little easier to deal with fraud. 'But I note with regret', he told me two years later, 'that in this area the DPP is still reluctant to prosecute and won't give reasons.' There is still a lack of staff and of expertise for this kind of work, in a country where people go to jail for minor shoplifting while more serious white-collar crimes go unpunished; it led one bishop to complain to me that justice in Ireland is weighted against the poor. Tax evasion, for example, is known to exist on a large scale (see p. 66), but no one has ever been sent to prison for it, and only recently has the law been changed to make this even possible. Meantime there are regular amnesties on undeclared tax money, which could net the Treasury up to £500 million a year.

Maybe these various kinds of abuse would be tolerated less, by officialdom and by the public, if only the Church were to take a stronger lead – or so it is argued by those who blame the bishops for putting their main stress on private 'sins' rather than public or financial ones (see p. 174). When in 1991–2 the business scandals were followed by the 'Miss X' abortion case, it was notable that Church leaders tended to keep quiet about the former, but joined loudly in the debate on abortion. The Church has denied any such bias. But so long as the Vatican holds to its line, the Irish bishops will follow – 'They seem more upset if I lust after my neighbour's wife, than if I embezzle large sums,' said one indignant liberal. Even many Catholics, while not putting it so sharply, will agree that if the bishops were to speak out more powerfully against business malpractice, then Government and public would be obliged to follow their lead – and the Church itself would win back some of the respect it has lost.

Complaints are common that this has become too self-seeking and materialistic a society. 'What we need is a new de Valera,' I was told by one local doctor. 'Old Dev was hopelessly old-fashioned in many ways, and we don't want to go back to his "frugal comforts". But at least he had idealism and principles.

Ireland could do with a modern-minded de Valera, to provide inspiring leadership in a new style. Mary Robinson might fit the bill – but not in her present job, she has no power.'

It is true that the Irish President has no political power: this is not an executive position as in France or the United States, but is more like the German or Italian Presidency. So Robinson could not at present play the role of some new-style de Valera, even if she wished. However, her job in its own way does carry much influence, especially as election to it is by direct popular mandate. She has thus been able to exert at least a kind of new moral leadership, in an Ireland much in need of it, since her victory in November 1990.

It was a narrow victory, over her Fianna Fáil opponent, yet it was a clear signal that pressure for change was increasing in Ireland. It was also symbolic of change. All six previous Presidents had been elderly male conservatives, all of them nominated by Fianna Fáil. Now the Irish people chose a youngish woman radical, who had already won fame as a barrister and a senator campaigning for feminist causes, for civil liberties and for reform in such areas as birth control. Robinson was seen as representing a new, more modern and liberal Ireland whose forces had been quietly growing. She has been able since her election to provide those forces with an inspiration and a focus, despite the strict constitutional constraints that forbid the President to interfere in politics or even to give views on public issues. She has breathed new vitality into the Presidency; and because of her personal qualities, and her radiant patriotism, she is massively popular even with many who do not share her 'moral' views. Her election was due in large part to women, who 'instead of rocking the cradle rocked the system', she said in her victory speech.

Mary Robinson was born in 1944 into a Mayo family of well-to-do conservative gentry, the Bourkes. Both her parents were doctors in Ballina, where she grew up a leggy tomboy, the only girl among four brothers. In childhood games she often cast herself as Robin Hood. She went to a convent boarding-school in Dublin, then to a finishing-school in Paris, where she acquired a feeling for Europe that has grown with the years. Academically gifted, she took a first in law at Trinity College, Dublin, then went on a scholarship to Harvard, where she was greatly influenced by the radical movement of the 1960s with its questioning of established values. Around this time she married a fellow law student from Trinity, Nicholas Robinson: he was a Protestant, and her strict Catholic parents refused to attend the wedding, but later they softened and accepted him.

Her career made a dazzling start. Aged twenty-five she was Trinity's youngest ever professor of law. She then spent twenty years as a senator and a barrister, fighting for various reforms and civil-rights causes, not always with success. Her efforts to get contraception legalized were blocked for many years; but she won women the right to sit on juries, and she secured a better deal for homosexuals and for children born out of wedlock. She has always had an idealistic belief in the role of law to promote social progress.

Her attempts to rise higher in national politics failed, for she was twice defeated in elections for the Dáil, as a Labour candidate. After some years in the Labour Party, she left it in 1985 in protest against the Anglo-Irish Agreement for the North: she thought this was unfair on the Unionists, whereas Labour warmly supported it. But in 1990 it was Labour that urged her to try for the Presidency; she accepted, standing as an independent candidate with Labour backing, against the two larger parties. At first her chances seemed remote, and the bookies were quoting odds of 100 to 1. Then the front-running Fianna Fáil candidate, Brian Lenihan, was involved in a relatively minor scandal and sacked by Haughey from the cabinet (he was Tánaiste). But even before this, Robinson's poll ratings had been rising fast, and it would be unfair to say that she won by default. She campaigned vigorously, carefully changing her public image from that of a rather austere legalist to someone more warm, relaxed and glamorous, a caring mother of three. And she appealed across the parties to a wide range of younger people wanting change. On the first round she secured 39 per cent of the vote, to Lenihan's 44 per cent: then on the run-off she picked up enough Fine Gael votes to move 5·5 points ahead of

Lenihan. It was the first time that the Fianna Fáil candidate had lost the Presidency.

For her seven-year mandate, the Robinsons now live in the official residence, Áras an Uachtaráin, a fine Georgian mansion in Phoenix Park, used by the Lord Lieutenant of Ireland under British rule. Robinson has been patently enjoying her Presidency, which has brought out new sides of her personality. Previously considered a somewhat starchy bluestocking, she has become more exuberant and enthusiastic, and sparkles when she meets new people. But she retains some of her stiff, shy nervousness, and her stubborn wilfulness, too.

After her earlier bold activities, the Presidency is in some ways a gag for her; and some friends feel that she is wasting herself in this largely ceremonial post. But this is not how she sees it. Cleverly she has used her legal skills to push its role to the allowed limits; and with zest and energy she has given it a new purpose. Knowing that her direct political powers are almost nil, she has set about trying to influence society in other ways, notably by meetings with people or groups who lie outside the normal circuits of public life. She makes a point of paying official visits to slum areas, to the unemployed in their homes, to dying rural villages, and to local women's groups involved in community work – milieux that previous presidents ignored.

'I am certain that grass roots activity of this kind is important for Ireland's future and deserves my support,' she told me during my interview with her at Áras an Uachtaráin. Of her role she said: 'It can be valuable to be the people's elected choice outside the prescribed agenda of politics, and to provide a "voice for the voiceless", as I have called it. The visits that I make to unlikely places are a form of influence on politics.' But when I tried to probe her views on some of the sensitive political issues of the day, such as the moral and family reforms, she answered very correctly: 'You know that I cannot tell you. But look at my track record.' I did.

The Irish President's role is not entirely ceremonial. As guardian of the Constitution, he or she has certain reserve powers, for example the right to refer a Bill to the Supreme Court to determine whether it is constitutional, and the right in some cases to be consulted as to whether a proposed reform should be put to referendum. The President also has the right to address the joint Houses of Parliament, the Oireachtas, and this Robinson has done. She cannot say anything that might influence policy. So in her many public speeches at home and abroad – and she is a gifted orator, with an elegant prose style and a rich contralto voice – she often resorts to a kind of coded language, making subtle allusions to her views in a way that an Irish audience will understand. Thus in the debate on the Maastricht referendum, she was able to urge a 'yes' vote without actually saying so.

Her popularity was resented by Haughey, who saw it as a threat to his own ego, and he made some attempts to curb her. In 1991 he even forbade her to go to Britain to deliver the BBC's annual Dimbleby Lecture (the President requires Government permission to carry out official engagements abroad). But under Reynolds, the tensions eased. And Robinson has paid many State visits abroad. In the United States, she gave lectures on feminism, AIDS and world poverty. In Paris she scored a triumph, not least because of her excellent French and her shining European-ism. She has been on official but not State visits to Britain. And she has been often to Northern Ireland, where some Unionist leaders have welcomed her as a voice of moderation. However, in 1993, with the aim of making the Catholics of West Belfast feel less marginalized, she publicly shook hands there with Gerry Adams, and this mistake lost her a good deal of the credit she had built up among Unionists.

Among those she has invited to Áras an Uachtaráin are working-class women's groups from West Belfast – Catholics and Protestants together. She is a feminist Irish-style, and has done much to encourage women to play a more active role in public life. While in favour of legalizing divorce, she is also still a practising Catholic, emotionally opposed to abortion. Yet in her old outspoken days she was highly critical of the Church. In 1990 she even described its 'patriarchal, male-dominated presence' as probably the worst single oppressive force subjugating women in Ireland. She cannot say that in public nowadays.

Mary Robinson's views on the Church and the moral issues are well known. But she is known also as a practising Catholic, a believer in family values, social justice, Irish cultural traditions – and all these ideals she *is* able to promote in her speeches, with a vibrant patriotism. This has won her popularity even with conservatives who would part company with her on some matters. She cannot produce any magic consensus in a society still in transition, still in uneasy debate with itself. As President, she cannot herself promote any change in the party structure, nor the outdated political system. So her election has brought no revolution – how could it? But her patent integrity and idealism are valuable to Ireland in its present mood.

Above all, limited in speech though she may be, her very presence as Head of State, with a Protestant husband, has been giving an impetus to the growth of a new kind of liberal and civic morality, modern and pluralist, distinct from that of old-style Catholicism. This is important, when so many Irish people, especially the young, have been turning against Church authority and are looking for some other moral leadership. In this limited way, maybe Mary Robinson *is* a modern-style de Valera. It is also important that this patrician from the provinces should be publicly extending so warm a hand to the 'voiceless' and the less privileged – in a society that likes to call itself 'classless' yet has wide extremes of rich and poor.

The cosy gossip of 'Dublin 4' – and the rich and poor of a 'classless' society

There are great differences of wealth and of lifestyle in Ireland: but it is not a class society quite in the English or even the French sense. The old Anglo-Irish ruling élite has largely disappeared, and Irish society today is ethnically very homogeneous: foreign immigrants are few, and nearly everyone derives directly or indirectly from the same kind of rural roots. The urban working class is of fairly recent growth, and remains quite small. And in some ways

Irish society is less like England's than America's: that is, status is less a matter of family background or education than of position and money – and the wealth disparities have even become more visible recently with the rise of a *nouveau riche* business class. But these social differences are softened by the strongly felt common bond of Irishness; by a chummy informality, also Irish; and by an egalitarian ethos that may be phoney in economic terms but is real in human ones. The Gaelic Games and Irish music are great levellers, as are funerals where rich and poor meet and talk. And in pubs over a pint of porter the new-rich tycoon may be warmly greeted by the small farmer – 'Bejasus, how are yer, Mick? – I knew yer father.' Haughey himself, with his simple background, was a paragon of this populism.

In this small country, everyone seems to know everyone else at a certain level – attractive in a way, though even some Irish can find it stifling and parochial. In the intense little goldfish bowl of the Dublin 'chattering classes', politicians, artists, doctors, academics and industrialists all mix together at the same pubs and parties, much more than in a larger capital of a larger country, such as London or Paris. Life is gossipy, personal, excitingly engrossing. Some of this activity may be out in bourgeois Ballsbridge or Rathmines, or in the homes of the well-to-do along the coast towards Bray. But the epicentre of this public social scene is a tiny segment of the heart of old Dublin, between St Stephen's Green and the Liffey. Here TDs from the Dáil mingle with media and theatre folk in the Shelbourne Hotel – in its lounge or its Horsehoe Bar, inner sanctum of this world – or in Doheny & Nesbitt's pub down the road, or at the Unicorn, a cramped, very simple sort of trattoria with a cult following. Or *Irish Times* columnists and Trinity academics consort with poets and legal eagles in the Palace Bar or Mulligan's. There is less heavy drinking nowadays, but still the same supremacy of racy gossip over intellectual analysis.

This is one facet of the world of notorious 'Dublin 4'. (Not to be confused with the Dublin 4 postal district from which its name derives. Dublin 4 is a kind of Kensington-cum-Hampstead, embracing the prosperous residential areas of Ballsbridge and

Donnybrook, with the RTE radio and television studios and the University College (UCD) campus.) 'Dublin 4' has been coined as the much-used byword for the Dublin intelligentsia, many of whom may live in Dublin 4 but others elsewhere – Garret FitzGerald, their prototype, lives in nearby Rathmines (Dublin 6), others down towards the coast near Dun Laoghaire. And there is more than one definition of 'Dublin 4'. It could be equated with the entire milieu of the media, politics and the professions. Or it can be used a little more narrowly to mean the modern liberal élites – those who share Mary Robinson's views, are critical of Fianna Fáil, the Church and old-style nationalism, and maybe write for the *Irish Times*. But go outside 'Dublin 4' and you may find its denizens quite widely resented for a we-know-best intellectual superiority – even by some who might qualify to join their ranks.

John Waters, for instance, that clever young maverick journalist, is a humble provincial from Roscommon who, Julien Sorel-like, has done very well in Dublin: he even writes a column in the *Irish Times*, spicing its bourgeois liberalism with a touch of the Jimmy Porter. He claims not to feel at home in 'Dublin 4', and he resents it for what he sees as its own contempt for places like Roscommon, and for the rough but 'real' world of working-class North Dublin (see p. 123). Or so he has written in his irritating but brilliant book *Jiving at the Crossroads* (1991): '"Dublin 4" was an attitude of mind, an attitude that had become impatient with the reality of life in modern Ireland ...' It was '... a class of people who had transcended their own class and background, who were out to culturally colonize the country, who believed themselves to have an almost divine right to dictate the way it should be run. The "Dublin 4" animal was polished and cosmopolitan, though not necessarily as privileged as the leafy avenues of Ballsbridge might lead the outsider to believe. It wanted no truck with the dark, irrational priest-ridden place it called "rural Ireland". For "Dublin 4", this place was just a bad dream, a mild irritation on the periphery of its consciousness, a darkness on the edge of town. It wanted an end to all this fanciful talk about an attachment to the land. It wanted Ireland to see itself as a modern, urban, industrialized democracy . . . All that was required was for the rest of the population to agree to lie down and die.'

Waters, however, is also a Robinson supporter, highly critical of Haughey and his like in Fianna Fáil, yet fascinated by them to the point where his barbs seem to contain a kind of hero-worship. The chief merit of his book is that it speaks up for a provincial Ireland little known to 'Dublin 4' – in this case, the Roscommon townlet of Castlerea where he grew up, in the flat and humdrum Irish Midlands. He describes it and other such places as having no real class structure but a hierarchy, 'in which every family, and every individual, has a fixed place. Everybody knows practically everybody else . . . Other than by leaving, it is almost impossible, within the ordinary activity of one's life, significantly to alter one's position in the pecking order. One might have a good job, and have built an expensive house in the town's most sought-after locality, but one remains, more or less, the person one started out as.'

So there is the life of Dublin, North and South; the life of these small towns (Ireland has few big ones); and the life of the countryside, of the small farmers (you must never call them peasants). These used to be a world apart. Today they are much better educated, their lifestyle has become more modern, they have new links with the towns where many of their relatives now live; and although some townsfolk may still look down on them as uncouth 'culchies' (bumpkins), their world and the urban world have been drawing closer, as in France (see p. 105). However, in rural areas and small towns alike there is a lack of strong local leadership, for several reasons. Not only has the Church's role declined, but Ireland has very little of a class of effective provincial *notables*, as in France. This may be due to the weakness of local government, and to the departure since independence of nearly all of the Anglo-Irish landed gentry who did provide some kind of lordly leadership from their 'big houses', for good or ill.

A few of these old families remain (see p. 321), but today they play very little part in local affairs. Many live in genteel semi-poverty. Few of them therefore have much contact with Ireland's own really wealthy set, which does exist, though it is small. This is the milieu of new money, of the international businessmen who came to the fore ten or so years ago, led by the controversial Smurfit and Desmond, and by such figures as Tony O'Reilly, the Irish tycoon who spends much of his time in Pittsburgh as chairman of Heinz (see p. 79). They and their children, and a few friends, lead a glamorous, exclusive life that sometimes features in the gossip columns but otherwise impinges little (save when there are scandals). At one recent charity ball in Co. Kildare (tickets £250 each), Smurfit turned up in a shiny blue helicopter, flanked by bodyguards. Many of these rich people also have houses abroad and wide international contacts. But, within Ireland, their set is hardly cosmopolitan. Even in the parallel set of the gentry, a figure like Vincent Poklewski-Koziell, a racy Polish count who boasts a friendship with Mick Jagger, is something of a rarity.

In and around Dublin there are other social sets too, and in this small, gregarious world they tend to overlap. There is the horsy set, centring round the breeders of the Curragh, in Co. Kildare, and the racing at Leopardstown. There is a new yuppy set of merchant bankers and stockbrokers, who are seen in the currently trendy restaurants such as Polo One and Locks. Their lifestyle is much the same as in London, save that they have rather less spending money: house prices may be lower, but so are salaries, while income tax is higher. And there is the literary and intellectual set, or rather sets: one of them is part of 'Dublin 4', another, led by the novelist Dermot Bolger (see pp. 247–9), prefers the lower-class Northside of the city.

Here Dublin's traditional working class, the world of the O'Casey plays, is fairly small; but the ranks of this milieu have been swelled in the past decades by the influx from the farms. Many poorer people live in dreary new dormitory suburbs (see p. 130), but there are still quite a few in the older central slum areas not yet renovated. This working-class Dublin today presents two contrasting images. There is the exuberant life-loving resilience depicted by Roddy Doyle (in *The Snapper, The Commitments,* etc.), which is perfectly real; but Doyle tends to gloss over the other side of the picture, the malaise of high long-term unemployment, the rise of petty crime and drugs, described maybe to excess by other new writers, such as Bolger (see pp. 247–9). It is not easy to draw a balance, and maybe O'Casey did so more subtly than his successors today; like his Paycock, poorer Dubliners have a natural joky cheerfulness that only half-conceals a deeper listless anxiety. They are much less poor than in his day, far better protected by the social net, but they are troubled by new tensions and uncertainties; Bolger has portrayed the sense of alienation of rural immigrants in their new suburbs. And there is a contrast, not only in income and lifestyles but in morale, between the poorer Northside and the better-off Southside of the city (these are shorthand terms, for in fact the geographical pattern is more complex). Another writer, Val Mulkerns, has sharply underlined this in *Very Like a Whale*, her novel about a young man from a cosy, decent bourgeois family who goes to teach in a slum-district school, thus entering a fearful milieu of drugs, rape, hooliganism and urban decay. Her book goes decidedly over the top, but it is spotlighting a real situation.

In income and wealth terms, the gulf between rich and poor may not be greater than in many comparable countries, but it is aggravated by a peculiar pattern of taxation. The Irish, notoriously, are the most highly taxed people in Europe. A reason often given is that they have been encouraged to aspire to the same levels of welfare and public services as in richer neighbouring countries, so the money for this can come only from high taxes. But in an effort to generate jobs, corporate tax for foreign-owned and manufacturing firms is kept low, at 10 per cent; so much of the burden has to be borne by individuals. Yet whereas income tax is ferociously high, tax on personal capital is negligible – a structure that unfairly hits the salaried lower to middle income groups much more than the rich.

In a country where the legacy of the Land Acts of the 1880s, enabling tenant farmers to own their land, has made possession of property so crucial and emotive a factor, it is electorally tempting for any party in power to refrain from taxing it. And this Fianna Fáil has done. Whereas Fine Gael in the 1970s imposed a property tax, Fianna Fáil then abolished it in 1977, together with the domestic rate. Today just a few larger private residences are taxed, and not heavily. What is more, there is no wealth tax either; this too was briefly introduced, then removed by Fianna Fáil, which argued that it was simply encouraging wealth to leave the country.

But with income tax it is quite another matter. There are fairly generous exemptions which help the poor: for a married couple, the first £6,800 of income is free of tax, and with child allowances this means that a family with five children will pay no tax on an income of £9,000. But soon after this, the blow becomes swingeing. The standard level is 27 per cent, but after only £13,000 a single person will reach the top bracket of 48 per cent; add in social security and other levies, and it means that on earnings beyond that level, he or she will be paying 55 pence in the £ in tax, as much as a millionaire in many countries. And a married couple with joint earnings in the fairly modest £21,000 range will be facing much the same burden. No wonder so many gifted young people choose to emigrate, even when they can find a good job in Ireland (see p. 315). There used to be a third higher bracket of 58 per cent, but this was abolished in 1992 – a further concession to the rich.

Over and above the low taxes on capital, the system favours better-off people in other ways, too. If they are self-employed in the liberal professions, or have business interests abroad, they have much more scope for tax evasion than salaried office or factory staff. And VAT, which rich and poor pay alike, remains unusually high in Ireland, even if in line with EU harmonization policies it has been reduced from 25 to 21 per cent since 1989. Many economists and politicians, notably in Fine Gael, have repeatedly urged that taxation should be reformed so as to shift the emphasis from income to property. But although the 1993 programme of the Fianna Fáil/Labour coalition promised to cease imposing the higher tax band on middle incomes, after a year in office it had still not put this into action. The best to be said of the taxation system is that the really well-off, who benefit from it so unjustly, are only a tiny minority; and poorer people, though they may have low wages, pay little tax and are helped by quite generous welfare allowances (see p. 83). There are still pockets of real poverty in Ireland, and the rising tide may not have lifted all boats, as was confidently predicted. But average prosperity has grown immensely in the thirty-five years since the Lemass era dawned.

3

MODERNIZING THE ECONOMY: BETTER LATE THAN NEVER

Ireland's economy and infrastructure have taken huge strides into the modern world in the past thirty or forty years. Consider just one example: the telephone service. In the early 1980s, at a cost to the state of some £1·4 billion, this was transformed from an antiquated joke, entirely non-digital, into an ultra-modern network, using Alcatel equipment from France. 'Until then,' one businessman told me, 'in the village in Kerry where I have a weekend home, the local exchange would close down at 2 p.m. on a Sunday, and I had to drive sixty miles to make a long-distance call. This year, I dialled Tokyo from a local call-box.' Firms in the provinces no longer waste hours trying to get through even to Dublin, let alone New York; and in nearly every village you see little yellow phonecard call-boxes, which actually do work.

Some ten or twenty years behind its richer neighbours, Ireland has been following the modern post-war path, as foreign hi-tech industries have arrived, living standards have risen, peasants have moved to the towns, and fitfully a new entrepreneurial ethos has begun to emerge. But the progress has been uneven, and there are plenty of people still left on the sidelines. In fact, this is still one of the three poorest countries of the EU: according to 1993 OECD figures, its annual GDP per head (c. $10,627) is well above that of Greece ($7,323) or Portugal ($8,364), but below that of Spain ($11,738) and far below the levels of Britain ($15,882) or France ($17,376).

Why this relative poverty? There could be some historical and physical reasons why Ireland stayed underdeveloped for so long. Its British colonizers sucked it for its farm produce but did little else to promote its economy; the industry they implanted was mainly in the North around Belfast, and this was lost to the Free State at independence. Ireland's peripheral position, 'the offshore island of an offshore island' as the phrase goes, has seldom been ideal for attracting investment, and the country has few mineral resources: despite much prospecting, no offshore oil has yet been found that is commercially exploitable. Moreover, much of the soil is too stony and infertile to offer its farmers a decent living. The Great Famine was a terrible blow, and the constant emigration since then has deprived Ireland of much of its best talent. Often it was the brightest ones who left, believing that only abroad could they succeed, not in Ireland's own beguiling but sluggish environment.

These may have been important factors, but some experts give a different slant. Professor Joseph Lee, for example, points out (op. cit., pp. 69, 513–28) that, at independence, 'Ireland's standard of living seems to have been about average for western Europe. It was, of course, only about two-thirds that of Britain. But the rest of western Europe averaged only about two-thirds that of Britain also'; in 1910, even Sweden and Norway had a lower per capita GNP than Ireland. In the next decades, however, Ireland had the lowest income growth of any European country except Britain; the more dynamic Scandinavian economies, even Finland's, pulled far ahead. Lee concludes, provocatively: 'Irish economic performance has been the least impressive in western Europe, perhaps in all Europe, in the twentieth century.' Not all economists would put it so strongly: but many would support the reasons that he adduces for Ireland's poor record. He puts it down more to human than to physical factors, deriving in part from history: the 'absence of an adequate performance ethic in the society'. To this lack of native enterprise and self-confidence could be added the short-sighted conservative policies of Ireland's post-independence rulers.

As already noted, the Cosgrave Government of the 1920s set a low priority on industry, and so did de Valera as Taoiseach in 1932–48 and 1951–4. Preaching a return to traditional rural values and the virtues of an Ireland 'satisfied with frugal comfort', he cared little for economic development. He tried to boost agriculture with subsidies, but did it so clumsily that the farming world went on stagnating. He was understandably angry at the continued economic dependence on Britain, which took some three-quarters of Irish exports; so his remedy was to wage a trade war with the old enemy, and he erected some of the world's highest tariff barriers, with the unrealistic aim of making Ireland self-sufficient in nearly all products. By the mid-1950s the impact of this protectionism was to render the economy moribund, just at a time when most of the Western world was forging rapidly ahead. Irish living standards were actually falling, and in the 1950s as many as 400,000 people emigrated. The sense of despondency was widespread.

There then took place one of the most important changes in modern Irish history, as a growing number of civil servants, and some politicians, began to press for a completely different strategy. Foremost among them was the brilliant young Kenneth Whitaker, who in 1956 became secretary of the department of finance. Described later by the *Irish Times* as 'the architect of modern Ireland', he was that rarity, a civil servant with creative vision and a taste for change and innovation. In what he later described as 'a dark night of soul-searching', he rethought the whole basis of official policy; and, influenced by the success of State planning in France and Italy, he began to promote ideas of free trade, foreign investment and planned growth that were still novel in Ireland. This led to his crucial report *Economic Development* (1958), which the Government accepted as the basis for a new strategy, Keynesian in character: the Programme for Economic Expansion. It was a remarkable turnabout, made possible because Whitaker's ideas were by now shared by many senior colleagues and by Fianna Fáil leaders – notably by the party's rising star, Seán Lemass, the modern pragmatist who in 1959 replaced the ageing de Valera as Taoiseach.

And so began the now legendary 'Lemass era' – though it might equally be called the Whitaker era – when Ireland made a decisive break with the autarkic de Valera philosophy and set about embracing Europe and the world. After 1959 the new policy went into top gear. Protectionism was phased out; the State

70

became much more involved in industrial planning; foreign investment, hitherto spurned, was now actively encouraged, with a
range of enticing new incentives. As a result, industrial growth
rose to 7 per cent a year and stayed at that level for a decade.
Ireland was now in a position to benefit from the general world
boom of the time, to escape from the confines of its narrow home
market, and to prepare for eventually joining the Common
Market, as it did in 1973. As economic self-confidence and prosperity grew, so emigration fell and many thousands of exiles returned
to work in the new Ireland: the annual net exodus dropped from
43,000 in 1956 to 11,000 in 1966.

Economic progress has continued since then, if erratically. EU
membership has brought various benefits, in terms both of new
markets and of the lavish aid that Ireland receives. And the GDP
growth rate reached the remarkably high levels of 6·5 per cent for
1989 and 8 per cent for 1990. It then slipped back to 2·5 per cent
for 1991 and 2 per cent for 1992 and for 1993, as recession began
to affect Ireland – but these figures were still above OECD and
EU averages. Most experts agree that the country's economic
performance in the past thirty years has been reasonably good,
given its legacy of underdevelopment. Especially since about 1988
it has weathered recession better than Britain or France, and has
maintained good levels of growth and balance of payments. But in
incomes it still lags well behind its richer neighbours. And various
doubts and difficulties remain today.

One of these concerns foreign investment. The growth rate
since the late 1950s may have been one of Europe's highest, but
this has been due quite largely to exports by the many
multinational firms that have moved in; and as these tend to
repatriate much of their profits, the real benefit to the economy is
limited. Some economists argue that the high growth rate is a bit
of a mirage, and most now agree that far more should be done to
encourage indigenous Irish firms. In sharp contrast to the old de
Valera days, Ireland's economy has today become very open:
exports account for some 75 per cent of industrial output, and
over a third of all industry is in foreign hands. But this could
simply make the country more vulnerable to world recession,

especially as foreign firms are the more likely to reduce staff or close their plants completely when the going gets rough.

A second problem concerns the high level of government spending, which more than once in the 1970s and 1980s led to large budget deficits and heavy public debt. First in the late 1970s Jack Lynch's Fianna Fáil Government recklessly increased public expenditure by 50 per cent; and in 1986–7 Fine Gael followed the same path to a lesser degree. Then the Haughey Government established a certain rigour, and its budget cuts brought results. Between 1983 and 1991 public spending was reduced from 49 to 37 per cent of GNP; and the national debt, which by 1987 had been driven up to almost 130 per cent of GNP, was brought down to 102 per cent by 1994. But today it still needs to fall further, to 75 per cent or less, if Ireland is to meet the requirements for entry into European Monetary Union.

There are several reasons why Irish Governments are under this constant pressure to spend heavily. With so many people out of work, and so many others still of school age in this young country, disproportionate sums need to be spent on welfare and on social needs such as education; moreover, the political system entices the parties to take a populist approach, giving the voters what they ask. And since the Irish have come to expect the same high level of welfare and services as richer nearby countries, this puts a heavier burden on the exchequer than Ireland can really afford. Is it not living above its means? As we have seen (p. 66), one result is the very high level of taxation; during Lynch's 'spending spree' period, taxation rose by over 30 per cent. And the distortions of the Irish fiscal system, with income tax so high and many other taxes so low, are regarded as not only socially unjust but a hamper on business incentive. Aware of this, the Government in the early 1990s made a few ad hoc changes. The 1994 Budget has now set up a more positive aspect to reform, but to apply it could be another matter.

A further problem relates to the role of the State, for Ireland presents the paradox of a free-market capitalist economy in which the State plays a large and assertive role. In this respect, it is more like France than Britain. Not only does the Government seek to direct industrial policy, but there are nearly a hundred State-sponsored bodies, most of them with strange Irish names, that take charge of everything from public transport and vocational training to electricity and peat-cutting. Many are run less than efficiently and make a loss, including Irish Steel and Bord na Móna, the peat development board. These firms are run on commercial lines, and the managements of some of them propose that privatization is the right answer. The Government is not ideologically opposed, but in a country with no great spirit of capitalist enterprise, it is not easy to find buyers. Many experts, however, regard the present State mechanism as too complex and clumsy for a country of this size.

Lastly, the high level of unemployment – over 21 per cent, according to one calculation (see p. 66), and still rising in 1994 – is seen as much the most serious of today's economic worries. On the positive side, the level of inflation has been kept low, down to 2 or 3 per cent in recent years, thanks in part to intelligent policies of wage restraint worked out with Ireland's generally moderate trade unions. But the wide gulf between rich and poor has not been reduced; nor has the labour harmony been of much help in creating jobs. For a number of reasons, demographic and agricultural as well as industrial, the Irish economy finds it peculiarly difficult to translate growth into jobs, so that even in a year of quite good expansion the numbers out of work may still rise. 'All the other economic indicators – inflation, trade balance, debt, growth – look fairly healthy today, save for this one,' a minister told me in 1993; 'it's a true Irish anomaly.' So these are today's main talking-points, endlessly debated in the usual forthright Irish manner.

Foreign hi-tech investors – but where are Ireland's own entrepreneurs?

The policy of heavy reliance on foreign investment is nowadays widely questioned. In today's world climate it clearly has its drawbacks, but in the earlier boom years it brought good results and was justified. Certainly when it began in the 1960s there seemed no better choice, for the Irish lacked industrial expertise of their own and realized that outside help was essential. Foreign firms began to arrive in the 1960s; then in 1969 the Industrial Development Authority was set up, an autonomous State body charged with encouraging investment, backed by a sizeable budget and a battery of grants and other incentives. Japanese, German and American firms in particular responded, eager to obtain a foothold in the EC, which Ireland was then joining. Its peripheral island location maybe had drawbacks, but there were other advantages.

The IDA put the accent on attracting light modern hi-tech industries of the kind that, in terms of transport costs, would not be too much handicapped by the geography. In the 1970s the emphasis was on electronics and chemicals; and no less than eight of the free world's top ten pharmaceutical companies set up factories in Ireland, led by Schering-Plough. Then in the 1980s it was the turn of computers, with the arrival of Digital, Apple and others. The investors settled mostly in the Dublin, Cork and Shannon areas, but also in some remote parts of the West.

In the past few difficult years, the rate of new investment has of course slowed right down, as in other countries. But it still goes on. Some foreign firms have pulled out, but the vast majority claim to be satisfied with their choice of Ireland. Today some 35 to 40 per cent of Irish industry is foreign-owned, accounting for over 90,000 jobs and over 70 per cent of manufactured exports; of the thousand or so foreign enterprises, some 350 are American, 240 British, 170 German and 35 Japanese.

Of the reasons given by foreign investors for choosing an Irish location, or for being happy with their choice, the most frequently cited are the IDA's incentives – capital grants of up to 60 per cent in many areas, freedom to repatriate profits, and an unusually low corporation tax rate of 10 per cent. Investors also quote the qualities of a workforce which is English-speaking (an asset for American companies), not prone to strikes, and generally well educated (see p. 215): Irish vocational training may not be exceptional, but the secondary schools turn out young people with good levels of literacy and mathematical ability.

One typical foreign-owned factory I visited was DDC in Cork, an American hi-tech electronics venture where Irish girls in blue head-masks, looking like a cross between nuns and astronauts, were operating mysterious black flapping equipment. 'DDC opened this plant in 1990, moving into Europe for "1992" reasons, to gain a place within the single market,' said the Scottish manager. 'Why Ireland? We wanted an English-speaking country, and we found the grants offered here were better than in Scotland, which we also considered. The educational level may not be quite up to Scottish standards, but it's much better than in America where the technicians are good but the unskilled workers far less so. And we were drawn to Cork by its university and the good air links with the US from Shannon. One minus: long-distance telephoning is fearfully expensive.' Several other firms gave me similar reasons for coming to Ireland, some adding that labour costs were much lower than in countries such as Britain. Another advantage could be the pool of highly skilled labour often provided by Irish emigrants wanting to return home (see p. 309). For example, when in 1992 the US microchip firm Intel was preparing to set up a major new plant near Dublin, the IDA advised it to recruit among Irish microchip engineers who had gone to work on the Continent for Philips and Siemens. Intel was able to find 150 qualified graduates, eager to seize the chance to return from exile to a good job.

This new US investment came at a time when the climate for attracting such ventures had inevitably grown less favourable. By the early 1990s not only was the world in recession, but the competition for attracting foreign investors had become more intense, notably with the entry of Spain and Portugal into the EC. So today Ireland now has to fight harder than in the buoyant 1970s. What is more, in these harsher times, some of the drawbacks of depending on foreign investment have become more apparent than in the easy years of fast growth.

Firstly among these, such investment is not always very stable. A multinational firm has a tendency – or so it is feared – to pull out of Ireland and switch to another country if this suits its world strategy. This could result from changes in technology, or recession, or possibly from its losing interest in Ireland at the end of its tax-break period. 'It could suddenly pull out the plug in Galway and set up in Taiwan, if it found that was cheaper,' said one cynic. For example, Ford and Dunlop shut down their factories in Cork in the 1970s, while in the 1980s some textile and computer firms closed in the Shannon area. By the early 1990s several US computer factories in the West of Ireland were drawing in their horns and shedding staff, owing to worldwide problems in that industry. In 1993 Digital closed its hardware plant in Galway completely, with a loss of 700 jobs, though it kept the software section open (see p. 140). And Asahi, a Japanese firm making synthetic fibres in Co. Mayo, had cut its workforce from 550 to 340 since the early 1980s. These are familiar problems in most countries today. But the Irish tend to fear that these foreign companies have little loyalty to Ireland and may ruthlessly switch their policies to suit their own interests, whereas a native Irish firm would have more sense of duty to its staff and a stronger feeling of local attachment.

Today it is also being asked whether the large sums spent by the Government, on grants and tax concessions, are altogether worth it in terms of the return. According to IDA figures, each job created by a foreign firm costs the State on average £13,000 in terms of grants and other aid. And then most of the firms' profits are allowed to flow freely out of Ireland, to the tune of up to £1 billion a year. Some critics argue that the 10 per cent corporation tax for these investors is over-generous, preventing the exchequer from gaining an adequate return. What is more, the IDA's programme of building ready-to-use light factories to entice investment has fallen foul of recession: several of these buildings have failed to find takers and they now lie empty, a burden on the IDA's budget.

Undoubtedly the foreign investment policy has brought, and continues to bring, great benefits – in terms of job creation, market contacts, technology transfer and management expertise. But many experts today will argue that it has been disappointing in its hoped-for spin-off effects on the rest of Irish industry. According to this view, not only is little of the profit reinvested in Ireland, but many foreign firms tend to operate as self-contained enclaves, rather than forming links with local Irish companies or encouraging subsidiary activity; most of their materials they buy in from abroad. This is partly the fault of the investors' own policies: but the Government and the IDA are also blamed, and so are native Irish firms for not taking up the challenge. The economist John FitzGerald (son of Garret) told me: 'Attracting foreign multinationals was necessary in the 1960s, to change the atmosphere in Ireland, and it is doubtful whether we could have done better with a different strategy. But the policy should have been refocused later: instead of devoting large sums to subsidizing foreign investors, more should have been spent on helping traditional Irish firms to grow bigger. As it is, we are stuck with this dichotomy between the very successful hi-tech foreign-owned sector, and the stick-in-the-mud, employment-intensive but relatively low-skilled older Irish industry.'

In line with this thinking, since the early 1990s the official emphasis has moved towards doing more to help indigenous firms. Here the problem is that Ireland still lacks a strong industrial class of its own, or a capitalist ethos. The Irish often display brilliant entrepreneurship when they emigrate, or go to work for foreign firms, but in a purely Irish context they have seldom found much incentive to develop it, either under British rule or more recently. Even today, Irish society is not fully geared towards encouraging this kind of success.

After independence, Irish capitalists tended to invest their money abroad, mostly in London, rather than use it to build up the Irish economy. Many of the most talented individuals, too, preferred to emigrate. Nor did the protectionist era exactly encourage modern dynamism among business people, cocooned within their tiny, sluggish home market. So after Lemass lifted the barriers, hundreds of little out-of-date firms were simply wiped out by the trade competition from Britain or the new foreign investors, and later from the Continent as well. Whole sectors virtually disappeared, mainly in textiles, footwear and engineering. The Government tried to promote some new industrial developments, notably the Shannon Free Airport venture (see p. 143); but the private sector did little to follow this lead. So today Ireland has remarkably few well-known native firms, at least in manufacturing. Exceptions are Waterford Crystal, which has been in trouble (see p. 137); Cement Roadstone; and the Smurfit packaging group, which operates mainly abroad (see below). As for Ireland's most famous traditional firm, Guinness & Sons, brewers of black creamy porter since 1759, it has now become a multinational based in London; the old brewery in Dublin is today merely a subsidiary of a worldwide empire, and the Guinness family own very few of the shares.

Today nearly all Irish firms are still too small to be able to export effectively; or they are still too heavily geared towards the British market and remain wary of venturing further afield. Most manufactured exports come from the multinationals. However, after years of prompting by independent economists, the Government has now finally committed itself to giving more support to native industry. In 1980 it commissioned an inquiry into industrial policy by the international consultancy firm Telesis. This criticized IDA policy and urged that more be done to strengthen selected Irish firms. But its findings were virtually ignored. In 1991, however, a Government by now more alert to the problem initiated another inquiry, by an Irish team under the prominent industrialist Jim Culliton. His report, while pointing out that foreign investment was still crucial, did urge the need to redress the balance by building up the indigenous sector; and it advised that better tax incentives be given to domestic firms. This time the Government took more notice. It is now slanting its grants less towards capital-intensive projects, and more towards job creation. And it is trying to encourage better 'linkage' between the multinationals and local Irish firms, so that the former can provide work for the latter.

There remains however the issue of *how* to stimulate Irish entrepreneurship. About this the Irish tend to be highly self-critical, as witness the view I was given by one leading economics writer, Paul Tansey: 'Why is domestic industry not succeeding? We have a low ratio of company start-ups, so it's clear that people don't want to go into business. Why? Because it involves high risks, without offering high enough rewards to make this worthwhile. People would rather opt for a high-status career in the professions, or a safe, well-pensioned post in the civil service, which today provides quite high salaries, often above £50,000 in its upper ranks. Or they will try to make money out of rents from property.

Ireland is simply not a profit-oriented society – it's a feature of many closed cultures and economies, as ours used to be for so long.' Others I met were just as outspoken. A civil servant said: 'The only business dynamism and risk-taking is in property deals and horse-trading, not in serious manufacturing.' And a merchant in Sligo blamed the famous Irish spirit of begrudgery: 'People who succeed here in Ireland are regarded with suspicion, yet if they leave and make a fortune abroad, then they're admired.' Might the problem also relate to the influence of the Catholic Church, which unlike Protestantism has no pronounced work ethic? In the period of British rule, much of the business enterprise came from the Dublin Protestants, but most of them have now gone (p. 176).

However, despite this somewhat negative picture, there are signs today that attitudes are beginning to change. Younger people have become more eager to go to the newly opened business schools, and a new breed of self-confident yuppies is emerging. Executives have returned from abroad with managerial skills, or they have trained with multinationals in Ireland. They have the abilities: but the readiness to take risks remains a rarer asset.

A handful of Irish entrepreneurs have become household names: but their successes have generally been in a foreign context, or in services or finance rather than in industry. Witness that trio of high-flyers, Tony O'Reilly, Tony Ryan and Michael Smurfit. O'Reilly, born and educated in Dublin, began his business career in Ireland, worked for H. J. Heinz there and in Britain, then rose up within that giant US food corporation to become its president and chief executive in Pittsburgh, with the highest salary of any American manager. He has also built up various interests in Ireland, including ownership of Independent Newspapers. Tony Ryan, running a purely Irish firm, has recently done less well. After working for Aer Lingus, he then built up the Shannon-based Guinness Peat Aviation into the world's largest aircraft leasing company and Ireland's biggest privately owned service firm. GPA, however, has now been hit badly by world recession, and in 1993–4 was having to restructure and make heavy cutbacks.

The third of the trio, Michael Smurfit, has made his vast fortune in the humdrum world of packaging, though his own jet-setting lifestyle is supremely glamorous. His father, who was English, set up a cardboard-box factory in Dublin which Smurfit later took over, and gradually expanded into a worldwide empire by acquiring or founding packaging companies in the USA, Britain and elsewhere. His group, Jefferson Smurfit, employs some 39,000 people, only 2,000 of them in Ireland itself; but it is Ireland's largest private company, the only one to be listed among the world's top 1,000. He operates from stylish modern offices in Donnybrook, Dublin, but for tax reasons he is domiciled in Monte Carlo. He is also a leading sponsor of Irish horse-racing, his passion. His image has now suffered somewhat from the Telecom Éireann affair. But he continues to show a brilliant flair for finance. A man of such talent and ambition could never be content within the narrow confines of Ireland, and inevitably he has sought his major successes abroad.

Not everyone can be an O'Reilly or a Smurfit, and today the main need is for medium- or small-scale entrepreneurs who will develop effectively inside Ireland. Just a few are emerging. In Galway I met Charles Coughlan, a manic, fast-talking whiz-kid who spent twenty years with a US multinational, then in 1980 founded his own firm, Precision Steel Components, making precision fasteners; he now has a staff of fifty and a turnover of some £1·7 million and exports 35 per cent of his output. Galway's university college encourages its graduates to set up their own little firms locally; and a Galway business-innovation centre has stimulated a range of small local activities, such as harp-making and knitwear. In Dublin, the minister of finance, Bertie Ahern, told me: 'For too long we've tried mainly to attract larger foreign firms, employing 500 people or more here. We have been slow to move, as the Germans and Japanese have now done, to an emphasis on smaller companies with a staff of 25 or so. But now we are changing our philosophy.'

There will still of course be an important role for the foreign investor, notably in hi-tech and in modern services, where Ireland's peripheral island position is less of a drawback. The Government has nurtured dreams of building up Dublin as a world hub of finance, a kind of mini-Zurich, and with this in view it recently created the International Financial Services Centre, a huge, gleaming building of black glass beside the river in central Dublin. Relying on its usual weaponry of tax incentives, the Government by 1993 had managed to attract some 200 companies to open offices there, most of them foreign, and the operation seemed to be going quite well, despite the recession.

In 1993 the new Fianna Fáil/Labour Government split the IDA into two parts, on the lines proposed by the Culliton Report. One agency will promote indigenous firms, the other will continue to woo foreign ones. Grants and tax concessions will continue at their former level. It remains to be seen whether this shift in strategy will have greater success in creating jobs – in a land where high unemployment is much the worst economic black spot.

Soaring unemployment: waiting for the birth rate's **deus ex machina**

From the 1920s right up until 1980, the official Irish unemployment rate was fairly low, varying between 5 and 8 per cent. In a sense this gave a false picture, for many people found work only by emigrating, while many others remained in poverty on small, overmanned family farms, where they were classified as 'self-employed', not completely out of work. Then in the 1980s urban unemployment took grip, and the official figure rose faster than in other countries at that time, reaching 17·7 per cent by 1987. Since the early 1990s Ireland, equal with Spain, has enjoyed the dubious distinction of having the highest jobless rate in the industrialized world, according to OECD.* And yet, strangely, in the same

---

* As in other countries, there are two ways of calculating the unemployment rate. The number of people claiming benefit was in 1994 just 300,000, or 21·5 per cent of the labour force. But under the International Labour Office definition of those perceiving themselves to be unemployed, the figure was 15·8 per cent, and this of course is the one the Government prefers to use. In either case, Ireland along with Spain still has the highest unemployment rate in the EU, in real terms.

period the economy itself was growing rapidly. In 1986–91 it expanded by some 27 per cent, the fastest rate in the EC, yet employment in those years increased by only 4 per cent. So why is there this mysterious inability of the Irish economy to translate growth into jobs?

Economists adduce five main reasons. One is the continuing rural exodus into the towns, as farming modernizes, the CAP cutbacks begin to bite and farmers' families swell the ranks of those seeking other work. This exodus has made its impact later than in most EC countries: in the late 1960s, 37 per cent of the active population was involved in agriculture, whereas the figure is now 11 per cent and still falling. Secondly, the Government's spending cuts of the 1980s reduced job outlets in the public sector. Thirdly, recent recession has led to cutbacks and closures especially among indigenous firms. Fourth, technological progress in the foreign-owned modern industries has enabled some of them to increase productivity and reduce staff. Yet these firms have meanwhile gone on expanding their exports, and this accounts largely for the high Irish growth rate, which thus is something of a mirage – 'our miracle of jobless growth', said one critic.

Lastly, and above all, the ranks of the jobless have been swollen by the reduced scope for emigration (see page 310) caused by recession abroad. With its traditionally high birth rate, Ireland has long relied on emigration to remedy its employment problem; and in the decades since independence, Britain above all has offered an abundant market. Most of the exiles have left by necessity, but some have gone willingly, to see the world and gain experience, hoping to return one day – as sometimes they have been able to do. Thus in the 1970s, when a booming Ireland was actually creating jobs while the British economy was stagnating, the total of those returning even exceeded that of emigrants by some 12,000 a year. Then in the early 1980s net emigration resumed. But within a few years all the principal destinations, the UK, the USA and Australia, were in recession and their supply of jobs was drying up, while Europe offered no major alternative. So the Irish stayed at home, or they returned to face the dole: between 1988 and 1991, annual net emigration dropped from

46,000 to just 1,000. The Government was able to claim that in roughly the same period some 40,000 new jobs were created in industry: but this was not enough to answer the needs of a growing labour market, swelled not only by the drop in emigration but by the high birth rate of twenty years previously. Today the number of youngsters entering the labour market each year still exceeds the total reaching retirement age.

It may seem surprising that such high unemployment has not led to greater social unrest. The experts predict that this could well develop, if the level were to rise any higher. But the Irish are cushioned by fairly generous unemployment benefits, whose basic £57 a week can in practice be doubled by child allowances; and as a full-time low-paid job might earn only about £120 a week, of which part goes in tax for a single person, the financial incentive to seek work can be slight. Some critics claim that the Government is 'subsidizing idleness', and they urge that the rates be cut. These are now somewhat higher than British ones, which of course increases the tendency for Irish emigrants losing their jobs in Britain to return to draw their dole in Ireland. In short, unemployment is costly to the economy: more serious, it is highly demoralizing to a large number of individuals, and thus to Irish society as a whole (see p. 234).

The problem has become *the* major national debate. Plenty of remedies are put forward, but it is hard to see what any Government could do beyond promoting industrial and rural development, and waiting for an end to world recession. Some experts urge that more should be done to retrain those put out of work; but this is expensive. A training authority, FÁS (pronounced 'faws', Foras Áisenna Saothair), has been running programmes for some 60,000 people a year, helped by the EC's Social Fund. But some of its projects have been simply a way of disguising unemployment. In 1993 the new Government began to create a more ambitious National Training Scheme, including a system of apprenticeship; but the Irish, unlike the Germans, have little tradition of this, and employers have always proved reluctant to help finance it. A more immediate way of alleviating unemployment might be to introduce temporary part-time work schemes, as in many countries, whereby those on the dole are given simple local community jobs to do, such as helping with the environment. The unions are sympathetic to this idea, as they are to reductions in overtime, and early retirement schemes: but they are less interested in job-sharing. They want stronger incentives for companies to invest their profits on job-creating schemes, and they want to see levies imposed on firms that refuse to do so.

Unemployment seems likely to continue at its present level for some time, and might even rise slightly. But then a *deus ex machina* will certainly appear in the form of the sharp demographic downturn in recent years (see p. 18). The hitherto high birth rate of this Catholic country began to dip in the mid-1960s, then fell much faster in the 1980s. The rate is now stabilized. It remains above the west European average, but only just. And from about the year 2000 this change will start to make an impact on the labour market through a big reduction in the number of school-leavers. This ought to alleviate not only unemployment but the age-old Irish scourge of emigration – but only if the economy as a whole fares well.

A smooth labour harmony, almost German-style

If the employment situation is bad, it is in no way due to poor labour relations, for these are remarkably smooth in Ireland – one of the brightest features of the political/economic scene. Dealings between unions, employers and ministers tend to be chummy and personal in the Irish manner; and although bargaining can be tough, common sense usually prevails. Thus a series of wage agreements have helped inflation and strikes alike to be kept to a low level.

In fact, the labour climate seems more like Germany's than Britain's. It is true that Ireland inherited its trade-union structure from the British, and for many years links were close: but since the coming of EC membership, Irish unions have tended to look much more to their new German partners for their model, rather than to the class-ridden British system. Co-management, however, is still much less developed than in Germany; and the fifty-seven Irish unions, varying greatly in size, are still far too numerous for their own good. As in Britain in the past, they defy attempts to amalgamate them. They are grouped within the Irish Congress of Trade Unions (ICTU); and the overall level of union membership, some 48 per cent, is above the EC average.

In ICTU's modern branch offices in Cork, I met Joe O'Flynn, neatly dressed like a bank manager, and a leader of the large white-collar Services, Industrial, Professional and Technical Union (SIPTU). He gave me a bright, optimistic picture which others would bear out: 'We have a policy of close cooperation with employers, there's no feeling of "them" and "us". In the Cork area, very few bosses are of the tough old-fashioned type, nearly all are open and modern-minded, and with them we share a true Irish sense of comradeship: our shop stewards have meals and drinks with them. It's all far better than in Britain, more like Germany, and very professional: our officials are trained in modern personnel and management skills. If union membership is so high, I think it's partly because of these good relations, for employees have no fear of being victimized if they join a union. Senior managers are often members, too. In Cork we've had no strike in the private sector for ten years. Strikes for us are a thing of the past.' Few British unionists would talk like that.

At the national level in Dublin, the Taoiseach and other ministers tend to be on easy first-name terms and in regular telephone contact with the main union leaders such as Peter Cassells, head of ICTU, and Bill Attley, head of SIPTU. Of recent Taoisigh, the liberal Garret FitzGerald was less successful at dealing with the unions, curiously enough, than the more autocratic Charles Haughey. One ICTU leader explained to me: 'Garret was too fussy and academic, with Thatcherite attitudes. But Charlie was more pragmatic, he had the common touch, he could feel out what the unions wanted, he saw the advantage to himself of good relations with us, and he publicly acknowledged our positive role. So he was able to deliver on the wage agreements. At a European level, he had good relations with that keen unionist, Jacques Delors.'

There had been some national wage agreements in the 1960s and '70s, and the policy intensified in 1987 when Haughey returned to power. The national debt was then high, and he decided to harness the unions' support for his efforts to bring the finances back into proper shape. He negotiated with them a Programme for National Recovery, whereby they agreed to give no-strike guarantees in return for promises of 2·5 per cent annual pay rises over a three-year period. Employees were none too pleased, for wages did not quite keep up with inflation, but the unions kept to the bargain. Then in 1990 Haughey proposed to extend the pact with a three-year Programme for Economic and Social Progress. This time, the unions negotiated more toughly, demanding higher wage rises and a greater say in formulating social policy. Finally a 4 per cent annual rise was agreed (inflation was now 3·5 per cent). But in 1991 the Government threatened to go back on the agreement as far as the public sector was concerned, claiming that such generous rises would upset its budgetary policy. There was a crisis, with the prospect of a general strike in the public services, but finally a compromise was reached.

So the PNR and PESP have in the main been a success: they have encouraged a wage restraint that has contributed to Ireland's good recent inflation record. Thanks also to them, and to the work of a labour court and a conciliation service (a little like ACAS in Britain), strikes in private industry have been rare. However, a few have broken out in the banks and in some public services, where small, diehard unions with an old-style ethos have clashed with equally out-of-date managements – a last vestige in Ireland of what cynics might describe as the British tradition. In the banks, the dispute was over a plan to extend opening hours. In the postal services, a lengthy strike in 1992 was provoked by a scheme, tactlessly applied, to introduce new work practices in the Dublin central sorting office. And in the same year the RTE's television programmes were blacked out for nine weeks when staff protested against plans to benefit from the new technology by reducing film-crew sizes. All these strikes had a Luddite element, but management were also to blame. In all cases, compromise solutions were finally reached.

Although the strike level is highest in public services and in semi-State enterprises, ironically it is here that labour relations have advanced furthest towards the enlightened German or Scandinavian model of co-management. Since 1977, staff representatives make up one-third of the boards of such bodies as the Post Office, Telecom Éireann and Aer Lingus; this system works quite well, and both sides claim to be happy with it. The unions have been pressing gently for its extension into larger private companies, but employers are wary, while IDA warns that it could deter American investors. The most that the unions have obtained is a formal commitment by firms to consider a voluntary system. Meanwhile, along with all the rest of the EU except Britain, Ireland did sign up for the controversial Social Chapter in the Maastricht Treaty, which gives legal backing to employees' rights of consultation. Employers remain wary that German-style *Mitbestimmung* might reduce firms' competitivity with the UK, still their main market. 'But just look at the Germans and Danes,' retort the unions: 'Are their firms so uncompetitive?'

The impact of Europe: spending the Brussels bonanza

Over and above the huge sums of special aid, membership since 1973 of the European Community (European Union) has brought a variety of other benefits to Ireland. One important one has been the sharp reduction in its over-dependence on Britain, which persisted long after it gained political freedom. In the 1960s over 70 per cent of all Irish exports were still going to the UK, and only 7 per cent to what are now the ten other countries of the EU. But then, with the opening up of new European markets, Britain's share of Irish exports fell to 34 per cent by 1987, while that of the rest of the EC rose to 39 per cent – a remarkable shift. Today Britain remains Ireland's best customer, but Germany is in second place. Similarly, when the European Monetary System was created in 1979, Ireland chose to join right away, while Britain stayed outside: thus the Irish punt broke away from its age-old fixed parity with sterling, and aligned itself instead on the stronger Deutschmark. Since the partial collapse of the EMS's exchange-rate mechanism in 1993, the punt's ties with the DM have loosened a little, but there is no question of its returning to the sterling fold.

Garret FitzGerald, by no means an anti-British statesman, gave me his view of the EC's salutary impact on Irish relations with Britain, both economic and human: 'Until the 1970s we were a largely agricultural country and the only market open to us was Britain, which had a cheap food policy and gave us very low prices: it was a classic neocolonial relationship. EC membership changed that in two ways. First, Britain lost the possibility of exploiting us, for it now had to pay the same food prices as the rest of the Community. Secondly, for our industrial goods we now gained access to the fast-growing EC market, instead of being confined to the slow-growing British market. EC entry also had a psychological effect on our relations with Britain. With the ending of economic dependence we acquired a new self-confidence and became an equal partner with Britain, in the new multilateral context of the EC. In fact, many other EC members are closer to us on any given issue than Britain. In the EC, we are in ad hoc alliance with different countries on different matters, and are no longer traumatized by the old intense bilateral relationship of a dependent character.'

On the broader political question of Ireland's role in Europe, there are still plenty of people, especially on the Left, who remain sceptical about the EU, and their voices were raised during the debate on the Maastricht Treaty (see p. 329). The economist the late Raymond Crotty, in particular, for years led a crusade against the EC, which he saw as a kind of conspiracy by the big landowners and other capitalists. Ireland, he told me in 1992, could have become a more prosperous *and* a more just society by staying out on its own, with a policy of rigorous nationalism. But his Bennite ideas find little echo among other economists, let alone in business circles, where nearly everyone believes that in economic terms the EC has been a boon for Ireland. It has boosted exports and growth, helped to attract foreign investment, and widened horizons. The price paid has been the closure of many small Irish firms, unable to cope with the new competition. As for the farmers, the Common Agricultural Policy (see pp. 97–8) brought big advantages in the 1970s to a country in which farming still plays so large a role; and today Ireland remains a major net beneficiary of EU aid in this sector – even if farmers angered by the recent CAP cut-backs do not always appreciate it.

It would be too cynical to suppose that the huge hand-outs from Brussels, given to Ireland as one of the EU's four poorer members, are the only reason why the Irish remain relatively so pro-European. But certainly the aid helps. At the time of the 1992 referendum on the Maastricht Treaty, one argument used by the Government for voting 'yes' (as the Irish did by 69 to 31 per cent) was that Ireland stood to gain several billions from the EC's enlarged Structural Funds. Reynolds told the voters that he expected £8 billion for 1994–9. When the EC proposed rather less, the Government angrily came near to vetoing the whole deal. Finally in September 1993 it settled for £7·2 billion, which was still generous, more per capita than the aid given to poorer Greece and Portugal. The Irish are clever at striking a hard bargain in the EC, and they know how to plead their cause.

Already in 1989–93 Ireland received some £3 billion from these Structural Funds, which have since been hugely expanded in order to compensate the less favoured countries and regions against the possibly negative impact of the '1992' Single Market (see p. 91). Money from the funds is reckoned by economists to add between 0·5 and 1 per cent to the Irish annual growth rate: i.e., in a year when growth might otherwise be 2 per cent of GDP, it becomes 2·5 to 3 per cent. In 1992, some 45 per cent of the money came from the Regional Fund and 37 per cent from the Social Fund; the rest, 18 per cent, was spent on 'agricultural guidance', which is a fund for such matters as rural development and sheep headage (see pp. 99 and 116) and comes in addition to the regular CAP market supports. The Social Fund is primarily for vocational education or retraining, with the aim of creating jobs. For example, at a heritage centre in Waterford, I met unemployed teenagers being trained to use computers, with EC aid. The Regional Fund is essentially for infrastructure and public works, e.g. new main roads, urban-renewal schemes, sewage works, even cultural ventures such as the restoration of Kilkenny Castle. The grants are substantial: 50 to 75 per cent of capital costs for public projects, usually 30 per cent for private ones. All the new trunk roads in the West have been built with this aid;* and all over Ireland you see blue placards with their familiar circle of twelve gold stars, proclaiming, 'This project is part financed by the European Community's Structural Funds.' Unlike some of Britain's remoter regions, the Irish feel no shame about publicly expressing gratitude for this EC largesse. Sometimes there is dissension between Dublin and Brussels on how the aid should be spent. The Irish Government first puts up its own proposals, and the EU Commission then decides whether these meet its own criteria. So both sides have to agree, and for some projects Brussels will refuse to give aid. Some independent economists argue that too much of the Social Fund is devoted to infrastructure and that money should also be spent on aid to industrial investment, but this is not EU practice.

A sharper debate is on regionalization. It is the preferred policy of the Commission to give most of its aid direct to regional authorities (as it does in decentralized countries like Spain and Germany), and then let them decide how the funds should be spent, thus bypassing national governments. However, the Irish Government refuses to regionalize (see p. 50). So the EU has no

---

* Road standards in Ireland vary greatly. The West has been given some priority, and the new express roads leading to towns such as Galway and Sligo are excellent. But, curiously, the main roads from Dublin to Cork, and from Dublin to Dundalk (for Belfast), are still patchy: many of the little towns along their route still have no bypasses, and traffic can snarl up for hours. These roads are now being modernized, but very slowly: 'We don't regard the Dublin–Belfast route as a high priority,' said one planning official: 'who wants to drive to Belfast, anyway?' This seems curious, in view of the government policy of closer North–South links. It is also true that many local businessmen fear that bypasses would spoil their trade, so in some towns they have managed to block government schemes for buying up the land for new ring roads.

choice but to channel almost all its aid via Dublin, and in the process to allow the whole Republic to be treated as a disfavoured region within the orbit of the Structural Funds. The Irish Government argues that this is only fair, for the Dublin region itself is underdeveloped, with high unemployment, and needs aid as well as the struggling West. This may be so. But the Western areas complain that Dublin as usual is neglecting them for its own purposes.

Lastly, when the Single Market came formally into operation in January 1993 and many barriers went down, the Irish were not so sure that *this* major new EC development was going to be as beneficial to them as others in the past. Firms in Ireland, as in other countries, did of course stand to benefit from the easier market access and movement of staff, from the reduction of tedious delays and paperwork over customs formalities, and so on. And certain sectors where Ireland is relatively strong, such as insurance, property development, and food processing, seemed likely to gain from the greater competition. But some sections of the Irish distribution system, clumsy and out of date, looked to be in danger as foreign services moved in. And although the Government was outwardly welcoming the Single Market, there were some private fears that Ireland's peripherality might be a handicap – as the economist Paul Tansey stressed to me: 'The Single Market could well accentuate the pull of industries and services towards the centre of the EC, with its excellent infrastructure and huge populations, to the disadvantage of outlying regions such as ours. We did negotiate excellent terms for the Structural Funds, which are intended quite largely to compensate the poorer or remoter areas against this attraction of the centre: but these funds are only temporary, whereas the drawbacks of our peripherality will be permanent. In the last analysis, who will want to invest in Ireland, if on the same conditions he can set up right in the heart of the EU?'

So today how does the future look for the Irish economy? When I asked the Taoiseach, Albert Reynolds, how he saw the prospects of Ireland narrowing the economic gap with her richer neighbours, he said: 'Further European integration is our best hope. I'm a believer in the Single Market, and in European Monetary Union.' In fact, Ireland today is fulfilling most of the criteria laid down for EMU convergence, save for the level of public debt.

Apart from the black spot of unemployment, the Irish economy today is in reasonably healthy shape, for a Europe still in recession. Irish Governments in the past few years have managed affairs skilfully. And the EU comparative figures for the years 1988–93 are striking. In that period, Irish annual GDP growth was 5·0 per cent, against an EU average of 1·7 per cent; annual inflation averaged 2·4 per cent, compared with an EU figure of 4·6 per cent; and the external-payments surplus was the highest in the EU. If this progress is maintained, Ireland will continue slowly to catch up with her wealthier partners. And this will become easier once the fall in the birth rate impinges on the labour market, thus lowering the high cost of unemployment.

The Irish have come to expect to live like north Europeans, yet the country's wealth is nearer to south European levels; and these popular demands put a constant strain on the budget, leading to repeated laments by the pundits that the nation is living above its means. Whereas the earlier Whitaker/Lemass adventure took place in a propitious time of world boom, the next stage of this still uncompleted economic revolution now has to face a much tougher world climate. This stage involves finding a new deal for Irish native industry – and also finding a new role for Ireland's smaller and poorer farmers.

4

THE SMALL FARMERS: MUCH LESS POVERTY, BUT A FUTURE FULL OF DOUBT

Agriculture in Ireland today, more than in most EU countries, faces the dilemma of how to reconcile two very different needs: on the one hand, the nation's economic need for efficient modern commercial farming, vital for the export trade; on the other, the human and social needs of the smaller, less efficient farmers, still so numerous. Their existence is now threatened, and with it the whole tissue of traditional Irish rural life.

Farming is still Ireland's major industry, accounting for 42 per cent of all foreign earnings; agricultural exports, consisting mainly of livestock, meat and dairy products, exceed imports by three to one. But most of this output comes from a relatively small number of large, well-organized, highly competitive farms in the south and south-east, a world away from the struggling small-holders on the poorer soil of the west and centre. Here some farms are properly mechanized but others remain antiquated: in Co. Limerick I found one man still using the rusty potato-sower that his grandfather had bought in 1911. Farming for many of these families is less a modern commercial activity than an ancestral way of life; the poorer ones depend on State hand-outs ('the farmers' dole'), or they take other part-time jobs to make a living. And they are pessimistic about their future.

The Common Agricultural Policy helped nearly all of them in the 1970s, dragging even the poorer ones out of their worst poverty. But it was then the same story as throughout the EC: the farmers had first been encouraged to invest and produce more, but this simply led to the notorious surpluses, to the beef and butter mountains, and so the quotas and other cut-backs were imposed.

Many Irish farmers today feel cheated by this. 'I was doing all right until this efficiency thing came in,' said one milk producer in Co. Mayo; 'but it now seems we were led up the wrong path. After investing in new equipment, I'm heavily in debt to the banks, but the EU quotas prevent me from expanding.'

Irish farmers, like the French, are great complainers; and they tend to forget how much their material life has improved since the old days. But their pessimism today does have some grounds. The CAP reforms of 1992 and the GATT deal of December 1993 are now imposing further cut-backs, which are intended to be borne mainly by the larger, richer farmers, while the poorer ones will be helped by direct grants; but in time the latter will suffer too, and many small farms will close. Agriculture's share of the Irish active population (13·8 per cent in 1993, the highest level in the EU after Greece and Portugal) has already fallen hugely in recent decades, and is bound to drop further as farming adjusts to the new conditions.

The life of the poorer country people has long been central to Irish culture and the Irish imagination. They used to be fearfully poor, most of them, and they carried a legacy of sufferings from the Famine and earlier; but they had dignity, wit and warmth, and a creative and original folk civilization that has inspired so much of Irish literature, from Yeats and Synge to Brian Friel. Today, how much of that culture survives, or can survive? In the past forty years, modern benefits have arrived. In place of their old hovels, many farmers have built themselves neat new white bungalows (with dubious aesthetic effect, see p. 154); they have videos and cars, and foreign goodies bought in the supermarkets. Some poverty remains, but not like it was in the old days, and most younger farmers now live tolerably well. Or else they leave, and this is the problem, for the mass farm exodus has left many rural communities half-deserted, bereft of their younger, more active members; and the impact of modernity, notably of television, has dealt a blow to the old folk culture, to the customs and crafts. Traditional music may be enjoying a revival, but there is no more storytelling on winter nights, no more summer dancing at Lughnasa. Some of the old village warmth is lost.

So are these poorer rural communities condemned to depopulate further, and to die? Or can they be given a new lease of life, through a diversification into new activities that will enable farmers to remain on the land? This today is a major talking-point. Ironically, the farmers most eager to stay on the land tend to be the older, more conservative ones who are the least able to adapt to the new changes now needed. For historical reasons, they remain fiercely attached to their own soil, and will proudly refuse to sell it outside the family. As they grow old, if there is no heir to take over, they will continue wearily farming their land, often maybe letting much of it run to seed, and refusing to retire. It could be argued that at least this inefficiency helps to relieve the EU surpluses: but it hardly makes for a dynamic local scene. So today, in line with EU policy, older farmers are being given new incentives to retire; and the younger, more active ones are being officially encouraged to diversify, if they can no longer make a living from the West's near-monoculture of livestock and dairy goods. The purpose is that these regions should now find some new future in forestry, or 'agri-tourism' (holidays on the farm), or modern cottage industries, organic farming or vegetable-growing, which till now has been strangely neglected. But will all this be enough to revive the romantic, menaced West of Ireland?

CAP reform: a cattle dealer from Sligo wields the big knife in Brussels

The lovely hills of Kerry and Connemara may seduce the tourist, but they are not so kind to the farmers who live from that soil. Most of it is too stony or too damp for much except livestock pasture. Even the potato, that former staple of the Irish rural diet, has been abandoned by most farmers. They find it difficult to market, and Ireland today actually imports potatoes on quite a scale. Governments in the past have made sporadic efforts to promote tillage, but this never caught on widely, and today 71 per cent of Irish farm output derives from cattle and milk – 'We have a cow-based economy here,' I was told in Co. Sligo. In the south and south-east, however, from Co. Cork through to the Dublin area, the land is better suited to cereals. Here barley, wheat and beet thrive, the plump dairy herds prosper too, and the fields are as lush and neat as in Norfolk or Normandy. In fact, the gulf between Ireland's rich and poor farms has tended to widen since the 1970s, aggravated by an unjust CAP system which till now has favoured the bigger farmers by paying its subsidies per quantity of produce.

The mentality of the smaller farmers has been shaped by their historical experience. Until the late nineteenth century nearly all of them were tenants with few rights, often ruthlessly exploited by absentee landlords: this added to their sufferings during the period of the Famine and after. Then the Land Acts of the 1880s gave many of them the rights of ownership, and this was consolidated by the Free State's land reforms of 1923, so to-day nearly all small farmers own their own land. But their family memories of these struggles remain so vivid that it helps to perpetuate the stubborn devotion to property among older farmers, even today. The younger ones at least are showing less interest.

The land reforms brought a greater sense of freedom, but not any sudden new prosperity. From the 1920s right up until the late 1950s, Irish farming changed hardly at all, stuck in the embrace of de Valera's conservative ideals of frugal rural simplicity. In 1958, when farming in many other countries was modernizing fast, techniques and lifestyles on the smaller Irish farms remained almost Victorian: for example, only one farm in twenty had an indoor lavatory, few had electricity. Farming families' horizons, however, were still very limited and their expectations low, and a farm of thirty acres or so was just about viable, though many were below this level. But then came the Lemass era, with its wind of change; at the same time, partly through radio and cinema small farmers were becoming more aware of the widening gulf between their lives and those of townspeople or the larger producers. So they grew more restive, no longer accepting emigration as the only remedy. Some of them took loans for buying tractors, cars and farm machinery, or for building new homes. Others took factory jobs, as Ireland industrialized.

And the exodus from the land continued, as it still does today. The statistics are remarkable. In 1926, some 52 per cent of the active population was working on the land; by 1961 it had fallen to 29 per cent, and today it is under 14 per cent. This has been due above all to mechanization, for a fifty-acre farm that used to require ten pairs of hands now needs only two or three. Also, young people will no longer accept the drudgery of farm work, if they can find better jobs in the towns, as was possible in the boom years. The employed farm labourer, once a common species, has virtually disappeared except from the larger farms. And the size of the average farm has been increasing, as many farmers die with no heir, or as some inheritors prefer to sell their land. The proportion of farms with fewer than 30 acres fell from 56 per cent in 1926 to 40 per cent in 1961 and 21 per cent today; in the same period, the percentage of farms of over 100 acres rose from 8·6 per cent in 1926 to 11·7 per cent in 1961 and 18 cent today. And the total number of Irish farms has dropped from 264,000 in 1926 to 209,000 in 1961 and under 120,000 today. Quite a transformation.

If Ireland in the early 1970s was so eager to join the European Community, one paramount reason was that with its large farming sector it stood to benefit greatly, seeing that so much of the EC's budget went on agricultural-price supports. And the Irish were not disappointed. First, EC entry removed the reliance on the low-price British market and pushed farmers' prices up to the much higher Continental levels; second, the farmers also gained the largesse of the CAP's price-guarantee and export-subsidy system, which covered all their main kinds of produce – beef, dairy products and most cereals, as well as pig-meat and sugar. Under this system, Irish net receipts from the EC reached £448 million a year by 1978; farmers' incomes rose rapidly during the 1970s, and signs of a new prosperity filled parts of the countryside. But this bonanza ended in 1979, when incomes fell quite sharply owing to external monetary factors; they then picked up again unevenly during the 1980s.

Ireland on balance has done very well from the CAP. But even in Ireland the CAP came under criticism during the 1980s – from economists, taxpayers and small farmers – for its two main iniquities: it encouraged over-production, and it benefited most the rich farmers who needed it least. The subsidies were paid per quantity of produce, and until quotas were introduced there were virtually no ceilings, so the more you produced, the more the CAP gave you. This delighted the larger farmers, but left the small ones grumbling that the cake was unfairly shared out, as of course it was. And the supports gave everyone an incentive to produce as much as they could, for a farmer's unsold stock was bought up by the bountiful CAP under the 'intervention' system. Thanks to this, and to technical progress, Irish farm output rose by 50 per cent in the period 1973–92, as its succulent beef and butter helped to raise the peaks of the CAP's 'mountains'.

In 1983–4 the EC began to take concerted measures to reduce these surpluses, notably in milk and cereals. Milk quotas were introduced. But Garret FitzGerald, then Taoiseach, arguing the special importance of dairy farming to Ireland's economy and to its rural society, managed to persuade his partners to grant him a special deal, which set the Irish quotas at a level 12 per cent higher than the EC average. It was a skilful piece of bargaining. Even so, the quotas were soon making even Irish dairy farmers feel the pinch. Unable to increase their milk output, some of them moved into beef production: but this simply increased the EC beef glut and sent prices falling. By 1990–91, owing to a number of factors including the impact of German unification, the prices of beef, lamb and milk were all tumbling; the farmers' unions claimed that real incomes had fallen by 16 per cent in 1990, though Government economists preferred to put the figure at 7 per cent. When I toured the rural West in 1992, I found little but gloom and indignation: 'I'm getting 20 per cent less for my lambs and calves than three years ago – what's the CAP for, if it can't do more to help us?' was one typical comment.

Farmers today may be disenchanted with the CAP. But most of them have done well out of it, and many have been resolute and skilful, even wily, in exploiting its advantages. For example, in the 1980s the CAP introduced special 'headage payments' for sheep-breeding in the Community's less-favoured areas, and most of Ireland was covered by this scheme. The grants were of various kinds, varying with the terrain; generally they offered between £10 and £30 per sheep annually, to a ceiling of between 200 and 1,000 sheep per farm. And many farmers leapt at this chance to add to their income; some moved specially into sheep-farming, and within a few years the total of breeding-ewes in Ireland had trebled, to 4·5 million. Most farmers applied the scheme fairly. But in some wilder areas such as Connemara it led to over-grazing on the hillsides, and this worried ecologists. In a few cases, farmers actually cheated by managing to get the same sheep counted twice by the CAP inspectors. It happened near the border, where there were unconfirmed stories of flocks being smuggled in and out of the North so as to draw two sets of payments. For the IRA, it was yet another form of fund-raising.

The Irish have also exploited to the hilt the CAP intervention funds, which remove the hassle of going out to fight in the market-place. It is true that some of the big dairies, such as Avonmore and Golden Vale, have done well with exports to Europe. But in the case of beef, reared on grass, Irish output is highly seasonal and cannot easily offer a regular supply. So the produce is 'sold into intervention', as CAP jargon puts it: that is, the CAP buys it up at a good price and stores it in the 'mountains', maybe selling it later. This happens with butter, too. In 1990 and 1991, as much as half of all Irish butter and beef went directly into intervention, while other beef was sold to non-EC countries with the help of the CAP's export subsidies (witness the Goodman affair). At one point, one-third of the 80,000-tonne EC butter mountain was Irish, even though Ireland produces only 5 per cent of all the EC's butter! So no wonder the Irish farmer has been keener on the EC than, say, the British taxpayer. But now at last the 1992 CAP reforms are forcing the Irish to change their habits.

By the early 1990s all EC Governments, even the French, were recognizing that quotas were not enough, and more radical means must be found of revising the absurd and costly system of supports and intervention, without damaging the small farmer too much.

Mounting American pressure in the GATT talks was adding to the urgency, but this was not the only factor. So the EC drew up the most far-reaching CAP reform proposals in its history. And their principal architect, the man who doggedly carried them to fruition amid the bickering lobbies of Brussels, was a tough, hard-headed ex-cattle-dealer from Sligo – the EC's redoubtable Commissioner for Agriculture in 1989–92, Ray MacSharry.

MacSharry was already a noted figure in Irish politics. Born in Sligo in 1938, he left school at fifteen, worked as a farmer, road haulier and cattle trader, and joined the Fianna Fáil Party, where he became a close ally of Charles Haughey. As his minister of finance in 1987–8, he imposed ruthless controls on public spending, and so won the nickname of 'Mack the Knife'. The same rigour he then applied to his job in Brussels, where in 1989 he became the one Irish Commissioner. He was known as a hard bargainer, pragmatic but combative – and, rare for an Irish politician, a teetotaller. Commissioners are supposed to serve Community interests, not their own national ones, and this rule MacSharry generally observed, though he is said on one occasion to have subsidized Irish greyhound breeders, and on another to have sent Irish Cheddar to Romania at EC expense, when what the Romanians had asked for was feta cheese.

Be that as it may, his *grand œuvre* in Brussels was the CAP reform, aimed at reducing subsidies by an overall net 30 per cent by switching the supports from the produce to the producers, via direct compensation to smaller farmers. MacSharry felt that these measures were right for Europe and appropriate also for Irish farming's particular needs: with his background, he understood the realities of the CAP problem, and he had firm ideas on how to cut its Gordian knot. He found an ally in the Commission's President, Jacques Delors, who also had small-farm roots (in the Auvergne). Together they steered the reform between the Scylla and Charybdis of contrasting British and French doubts. At the same time, MacSharry stood up firmly to US demands in the GATT negotiations, arguing that the EC had now agreed to major concessions and could not be expected to go further.

Adopted in 1992, the CAP reform began coming into force in

1993. Its guiding principle is to support the producer with direct aid measures linked to the size of farm and number of animals, rather than with guaranteed prices regardless of output, as hitherto. In brief, intervention buying is being scaled down; other price supports are being reduced, too, and so are milk quotas. The major cuts in subsidies for cereals, and the new 'set-asides' mainly for cereals (i.e. some land to lie fallow), are hitting the big French wheat barons far more than the Irish, not great growers of cereals (fortunately for MacSharry's domestic popularity, one might say). In return for these massive savings, farmers are being compensated by direct payments, but only up to a certain ceiling (i.e., for cattle, the limit is be 180 animals per farm). Thus the large-scale farmers will bear the brunt of the cuts. MacSharry said: 'We must stop paying huge sums to factory farmers who pollute the environment and add to the surplus stocks.' His critics suggested that he was trying to 'Sligo-ize' European agriculture by favouring smaller farmers.

Reactions in Ireland to the CAP reform were mixed. The farm unions, notably the Irish Farmers' Association (IFA) led by the big producers, were angry: they labelled MacSharry 'a second Cromwell', claiming that his reforms would wreak havoc across rural Ireland. They argued that it was wrong to introduce a kind of deficiency-payments system which would create a 'hand-out mentality': but their leaders were probably more concerned with their own falling profits. As for the small farmers, many were anxious, but not openly hostile. The reform did not prevent a seven-to-one vote in rural areas in favour of the Maastricht Treaty, in the 1992 referendum, though admittedly the CAP reform was not part of 'Maastricht'.

A battle of statistics ensued as to whether the reform would harm or help Irish farming. The unions claimed that it would cost Irish farmers at least £100 million a year. But the minister of agriculture, Joe Walsh, loyal to his Fianna Fáil colleague in Brussels, retorted that farmers would probably benefit by about £80 million. Walsh said to me: 'The reform is a bit of a curate's egg, but we had no option but to go along with it. On balance, Ireland should gain, as we have so many small farmers and relatively few big ones.' Some other comments were less equivocal. The *Irish Times* even wrote: 'The reform marks a major, radical change which is good for Irish and European agriculture. It will bring the Irish farming industry closer to the market-place and away from its heavy over-reliance on EC intervention.' But its success will depend on how the Irish farmers respond to this challenge. The richer ones will suffer large cuts in their subsidies: but they can afford it, and should be able to adapt. The more efficient medium-sized farmers may do well; and if the smaller marginal farms will now continue to disappear, this was bound to happen anyway. At least the new CAP will be far less unjust, and less wasteful, than the old system.

It may even help to rationalize the Irish meat industry, where muddle and malpractice have long been legendary. In Ray MacSharry's own Co. Sligo, one young cattle breeder told me: 'Selling meat in Ireland is a nightmare, I can assure you. The meat trade is chaos, a mafia that the Government seems unable to control; it's awash with cash, so there are endless opportunities for corruption – as the Goodman affair shows' (see p. 53). Not all would put it so strongly, but many breeders do feel that they are in the hands of ill-organized and greedy middlemen. And as the output is so seasonal, even the best abattoir or meat trader may find it hard to operate an efficient business; hence the recent spectacular collapses, such as that of the UMP meat firm in Co. Mayo. But now, as scope is reduced for the easy outlet of intervention dumping, meat firms will be forced to reorganize; they will have to either fight harder for real commercial sales abroad, or else put far more emphasis on meat-processing, rather than simply slaughtering and selling carcasses.

The farmers that I visited in the west and north-west of Ireland late in 1992, just before the MacSharry reforms began to take effect, were none of them very confident about the future of agriculture in their areas. Seán Clarke, in his late forties, is a medium-sized farmer with ninety acres of rolling pasture land in north Mayo, near Ballina, where Mary Robinson comes from. He has thirty-eight dairy cows, and he rears calves for slaughter. With his wife and four children he lives in a modern house with nondescript furnishing. Though his smile was warm, he did not speak very cheerfully. 'My grandfather owned seventeen acres here, and my father and I have gradually extended the farm since then, by buying up land. But costs keep rising, so you have to run to stand still: forty acres used to be a viable size, but today ninety seem hardly enough, and tomorrow it might be twice that – who knows? I just can't afford to buy yet more land, I'm too much in debt. The EC helped us a lot at first, but it has profited mainly the middlemen, and the milk quotas prevent us from earning more. Yes, of course I have a better living standard than my father did, and less physical drudgery. But I have to work just as long hours, and we take virtually no holidays. None of my kids are keen to take over the farm, so I don't know what its future will be. Foreigners are buying up the land round here.'

Over in Co. Leitrim, in pretty country near the border, Frank McGuinness combines sheep-breeding with tourism: 'The EC headage payments, £25 per animal per year, make it just about worthwhile for me to keep my forty sheep, which otherwise would make a loss. Lamb prices fell a few years ago, so the EC brought in these payments to help the small farmers: as a result, far more people moved into sheep, production soared, and so now prices have again plummeted – a typical crazy EC vicious circle. Why can't they get their act together? But sheep now account for only a small part of our own income. We're moving into agri-tourism.'

During the final GATT negotiations of the Uruguay Round in 1993, the farm lobby put pressure on the Government to secure a better deal from the Americans. Just as the French farmers were anxious mainly about their cereals trade, so Irish farmers were worried that their beef and dairy exports outside the EC would suffer under the GATT agreement. So Ireland discreetly backed the French position on farming. The final compromise reached with the USA in December satisfied the Government, which felt certain that Ireland's economy overall, like others, would benefit from GATT's new trade deal. But the farmers were less happy. Their beef sales to Third World countries would now be limited, and they would have to make up for this by increased trade within Europe. In 1994 they were anxiously waiting to see how the new GATT rules and the CAP reforms would affect them in practice.

Today many of them feel, not unfairly, that they have been cheated and misled by the shifts in EC and Government policy of the past years. First in the 1960s and '70s, as in other countries, they were urged to increase productivity, so the more enterprising of them invested in new equipment and ran up debts. Then in the 1980s they were told to cut back, because of the surpluses, and were faced with quotas on milk and cereals. They may recognize that the quota system is necessary, but they complain that it prevents them from becoming more efficient and prosperous, since they cannot increase their output – except by buying other farmers' quotas, as is seldom possible. 'It's a scandalous situation,' said one dairyman near Limerick, echoing a view I heard often: 'The Third World is starving, and here are we being told to produce less. The EC should subsidize us to export our food massively to poorer countries.' Alas, it is not a solution that many politicians find feasible. Instead, the logic of the CAP reforms will pursue its course. More land will be taken out of production; other uses than farming will be found for the countryside. Backward farmers, useless to the economy, will continue to disappear; and rural Ireland will continue its inexorable path of change, for better or for worse.

The 'mountainy men' and the end of an old folk culture

At a human level, there have been both gains and losses in the huge changes that have swept through Irish rural life in the past few decades. Gains, certainly, in material conditions and in individual freedom; losses, probably, in the close warmth of community and the vigour of an old folk culture.

As late as the 1920s and '30s, the rural world still retained many of the traditions of a much earlier age, especially in the West; and there are plenty of old people today who remember that time, from their childhood. On winter nights *seanachaí* (storytellers) recounted the old tales and legends, and in summer there was dancing at the crossroads; costumed straw-boys and wren-boys paid visits, and people still believed many old *piseoga* (superstitions). A housewife would churn the milk at home, bake her own bread, and often do the cooking above a peat fire on the open hearth. Sickles and scythes were still used for harvesting, rough farm furniture was made locally from wickerwork, and carts drawn by horse or donkey were still far commoner than cars or tractors, even than bicycles. It was still almost the world of Synge's *Playboy*, set in Mayo in 1907.

Little of that folk civilization today survives in daily usage; life has become more comfortable, if less picturesque. Most homes except the poorest now have television and electric cookers, while modern utility furniture has tended to replace the old handmade items, now relegated to the folk museums or to atmospheric haunts for tourists; the pony-trap, too, is mainly for the tourist. The farmer prefers his Nissan or Opel, even if some of his farm equipment may still be quite antiquated. Radio and TV have killed off the *seanachaí*, and discos have replaced crossroads dancing. However, the recent conscious revival of Gaelic culture (see p. 276), coming often from the city more than the country, means that again there are plenty of *céilthe* with Irish music. And in some places country people still practise the old folk-medicine cures (see p. 339).

Maybe more important than these changes in culture and lifestyle are the shifts in social and family patterns and attitudes. The sociologist Hugh Brody, in his book *Inishkillane: Change and Decline in the West of Ireland* (1973), gave a sombre picture of life in a village in Co. Clare around 1970. He contrasted the villagers' former community warmth and security, despite their poverty, with the 'demoralization' caused by what he called 'the impact of urban capitalism', i.e., the commercial influences that came in from outside during the 1960s and earlier. Contact with a wider outside world, he said, damaged their faith in their own society and values, giving them a complex of inferiority; the rise to power in particular of the local tradesman, the *gombeen* man (Irish

105

pejorative term for profiteer), brought in alien, corrupting money values. The villagers' old stern sense of family duty was eroded; free mutual aid between farmers became replaced by individualism; the pubs, once full of jolly, drunken singing, fell empty and silent except during the short tourist season. The villagers felt a sense of loneliness and pessimism, as they 'lost belief in the social advantages or moral worth of their own small society'.

There may be much truth in this, but it is not the whole picture. Rural communities may be breaking up, they may have lost their old certainties, they may be anxious about the future. But not only do people have far less drudgery, better creature comforts, better social and medical services, than in the old days; they also have more freedom in their personal lives. Authors other than Brody, for example Patrick Kavanagh in his wonderful epic poem *The Great Hunger* (1942), have drawn a picture of an old rural world that was stifling and desolating in its narrowness, under the pressures of a deeply puritanical Church and of family rigours (see pp. 180 and 202). Were people happier or not in the old days, when their expectations were so much less high? It is not easy to draw a fair balance. The old tight community spirit may have waned, but are not new-style community ventures now appearing? The sociologist Professor Damian Hannan suggested to me: 'Certainly Brody is right to say that the old holistic self-contained rural culture has gone. But the pattern varies greatly from place to place. You can go to parts of Mayo or Leitrim which are just as demoralized as he describes; all the young people have left, just a few old ones remain. But in some other places the sense of community is still strong, and is being used to regenerate much voluntary activity.' Or put another way, rural society is polarizing. The really poor, the sad cases such as lonely bachelors, are being marginalized; but other families are adapting to the modern world as their lives become increasingly like those of city folk.

Liam and Maureen Meehan, for example, are a go-ahead couple aged around forty, with an eighty-acre dairy farm in Co. Clare, not far from the village which Brody studied. Liam showed me his Mercedes, his video and fax, and as we drank Jameson in their airy modern sitting-room he said: 'The changes since my boyhood are unbelievable. My father did not marry till he was fifty-one, and my mother was far younger – late marriage for men was still quite common then. They had no car, no electricity; I used to cycle twenty miles with my father to cattle fairs. I left school at twelve, and took over this farm when he died, with just nine cows. Now I have fifty. Maureen and I were very poor at first, we lived in a caravan till we built this house. We couldn't afford a honeymoon, but now we've just been on holiday to Tenerife. And yet, I think possibly people were happier in the old days, they had more time, were more self-sufficient. There is not much future for farming here, so we are diversifying into tourism, getting our neighbours together to start holiday activities round our lake. That's the new community spirit for you.'

But not everyone I met was so sanguine. A woman in a tiny village in Co. Limerick said: 'The last shop here has just closed, and the school, and the post office, so we have to use the nearest small town. All is being regrouped: it's hard on elderly people without a car. Social life here is declining. And small farmers with only five or six cows are being forced out of business.' And Seán Clarke in Mayo, with his sizeable dairy farm, told me how his life had changed: 'In the 1950s my parents on this farm had just horses, no car, and no running water – before going to school, I would walk over the fields to draw water from a well for my mother, who made her own butter. We had three cows, and we grew potatoes and vegetables and sold eggs. But this kind of small-scale mixed farming has almost disappeared, it makes no money. We used to scythe the grass for hay – it was back-breaking. Today there is far less of this drudgery, yet I think I work as long hours as my father did, what with all the paperwork. And community life has changed. In the old days, there was so much mutual self-help: as a boy I used to be sent round to other farms to help them pick potatoes or gather grain, and they would do the same for us, all for free. But now people are more separate from each other, more egotistical. You are on your own much more, and you either make it or you don't.'

★

The small, marginalized farmers survive either through what is called the 'farmers' dole' or by having another job part-time. It is reckoned that only about a third of Irish farms are viable as full-time operations; another third subsist with the dole; and a third are part-time. That is, many farming families also run a shop or a pub, or they do odd jobs; or the wife, who used to be expected to help with the farm full-time, goes out and gets other work, maybe in an office. In farming households the percentage of income from non-farm sources has increased since 1973 from 30 to 46 per cent. It is a trend common throughout the EC.

Some of this extra income is from the farmers' dole, that is, from the State assistance payments that are given to poorer farmers on a means-test basis. It is not quite an unemployment benefit, for the farmers do derive some earnings from the farm: it is more like a top-up, to the level of the normal dole. And many farming families badly need it, as they struggle with isolation and poverty in the wilder parts of the West: many live not even near a village but on lonely moorlands or uplands – 'mountainy people', as the Irish call them. It could, of course, be argued that rural poverty is more endurable than the urban variety (see pp. 231–2). And even the poor, if they own their own land, can at least take some pride in the social status of farmer, and remain respected members of the community.

This may explain the tendency of many older farmers to cling on to their land unproductively, rather than sell it and retire with dignity. This relates to historic attitudes to land, in a country where possession of it still carries so much prestige.* In Mayo, I visited a man in his sixties with forty acres stretched across a fertile valley. He said that his grandfather had been the tenant there of a harsh English landlord, long since gone, and the land had become theirs in the 1880s. His five children had all left, his wife was dead, and he farmed the property alone. Germans had come wanting to buy it for holiday purposes, but he had refused: he loved his land,

---

* John B. Keane's novel *The Field*, filmed in 1991 by Jim Sheridan, suggested that even a long-standing tenancy of a piece of land, rather than legal ownership, can arouse just as fierce emotions of devotion and possession.

and where else was he to go? The authorities had come, urging him to rationalize his fragmented farm by exchanging some fields with neighbours, so that they could farm more effectively. Again he refused. What he cared for was *his* fields, the ones his forebears had acquired after all their sufferings. Today, amid some squalor, he subsisted with just a few cows and vegetables, and the dole.

It could be argued that a farmer has a perfect right to use his own land as he wishes. But in many places the clinging to it is making it harder for younger, more active people to acquire it and use it more productively for other purposes. And this annoys reformers who are trying to revitalize the West. 'Land is like religion, people just can't let it go, they hang on to it irrationally,' said one economist scathingly. 'The older farmers are too ill-educated to use the land more effectively. There's no retirement culture, so they go on till they drop.' And when a farmer dies, or if he does retire, he will nearly always try to leave his property within the family; almost 90 per cent of transfers are by inheritance, so that little land comes on to the open market, and this makes it harder for go-ahead farmers to expand their acreage. Official schemes to entice older farmers to retire have met with little response so far: but today under the new CAP reform the incentives are being increased.

Quite a number of the older farmers of this kind are solitary bachelors – a sad Irish rural phenomenon linked to past customs of marriage and family. Traditionally the eldest son would inherit the farm. But as farming has grown less viable, this privilege has become more of an obligation, and often today the farm is taken over by whichever son is prepared to stay. Until not long ago it was the custom that the inheritor would remain on the farm unwed, until all his siblings had wed or emigrated. Hence the practice of very late marriages for farmers, with 'boyhood' lasting into middle age. Usually it was the girls who left first, unwilling to accept the drudgery of being a farmer's wife (see p. 202). So by the time the unwed heir to the farm came to look for a spouse, there was not much choice locally. Still emotionally tied to his parents, and sexually innocent, if not repressed, he was often ill-equipped for seeking or finding a girl, so he never married. Today you can see them still, propping up the bars of village pubs, these 'mountainy men' in their later years, often leading very isolated lives. Many are clinically depressed, suffering from 'the nerves' as it is called, but few take their own lives. Today this generation is passing away, and the young behave quite differently; they now face the newer challenge of how to find quite other uses for the remoter countryside, in place of lonely subsistence farming.

The fight to save the rural West: peasant farmers turn to forestry and agri-tourism

Today it is official EC policy, as well as Irish Government policy, to encourage smaller farmers to diversify into other activities: the increases in the Structural Funds are being used partly for that purpose. For many farmers it could be the only means for them to survive on the land, and this is important for the whole environment, not just for their own future; if too many of them leave, then the schools, shops and social services close down, the villages die, the isolation increases for those who remain, and the remoter rural areas become a desert.

It could be asked how much this would really matter. After all, large parts of North America are completely empty. But western Europe, Ireland included, has an ancient tradition of settled rural civilization and cannot be destined to share the vast silences of Wyoming. If the small farms are no longer viable and their food output is no longer needed, then the countryside must be given other uses and farmers must find other things to do. In France, there has been much talk of their being paid by the State to be 'guardians of nature'. In Ireland, the accent is rather on using public grants to help them extend into forestry, agri-tourism, local mini-industries, and so on; or to move into other or specialized food products, if the markets can be found, so as to fill the gap caused by the inevitable decline of livestock and dairy farming.

Take, for example, the strange saga of Irish vegetables. Oddly, the Irish have never been great vegetable eaters – apart from potatoes, whose crop failure in the 1840s cost a million lives. It is true that until about 1970 many small farmers did grow a few potatoes and other vegetables, to sell locally as well as for their own use. But then most of them stopped. Vegetables were hard work, and were not covered by the EC price supports, so it was far easier, and more secure and profitable, to concentrate on milk and livestock. Moreover, it became harder to find hired labourers ready to help with the menial work of vegetable-picking; also the markets were ill organized, so it was not easy to get good prices. 'I found that we couldn't compete with the larger, more efficient foreign producers, so I gave up beet and potatoes and moved into cattle,' one Galway farmer told me.

However, in the 1980s the Irish public began to buy far more vegetables, spurred on by the food writers, the health writers, and the general new vogue for things European (see p. 223). So the anomaly exists today of this agricultural country, with its small population, actually importing a large percentage of the ordinary vegetables it could easily grow itself, such as carrots, onions, broccoli, even potatoes, as well as fruit such as apples. Some 85 per cent of Irish processed potato chips come from abroad, and 1,000 tonnes of seed potatoes come each year from Scotland! Irish vegetables tend to be badly selected and packaged, often sold in rough paper bags, and they have a poor image; so the public would rather buy, say, Dutch or Spanish.

The Department of Agriculture today is urging the farmers to grow more vegetables on a proper commercial scale, and the distributors to improve their networks. Some cooperative chains have taken up the challenge. But individual farmers tend to remain wary, apart from some successes in particular fields. New mushroom-growing ventures have broken into the UK market on a big scale; and in Co. Mayo I found one farmer moving into seed potatoes, another into growing edible seaweed. In Limerick, the Shannon Development Company (see p. 143) has set up a go-ahead new Food Centre that encourages farmers to respond to the sophisticated tastes of Europe, now invading Ireland too. As a result, in Clare and Limerick a few farms are moving down paths till now undreamed-of in these parts – growing garlic and unusual herbs, or breeding deer for venison. 'We are changing the Irish eating experience,' said the Centre's director excitedly; 'but we're not moving into snails. The climate is too damp.'

The Centre also encourages organic farming, whose produce finds a growing market both in Ireland and abroad, in today's health-conscious age. German and English settlers pioneered this kind of farming in Ireland a few years ago (see p. 339), and it is now catching on with the Irish too, practised by some 500 farmers. In the hills of Co. Leitrim, right by the border with the North, Rod Alston arrived from Manchester in the 1970s with 'green' ideals of simple self-sufficency, and bought a 21-acre plot in an area called Eden, which means 'brow' in Gaelic. It may not be quite a Garden of Eden, especially with the IRA close at hand, but he and his Irish wife have built it into a successful little business. They sell vegetables and herbs, and milk and cheese from their goats – all organically produced. 'Tastes are changing, the Irish are eating far more salads and herbs than before,' they said. 'We organic growers are returning to the pure farming styles of the old days, before those dreadful fertilizers came in.'

Could forestry, too, provide new land uses that would help to keep some farmers in work? Certainly the potential is there, for Ireland's still scanty reserves of forest could be massively expanded. In medieval times, much of the country was under vast tracts of oak and elm. Gradually these disappeared, and by the 1920s only 1·5 per cent of the land was wooded. Since then, an official policy of afforestation has gradually gathered pace, and today the figure is up to 7 per cent, most of it conifer – but this remains far below the EC average of 24 per cent. A State forestry board does its own planting; and private investors have joined in too, notably banks and insurance companies. They buy up land for forest, encouraged by the sizeable EU and Irish grants now available. But the farmers themselves, for a number of reasons, have proved reluctant to plant trees on their own land.

'Unlike, say, the Black Forest, Ireland has no tree culture,' said one landowner; 'for the peasants, the tree has always been a Protestant landlord symbol – cut it down as soon as it pokes above the hedge!' What's more, Irish farmers have no tradition of the long-term investment required for slow-growing trees. Like any farmers, they are wary of change; and they see forestry suspiciously as an omen of the demise of their habitual agriculture. Above all, they fear the claustrophobia of a landscape sombrely cloaked in pine-trees, where familiar vistas would be blocked and neighbours could no longer see each other's houses across the valley. 'Forests may be a necessary way of the future, but they're lonely and monotonous,' was a view I heard many times.

These feelings find an echo among environmentalists, who have raised a national debate as to whether the right kind of trees are being planted, in the right places: they want fewer conifers, more hardwoods. There may be a strong economic case for more forestry in Ireland, but the aesthetic and ecological case is much more dubious; and although the Government is pushing hard for more tree-planting, much of its planning has been badly thought out and ill coordinated. Curiously, forestry comes under the department of energy, not that of agriculture.

Until now, the accent has been on planting conifers – notably the Sitka spruce, a North American variety that is cheap and grows to maturity quite fast, in about forty years. But it yields poor-quality timber; and if planted by waterways it can produce an acidity that will damage fish and insect life – or so the ecologists claim. Their other complaint is aesthetic, that great swathes of recent plantations of these pine-trees have already spoiled the look of glorious wild uplands, in parts of Connemara and elsewhere. One environmentalist complained, 'Do we really want our hillsides covered with straight lines of these dreary little Christmas trees, planted by the forestry board or by foreign investors?' But unfortunately, planning permission is not required for developments of fewer than 200 hectares. So a clever investor can plant a clump of 195 ha, then leave a space, then plant another 195, and escape all control.

It is true that in many parts of Ireland the bogland soil is unsuited to beautiful hardwoods such as oak and beech; if these areas are to be afforested, dull conifers are probably the only answer. But the tree-lovers' lobbies, now vocal in Ireland, have been campaigning for much more planting of hardwoods wherever possible; and they have finally made some impact on official minds. Grants for hardwoods have been increased to about £2,000 per hectare, against £1,100 for conifers – some compensation for the fact that an oak takes three times as long as a Sitka to grow to full height. Whereas in 1989 only 3 per cent of new tree-planting was of hardwoods, by 1992 it had reached 10 per cent. EU policy strongly favours hardwoods.

Since the late 1980s, a number of farmers have finally become more interested in forestry, recognizing that the CAP reforms and other changes may leave them with few other realistic choices. The existing Irish forests are mainly in the Wicklow mountains south of Dublin, and in scattered parts of the south-west and west; but there is a wide stretch of low hills in the north-west, the 'drumlin belt' running from Monaghan to Galway, that is not ideal for dairying and could benefit from a change to forestry. Here some farmers' cooperatives are now active. In the early 1980s, private planting in Ireland accounted for only about 300 hectares a year: but by 1992 the figure had reached 9,345 ha, of which a remarkable 70 per cent was done by individual farmers or cooperatives, and the rest by banks and other non-farming investors, who will often lease land from farmers not wishing to sell it. Coillte Teoranta, the State-owned forestry board, contributed a further 12,000 ha. In fact, Ireland is now making up for lost time by planting trees at a faster rate than any other EU country, and the amount of land under forest is expected to rise from 7 to 10 per cent by the year 2000.

However, it is far from certain how much this might benefit either the farmers or the Irish economy as a whole. Within ten years, Ireland should for the first time become a net exporter of timber, and this will help to compensate for the decline in dairy and livestock exports. New factories could be created for wood-pulp and construction timber; and locally there could be new spin-offs for carpenters and other craftsmen. But modern forestry is not at all labour-intensive; and the farmers know well that tending a huge expanse of Sitka spruce, or even a handsome oak-wood, is not going to make up fully for the cutbacks in beef and creameries. Other new outlets too will be needed, such as farm tourism.

It is a romantic, *Heidi*-esque ideal, the holiday on the farm – urban children learning how cows are milked, Daddy taking a turn at haymaking after his months of office stress, villagers and city-dwellers singing folk-songs together under the stars. Farmers in Germany, France and elsewhere have done well with these *vacances à la ferme*, popular in a 'green' age; now the Irish are taking them up, too, as a means of adding to farmers' incomes, maybe also of bringing city and country people into better contact. The trend is encouraged by the EU, with its new 'Leader' programmes for rural development (see below). But just how large is the market in Europe for this kind of modest, homespun holiday? And how many farmers are really prepared to become part-time hoteliers and *animateurs*?

Certainly the west of Ireland's future will rely heavily on tourism. Some of this may be the luxury tourism of golf-courses and marinas, or the mass tourism of coach parties and big modern hotels. But an excess of this could spoil the very qualities of gentle remoteness and simplicity that are such a large part of Ireland's appeal (see p. 149). The Government is aware of this. And today its gospel is that Ireland's farms are themselves a tourist asset, for there will also be a growing demand in Europe for simple, healthy rural holidays close to local people. Farmers are being incited to convert parts of their homes or outhouses into modern self-catering units, or rooms for bed-and-breakfast, maybe dinner too, for holidays that can integrate the visitor into daily rural life. Foreigners, American and Japanese as well as European, are generally delighted. The farmers themselves still tend to be wary of embarking on such projects, but the potential is there. One family in Kerry, unable to make ends meet with their farm, have turned part of it into a small zoo and aviary, attracting thousands of visitors.

One successful venture is in the rolling Ballyhoura countryside south of Limerick. Here, where the villages were slowly dying and the young people drifting away, a group of families have banded together to form a kind of cooperative for tourism and rural development: Ballyhoura Fáilte (welcome). Some have turned their working farms into guest-houses, such as Séamus and Frances O'Donnell. 'Our guests', they told me, 'love to help us feed the lambs and make the hay, hold parties with us in the meadows, watch the cows be milked and the chickens hatch. Some of these city kids don't even know that eggs come from hens.' Another farmer, Paddy Finton, has diversified into lecturing. Over coffee and porter cake on his little family farm, he will recount its history since the Famine, tell how his lifestyle has changed since the coming of milking machines, and explain the ancient legends of King Oisin on the Ballyhoura hills.

Guests can also inspect other local farm activities, such as cheese-making, a honey farm, a deer farm, a noisy cattle auction; they can visit Rosie, who talks with her pigs and breeds fluffy, neurotic Angoras; or take riding lessons from Lila, whose love of her horses shines with a bright passion; or make day-trips to Cork or Kerry, Clare or Kilkenny; or spend their evenings at *ceilthe* in the pubs. These are holidays for those who like mud on their boots, warm Irish conversation (lots of it), home-made soups, rough brown soda bread, meat from the farm. Ballyhoura Fáilte now markets its holidays in France and Germany; and in a bright new education centre it holds English-language courses for foreigners. The EU provides some funds. 'The tourist season is short, and tourism cannot change everything,' says Frances O'Donnell; 'but it is certainly giving this area a new lease of life.'

Ballyhoura Fáilte today extends also into village renovation, vocational training, small businesses, farming and forestry; as such, it is one of a number of 'integrated' rural-development ventures that have sprung up recently in the west of Ireland, aimed at job creation and at restoring a sense of hope and purpose to areas in decline. Some of the ventures are aided by the EU's Structural Funds and notably by its Leader programme, which began in 1992. This is funding some one hundred development projects of which seventeen are in Ireland, including Ballyhoura; the money comes to them directly, not via Dublin, and is for the pump-priming of genuine locally based initiatives.

In the past, various well-intentioned job-creation schemes in rural areas, run by such bodies as the IDA, failed to be fully effective because they were insensitively implanted from outside, without properly harnessing local resources. So today the accent is all on 'bottom-up' ventures, as they are called, where the initiatives and the leadership are local, using local assets and talents – as in Ballyhoura. 'People have become too dependent on State initiatives and State hand-outs,' said one local activist; 'they must do more to help themselves, even if they will still need money from outside.' But there are problems. In many places the more dynamic local leaders have emigrated, leaving only the weak and passive. And these new rural ventures require a new mentality of cooperative effort which curiously is not in local Irish tradition. The old rural communities may have had a strong sense of solidarity and mutual help: but it was based around family and defined rituals such as harvesting, and today it has waned. 'Most people have become too individualistic, they won't bother to take part in the new community action,' was a complaint I heard repeatedly on visits to rural projects in the West.

A priest, Father Harry Bohan, pioneered rural development in Clare in the early 1970s. In his native village of Feakle, he encouraged people to build new homes, new cottages for summer rental, open a hotel and a new shop: this drew some emigrants to return to the village with their families, and the school got an extra teacher. The venture was a modest success. Up in western Connemara, near Clifden, I visited an EU-backed 'combat poverty' venture. Here the tourists crowd in summer to wild, hilly scenery among the loveliest in Ireland; but the season is short, and two-thirds of the houses are summer dwellings empty in winter, when the isolation is fearful on the tiny, poor farms of the sweeping bogland. Sixty per cent of families still have no telephone, and 30 per cent have no car. Here the anti-poverty project tries to help elderly or unemployed people, and lonely housewives. It has initiated a bus service which tours the more isolated farms; and in its youth centre it trains young people in skills that they can maybe use locally, rather than having to emigrate. 'Little rural ventures such as ours can play a useful social role, and can help morale,' said the project's leader; 'but economically they can only scratch at the surface of the basic local problems of unemployment and poverty.'

In eastern Mayo I was directed to one interesting success story. Kiltimagh, a big village near the Knock pilgrimage shrine, used to be a byword in Ireland for provincial lethargy – the sticks! It produced some talented people, but they all emigrated, as did Tom Flatley, now a millionaire in Boston. However, one who stayed was John Higgins, a teacher; he decided to revitalize the place, and in the late 1980s he launched a rural-development project. His energy and leadership have worked wonders. In the space of two years, local unemployment was halved and forty-five jobs created. New shops were opened, a clinic, guest-houses for Knock pilgrims, and some small firms, one of them making furniture. Higgins started a harvest festival; and he had some of the old buildings restored, so that Kiltimagh today looks far more neat and graceful than the average down-at-heel Irish village. 'Some people are still expecting me to land some big multinational factory,' he told me, 'but that is not what I'm about. My funding has come from local sponsors, plus some from the State. But we depend on no government department: Dublin bureaucracy has killed too many local schemes.' Kiltimagh may be a rare star example: but it shows what pure local initiative can do.

A handful of other ventures are closer to the kibbutz, or to the hippie commune ideal of the 1970s. In Clare, near Corofin, some young small farmers and their families have grouped themselves into a kind of commune, in a big tumbledown farmhouse. Here they manage to scratch a basic living from building work, stone-cutting and stone-laying (using slabs of black stone from the nearby Burren), and selling honey and organic products. The work and the money are all shared. The driving force, Michael Neylan, a sharp-minded, somewhat cranky idealist, told me: 'OK, small farms here may no longer be viable. But neither the rural development model, nor the Shannon industrial model, seems to us to provide an alternative. This area's future looks bleak. We just cannot survive in an open economy: so instead our group is trying this autarkic semi-closed economy, a bit like a kibbutz. Can it set a trend? Maybe not. The farmers are simply not used to pooling their work or their land. What we do here goes right against their tradition.'

Up in Co. Roscommon, in one of the most depopulated corners of Ireland, I found a pioneering venture that reminded me of the Cévennes in France in the 1970s, when middle-class migrants from Paris would try to make a simple living on the stony uplands, from goat-breeding or rural crafts. Here by a lake in Roscommon, down a lonely side-road, a group of young professional families from Dublin have bought up some poor bits of land, brought their modern skills with them, and with a sense of social commitment are trying to revitalize this dying region. These 'blow-ins' (as the Irish call newcomers to an area) do not exactly form a commune: but they live simply, share most of their resources, and try to be largely self-sufficient. Dick Hinchy, who gave up a well-paid job as a graphic designer in Dublin, told me their story: 'My wife and I were fed up with the rat-race, so we came here and bought eleven acres. Others of our group are technicians or craftsmen, able to do car-repairs or plumbing, for instance. So we can contribute locally, in an area that has been losing its service firms as people drift away. For example, as a designer I can work for local shops and the tourist trade: they need me. Some others of our group are potters, painters, photographers, musicians; one even has a tiny recording studio. Small is beautiful!' Many other blow-ins in these regions are foreigners, mostly German (see p. 336). Hinchy's group also edit a 'magazine of alternative living', *Common Ground*, rather like *Whole Earth*. He went on: 'We grow much of our own food, keep farmyard animals, do our own repairs. Our lifestyle is more like that of the peasants of the 1950s than of today – we blow-ins are the only ones still keeping alive the de Valera values of rural frugality! We earn a little money locally, and many of us also draw the dole. We grow expert at milking the grant system, too. Are we parasites, cheating society? No. Without us and our children, the local schools might close, and the post offices. We are too few and too marginal to save the West on our own. But we can set a trend.' I found his arguments plausible, and the whole experiment quite inspiring.

Mushroom-growers and organic farmers, planters of oak or conifer, Ballyhoura guest-house owners, Mayo village job-creators, blow-ins from Dublin in deepest Roscommon – can these and other diverse little ventures add up to something big enough to stem the continued decline of the rural West? Or can they only scratch the surface of the problem? The old timeless order of farming will continue to fade and change, and matters may get worse before they get better. But I met optimists who believe that a corner is being turned, that small farmers and others in the West, after apathetic decades of depending on initiatives from outside, are beginning to take their destiny in their own hands, as in Kiltimagh and Ballyhoura. 'What we are doing now is the last chance for this region,' said the leader of one rural-resources project in Mayo. 'If we fail, then it's all up. Nothing will halt the remorseless drift towards Dublin.'

5

A SWOLLEN METROPOLIS AND ITS STRUGGLING REGIONS

By no means all the emigrants from the West go abroad. Many of them make for Dublin, which has swelled in size from 470,000 inhabitants in 1936 to over a million today (suburbs included), almost one-third of the Republic's total. As the drift has continued from west to east, the population of Connacht (the five north-western counties of Galway, Mayo, Sligo, Leitrim and Roscommon) has fallen from 647,000 in 1905 to 431,000 today.

The capital dominates the rest of the country to a degree unusual in Europe – even more than, say, Paris dominates France. This is a matter of politics, culture and economy, not just of population, and it is not entirely healthy. Much is due to the centralized system of government, which in turn draws to Dublin the principal business milieux, and most of the cultural and intellectual talent. No other town is of any great importance: even Cork has only one-eighth of Dublin's size, and it begrudges Dublin's hegemony, yet can do little against it. Some other towns, notably Galway, have been growing livelier in recent years, it is true; some big new firms have set up in the regions; theatres have opened; some brilliant professors enliven local campuses. But Dublin is still where the action is; and the milieu of its intelligentsia, the so-called 'Dublin 4', seems in many ways closer to London than to Ireland's own rural world. But Dublin today has its own problems. It has been changing fast, and not entirely for the better – as any Dubliner will tell you.

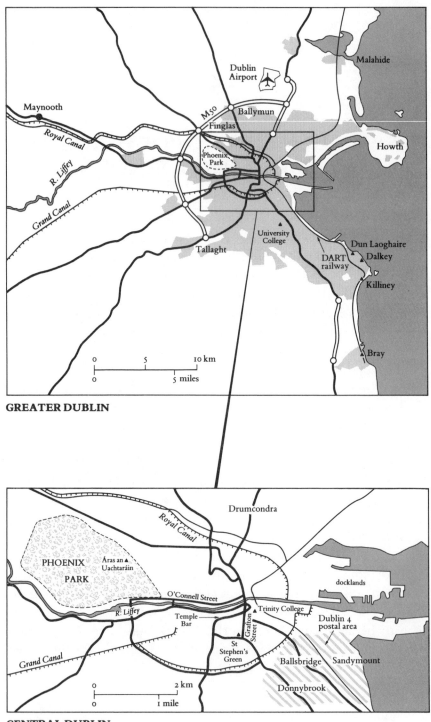

GREATER DUBLIN

Dublin Airport
Malahide
Maynooth
M50
Ballymun
Finglas
Royal Canal
R. Liffey
Phoenix Park
Howth
Grand Canal
Tallaght
University College
DART railway
Dun Laoghaire
Dalkey
Killiney
Bray

0 — 5 — 10 km
0 — 5 miles

CENTRAL DUBLIN

Drumcondra
Royal Canal
PHOENIX PARK
Áras an Uachtaráin
docklands
O'Connell Street
R. Liffey
Trinity College
Dublin 4 postal area
Temple Bar
Grafton Street
Grand Canal
St Stephen's Green
Ballsbridge
Sandymount
Donnybrook

0 — 2 km
0 — 1 mile

In Dublin's partly fair city: escape from a legacy of planning neglect

The river Liffey divides Dublin in two, socially as well as physically. The Northside, as it is called, is the more down-to-earth, the
Southside more bourgeois; and each regards the other with a
certain half-humorous scorn. North of the river are the older
working-class districts, and beyond them the desolate new housing
estates, such as the stark tower blocks of Ballymun, where parts of
The Commitments were filmed. South of the river, the south-west
has its poorer areas, too: but the south-east is overwhelmingly
middle-class. Here near the centre is Dublin 4, the postal district
that has become a nickname for the city's intelligentsia (see p. 62),
dwelling in big Victorian mansions or newer villas with gardens.
Others of this class live farther out along the coast, towards Dun
Laoghaire and Bray, in prosperous commuter suburbs once
favoured by the English. Northsiders consider these areas altogether too anglicized, full of 'people talking with pseudo-English
accents', and they claim – maybe rightly – that their own Dublin
is more natural, more gutsy, more *Irish*. Southsiders in turn think
the Northside too rough, and hold it responsible for the growth of
crime and drugs in the city. The mutual jibes are an endless source
of pub banter.

Lively but messy, Dublin is more a state of mind than a city of
great visual beauty. Human qualities come first – the gregarious
intimacy, rare in a town of this size, the vivacious gossip, the
cultural fizz, the wit and repartee at every social level (e.g. the
London journalist Angela Lambert's exchange with a taxi-driver.
She: 'I'm not going far.' He: 'I didn't think you looked that kind
of girl'). As the city has swelled in size, and people have moved
out to suburbs, something of this old warmth and intimacy has
been lost, inevitably; and plenty of Dubliners today lament that
the city is not what it was, as they songfully recall 'Dublin in the
rare oul' times'. Yet enough of its special quality survives to
explain its hold over the sentimental loyalty of Dubliners, and its
continuing appeal to visitors.

Visually, Dublin is admired above all for its downtown district

of redbrick Georgian terraces, or what is left of them; and there
are some elegant public buildings, too, such as the newly restored
Customs House (built 1791) by the river. But vast tracts of the city
are a shabby, run-down mess, unworthy of a modern European
capital. This is due partly to past neglect and shortage of money
for renewal. It may relate also to the Irish lack of any strong visual
sense or concern with tidiness. And some of it results from decades
of bad planning by Dublin Corporation, conniving at ruthless
property development.

Several Georgian terraces have been pulled down or left to
decay. St Stephen's Green, the spacious garden square at the heart
of the city, has been spoilt by insensitive redevelopment along two
sides. The banks of the Liffey once had a quiet provincial charm,
but are now lined with decaying older buildings and ugly new
ones. And broad O'Connell Street, formerly so fashionable, has
descended into tatty commercial vulgarity, like most of this old
Joycean core of Dublin north of the river. Of the city's various
large modern buildings, many are hideous, others are quite attractive but badly sited, out of tune with their surroundings; in
architecture as in design, Dublin has little feeling for the modern,
and seems to know neither how to use it to advantage nor how to
resist it, thus often ending up with the worst of both worlds.

This state of affairs has prompted an ongoing public debate in
recent years, as a vociferous conservationist lobby joins battle with
the city planners and developers. One lobby leader, Frank
McDonald, crusading environment correspondent of the *Irish
Times*, has called Dublin, with a touch of hyperbole, 'probably the
shabbiest, most derelict capital in Europe'. He castigates the city
managers for their lack of feeling for the city's looks and fabric,
and has quoted a 1988 EC report that placed Dublin 101st among
177 European cities, in terms of planning and amenities. Some
conservationists, it seems, regard any modern change as bad, and
want to preserve the old city in aspic. Others, more sensibly, agree
that Dublin must change as modern life changes. But the city finds
it peculiarly hard to combine sensitive restoration with efficient
and attractive modernization. So it does neither very well.

★

Until the end of the 1950s there was very little new building in Dublin and the city centre grew badly run down, but at least it was not despoiled. Then, with the prosperity boom of the 1960s, the property developers moved in − 'the men in the mohair suits', as the catchphrase went − and began to build new office blocks and to demolish some Georgian terraces. Governments of the day actively supported them, for economic reasons, while public opinion remained mostly indifferent. Amazingly, there was a widespread feeling in those days that Georgian Dublin, as the legacy of British colonialism, was not worth preserving! In handsome Fitzwilliam Street, one long row of Georgian brick mansions was pulled down to make way for the particularly hideous new modernistic headquarters of the Electricity Supply Board.

Towards 1970 a small conservationist group finally began to make its voice heard, led by a few individuals such as Frank McDonald, David Norris the 'gay rights' campaigner, Deirdre Kelly who formed the Living City Group, and members of An Taisce, Ireland's National Trust. Their first *cause célèbre* came in 1970 when property developers with government backing launched plans for demolishing some Georgian houses right on St Stephen's Green, at the corner of Hume Street, and replacing them with modern concrete offices. The crusaders contested this with sit-ins, supported by a number of liberals including Garret FitzGerald; the young Mary Robinson was there too, on the back of a lorry. There was much furore, as one minister taunted the squatters, 'you long-haired intellectuals, you are the allies of English belted earls!' Finally a wavering Fianna Fáil Government obliged the developers to accept a compromise − the Georgian houses would go, but would be replaced with Georgian-style pastiche buildings rather than glass-and-concrete. These stand there today, not beautiful but at least not an assertive eyesore.

So the result was a draw, from which the conservationists took some heart. But they were to suffer some real defeats in the 1970s, notably when the City Corporation proposed to erect two large concrete blocks for its own new offices, at Wood Quay by the

Liffey, on the site of an old Viking settlement. The crusaders stirred up enough interest among Dubliners to stage a march of 20,000 people against the scheme – but to no avail. And so today these ten-storey brutalist slabs rise up by Wood Quay, grotesquely out of place, described by McDonald as 'concrete bunkers like Nazi wartime blockhouses'. Across the river, by O'Connell Bridge, the British property firm Arlington Securities acquired a whole quay-front of Georgian houses in the 1980s, with the aim of creating a large modern shopping centre with a bus station on its roof. The project happily came to nothing: but the fine old houses have been left in limbo, unrestored, adding to the general sense of dereliction along the Liffey quays.

Sam Stephenson, Ireland's best-known and most controversial architect, was responsible alike for the Wood Quay blocks, the ESB headquarters, and the modernistic Central Bank building next to bohemian Temple Bar. When I met him, he sought to justify his philosophy: 'public buildings need to be large and assertive, to make a big statement. And a lot of nonsense is talked in defence of old buildings, which seem to acquire a veneration for beauty just by being old. The conservationists are absurd, they want nothing to change' – remarks capped only by the city manager's PRO, Noel Carroll, who said to me, 'That Georgian stuff was never intended to last for ever.'

It is the notorious weakness of democratic local government in Ireland (see p. 48) that lies at the heart of Dublin's renewal and planning problems. The councillors of Dublin Corporation have little power, and the effective authority rests with the city manager, who is not elected by them but appointed by the Government. The manager since 1979, Frank Feely, is a clerk and accountant by background, a jovial and approachable man with a flair for public relations but little feeling for architecture or for human-scale planning; and most of his senior staff are equally philistine. He tends to do the bidding of the Government, which is the real ruler of Dublin – and governments have made economics their priority. Their concerns have been (a) to endow the city with new offices that will attract new business, and (b) to provide the construction industry with work that creates jobs. These are sensible aims in themselves, but restoration and sensitive planning have been largely forgotten, and most of the improvements in this field have resulted only from cajoling and persuasion by conservation groups. It is so different from the situation in many Continental cities – in Paris, for example, admittedly a much richer town, where an equally autocratic regime has shown a true concern for the city's fabric, and has combined elegant restoration (e.g. in the Marais) with some striking and beautiful modern public buildings.

In the past ten or fifteen years the climate has improved, it is true. The warnings of the conservationists have won through to ordinary public opinion, which is now more alert; and the authorities in turn have at last begun to show more concern. Georgian terraces are no longer being pulled down; recent planning laws now make harder the kind of wanton demolition that used to happen without even a public hearing. Charles Haughey, long a close ally of the property developers, began in his final years as Taoiseach to show himself a convert to conservation, and in 1988 he set up the National Heritage Council. Since then, State funds have been used for the tasteful restoration of some major public buildings, including the Customs House and Dublin Castle. And in the 1991 city council elections, the Fianna Fáil majority was replaced by a new centre–left coalition which included four Greens. This drew up a new civic charter for improving Dublin, and it began to put pressure on Feely and his bureaucrats.

The most appealing new development is the conversion of the little Temple Bar district, in the heart of the city, into a kind of bohemian Left Bank. Squeezed between the river and Dame Street, this is an old area of narrow cobbled streets with buildings in an intriguing jumble of styles, many of them eighteenth-century. Once full of craftsmen, it had become almost derelict by the late 1970s, when the public transport authority (CIE) decided, with government backing, to buy it up and turn it into a big bus station. But CIE spent years finalizing its plans, and meanwhile various little 'alternative' enterprises, pop studios, junk shops, arty galleries and so on, began to move into the empty buildings. A tiny Latin Quarter was emerging spontaneously. The conservationists saw the charm of this, and so An Taisce (the National Trust) began to lobby the Government to spare Temple Bar – with success. In 1987 Haughey made a spectacular turnabout, declaring that the area was after all 'historic and attractive': it must be kept and refurbished, and, 'I wouldn't let CIE near it.' So instead he set up an official agency to restore the 28-acre central site, helped by EC structural funding. The aim was to turn it into an informal area of culture and culture-geared commerce. By 1993 a new Irish Film Centre had opened there, a photographic centre and a fringe theatre, and the area was filling up with little bistros, boutiques, craft studios, rock venues and the like, all very casual and untidy in the Irish manner, but full of life, and not yet too trendy and glossy *à la* Covent Garden. In summer there are street musicians and plenty of tourists; some old traditional craft shops are being restored; trees are being planted in new piazzas; and housing for 3,000 people is being built or renovated so that the area can also be a living community. In short, Temple Bar is the kind of environmental project that Dublin needs, and it marks an encouraging change in official thinking.

Temple Bar's housing belongs to a new policy of drawing people back to live in the inner city, after seventy years of outward drift during which the population of the central area (bordered by the canals) has fallen from 250,000 in 1926 to 75,000 today. It is a trend common to many Western cities, partly inevitable, but in Dublin it has arguably gone too far and been badly managed.

The city used to have some of the worst slums in Europe. Maybe they nourished a warm human solidarity and even inspired some fine literature (e.g. O'Casey's plays), but they were neither cosy nor hygienic. In the 1920s the corporation, with limited means but the best of motives, began to pull down some of the worst tenements and move people out to new housing estates. In recent decades this outward process has gathered pace, and taken new forms: in a word, the middle class has moved out of its own accord and gladly, the working class rather less willingly. Dismayed by the new commercial congestion and the rise of petty crime, most of the middle-class inhabitants of the old city centre have migrated to more serene and spacious purlieus, either just across the canal to Dublin 4 and Dublin 6, or further out to the south-east. Many in the working class, maybe more sentimental or habit-bound, might have preferred to stay in their old familiar surroundings and to have their council flats renovated. But the corporation, firstly, found that this would be more costly than building new homes for them; secondly, it wanted to clear parts of the central area for new business activity. In the 1980s, most of Seán O'Casey's tenements in the Gardiner Street area were pulled down, and a sorry wasteland was left, waiting for the developers. Many inner-city schools and hospitals began to close, as giant new low-cost suburbs were built on the city's periphery, to the north and west.

In many European cities, by the 1980s some people were moving back to live in the centre, and belatedly Dublin began to follow this trend. Led by the militant Deirdre Kelly with her Living City Group, and by Frank McDonald with a polemical series of articles in the *Irish Times*, the conservationists opened a campaign, stressing the harm it would do to the inner city if all its residents left. 'As usual, we had to drag the corporation into doing anything positive,' McDonald told me; 'at first they would not admit there was any problem.' But finally the authorities began to promote a few new building projects in the central area, alike for rental or for ownership, and for all social classes. There have been plenty of takers, though the process has not yet gone far. These little clusters of new low-rise housing are mostly attractive; and Temple Bar is part of the programme.

Of the dormitory suburbs created earlier by the corporation to cater for slum evacuees and for rural immigrants to the city, the most notorious is Ballymun. Built in the 1960s on the northern edge of Dublin, it stands today as grim testimony to the high-rise, low-cost mistakes of that period. Its main feature is seven sixteen-storey grey towers, pleasantly spaced and sited but very badly constructed and equipped. By about 1990 they were occupied mainly by the lowest income groups, some 70 per cent of them unemployed (the well-known Jesuit priest Peter McVerry was running his hostel for homeless teenagers in one tower, see p. 233).

Upkeep was such that many of the lifts had broken down, the concrete stairways were filthy with litter, windows were smashed, crude graffiti were everywhere; the buildings had no doors, so any marauders could walk in, plus a few tragic individuals who found jumping from upper-floor balconies a convenient way to die. Finally the corporation did start refurbishing the towers, as best it could: lifts were repaired, and locked doors with an intercom system were put in, which at least kept out trespassers and deterred the would-be suicides. Ballymun was the location used for parts of *The Commitments*, notably the scene – considered very 'Oirish' by some critics – where a white horse is taken up in a lift. It at least made the point that Ballymun, like other new suburbs, has an interface with pastoral farmland, where the kids of local peasants and of the urban poor play together.

'We have learned from our earlier blunders, we have built no more Ballymuns,' an official told me. Indeed in the 1970s, following the trend in Britain against high-rise blocks, the corporation swung to the other extreme and started to build very spacious low-rise suburbs. With the growing need for new housing as the city's population swells, some of these places have now mushroomed to quite a size: Finglas in the north-west has 60,000 people, while notorious Tallaght, a 'new town' just outside the city to the south-west, has reached 80,000, making it the third largest conurbation in the Republic, ahead of Limerick.

Dublin's environmentalists have strongly criticized these developments for their inept, inhuman planning. Their complaints are that basic amenities have been slow to arrive, such as post offices, cinemas, shops, or new firms that could provide jobs locally; public transport is seriously inadequate; the extreme spaciousness, with drearily identical little houses separated by wide, dull roads, lessens the sense of community warmth that city dwellers need; and, since it is mainly young families who move out to Tallaght (half of its inhabitants are under nineteen) while the grandparents tend to stay near the centre, families are dispersed and 'age-group ghettos' are created. There is truth in all of this. On the other hand, those who actually live in these suburbs are often quite contented – at least they are far better housed than in their old slums, or at Ballymun – and they resent the tendency of the liberal media, fiercely anti-corporation, to focus on Tallaght as a nightmare place where life is unliveable.

The novelist Dermot Bolger took me out to Finglas, where he lives and where he set *The Journey Home* (see p. 247). It seemed no worse than most of the larger housing estates built in Britain at the same period. The rows of little semi-detached houses were monotonous but not too ugly, and the ones we visited, though small, looked quite comfortable. Yes, it was all too spread-out, but the views towards the Wicklow mountains were exhilarating, with meadows close by. Also quite close were new shopping centres, schools, churches and so on. Bolger said that people were now quite happy, apart from the worry of unemployment, and crime and vandalism were much less of a problem than downtown.

Over in Tallaght, which is newer, matters may not be so bright. Yet here, too, proper amenities are belatedly arriving, including hospitals and a technical college – but not pubs, which remain scarce owing to the quirks of the licensing laws. For Dubliners who love their pubby 'crack' this is quite a blow to social enjoyment. However, one inhabitant of Tallaght, the writer Kieran Fagan, has defended it against the moaning of the media, in a book, *Invisible Dublin*, published by Bolger in 1991: 'Tallaght is not as bad as all that ... there's 80,000 people out there, living perfectly normal lives ... In fact they are infused with something which more than compensates for their unhealthy junk food diets. THEY ARE FILLED WITH COMMUNITY SPIRIT ... There was a great flowering of residents' and tenants' associations ...' Fagan also speaks of 'the best shopping centre in Ireland', which has provided 1,500 jobs, and of other new amenities: 'There's a swimming-pool, a bowling-alley, two libraries and five bus routes within ten minutes' walk from my house.' But wild adolescents do sometimes steal cars.

Certainly the planning of these suburbs could have been managed better. No development agencies were created for them, which, as in Britain, could have overseen the buying of land, the overall layout, the provision of amenities. The planning was ad hoc, echoing many of the mistakes that the French had made with their early *grands ensembles* in the Paris region. First came the houses and some roads, and only later were the proper facilities of a town provided; so for some time the first inhabitants lived in a kind of wilderness, having to commute to find many essential services. Gradually however the amenities *have* arrived; and finally the new suburbs have begun to forge their own identity and sense of community, helped by the Irish neighbourly spirit. However, the massive rehousing of Dubliners in the past twenty or so years has aggravated a class segregation that was much less evident in old downtown Dublin. One token of this: the percentage of young people going on to higher education is between 26 and 44 per cent in the south-eastern suburbs, only 6 to 7 per cent in Tallaght and Finglas.

Today the major debate on Dublin's future is over roads and public transport, and it is here that Feely and his planners are now under heaviest attack from the conservationists. The huge growth of car traffic has congested a city that seriously lacks good, broad roads, and the public-transport system is too undeveloped to provide an attractive alternative: hence some 52 per cent of commuters come into the city by car, and only 34 per cent by bus or train. The fast and efficient little DART electric railway uses a line built by the English back in the 1840s and usefully serves the north-east and south-east suburbs, running from Howth via the city centre to well-to-do Killiney and Bray. But this at present is Dublin's only local railway. And the ubiquitous orange double-decker buses that serve the rest of the city are slow, shabby and often infrequent.

The corporation's answer has been to throw roads at the problem. Certainly many car-users caught in the jams feel that new, modern roads are badly needed, especially at the approaches to the central area: but this would entail much demolition, and here the conservationists have declared open war. They are angered above all at the current construction of a new Inner Tangent just west of the city centre, sending dual carriageways through old residential areas: in the Liberties district close to St Patrick's

Cathedral, several atmospheric old pubs and corner shops have been pulled down to make way for the broad new road. In the early 1990s this became another *cause célèbre*, but the conservationists failed to win. One reason: the authorities have never sanctioned the holding of proper public inquiries before road schemes are adopted.

I cannot myself agree entirely with the more extreme conservationist case against any new road-building. Dublin still badly needs better access routes; and until the M50 western ring motorway is laboriously completed, to drive round the north-west side of the city, for example to get to the airport from the west, will remain a nightmare. Plans for an eastern bypass through the port area, linking north and south Dublin, have been shelved indefinitely under conservationist pressure.

The trouble is that Dublin, slow as usual, has come very late into the great debate for and against the motor car. Most other West European cities had already completed their major road schemes when measures to restrict private car use came into vogue. But today Dublin is having to tackle the car problem without the adequate infrastructure, and without any overall coordinated transport and roads policy. Responsibility is divided between various government departments, the Irish public transport authority (CIE), the city's roads department, and the Garda which deals with traffic: often they are at cross-purposes.

Certainly the conservationists are right that far more should be done to improve Dublin's public transport, which in the National Development Plan for 1989–93 received only £36 million of government funds, against £212 million for roads. At least, an old light railway is now being reopened parallel to the DART line and further inland. But there is a need for many more buses and bus lanes, or maybe trams (a metro is not feasible). However, proposals to restrict car use have come up against politicians' fear of upsetting voters. When asked about the need for better public transport, Haughey once said cynically, 'You just can't get Dubliners out of their cars.' To which one conservationist retorted, 'When was Charlie last on a bus?'

Few pedestrian zones have been created in central Dublin, apart from Grafton Street with its busy shops, which was cleared of traffic in 1988. Elsewhere the car reigns. Yet the city's parking system is a farce: there are meters in the whole central area, but the regulations are simply not enforced. Cars parked wrongly are never clamped, rarely towed away, and seldom even given parking fines, for the wardens are too lax: a survey carried out by Trinity College in 1989 found that of cars parked on yellow lines in the central area one morning, less than one per cent had received tickets, and less than two per cent of those parked at meters whose time had expired. No wonder so many people drive into town, when they can so easily do so for free! Yet if the wardens did their job properly, as in Britain or Germany, it might raise a public outcry that few politicians would want to risk. 'It's a good example of the absence of consensus about the need for rules in Irish society,' said one critic. And the city's PRO, Noel Carroll, even remarked to me blithely: 'The imposing of rigid controls is not in the Irish psyche: we are not a German city! I personally find our public-transport system very good, and our roads well adapted. We have to respect the legitimate aspirations of car users. The *Irish Times* carries advertisements for cars, but also editorials denouncing them. Is that logical?'

Dermot Bolger has written of his beloved Dublin: 'It is alive and vibrant with new people, with new blood, new streets, new placenames ... it is a living city. A city is like a person, it is always changing.' Some of the change is for the worse, beyond doubt. The planners have made their ravages, and much of Joyce's Northside Dublin is no more: no. 7 Eccles Street, where he set the home of Leopold Bloom, has been pulled down. Yet in some other respects, mental rather than visual, something of the spirit of Joyce, or of Behan or O'Casey, survives. Writers may no longer frequent the pubs so much (see p. 236), but other Dubliners do, massively. The famous pubs are still there, with their quaint period décor; and sometimes in the streets in summer, life is still lived with a peculiar gregarious intensity that seems more Mediterranean than northern. Few people may inhabit the centre any more, but they go there for entertainment as well as work, and this centre is still compact enough to retain a certain vivacious intimacy. Here in the heart of the city is Trinity with its 8,000 students, spilling out into car-free Grafton Street where street musicians play. Dublin remains a less cosmopolitan city than most of its size in western Europe, but it is a magnet for the rest of Ireland, alive with the accents of Kerry, Mayo and Donegal. The main provincial centres are humble by comparison – even Cork.

Cork, Limerick, Galway: resentment and renaissance

The Republic's other main towns, Cork, Waterford, Limerick and Galway, are all quite tiny places compared with the assertive capital: even Cork has a mere eighth of Dublin's population. They are all sea or river ports, with Atlantic trading traditions going back to Viking or Norman times. Each has a keen sense of its own local identity, but fortunes tend to fluctuate; today, the contrast is striking between the youthful excitement and bustle of Galway and the quiet stagnation of Waterford.

Cork likes to call itself 'Ireland's real capital', which it certainly isn't. This second city of the Republic is consumed by its resentment of Dublin – a serious matter, but also a kind of stock joke. Its people are robust individualists who think highly of themselves; their fierce loyalty towards their proud old mercantile city reminded me of the city-state patriotism of Italian towns, or of a city such as Toulouse. Corkonians are even more humorous and voluble than most Irish; great lovers of 'the crack', they will gladly talk the night away in their throaty, singsong accents. And their favourite topic is the arrogance of Dubliners, always trying to do them down. Notably they hate the centralist system that Dublin represents – the fact that they must travel to the capital to get the smallest matter settled, and the lack of adequate municipal funds for their city's upkeep.

With only 140,000 people it is not a large town, but it has the looks and feel of a real city, much more than Limerick or Galway. Its old town centre is enfolded gracefully between two arms of the river Lee, and it has some character, even if very few pre-eighteenth-century buildings survive; the river walks are pleasant, the alleys of new pedestrian zones are busy and quaint, some streets bear proud names such as Grand Parade and South Mall. And yet, with many houses in poor repair, Cork's overall impression is one of faded grandeur, slightly melancholy; of having seen better days.

As in a sense it has. Its fine natural harbour has made it an important seaport since early times, and in the seventeenth and eighteenth centuries it knew something of a golden age of commerce and industry. For centuries it was dominated by well-to-do 'merchant prince' families, somewhat in the Hanseatic tradition: but they have now nearly all died out – 'replaced by the multi-nationals', I was told. Cork's industrial tradition took a knock in the 1970s when the Ford and Dunlop factories both closed. But since then a number of hi-tech firms have arrived, notably in electronics and pharmaceuticals (Apple has a sizeable new plant), and today industry is again doing fairly well. The port, and the southerly Atlantic position, make Cork one of Ireland's most popular venues for foreign investors. Even so, unemployment is high, especially in the drab 1960s housing estates on the north side of town.

One well-known Cork man was Seán O'Faoláin. Another was Jack Lynch of Fianna Fáil, who as Taoiseach in 1966–73 and 1977–9 did a great deal for the city (see p. 32). When he then lost his power struggle with Haughey, Corkonians registered their displeasure by switching their votes from Fianna Fáil – and for this Haughey never forgave them. As Taoiseach, he penalized Cork – or so local people believe – by holding back subsidies and refusing to give cabinet posts to Cork politicians. Such is Irish politics – and it added to the local anti-Dublin resentment. Cork people even accuse the Dublin-based Arts Council of causing the closure in 1990 of their well-known ballet company, under pressure from Haughey (see p. 263). However, despite this loss, the city retains a fairly active cultural life, as well as a vigorous intellectual life centred on University College with its many brilliant professors, among them the historian Joseph Lee.

Cork's city council, like so many in Ireland, is seldom a very effective body. But the town was fortunate in its unusually enlightened and go-ahead city manager in 1974–86, Joe McHugh.

He was able to kill a scheme for driving a motorway along the river banks, and to prevent developers from demolishing old houses. Irish city managers can sometimes be reactionary; but there are also times when they show more sensitivity than philistine councillors. Helped by EU funds, Cork has now built itself new ring roads, soon to be completed by a long tunnel under the Lee east of the city. Plans for this were first drawn up in 1980, then shelved while lobbies fought over the rival merits of a tunnel and a bridge, and only in 1992 did work start – 'Typical of how long things take in Ireland,' said one Cork man.

Cork is the capital of one of the most prosperous of Irish counties, where the coastline of the 'Irish Riviera' stretches westward past neat resorts such as Kinsale and Schull, today popular with foreign settlers, English, German and others. This is quite a sophisticated area, where the yachting is excellent and the food can be rather good. Inland, on the fertile rolling plains, the dairy and wheat farms are much larger and more successful than the Irish average. And beyond is Kerry, scenic but still rather poor. The people of Cork, who fancy themselves as urbane, tend to scorn their Kerry neighbours as out-and-out 'coulchies': hence the spate of Cork jokes about Kerry, such as, 'A Corkman is a Kerryman with shoes on.'

Waterford, with 40,000 people, is the largest town of the south-east, a river port with an industrial tradition, but today a rather depressed little place. For years it has depended too heavily on its major firm, Waterford Crystal, glass-makers, which recently has been forced to shed a third of its 3,000 workforce and has also been plagued by long strikes. The city has acquired a bad image. With the help of EU money it has done some urban renovation, and it has a lively theatre company and a new £36 million regional hospital. But plans for a big new downtown shopping centre were shelved when the main backers pulled out, losing confidence in the town, and in 1992 all I could see of the site was a vast gaping hole. Waterford on a wet day I found a most gloomy experience, save for the lively music in the pubs.

★

Limerick, by contrast, till recently had a far worse image, as dreary, drab and narrow-minded, but today it is in the throes of a revival. This city at the head of the Shannon estuary is the Republic's third largest (pop. 80,000 with suburbs) and has enjoyed a notable history. In the early Middle Ages it was a seat of Irish kings, then an English trading colony and walled outpost, where King John built a fortress; in 1691 it endured a famous siege. Then in more recent times it became known as a bastion of hard-line religious conservatism, but also of labour militancy, leading to confrontations between Church and workers. It was anti-Semitic too. One writer described Limerick in the 1950s as 'a tight-assed sort of place, a city of priest-ridden hypocrites'. Others found it backward, snobbish and gloomily provincial; and this reputation persisted until the 1980s.★

Limerick's revitalization has been due above all to the proximity of the Shannon Airport industrial development (see p. 143), which drew various new hi-tech firms to the area. This also prompted the creation of Limerick's new university, today the most go-ahead in Ireland, geared towards high-level research and techno-logy (see p. 220). It is set just outside town on a spacious modern campus, with an adjacent 'science park' of research firms. All these ventures have brought in new blood, gradually shaking the town out of its lethargy. But while this vibrant new Limerick was arising on the outskirts, the architectural and social fabric of the old town continued to crumble.

Finally in the 1980s a group of citizens set up a Civic Trust, the first of its kind in Ireland, and began to press for urban renewal. The State-owned Shannon company, the city council and the EC all responded with funds, and today the work of restoration is the most impressive of any town in the Republic. In the decaying medieval district by the river, King John's old castle has now been splendidly restored from near-dereliction and endowed with a fine museum; some other ancient buildings have also been renovated; a

---

★ The comic five-line poems that bear the city's name have very little con-nection with it. They are thought to originate from the chorus of an eighteenth-century soldiers' song, 'Will You Come Up to Limerick?'

bright and smart new city hall has been built nearby, and there's a neat new park by the Shannon. So tourists are at last being wooed to Limerick. But many parts of it remain seedily run-down, notably the main downtown grid of hideously tawdry shopping streets.

Limerick's worst problems, however, are social. This is probably the most polarized of Irish towns, even more than Dublin: on the one side, the well-paid staff of the new hi-tech firms and the university; on the other, the poverty and deprivation of the older working-class housing estates. Here crime, vandalism and violence became so blatant in the 1970s and '80s that Limerick won the nickname of 'Stab City', to the fury of local politicians. Happily, the violence has since diminished, while concerted action by welfare bodies such as the EU-backed 'combat poverty' groups has brought a few results. But the unemployment level is up to 80 per cent on some of the ghetto-like housing estates, which have decayed into slums that ought to be pulled down, like Ballymun in Dublin. Some radical critics complain that more money should be spent on fighting these social ills, rather than on tasteful restoration of medieval buildings.

Political and social debate is sharp in a town dominated by a cluster of colourful rival personalities. The Left is led by Jim Kemmy, Labour TD and former lord mayor, a burly ex-stonemason and self-made man. On social and moral issues he often clashes in public with Limerick's notorious bishop, Jeremiah Newman, an elderly scholar who is the most outspokenly conservative of all senior Irish clergy (see p. 163). So it would seem that the Limerick tradition of Church/Labour confrontation is still alive and well. Then there is Professor Edward Walsh, the élitist president of the university who believes in the panacea of modern technology. He hardly sees eye-to-eye with Kemmy, who is also in some rivalry with Des O'Malley, a Limerick man and local TD, instrumental in securing State funds for the urban renewal. The conflicts are real, even if they tend to get cloaked in the usual Irish easygoing bonhomie.

Galway, in contrast to Limerick, is generally seen today as the most lively and seductive of Irish provincial towns. A cult has developed round it, as a Mecca of youth and a hub of artistic exuberance, where local students, foreign tourists, electronics engineers, guitarists and Irish-speakers rub shoulders in narrow old streets crammed with every kind of folksy restaurant, fringe theatre or musical pub. 'It's a mini-Amsterdam,' was one comment I heard, 'just as bohemian but more intimate.' And the town's hectic growth and cosmopolitan bustle come as quite a surprise in the heart of the declining, depopulating West.

This is not its first golden age. In the fifteenth and sixteenth centuries this little port on Galway Bay was a tiny city-state ruled by a merchant oligarchy, trading with France, Spain and the Baltic, and quite prosperous. In the 1960s it was quiet and almost forgotten, but then it suddenly began to grow, at a faster rate than other Irish towns, from a population of 22,000 in 1960 to 51,000 today (70,000 including suburbs). As in Limerick, but in a different manner, new industry and the university have played major parts – and so has tourism. In an area with no industrial tradition, the IDA set out to attract foreign investors, and a number responded, such as the American computer firm Digital, in the 1970s. But then in 1993 Galway suffered its worst blow for some years when Digital, hit worldwide by the recession, closed down its whole hardware plant there, with a loss of 700 jobs. It did keep open its smaller software plant, and the IDA was able to find some replacement firms, too. But the blow to Galway's golden image has been real.

University College, Galway, founded back in 1845 (see p. 217), has been expanding fast, especially on the arts side, and so has done much to vitalize the town's cultural life. The tourist trade, too, has blossomed, for Galway is the gateway to Connemara, the Burren and the Aran Islands. These factors together have had a multiplier effect, so that Galway has come to be seen as a stimulating place to live, with a lovely setting, fine beaches and scenery close by, and pure air. It is a magnet that has drawn Dubliners and foreigners to settle, as well as poorer emigrants from the doomed farms of its own hinterland: but the contrast between booming Galway city and declining Galway county is something of an anxiety to politicians and planners.

It is not an especially beautiful city, and few of its pre-eighteenth-century mansions survive. But some tactful urban renewal has recently improved the old quarter of narrow little streets near the port and the river Corrib: disused warehouses have been restored as shops, flats and offices, while a handsome new shopping complex cleverly incorporates part of the ancient city wall. In term time or in tourist time, the youthful animation in this downtown area is intense. As the university with its 6,000 students is close to the centre, not out in the suburbs as at Limerick, this smallish town has a strong student flavour, allied to that of a tourist resort – all very casual, spontaneous and unsmart. Restaurants and bars of every kind keep opening; festivals crowd the calendar; the summer arts festival is the largest in Ireland; and the Druid repertory theatre is Ireland's best. There is also an Irish-language theatre, which thrives, for Galway prides itself as a centre of Gaelic tradition and is close to the largest *Gaeltacht* area (see p. 297). Plenty of other languages and accents can be heard too, in this town of German backpackers, Scottish poets, Japanese technicians, French waitresses and half-drunk English 'crusties' (latter-day hippies). 'I never want to leave and go back home to dull old Cork,' said one student I met. Fancy hearing that from a Cork girl.

But what of Galway county, and the rest of the rural West?

Shannon and Knock: technocrats and priests to the aid of the menaced West

In 1968 the late John Healy, a leading Dublin journalist, published a polemical little book, *The Death of an Irish Town*, that gave a searing picture of his own birthplace, Charlestown, an average little rural town in eastern Mayo, on the main Galway–Sligo road. He described how a once lively if hardly prosperous community had been gradually ruined by emigration. Shops closed through lack of business; the nearby farmsteads were abandoned; post-primary education was neglected. He found that of his own local

141

primary class of boys in the 1940s, only three remained in Charlestown twenty years later; the others were all in Dublin, London, America or elsewhere. And he described 'a numbing passivity that helps a town to die . . . our people have lost pride in their town'. With passionate rhetoric, he argued that more resolute official policies could have done much to stem the exodus from the West, and he later gave his book a second title, *No One Shouted STOP!*

The emigration of that period was to a great extent inevitable. But Healy was right to assert that more action could have been taken sooner to mitigate its effects – if only Dublin had been more alert to the problem, and if local people had been better equipped to stand and fight their ground, instead of just leaving. Today, however, plenty of voices are shouting STOP – for example, the bishops of the West, who in 1991 launched a crusade to save the region from further decline. As I noted in the last chapter, there are now plenty of new initiatives, both local and officially inspired, to harness the West's resources for new activities. New airports have been opened and main roads built, making the region far less isolated than it used to be. But as agriculture changes, the exodus is likely to continue. And rightly or wrongly the West still feels neglected; it still rails bitterly at Dublin for failing to adapt its policies to meet local needs.

There has never been any overall regional development strategy for Ireland, in the manner say of France. In the late 1960s the Government did commission the English planning expert Colin Buchanan to propose one, and he came up with a plan for nine specific regional growth centres, but the scheme was shot down by Fianna Fáil politicians alarmed at the jealousies this might create among their electors. So the Government has simply allowed investors to settle wherever they wish, influencing them only with its cash inducements, highest for the West.

The one coordinated regional State effort has been in the Shannon-estuary area, thanks to the presence there of a major airport. This, the most westerly in Europe, was built in the 1940s primarily as a refuelling halt, at a time when it was still hard for aircraft to cross the Atlantic in one hop. Then the long-range jets came in, threatening Shannon Airport's future. But rather than sacrifice it, the Government decided to expand it as a stopover (banning direct transatlantic flights to Dublin, see below) and to use it as a hub for activating this depressed, isolated part of Ireland. So in 1959 it set up the Shannon Free Airport Company, usually known as Shannon Development, or Sfadco for short. This semi-State firm created what is said to be the world's first airport tax-free industrial zone; and it was in the forefront of the Lemass campaign of the 1960s to attract foreign investors to Ireland – with some success.

In their airy office by the airport, with the EU flag flying outside, Sfadco officials talk confidently about their mission to help the West – 'We are a catalyst for this whole area' – with a technocratic enthusiasm that I found unusual in Ireland, more like France. The airport and the new industries between them have created some 8,000 jobs locally; and a whole new town, Shannon, has grown up. Some firms are industrial, such as Alumina, a giant Canadian-owned aluminium plant that belches away on an island across the estuary. Others are in services, such as Guinness Peat Aviation, the big aircraft-leasing company, Irish-owned, which was doing well until it was badly hit by recession in 1992. Sfadco and the airport have also stimulated tourism: for many Americans arriving in their jumbos, this area is their first taste of Ireland, and they have the delights of Bunratty's medieval banquets close by. All in all, Sfadco has certainly done much for this part of Ireland, and its work has sparked off the revival of nearby Limerick City. But now in a time of recession its power to create new jobs is proving fragile.

Moreover, right up until 1994 the success of the airport was made possible only by restricting the flying rights of major airlines. From the beginning of the jet age, the Irish Government imposed a compulsory Shannon stopover on all scheduled flights between Dublin and North America; this, it argued, was the only way to save the airport, so vital for the West. But many Dublin passengers were irked by the ninety-minute stop at Shannon, and could even find it quicker to get to or from America by flying via a British airport. American airlines were also being deterred, and in the early 1990s only Delta was flying direct to Ireland. Aer Lingus, too, the Irish State airline, claimed to be losing traffic on its transatlantic flights, because of the stopover.

In 1992 the issue re-emerged. Aer Lingus began to demand that the stopover be modified, and was backed by high-level business interests in Dublin who wanted to see their airport developed as a European 'hub'. Dublin and Aer Lingus clearly had a case, on rational economic grounds. But Shannon also had a case, on regional grounds; and it was backed by some powerful politicians, including Des O'Malley, a Limerick man, and Labour's Dick Spring, from nearby Kerry, who said that purely commercial needs should not be allowed to override the valid needs of the West. Tensions rose. Some 30,000 people attended a 'Save Shannon' rally in Limerick, waving black banners. It was claimed that without the stopover Shannon would lose much of its business and firms might leave; also, that two-thirds of the passengers on this route did in fact alight or board at Shannon, not Dublin, indicating the importance of the airport for tourism.

By 1993 Aer Lingus was in heavy debt, hit by world recession, and it badly needed help: but Spring was now Tánaiste, in a strong position to defend Shannon's interests. After months of tough negotiations, finally a simple compromise solution was found. From April 1994, Aer Lingus would have one daily direct flight Shannon–New York, and another Shannon–Dublin–New York (*sic*) and back the same way. So no more compulsory Shannon stopover; instead, Aer Lingus will operate non-stop flights from *both* airports, and foreign airlines can also fly non-stop Dublin–New York if they choose. There were some grumbles in the Shannon area; but basically both lobbies, and Aer Lingus, are satisfied. Why couldn't the solution have come sooner?

Outside Sfadco's own area, a number of other foreign investment projects in the West have done fairly well. At Killala, on the north Mayo coast, in 1974 the big Japanese chemicals firm, Asahi, set up a plant for making synthetic fibres which now employs some 340 staff; some local emigrants returned from England to work for it. Asahi has implanted a Japanese system of disciplined teamwork, known as 'the See, Think, Plan, Do philosophy', not exactly in the Irish tradition, but it seems to have been accepted. On the factory walls I saw placards, 'See, think, plan, practise and do, at all times and in all events for Ireland.' Perhaps the appeal to patriotism does the trick. Nearby, at Ballina, a Ruhr toolmaking firm, Heyner, has named its Irish subsidiary Shamrock Forge, but the managerial ethos is German. The German manager, wearing a flamboyant Tracht outfit of green silk and leather, told me that he was pleased with low Irish labour costs but sometimes irritated by Irish slowness. 'He's a bit bossy,' I was told locally. 'He doesn't see that the shortest distance between two points may be a straight line for a German, but it's a zigzag for the Irish.'

One significant recent trend has been the decision by some big American service firms to transfer parts of their main US operation to the west of Ireland – the so-called 'growth of the global office'. New York Life Insurance now processes its domestic claims in a village in Kerry; the publishers McGraw-Hill run their worldwide magazine subscription renewals from Galway. These and other firms are drawn not only by the low costs and good workforce, but by the five-hour time differential with the US. This enables them to get much of their routine work done while America is asleep, and have it shipped back during the computer terminals' 'down time' when costs are low: it saves both money and time. A New York firm will send over its material in the evening, by computer link, the Irish will work on it in the morning, and New York will get it back by the time its own offices open – simple! These ventures have so far created about a thousand jobs in the west of Ireland, and more are planned. One attraction for the investors is that good skilled office-workers are much easier to find than in the USA. At McGraw-Hill in Galway, where forty girls were tapping away at their keyboards, a young manager told me: 'Some of them are local farmers' daughters, and they are far better educated than in America, especially in geography. They know where places are in the world. American girls have no idea, so the letters are constantly misaddressed.'

Foreign investments of this kind, though useful, can only be part of the answer to the crisis of the West. Everyone today agrees that more of the effort must come from local initatives, helped by outside funding. But the weakness of local government in Ireland, and the absence of any regional structure, are handicaps: therefore much has to depend on ad hoc ventures by dynamic individuals. In 1991 the bishops of the West launched their own crusade, led by none other than Bishop Casey of Galway (see p. 167), who whatever his other failings was a man of true social concern, the kind of inspiring activist that the West needs. He told me shortly before his resignation in 1992: 'This region is dying, it will be dead in ten years unless something is done. So we bishops commissioned a full economic study; we held a series of public seminars, and we have been lobbying in Dublin and Brussels to get the authorities to act. The EC Commission has promised to help. But as Ireland is all one region, the EC money is badly allotted. Far too much of it goes to the Dublin area.' A familiar complaint in the West.

Interestingly, a number of bishops and priests have played pioneering roles in the economic fight for the West. Father Harry Bohan's rural development work in Clare I have already mentioned. Earlier, in the 1950s, Father James McDyer became something of a legend in Ireland for his efforts to rescue his remote parish of Glencolumbkille in Donegal, afflicted by steady emigration. He united the villagers in cooperative job-creation schemes, at a time when these were still unheard of in the rural West. He started workshops, got new houses built and a parish hall, created festivals, opened a folk museum; and for some years he managed to halt the steady exodus of young people. Today, a little of his legacy still survives, in a village that is now a modestly flourishing summer resort. But when he urgently preached his gospel of rural self-help across the rest of the West, it fell mainly on deaf ears. Nor did he get much support from officialdom in Dublin. He was a prophet in advance of his time.

An even more remarkable saga was that of the priest of the Knock pilgrimage shrine (see p. 161), who built an international airport in the wilds of Mayo. Knock, where the Virgin allegedly made apparitions in 1879, is Ireland's leading Marian pilgrimage centre and claims to be the foremost in Europe after Lourdes and Fátima, in terms of numbers of visitors. When the Pope came for its centenary in 1979, a crowd of 350,000 turned up in the little Mayo village and there was chaos. This gave the priest of the shrine, Monsignor James Horan, the idea of building an airport, for his pilgrims and for the north-west as a whole. Many people thought he was crazy. But he managed to persuade the Haughey Government to provide funds (by happy chance, the minister of transport, Padraig Flynn, was a local man, from Castlebar). The initial plan was for a modest 2,000-ft airstrip: but Horan was a visionary who got carried away by his own ambitions, and soon he won the finance for a 6,000-ft runway able to take jets. Work began. Then in 1982 Fine Gael came to power, suspicious of the project, and suspended all further finance. So Horan launched his own fund, appealing to Mayo emigrants in America and to local people: he would go round the pubs with an accordeon and collecting-box, and he managed to raise over £2 million. He also surreptitiously got the runway extended by a further 2,000 ft so that it could take jumbos, without Dublin quite realizing what he was doing.

In 1986 the airport officially opened and the first US jets began to arrive. Horan himself died a few months later, aged seventy-four, on a visit to Lourdes. Today he is venerated as a local hero, and his gamble has just about paid off; what was at first seen by many as a waste of public money is now a modest success, in economic terms. Horan International Airport stands proudly in what seems like the middle of nowhere, on a plateau ten miles from Knock and close to Healy's Castletown; privately owned by a trust, it has scheduled flights to Dublin, London and Manchester, and attracts US charters in summer. Its main traffic is not in fact pilgrims but tourists, business people and Mayo emigrants on return visits. It may not have changed the face of Mayo, and it is tiny compared with Shannon: but it is helping to bring new life to an area that John Healy twenty years ago saw as dying, if not dead. And all thanks to a parish priest.

Various other scattered local ventures are also working to help the West, such as the one I described at Kiltimagh (see p. 118). At Bellmullet, in the farthest remote corner of north-west Mayo, the villagers have raised funds for building a golf-course for American tourists. At Killala, also in Mayo, emigrants have returned from Britain and America to work in new little factories started by local people. And in Galway a 'Business Innovation Centre' has sponsored a strange variety of new activities in the region, from harp-making and shark-fishing to sand-blasting of signposts on rock.

One ingenious remedy for rural depopulation, now being tried out, is that urban long-term unemployed should be resettled in the countryside. Under one pilot scheme backed by the EU, a number of out-of-work Dublin families have been persuaded to move to Co. Clare, where there is plenty of vacant rural housing. 'This is rural emigration come full circle,' said one pioneer of the project. 'The newcomers can grow their own vegetables, maybe find odd jobs to do. They have lower living costs than in their city slums, and a better quality of life.'

Certainly a new spirit is stirring in the West. 'For too long we have depended passively on outside help: now at last we are helping ourselves,' was a view I heard many times. But the change may have come a little late. The brave new local initiatives are still few and tiny compared with the scale of the problem, and rural emigration seems set to continue, for there are far too few skilled jobs available for a younger generation increasingly well educated. Many local people remain gloomy about the region's prospects. When in 1992 a big meat-processing factory went bankrupt at Ballyhaunis in Mayo, threatening the loss of 600 jobs, it sent shivers throughout the West from Donegal to Kerry.

Probably the future of the economy lies more in the small local self-help ventures than in larger-scale foreign investment. It will lie also in forestry, and new kinds of farming – and in developing the region's few towns as poles of attraction. The success of Galway City is important for the West. It means that some of the rural emigrants will at least be tempted to stay in that area, rather than drift to Dublin or abroad. The future lies also in tourism. But if this is developed too massively, it could become the enemy of one of the West's supreme assets: a clean, unspoilt environment.

The environment: a battle for the Burren, and bungalow blight

The charms of Ireland have turned tourism into a major economic asset, accounting for over 7 per cent of GNP. It provides about 100,000 full-time all-year jobs; and it earns over £1 billion from the three million or so annual foreign visitors, of whom the British are much the most numerous, with the Americans in second place. French, German and Italian numbers are growing fast.

The new vogue for 'agri-tourism' (farm holidays) is a small part of a wider government strategy of tourist development, notably for the West. It has encouraged the building of scores of golf-courses, for which there is plenty of space and a ready clientele, notably American, German and Japanese. It has also promoted lake and river cruises, ocean marinas and horse-riding centres; new 'heritage centres' where the descendants of émigrés can seek out their Irish roots (see pp. 319–20); and summer festivals of all kinds, such as the Galway Oyster Festival, the Wexford Opera Festival, the Yeats and Merriman literary festivals, and at Lisdoonvarna in Co. Clare a folk event where traditionally brides used to be bartered.

The danger certainly exists that mass tourism could begin to spoil Ireland, as parts of the Mediterranean coast have been spoilt. Happily, there is little sign of it yet – few eyesores of the kind familiar in Spain or Greece, even on the Côte d'Azur. The new rural hotels tend to be fairly small, and well sited to blend with the landscape; many are converted stately homes (see p. 326). The Club Méditerranée finally arrived in Ireland in 1992, on the Kerry coast, but with a discreet eighty-room hotel for golfers, not one of its usual huge holiday 'villages'. In fact, much of the tourism in Ireland is still individual, eclectic and human in scale, from farmhouse B&Bs to hired Gypsy caravans and singsongs in pubs; and even in high summer many of the lovely beaches and beauty spots remain remarkably uncrowded. However, there is now growing pressure from promoters for larger-scale mass-tourist operations; and it is not certain how far the Government may resist this lucrative temptation, despite its declared policy of avoiding the mistakes of southern Europe. It would be a sad irony if too much hectic modern tourism were to damage the very qualities of quiet remoteness and quirky gentleness that tourists come to Ireland to find.

As in the case of Dublin town planning, so also in rural matters, the Irish today are becoming much more environment-conscious. When there is possible ecological danger from some new project, pressure groups will take action, and the public will show interest – far more than twenty years ago. This was seen in 1992–3 in the notorious case of the planned 'interpretative centre' in the Burren, Co. Clare. It has been the sharpest environmental controversy of recent years, and is revealing of the way that public opinion operates in Ireland.

It is government policy to endow major tourist sites with these modern-style centres, which use videos, lectures and wall displays to explain about the site. The idea is good, and it can work well, for example in the new interpretative centre near Glendalough monastery, Co. Wicklow. But the planning and building of these centres is in the hands of the Office of Public Works, a not very cultural State body that has not always been sensitive in its exact choice of location – or so it has been argued, notably in the case of the Burren, that wild, strange and beautiful region of limestone rocks and flower-clad moorland, south of Galway Bay. Here the OPW wanted to build a centre in a disused quarry at Mullaghmore, just inside the Burren. But the environmentalists took up arms, led by An Taisce (Ireland's National Trust) and backed by the World Wildlife Fund. They pleaded that to put this big centre *inside* the Burren would not only be unsightly, but the sewage and refuse created by the tourists would damage the area's delicate ecology, its rare wild flowers and plants, its unusual turloughs (rock pools). The leader of the campaign, Dr Emer Colleran, a Galway microbiologist and former president of An Taisce, told me: 'The Burren wilderness has a superb richness, botanical and geological, and a special spiritual quality. To implant a major tourist centre there would be like painting a moustache

150

on the Mona Lisa! We are not against interpretative centres as such, they are useful: but they should be located not *at* the beauty spots but further back, in nearby villages. This is now the practice in other countries, and the OPW are out of date. I accept that they are careful people, they do care about ecology: but they have simply got their facts wrong. And I'm a scientist, I know.'

Most local people however were in favour of the OPW project, including Clare County Council, Clare TDs, Sfadco, and hoteliers eager for more business; and they all tended to feel that the environmentalists were making too much fuss about not very much. Moreover, the OPW as a State body was exempt from planning permission, so there was no formal means of appeal against it – very different from the position in Britain, where any such project would get a full public inquiry. The OPW was dependent on EC money for 75 per cent of the costs of the centre, so Dr Colleran and her friends lobbied the EC and persuaded them to make a full environmental study. But the EC too came down on the side of the OPW and committed its funds. So late in 1992 work on the project began.

There were disputes at the same time over two other proposed new interpretative centres, one in the Boyne valley, the other at Sally Gap in the Wicklow Mountains south of Dublin, where the battle against the OPW was led by the colourful local seigneur, Garech Browne of the Guinness family (see p. 324). He told me: 'They want to put a centre with a huge car park right at the top of my drive. It would ruin the environment. Luckily the county council are on my side, and some government ministers: but they seem to have little clout against the OPW, which is arrogant and all-powerful. It regards us as a bunch of élitist snobs trying to keep mass tourism from our back garden. But we are *right* to do so. In other countries, for example in Britain's Lake District, the dangers of this kind of tourism have now been learned. Ireland, as usual, is belatedly getting round to a bad habit that others have outgrown.'

The climax to these strange affairs came in 1993. The conservationist lobbies at all three sites took the OPW to court.

But the OPW, having been given a Government go-ahead, began work as fast as possible, hoping to achieve a *fait accompli*: over £1 million was spent, and a huge hole was dug in the Burren. Then the Supreme Court produced the dramatic ruling that the State was wrong to suppose that it enjoyed exemption from planning control under the 1963 Planning Act, so the OPW must first seek permission. This changed the picture, and the conservationists were delighted. The OPW judiciously scaled down its three projects, and began a tactful canvassing of local opinion, before starting to face An Bord Pleanála, the State planning board. It was a victory for democracy over the autocratic State – but not yet the end of a muddled dispute that the *Irish Times* called 'an unmitigated public-relations disaster' for the OPW. And Ireland remains backward in its system of holding public inquiries to deal with such matters. Decisions still tend to be taken behind closed doors by officials, whenever they can get away with it.

Another controversy in 1992 concerned plans for gold-mining in south-west Mayo, between Westport and Leenane. This is a remote scenic area very like nearby Connemara, popular with salmon fishers and hikers. Two prospecting companies struck gold, thought to be worth some £400 million, and demanded mining rights from the Government. They promised that the work would create plenty of new jobs, in an area badly in need of them. But many local people grew worried, and found strong backing from environmentalists: David Bellamy came over to help them. 'Mining involves cyanide and rock-blasting, and would create massive toxic waste,' said one hotelier with a salmon-fishing reserve; 'it would spell disaster to the fishing and tourist businesses we have created here, and to farming.' At first Mayo County Council sat on the fence, concerned about the danger of pollution but enticed by the job prospects; finally, under local pressure, it came out in favour of a ban on all mining in the region. But this annoyed the Government, which set high priority on jobs and seemed to believe the companies' assurances that the mining could be 'environmentally acceptable'. The companies appealed to the Irish High Court against the council's ban, and in November 1992 the court pronounced in their favour, declaring it illegal.

Many local people were left aghast, farmers and hoteliers alike. Peter Mantle, an Englishman running a small private hotel on his salmon and sea-trout fishery, told me: 'A clean environment is one of the star assets of this part of Ireland – why ruin it? Who will want to come on holiday to a blasted gold-mine? And jobs aren't everything: the mining will last maybe ten years, but the ecological damage could be permanent. My wife and I left the London rat-race to live in this paradise, but now we are under assault on all sides. The lovely hills are being spoilt by sitka spruce, and the pastures by over-grazing of sheep, thanks to the EC headage payments. And now comes this gold-mine.' However, though the mining companies had apparently won their case, by the spring of 1994 they had not yet started work. The strength of local opposition, plus the falling world price of gold, seemed to be giving them second thoughts about the whole project. So the ecologists were keeping their fingers crossed.

As for industrial pollution, this is less often a problem in Ireland, if only because there is not so much older heavy industry. However, there have been complaints about modern chemicals factories in the Cork area. When the American company Merrell Dow proposed to set up a plant near Cork, a local lobby waged a campaign against it, and the firm backed out. Farming tends to cause more problems than industry; many farmers create pollution through clumsy use of fertilizers, or effluent from silage, and this is not easy for the Government to control.

Nuclear hazards are not an issue, for there is a political consensus that for environmental reasons Ireland should not build nuclear power stations. So a country with few natural energy resources has to rely heavily on imported oil and coal: oil fulfils some 48 per cent of energy needs, against 22 per cent from coal, 16 per cent from natural gas, 13 per cent from peat. The coal-mines, never prolific, are now virtually exhausted. Sizeable natural-gas deposits have been found off the Cork coast and are being exploited. But the search for offshore oil has proved elusive. Electricity, very expensive in Ireland, comes largely from natural gas, but oil, coal and hydro also contribute – and so does peat, that major feature of the old rural Ireland.

More commonly known as 'turf' in Ireland, peat is decayed semi-carbonized bog vegetation, and it has long been a staple form of domestic heating in the Irish countryside. It is found especially in the flat, gloomy boglands of the Irish Midlands, where the State peat board, Bord Na Móna, today owns large tracts of land and uses complex modern machinery to harvest the peat from the bogs. Most of this it sells to the electricity board, and some to the public in the form of briquettes for household heating. Other peat is still dug privately, by more old-fashioned means. As close to Dublin as the Wicklow Mountains, some peat bogs belong to big landowners who lease out parts of it to Dubliners – not just to the poor, but to middle-class families who come out at the weekends, dig it by hand and take it home for their winter fuel; in two days they can gather enough for all winter. On many a hillside you can see what from a distance look like white flocks of grazing sheep; they turn out to be scattered plastic bags used for collecting the peat.

The Irish are not always the tidiest or most aesthetically minded of people. They may have created few tourist eyesores to spoil the landscape, but they have been less careful with small-scale private home-building. Parts of their lovely country have become infected with the notorious epidemic of 'bungalow blight' – little white modern houses strewn across valleys and hillsides. This much-lamented trend began in the late 1960s when the Government, with the best of intentions, tried to help small farmers and others to build new, comfortable homes cheaply, in place of their old cottages. It produced a series of standard architectural plans, which anyone could buy in a shop for £1 or so each, and then use for constructing a house with the help of a local builder, thus avoiding architects' fees. A book, *Bungalow Bliss*, advised the public on how best to use these plans, and it became a best seller.

It was a time when the farmers were growing more prosperous, and thousands seized on this chance to move into the modern world. Their old picturesque cottages were very often poky, damp, almost impossible to modernize; and they could hardly be blamed for wanting to build a new home on their own land, with larger rooms, proper plumbing and heating, and space for their new luxuries such as washing-machines. The cottages were often kept for use as garage or outhouse. However, many other rural bungalows were also built, not by farmers, but by townsfolk as commuter or holiday homes; and these began to line the country roads, turning the bliss into blight. Today you see them everywhere, built sometimes of local granite, more often of cheaper concrete blocks, and nearly always painted white; they may be cosy to live in, but they blend less well with the landscape than the old grey thatched cottages. Some even have absurd fancy embellishments, such as Greek porticos or Spanish patios (ideas maybe picked up on foreign holidays), which have led to the nickname 'Hiberno-Dallas'. Until recently, planning rules were lax, and anyone could build almost anywhere. Today the rules have been tightened, and new bungalows are not allowed in scenic locations: 'The Irish norm used to be the absolute rights of private property,' an An Taisce official told me, 'but now a social norm of the public right to control that property is coming in. That's new for Ireland.' But it comes after much damage has already been done.

It is often said that although the Irish are masters of words, of anecdote, wit and poetry, they lack a strong visual sense of style. It shows in their buildings and décor. There is little native architectural tradition, save for that imported by the British, mainly in the Georgian period; but nor is there much feeling for attractive modern design or building. This helps to account for the dreary look of so many Irish towns and villages, which give the appearance of being poorer and more backward than they really are.

The Irish have little taste for modern architecture. It is true that the Ambrose Kelly partnership has produced some interesting new work, somewhat in the James Stirling idiom, in Limerick and other towns. But the modernism of Sam Stephenson sits ill upon the streets of Dublin. What the Irish prefer is the nostalgic retro style, and this is now in fashion for façades and shopfronts. In the 1960s and '70s, ugly modern plastic came into vogue for a while, but today there is a reaction against this, and many shops and restaurants have deliberately restyled their façades in a quaint nineteenth-century idiom. It lends to some Irish main streets an old-fashioned Dickensian look that many tourists no doubt find charming and 'typically Irish'. Certainly it is authentic. But the preponderance of dark brown adds a sombre touch. And whereas some façades have been carefully restored, a great many others remain tatty and decayed – less through lack of money for renewal than because so many Irish people just do not care or notice how things look. There is little of the colourful chic and neat visual flair that you will find in southern parts of Europe just as poor as Ireland, or poorer – for example, the villages of Portugal, Andalusia or the Greek islands. Nor is tidiness an Irish forte. Mary Harney, when minister of state for the environment, said to me: 'We have a major national problem with litter. We are a dirty nation, and a lawless society, so we just throw things anywhere. I'm trying to educate people, but it's an uphill task.'

6

CHANGES IN SOCIETY AND MORALS: TOWARDS A MORE SECULAR IRELAND

The changes in rural life, the growth of modern prosperity and of modern urban problems, have been accompanied by other far-reaching changes in Irish society. This chapter looks first at the Catholic Church and its declining influence; then at the great national debate on the sexual moral issues, as birth control is finally accepted but abortion stays illegal; then at the changing position of women, and the new divorce referendum. Next I look at education, where again the Church's direct role is waning; and at some of the changes in lifestyles.

The Pope's last bastion: authority contested, celibacy under strain

The phrase 'moral vacuum' frequently recurs today in talks with observers of Irish society. They speak of a gap left by the decline of the Church's old moral authority, with none other taking its place. I heard this from Dr Garret FitzGerald. And I heard it from a Jesuit priest in Dublin, talking off the record: 'The Church is losing respect among younger people, since it is so out of touch on private morality. This is tragic, for it thus forfeits the authority to take the lead in today's real battle, which is not against condoms but against poverty, corruption and social injustice. The moral vacuum is serious.' But from the Church's point of view, how can it adapt to a changing society, yet retain its sacred and eternal principles? It is the dilemma of Catholic priests around the world, especially acute under an Irish Church hierarchy so vehemently loyal to the Vatican.

This Catholic Church in Ireland, which for good or ill has done so much to shape and mark the Irish people, is today in crisis. Yet it remains more powerful here than anywhere else in Europe, even Poland. Some 95 per cent of the Republic's citizens are Catholic, and of these as many as 82 per cent still go to Mass regularly – much the highest figure in Europe. But the Church's influence, once so massive, has been declining steadily in the past thirty years, as society grows more secular. Many practising Catholics no longer follow its moral laws in their private lives. They may still believe in God, and be on affectionate terms with their parish priest; but they have grown critical of the Church as an institution. Many of them regard it as too secretive and authoritarian, too much concerned with the sexual moral issues, and too little with wider social problems.

And the hierarchy of the Church does not find it easy to adapt to the new challenges. Most of the bishops are elderly, and many appear simply bewildered by the changes – 'It is sad to see what is happening to our wonderful Irish people,' said one of those I met. 'The old social and moral controls of rural society are disappearing, and people are lost in a new, permissive urban world.' He may be right. But increasingly people do not listen to the Church's own solutions. It remains more directly obedient to the Vatican, hence to a conservative Pope, than in other countries. Its discipline is tight, and outwardly it appears a monolith, speaking with one voice. However, behind the scenes a growing minority of liberal clergy, mainly in the orders such as the Jesuits, are becoming critical. Their influence for the moment is limited. But this could change.

One must look in history for clues as to why the Catholic Church has enjoyed such exceptional power in Ireland, and why the Irish have tended to be such a religious people. It could be that the Irish Celtic persona, like the Breton, with its sense of mystery and mysticism, its concern with wild spirits, magic and legends, going back to pre-Christian days, has nurtured in this people a natural religious sense. Then, after the Reformation, the Irish stuck with the Church of Rome because their English overlords did not; and it so happened that this Latin-inspired Catholicism suited their wayward temperament much better than the sterner, more disciplined Protestantism of Northern Europe would have done. Or that is one interpretation. Then in the nineteenth century the Catholic Church became identified in people's minds with their Irishness, and thus became a symbol of resistance to the Protestant British, even though it did not itself play any dominant role in the struggle for freedom. After independence it continued to benefit from this nationalist kudos, rather like the Church in Poland.

It was also in a spirit of opposition to British rule that in the period 1870–78 the Irish Church was set firmly on the ultramontane path of absolute loyalty to Rome – the path it still follows today – by the powerful Archbishop of Dublin, Cardinal Paul Cullen. He created the authoritarian structure that still persists. And through its control of most school education the Church was able to keep the people obedient to its values, and thus to impose a puritan ethic on a nation that in earlier days had been sexually quite free-and-easy.

During the first decades after independence, the Church exercised considerable influence over government policies, notably in family, social and cultural matters. Both of the main political parties depended on the pious conservative rural vote, and so they did not dare to offend the hierarchy. The Church lent its weight to the censorship laws of the 1920s (see p. 238) and it firmly excluded sex education from school curricula.

One notorious case, in 1951, was that of the 'mother and child scheme'. At a time when the Irish public health services were still poorly developed, the young, radically minded health minister in a Fine Gael-led coalition, Noel Browne, put forward a plan for a free health scheme for pregnant mothers and proper postnatal care for mothers and babies. But the Church resented this intrusion by the State into its own field of welfare (it ran most of the hospitals), so it declared the scheme 'contrary to Catholic social teaching'. It put strong pressure on the Government to drop the scheme, which it did – and Noel Browne resigned, after being told by Seán MacBride, a senior minister, 'You cannot afford to fight the Church.' Browne, bitterly anti-clerical, has given a sharp account of this episode in his autobiography, *Against the Tide* (1986), where he tells how his ardent youthful Catholicism turned to disillusion when he found that the Church, as he saw it, cared less about helping people than about keeping its own power. He was angry that the Church 'assumed it had the right to dictate policy to the Government'. And he quoted a remarkable pronouncement in 1951 by the ultra-conservative Archbishop Kinane of Cashel: 'Subjects should not oppose their Bishops' teaching by word, by act or in any other way . . . God is the author of organized civil society and hence political and social activities are subject to God's moral law, of which the Church is the divinely constituted interpreter and guardian.'

No Irish prelate would talk like that nowadays. Roughly since the 1960s times have been changing, as Ireland has opened out to foreign influences, and people have become better educated and less instinctively obedient to Church doctrines. The phrase in the 1937 Constitution that recognized the 'special position' of the Catholic Church was removed by referendum in 1972. And today, although the Church remains adamant on a few key issues, notably divorce and abortion, it interferes less than it used in most other State policies – and Governments in turn defer to it less. 'In the 1950s', said one liberal-minded bishop I met, 'the Taoiseach would feel obliged to seek the Archbishop's permission even to open a new building in Dublin. He doesn't any more – and I for one am glad that we no longer meddle in politics to that degree.' Of course, the Church does still possess much power in Ireland, for example in the running of schools, but even here its direct influence is waning, as more lay teachers are appointed and the schools become much more secular (see pp. 209–14).

It is true, however, that, among ordinary people, Christian belief and practice has declined less than in most Western countries. The rate of regular attendance at Mass has fallen from 91 per cent in 1974 to about 82 per cent today – but this compares with a mere 14 per cent in supposedly Catholic France! Even in Dublin, where some working-class areas today seem quite pagan, the Mass-going figure remains as high as 69 per cent; and in rural Ireland, where most homes are still decorated with crucifixes, madonnas or portraits of the Pope, it is 89 per cent.

In these less sophisticated areas, many people still feel a strong need for the magic and mystery that the Church can offer; they still believe in moving statues, apparitions and other miracles. To see this kind of old-style religious fervour in action, it is worth visiting the shrine at Knock in Mayo (see p. 146), 'the Lourdes of the North', where in 1879 fifteen villagers claimed to have seen an apparition of the Virgin, Joseph, St John and angels, lasting two hours, and mobile. Today, of Knock's 1·5 million annual pilgrims over 80 per cent are Irish. On some Sundays, up to 20,000 people crowd the huge basilica, built for the Pope's visit in 1979; there are torchlight processions, and queues at the row of nine modern taps selling 'holy water'. Some miracle cures are claimed. For example, in 1990 a woman from Athlone was suddenly cured of multiple sclerosis during a service in the basilica. The official Church, not wanting to be laughed at, remains wary of calling such cases divine miracles, and prefers to suggest that there may have been medical explanations for them. Most amazing is Knock's success with confessionals; under public demand, a big new chapel was opened in 1991 with enough cubicles for fifty priests to hear confession at the same time, and every Sunday they are very busy. In Ireland as a whole the practice of saying confession has dropped off sharply (due in part to the spread of contraception, it is thought). But the pilgrims to Knock readily go to confession, maybe because they have an anonymity that they cannot find at home.

There are many reasons why the figures for regular churchgoing remain so high in Ireland. Some people may attend Mass primarily out of social convention; or through fear of gossip if their absence is noted, at least in villages. But a great many do also retain a genuine Christian belief in God; and they will draw a distinction between this true spiritual faith and the moral doctrines of the Church, which they do not always obey. The Church and its sacraments have become far less central to their lives than formerly. And there are plenty of young people with a real sense of Christian values, and concern for social justice, who do not go to church unless they have to. In the eighteen to twenty-five age group, weekly Mass attendance has fallen since 1974 from over 70 per cent to a mere 56 per cent – maybe a pointer for the future.

In this shifting climate, the role of the parish priest has been changing. He used to be the undisputed leader of the village, a man maybe of great personal kindness but stern on the moral issues, where generally his word was obeyed. His warnings of hell-fire were taken seriously, and he could force an erring couple to the altar or break an illicit liaison. Today, he generally keeps a much lower profile on matters of this kind (see p. 199). He will still be liked and respected for his own human qualities, but he is no longer the dominant local figure by virtue of his position as priest, and no longer chosen ex officio as president of local clubs. His moral authority no longer comes with the job: he has to earn it.

The senior Irish bishops are not finding it easy to adapt to this new and fluid situation. They were brought up to expect the Church to enjoy absolute authority, and to be obeyed. Now they find themselves criticized on all sides, especially in the Press and media, and even by some of their own priests. A few of the more liberal bishops are quite glad of these new challenges, but the majority are confused and anxious, unsure how to come to terms with a new pluralist society in which the Church has to compete with other values and other voices than its own, paraded nightly on the nation's television screens.

If the Irish hierarchy is so much more conservative than in most of Catholic Europe, one explanation lies with the Vatican. When Pope John Paul II visited Ireland in September 1979, within a year of his taking office, he was greeted everywhere by huge adulatory crowds; over a million people attended Mass with him in Phoenix Park, Dublin. He was deeply touched; and today it is often said that he regards Ireland as the last reliable stronghold of Catholicism in Europe – as much as his native Poland – at a time when even in Italy the faith has been receding so fast. So the Pope puts a priority on holding Ireland to his own particular Christian vision. And as all appointments of Irish bishops are made by the Vatican, it is the conservatives who are chosen, especially for the senior posts. The two most recent Archbishops of Dublin have been firm papal loyalists. And Cardinal Cahal Daly, who in 1990 was appointed Archbishop of Armagh and Primate of All Ireland,★ though a moderate in terms of Northern Ireland politics, is highly conservative on the moral and doctrinal issues. Some less senior prelates are more liberal, such as Brendan Comiskey, Bishop of Ferns and Wexford, who in private is ready to argue against the papal line on such matters as celibacy for priests. But men with these views seldom reach the highest posts.

The archetype of conservative Irish bishops, and perhaps the best known, is Jeremiah Newman, Bishop of Limerick, now in his late sixties. He is a scholarly man with a boyish charm, who received me with great warmth and courtesy in his lovely library full of old books. He enthused when we talked about the Middle Ages, and life at Oxford in the old days. Then we turned to religion and the present day. 'Of course the Church *must* be authoritarian,' he said. 'Christ gave the Church immutable moral laws, which do not change with mere changes in society, and the bishops have to ensure that these are obeyed.' He had recently spoken out against Protestantism for being too lax in upholding these eternal principles. He is also known locally as a male chauvinist, hostile to women having any role in running the Church, and he spoke to me of 'nuns who stupidly become infected with feminism, wanting to leave their convents and do social work, wearing ordinary clothes' (see below). To my questions about whether the Church should adapt to social change and new ideas, he said plaintively: 'But, John, what's wrong with tradition? That's the way it's always been up till now, and I just don't understand why it's all going wrong. Why are the media so vitriolic towards us? *Why?*' He struck me as a nice old boy but bewildered and out of touch with today's world; others who know him have felt the same, and have talked to me about his fondness for whiskey, sometimes evident when he speaks in public.

★ The Catholic Church, like the Church of Ireland (Protestant), is organized on an all-Ireland basis, and its Primate is also Archbishop of Armagh, in the North. There are four archbishops and thirty-one bishops.

But when I met him, he was on the wagon. 'I'm so lonely,' he said, 'living here on my own with two elderly nuns to look after me.' As a scholarly don on some campus, he would be regarded as a charming, harmless old diehard; as a bishop giving pastoral care to a rough, tough city like Limerick, he seems out of place.

However, in contrast to so many bishops, a number of the more junior priests are today quite liberal. Some of them, partly as a means of escape from the conservative clerical climate in Ireland, go out as missionaries to the Third World, where the Irish have a long and honourable tradition of such work. There they sometimes get caught up in 'liberation theology' and then return home even more radicalized, to add their weight to the efforts to modernize the Irish Church. In fact, behind its disciplined façade, quite a debate is today going on within this Church, as some clergy dare to urge the bishops in private to modify their line on issues such as birth control. But in public, these critics are careful to toe the official line – partly out of loyalty, and partly through prudent self-interest, for a dissident priest will be harassed by the hierarchy and could find himself transferred to some remote and inferior post, by way of punishment. The liberal element in the Church is still small and fragmented, and has no major personality around whom to rally. Its power is thus limited. The average parish priest, though he has become more tolerant, remains conservative and happy to follow his bishop.

It is the religious orders, the Jesuits, Dominicans and others, who are generally more radical and outspoken than the parish clergy. Being less directly under the control of the hierarchy, they feel freer to speak out. Some 200 of these orders, with 16,000 members, are grouped in a body called the Conference of Major Religious Superiors, which takes a Leftish line on social matters and is constantly pressing the Government to do more for the poor and unemployed. It lobbies the bishops, too, as a spokesman told me: 'We discreetly do battle with the hierarchy all the time, urging them to be less secretive and authoritarian. We also want them to speak out more strongly against poverty, corruption and social injustice in Ireland, and to keep a lower profile on the issues of sexual morality, where the Church is in danger of losing the younger generation. We are making some progress, but it's slow. There can't be much real change under the present Pope.'

A few individuals in these orders have become famous in Ireland for their crusading social work. Peter McVerry, a Jesuit, runs a hostel for homeless teenagers in the Ballymun slum district of Dublin (see pp. 129 and 233). 'It is God's will that poverty and deprivation should be tackled,' he told me, 'so the Church should put far more stress on this, and shut up about the sexual issues. Priests are simply not trained to understand these things, their education is far too theological. But I do not want to get drawn publicly into the great moral debate: it could prejudice my real work, which is to push the State to spend far more on helping the poor and homeless.'

Sister Stanislaus Kennedy, the nun known to all the Irish as 'Sister Stan', is another tireless campaigner against poverty, a Mother Teresa figure. When she began her work in the 1970s, she openly criticized the bishops for living too comfortably and neglecting the poor. They were none too pleased; but today they actively support her work, and she has become quite an Establishment figure, serving on various government commissions that deal with poverty; her book, *One Million Poor*, was launched by Garret FitzGerald as Taoiseach. She also runs an agency in Dublin for helping the homeless, the destitute, deserted wives with children, indeed anyone in distress. And she states that nuns today can follow their vocation just as well by going to live and work among the poor as by staying within the convent walls.

This is just what many Irish nuns are now doing. As in other countries, vocations have been falling off, and today the young women who enter the orders are less than half as numerous as the older ones who die or leave. Many convents, and monasteries too, are closing down, but not just because of this drop in numbers. It is also because the nuns have found other tasks; these are the ones who stay in their orders but go to live in little groups on housing estates, where they wear jumpers and jeans or other mufti, and do various kinds of social work, under the aegis of their orders. 'We are far closer to ordinary people than nuns used to be,' said the sister in charge of one group, from the Good Shepherd order, whom I visited in their council house in a grim slum district of Waterford, rife with vandalism, drugs and high unemployment. 'We try to help the women whose husbands have no jobs, and young girls with unwanted pregnancies. This is real Christian work, of great value. Our first priority here is not pushing people to Mass but helping them to find self-respect and to come to terms with their problems.' Several nuns in this kind of work told me that they favoured birth control (but they cannot say so publicly) and would privately give advice on how to obtain it. In Limerick there is even a sister who sometimes will secretly help women to go to England for an abortion – this, under Bishop Newman's nose.

Many radical Irish Christians feel that the Church has got its priorities wrong in stressing private sexual morality rather than public social justice. It is true that the hierarchy today is readier than twenty years ago to speak out against poverty and other distress, to support the work of people like McVerry and 'Stan', and to urge the Government to act. It also has a generous record of aid to the Third World. But at home it remains curiously reticent about high-level corruption, in politics or business. When recently Ireland was shaken by scandals of this kind, the bishops raised little protest, disappointing many of their faithful by their failure to exert their moral authority. Were they afraid of alienating senior politicians or big industrialists, whose support they need? This has been suggested. And certainly it is true that the Catholic ethos, especially in Ireland, has tended to focus on individual and private morality, to the neglect of public morality and civic responsibility.

The Catholic Church's obsession with sexual guilt, and what may seem to an outsider its fear of sex, are not unique to Ireland, but in Ireland they have marked society more deeply than in most countries. How did this happen? In the nineteenth century, it may even have been a reflection of the Victorian puritan ethos in Britain, though the Irish might not wish to think so. There were also economic factors: late marriage, and chastity outside marriage, were used as a way of keeping down the population, after the ordeal of the Famine. Then, as historians have noted, until quite recently the Irish Church seemed to regard sexual immorality as the only immorality, while turning a blind eye to social injustices. Today, now that so much private behaviour and public opinion have moved in a permissive direction, most clergy prefer to keep a prudent low profile about the 'moral' issues. But the Church is still *perceived* as being obsessed with sexual morality, and with good reason, for the views of many bishops have not changed. Some critics would even suggest that celibate clergy are not the right people to understand sex or to pronounce on its morality. Senator David Norris, Ireland's leading gay-rights campaigner and a much-respected figure (see p. 187), suggested to me: 'I feel some compassion for these elderly men who have sacrificed the joy of sexuality. So I'm not surprised that the hierarchy are abnormally obsessed with other people's sex lives.' So this leads us to the issue of priestly celibacy – and to the famous affair of Bishop Casey of Galway.

Dr Éamonn Casey was an enigmatic, even tragic figure. For many years, until his sudden resignation in 1992, he was much the most popular of Irish bishops, admired alike for his energetic campaigning for the poor and deprived, and for his jovial, warm, sociable personality. He stood out from the run of bishops as an almost Rabelaisian figure, an extrovert showman and joker, lover of song and drink and fast cars. He was also an unusually compassionate man with a big social conscience, a champion of human rights in Latin America. 'He embodies Irish Catholicism's human face,' wrote the *Irish Times*. All too human, it transpired, when the news came out of his former secret love-affair as Bishop of Kerry, and his teenage son in America.

Casey came from a modest background in rural Kerry and never lost his thick local brogue. He took a doctorate in philosophy at Maynooth (see p. 171), and later moved to Slough, near London, as chaplain to the big Irish community in that area. Here he worked especially for the homeless, and in the 1960s was co-founder and later chairman of Shelter, the organization that did so much to bring them help. Colleagues described him as 'a human dynamo', working non-stop with passionate conviction. In 1969, at the age of forty-two, he was appointed to his native Kerry as Ireland's youngest bishop. Seven years later he became Bishop of Galway, where he led the local bishops in a campaign to stem the decline of the West. He was also made chairman of Trócaire, the Irish Church's agency for aid to the Third World, and this absorbed much of his energy and passion. He publicly denounced the selfishness of capitalism and the evils of Third World poverty. He went to El Salvador, where he was shocked by the human-rights abuses of the US-backed regime there: as a result, when President Reagan visited Galway, Casey pointedly refused to meet him. He was exceptional among Irish bishops in the sharpness of his attacks on inequality and social injustice, both at home and abroad. This made him some enemies, but it also won him huge popularity in Galway – as did his breezy, fun-loving personality. In London in 1986 he was fined and banned from driving for twelve months, for speeding while under the influence of alcohol, but he quickly apologized to his diocese, and became even more popular. The Irish like a man who will admit to his human weaknesses.

My wife and I had lunch with him in Galway in March 1992, two months before he resigned. He took us out in his BMW to a village on the coast, where little girls bounced up to him and he patted them on the head, thanking them for their day's fasting on behalf of Trócaire. We were soon under the spell of his vivacity and charm; his energy was amazing for a man of sixty-five. But his ideas were more rigid. He denounced the ills of excessive drinking, which he linked to the rise of sex. He spoke of his work for unwed teenage pregnant girls, helping them to have their babies adopted. He said: 'One cannot pick and choose with the Church's teaching, one has to accept it all, or stop being a Christian. Restraint and self-sacrifice are the basis of what we preach. My policy is to be very firm and rigid on these sacred principles, but sympathetic and tolerant towards individual cases of sin.' He was soon to need such tolerance. Politically radical, he had always been known as highly orthodox on the moral issues. But his public preachings against extramarital sex were now to ring hollow.

In May 1992 Casey suddenly resigned and vanished to the United States. At the same time Annie Murphy, an American living in Connecticut, twenty-one years his junior, made public her version of their eighteen-month love-affair in 1973–4 in Kerry, when he was bishop there. 'It was magical, like gossamer wings,' she said, adding that when she became pregnant, he pushed her hard to have the child adopted. She refused, and after their son Peter was born, she returned with him to America. After this, Casey made her regular payments, but refused any direct contact with the boy.

A few days later, Casey himself virtually corroborated this account. In a statement he said, 'I have grievously wronged Peter and his mother . . . I have also sinned grievously against God.' He said he had paid her out of his own salary, save for a sum of £70,000 in 1990 which he had drawn from diocesan funds. This had since been paid back with interest by several donors – but only *after* his resignation. Casey spent the next months incognito in a monastery in the USA, after which, with Vatican permission, he moved to Ecuador, to end his days there as a missionary. And Murphy had the bad taste to publish her own detailed and lurid account of their affair in a best-selling book.

After the scandal broke, the Vatican kept a discreet silence. But across the world there were banner headlines, and in Ireland itself a cascade of moral turmoil, at a time when society was already in crisis over abortion (it was just after the affair of the raped fourteen-year-old – see p. 190). Opinions on Casey were divided. Some people were simply shocked by his sexual 'sin'; or they saw him as a humbug who had failed to practise the moral code he preached from the pulpit. But others were more generous. They saw Casey as a victim of the Church's own hypocrisy, of its outdated views on celibacy; they even found it no coincidence that a man of such energy and warmth should have needed to give his love for a woman full expression. Was his 'human frailty' a negation of his many virtues, or in some way a part of them, for a priest who could not divorce his sexuality from his Christian humanism?

Many clerics spoke up with personal sympathy for Casey,

including his own archbishop, the saintly and much-loved Joseph Cassidy of Tuam. One liberal nun in Galway even said, 'The only wrong thing he did was to love a woman. He's only broken Church law, and we all know Church laws can change' – and many good Irish Catholics quietly agreed. Yet although Casey was relatively little blamed for having a love affair, he was widely criticized for the way he had handled its consequences. The English Jesuit writer Peter Hebblethwaite described as 'moral abortion' his attempts to get Annie to have the child adopted: 'He advised her to "give it to God" – how very convenient for him.' And then there was the murky matter of the borrowed diocesan funds. Probably Casey ought to have resigned as soon as Annie became pregnant, or at the start of the love affair, and then pursued his Samaritan vocation as a layman. But instead he put his episcopal career, and the Church's reputation, ahead of his human duty (the Vatican, it was said, had urged him not to resign).

The affair reopened the old debate about priestly celibacy. Across the centuries, in Ireland as elsewhere, Catholic priests have not always kept to their vows of chastity. Some have had long-term liaisons; and if a baby resulted, it was usually sent quietly into adoption and the whole thing hushed up. Only today are these matters becoming more openly talked about (at least one other Irish bishop is rumoured to have a regular mistress and another to have a live-in male lover). And only today are the celibacy vows driving so many priests to leave the Church: since 1970, over 100,000 priests worldwide, some of them Irish, have abandoned their vocation in order to marry. In Co. Cavan recently, a priest eloped with a nun. On the Aran Islands, another priest began an affair with the wife of a local policeman. They moved to America, where she obtained a divorce, he got himself defrocked, and they married. And they are now back on the island, where the Garda sergeant is living with another woman! All this is more or less accepted locally, something inconceivable even twenty years ago.

Pope John Paul retains a firm stand on celibacy, and the Casey affair is unlikely to have swayed him. But in Ireland, according to a poll in 1993, 69 per cent of people are now in favour of ending the celibacy rule – and that would include a growing minority of priests themselves. Soon after the Casey affair, one senior bishop told me privately: 'Marriage for priests will certainly come, in time, but not under this Pope. Some priests are just not cut out for celibacy, and could probably do their job better with the help of a loving wife, as in the Protestant Churches. But others *can* accept the discipline of chastity. We should simply be allowed to choose.' And in Galway I heard the same from a liberal priest who knew Casey well: 'Ending the celibacy rule would have saved Casey. A married priest with a family would be better able to share human experience and understand people. Many of my colleagues feel as I do, and we'd like to challenge the Pope, but we dare not speak out publicly against the hierarchy.' As it is, Casey was an excellent man in the wrong job.

This celibacy rule, as in other Catholic countries, is a main reason for the decline in recruits to the priesthood and religious orders. The orders, of nuns, monks, etc., are the worst affected; their members have dropped in number by about a third since 1970, and some 40 per cent of them are now aged over sixty. In the same period, the total of young men entering the priesthood each year has fallen by 30 per cent; and some two-thirds of seminary students leave before the end of their seven-year course, whereas it used to be only a third. They lose their sense of vocation, or they are tempted by other careers or by marriage.

The hierarchy claims to be not yet too disturbed by this trend, for Ireland is still plentifully stocked with priests. More worrying to some bishops is the fall in quality. 'We get far fewer really bright, intellectual recruits than we used,' one of them told me. 'In the old days, St Patrick had wooden chalices but golden priests; now Ireland has golden chalices and wooden priests, or so it's said.' I was not impressed myself by the tame group of theology students I met at St Patrick's College, Maynooth, the national seminary of Ireland. When asked why they wanted to become priests, two of them said, 'My bishop thought I should, so he sent me here,' and another, 'I want to administer the sacraments.'

Maynooth, as it is known for short, in the little town of that name just west of Dublin, has long been one of Ireland's most powerful institutions. Curiously, it was set up in 1795 by the

British authorities, worried about the radical impact of Irish priests returning from the French Revolution. Until quite recently, it was purely a college for training priests and for promoting orthodox theology, and its conservative influence on nineteenth- and twentieth-century Irish life was huge: Seán O'Casey described the great spire of its church as 'like a dagger through the heart of Ireland'. Its word was moral law ('This ye may do, but that ye may nooth,' went an old joke). Then in the 1960s, with university expansion and the advent of the liberal ideas of Vatican II, Maynooth was enlarged to include other faculties. Today, of its 3,400 students, only 10 per cent are training for the priesthood; in most respects it is much like any other university, full of lay teachers (some of them Protestant) and girl students in jeans. Its central campus of stately Victorian buildings has something of an English redbrick ambience.

Maynooth, however, is still owned and run by the Church, and the thirty-four Irish bishops use it as a headquarters. Here they hold their thrice-yearly conferences, deliberating behind closed doors and announcing only certain decisions. So Maynooth is a byword for the authority *and* secrecy of the Church, today much criticized. Some bishops would like to see a change, as the liberal Bishop Comiskey of Ferns told me: 'In the United States, where I used to live, the bishops' conferences are held mainly in public, in front of the media. But in Ireland many bishops are still horrified by this idea. They have little sense of public relations. Nearly half the bishops would like a change, including Cardinal Daly. But plenty of the older, influential ones want the status quo – and we work on consensus.'

In its cooperation with the laity and especially with women lay workers, the Irish Church is just beginning to follow the trend of some other countries. Its clergy have always felt a strong sense of hierarchy, wanting to keep aloof from the people and to manage local parish affairs in their own way, with their own staff. 'This image has done a lot of harm,' said a priest I met in Galway. 'But in some parishes here we have now set up pastoral teams of voluntary workers, mostly women, who help us run the parish, and have a say in how it is run. It is a scheme we have copied from the American and Australian churches and it's new for Ireland. We try to promote the idea that the Church *is* the people, not some authoritarian body preaching to them from on high. I would also like to see women priests one day, but that won't happen under the present Pope.' These changes are still contested by the old guard: Bishop Newman is not in favour even of lay women helping to run the diocese.

In Ireland more than in most countries, the basic dilemma facing the Catholic Church today is intellectual and theological: how can it coexist with a pluralist society whose views are not always its own, when it regards its own divine laws as superior to the mere human laws of democracy? How can it thus accept that a government should pass a law contrary to its own teaching, for example on divorce? Bishop Comiskey told me that he saw this as a debate between the Thomist and John Stuart Mill views: 'The old Thomist doctrine of the Church is that only its own laws are valid, being divine, and it cannot accept temporal laws. This is still the Church's teaching in a way, and is upheld by many bishops. But others, such as myself, would rather admit Mill's interpretation, whereby State law is a consensus of different views and the Church should be ready to live with this and accept that its own law is not absolute. Thus, in a referendum or other national debate, the Church should promote its own view-point but accept the result if defeated.' Others, however, put it differently. For Bishop Newman, 'Christ gave to the Church certain moral laws which are immutable and eternal. It is our sacred mission to uphold these, so we have no choice but to be authoritarian.'

The Church has still not resolved this dilemma. It still finds it hard to accept that changes in society should be any cause for changing its own doctrines; or that to be more flexible on some issues, notably the sexual ones, might win it back some of the support it has lost. It is fearful of making any concessions that might open a floodgate; and when it shifts its position, it is only under strong public pressure. One could argue that the Church is courageously sticking to its own principles. But the net result is that it has been losing much of its old moral authority in Irish society.

Many Irish commentators speak of a sense of moral vacuum in society. The Church may have been rigid and harsh in many ways: but it gave security, and a moral framework for people's lives. Today they have more personal freedom, but many of them feel vaguely adrift, for the decline of Church authority has not been compensated by any other code of values, save for a vague liberalism. As many people see it, by putting its stress on private and family morality and individual salvation, the Church neglects the ethic of civic responsibility; it seems more worried about sex than corruption, or even poverty; and although it inveighs against consumerist materialism, it offers little satisfactory alternative. Garret FitzGerald gave a forceful analysis, in an *Irish Times* article of 8 August 1992:

'. . . The institutional Church lost virtually all moral credibility with the great majority of people – inside as well as outside the Catholic Church – by its insistence on elevating the issue of the possible impact of contraception on sexual *mores* to the level of an absolute that must take precedence over *all* other considerations . . . That the institutional Church appears to have failed to recognize the damage it has thus done to its own moral authority is not only tragic for the Church itself; it has also undermined its capacity to contribute to the stability of society, especially in Ireland, as well as weakening its conscience-forming role in relation to social justice – which is badly needed in our modern individualist society. For our community is at present deeply pervaded by the powerful influence of a modern individualism that is preaching, without effective intellectual challenge, both a superficially attractive hedonistic message and at another level a self-serving economic materialism. And unhappily the moral vacuum that has increasingly been left by a disorientated institutional Church is not being filled by any alternative force.'

Dr FitzGerald laments that there is no proper public intellectual debate on these vital questions, in an Ireland where the Church and the media conduct a dialogue of the deaf. He blames the media for tending to accept 'liberal' anti-Church positions uncritically,

and the Church for its inability to admit past mistakes: 'The relationship between the Church and the media is significantly less
healthy and happy in Ireland than anywhere else in the developed
world.' Certainly some senior churchmen seem paranoid in their
horror of what they see as victimization by the media. 'The liberal
press and television hate our guts, I'm sure of it. They blame us
for being fixated on sex, but *they* are the real culprits, absorbed in
their hedonistic morass,' was the sharp language I heard from the
conservative Bishop Murphy of Cork, though he went on: 'But I
think it's good for the Church to have lost the old rural certainties
and to be in this new urban situation where it has to fight to hold
its ground.'

This crisis in the Church is painful to many Irish people, who
even if they are not great churchgoers still have Catholicism in
their bones and have been schooled to see the Irish Church as part
of their nationhood. Bishop Murphy's namesake in Cork, the
somewhat anti-clerical former Senator John A. Murphy, a man in
his sixties, said to me: 'The Catholic Church is part of what we
are. Many of us have some relative who is a priest, present at all
family occasions. And as with Joyce and his generation, the childhood influences within us are such that many of us have never
escaped from Catholicism, and thus we keep a residual affection
towards the Church, in many of its activities. So at least till recently
we have never had in Ireland the confrontational anti-clericalism
so common on the Continent. But the young generation are
different: they have no such hang-ups, and don't understand this
Joycean mix of guilt and nostalgia towards the Church.'

So there is still this fund of popular goodwill, which the Church
could respond to better than it does. Ireland still has many excellent
priests, men of great goodness and kindness who are loved and
admired by their parishioners. Many are working for social
progress, like Peter McVerry, or like those who have recently
fought to develop the West – Father James McDyer in Donegal,
Monsignor James Horan of Knock (see p. 147). Today, a Church
with a changed attitude could still win back much of the ground it
has lost in Ireland, and help to provide an enlightened modern
lead that this confused society needs. Whether it can do so may

depend on the Vatican, on its readiness to appoint younger, more open-minded bishops.

Meantime, the Catholic Church possibly suffers from enjoying a near-monopoly of Christianity in the Republic. In Germany, the Protestant and Catholic Churches have a sixty/forty share of the population (in the old West Germany it was fifty/fifty), and this gives them a spur of competition that is fruitful. In Northern Ireland, too, the Churches today are fairly evenly balanced, and mostly the senior clergy work well together in efforts for peace and reconciliation, despite fringe Paisleyite anti-papism (see p. 419). In the Republic, ecumenical relations are also rather good, and the legacy of the struggle against the British has left few tensions at a daily level between Catholics and Protestants. But there are so very few Protestants left – and even for the Catholic Church that may not be healthy.

Since 1920, the Protestant numbers in the South have declined from over 10 per cent to a bare 3 per cent of the population. So they were never more than a small minority, but in the days of British rule they had major influence. Most of the Ascendancy was Protestant (see p. 321); so were many ordinary Irish families who had 'taken soup', i.e. adopted the religion of the colonizers, in the nineteenth century or earlier. Protestants were mainly middle-class or small shopkeeper class, with rather few workers or peasants. They dominated Irish business life, controlling most of the larger banks, trading firms and industries, such as Guinness. They owned the *Irish Times*. And they included several leading Irish figures, even some with strong nationalist sympathies such as W. B. Yeats and Douglas Hyde, who founded the Gaelic League and later became the Republic's first President.

At the time of independence and after, a great many Protestants were virtually pushed out of Ireland or made to feel unwelcome, or at least they felt it was no longer the place for them. That is the main reason why their proportion has fallen: but there are others, too. One, the birth rate has been much higher among Catholics, at least until very recently. Two, in the case of mixed marriages, today quite common, many parents have stayed obedient to the

Vatican's *Ne Temere* edict, obliging them to bring up their children as Catholics.

The main Protestant church is the Church of Ireland, sister to the Church of England. It operates on a pan-Ireland basis, and its primate is the Archbishop of Armagh, across the border. In the North, it is still flourishing, but in the Republic it is in trouble. With congregations dwindling and costs rising, hundreds of local churches have had to close, and a rural vicar will now look after a number of parishes. With funds so short, many church buildings are in a poor state: even St Patrick's Cathedral in Dublin has had to rely on the City Corporation for its repairs.

Up until the Lemass era of the early 1960s, which changed Ireland so much, Protestants still played a sizeable role in Dublin business life, and Catholics might even find it hard to reach senior positions in their firms. The same was true in some other towns. In Sligo, until the 1970s commerce was dominated by a group of well-to-do Protestant families, very conservative, who barred the way to outside competition. But this has now changed, as the big Dublin stores such as Quinn and Dunne have moved in. Yeats's mother's family, the Pollexfens, used to be leading merchants in Sligo, but have moved away long ago.

Today, Protestant influence has everywhere declined; yet it still makes itself felt, out of proportion to its numbers. And it remains quite largely middle-class. There are still a fair number of Protestant firms in Dublin, which even some Catholics regard as being more hard-working, efficient and upright than the average, thanks to the so-called Protestant ethic. Since 1986 the *Irish Times* has had its first Catholic editor, Conor Brady, but several of his senior staff are Protestant, and the paper's freethinking ethos is still imbued with a Protestant liberalism. In education, the Church of Ireland still runs a large number of schools (see p. 211). Trinity College, Dublin, another former bastion of Protestantism, today has a Catholic president, Thomas Mitchell, and a majority of Catholic students, but here again some Protestant spirit survives.

The most positive change is that Catholics and Protestants are no longer at loggerheads, as they used to be. 'Because we are now so few, we are considered harmless and left alone,' suggested one Protestant landowner with a touch of cynicism. The new spirit of ecumenicism has spread over from Europe into the Republic, even if it has not yet touched everyone in the North. As recently as 1949, under de Valera, the Irish Government was prevented by the Catholic Church from attending the Protestant funeral service for the Irish President, Douglas Hyde! Until 1970, Catholic students were forbidden by their bishops to attend Trinity College, and disobedience was declared by the Archbishop to be 'mortal sin'; but today some 60 per cent of Trinity students, and many of the teachers, are Catholic. In Cork in 1964, Catholic clergy and teachers refused to enter the Church of Ireland cathedral for the funeral service of a much-loved local professor, since to attend a Protestant service was decreed 'sinful'. Today, the young auxiliary bishop goes into that cathedral to preach at ecumenical services. In Limerick, Bishop Newman may inveigh against the 'lax' Protestant ethos: but he is on cordial personal terms with the Church of Ireland bishop.

Today the two Churches may still be in rivalry over control of schools, or hospitals. But young Catholics and Protestants scarcely notice the difference between each other; and intermarriage, still rare thirty or so years ago (cf. William Trevor's novella of small-town life, *Reading Turgenev*, see p. 203), is now common. 'In the 1960s', says Susan Parkes, a lecturer at Trinity, 'we Protestants were still in a kind of ghetto. But now we have broken out. Even so, Protestants still like to keep their own identity, their own sense of community. There are still many of us who prefer to have a fellow-Protestant as our doctor or solicitor. It is a little bit like being Jewish in London or Paris. But our decline in numbers is bound to continue.'

Birth control comes in, abortion stays out: a passionate national debate

The crisis of the Catholic Church is bound up closely with Ireland's extraordinary national crisis over sexual and family moral-ity – issues that make far more impact on politics than elsewhere in Western Europe. In the 'Miss X' affair of 1992, when a raped girl of fourteen was at first legally prevented from going to

London for an abortion, the nation talked of little else for weeks; the abortion issue then dominated the referendum debate on the Maastricht Treaty, for there was a link between the two. Even the sale of the common condom has aroused passionate nationwide controversy.

Many Catholics have long been proud of what they see as Ireland's moral 'uniqueness', its defence of old-style Christian values in a world that is forgetting them. Ireland continued to outlaw birth control, abortion, homosexuality, even divorce, long after other West European countries had come to accept them. But Irish society has been changing, and many younger people no longer follow the Church's teaching on birth control or sex outside marriage. The nation is deeply divided on these issues; but despite vociferous conservative opposition, the Government in the past few years has finally been dragged by liberal opinion and popular practice into accepting widespread reform.

So the Irish are in the thick of a kind of sexual revolution, in a muddled sort of way. Under pressure from a small but influential liberal lobby (Mary Robinson was one of its leaders, before she became President) the Government has gradually legalized the sale of contraceptives. In 1993 Parliament finally repealed the old law making homosexual practice a criminal offence. And if civil divorce is accepted, as seems likely, in a referendum now set for early 1995, then Ireland will cease to be the one European country where this is still illegal. Only on abortion, a morally trickier subject, are the Irish still much more reticent. The vast majority remain opposed to its being legalized in Ireland itself; yet they have now voted in favour of free information on how to get an abortion abroad. And so, amid this kind of hypocrisy, and much moral confusion, the Irish have slowly and erratically been catching up with European practice in these matters.

The Church used to breathe fire from the pulpit against sexual sin. In the past few years, not wanting to lose too much support from younger people, it has been keeping a lower profile in public, and on matters such as abortion it prefers to let the campaigning be done by militant Catholic lay groups. But the bishops still hold firmly to the Pope's doctrines, which he powerfully reaffirmed in 1993; and bishops and conservative lay leaders still have much influence over the political parties. So governments have tended to dither and procrastinate on reform measures. They know that middle-class Dublin, even working-class Dublin, tends to think differently on these issues from traditional rural Ireland. I met a girl from Co. Cavan living in London, who said, 'If I prefer to live and work here, it's in part because of the climate in my village. The local doctor won't prescribe me the pill because I'm single. The chemist will sell me condoms but then he gossips. And I have arguments with my old school-friends whose view of unwed teenage pregnancies is, "God will look after the babies, no need for *us* to worry." The law may be changing, but, in villagers' minds, the sexual revolution isn't completed yet, I can tell you.'

She is right, for the law lags behind some sections of public opinion and practice, but is far ahead of others, and this leads to endless charges of hypocrisy. Many of those who do not want abortion legalized in Ireland will accept that thousands of Irish women each year should travel to England for it, and should now be able to get free advice about it in Ireland. There is no divorce but marriage breakup is common, and couples who then cohabit 'illicitly' are socially accepted – even cabinet ministers do it. And so on. Even though public mores are changing, and tolerance of individual conduct is growing, a great many Irish have been reluctant to change the laws that enshrine their old Catholic ideals. Hence the blaze of public debate on issues that two generations ago were never discussed in public.

Historians tell us★ that Irish puritanism about sex dates largely from the post-Famine period, when efforts were made to check a rise in population by encouraging very late marriage (see p. 201), combined with celibacy and chastity. This was the policy of farmers, who saw the economic dangers of large families, and it fitted in with the Church's own anti-sex ethos, preached from every pulpit. Sex outside marriage was rare, love affairs were furtive or stamped out. This puritanism was then taken up by the

★ For example, Lee, op. cit., p. 645.

conservative governments of the Free State. Sex was not a subject for public discussion. The arguments concerning divorce, or birth control, or help for unwed mothers, were simply never mooted on State radio or in the newspapers; and cases of rape, wife-beating, illegitimate birth, even suicide, went unreported. Everyone knew these things happened, no one spoke of them except in whispers.

The barriers began to break in the 1960s as Ireland opened up to the world; modern consumerism arrived, young people returned home from more liberal societies, and the English 'permissive' revolution of the sixties made its impact, especially via TV programmes – 'There was no sex in Ireland until the BBC came,' lamented the diehard Fianna Fáil TD, Oliver Flanagan, in a famous phrase. Then on Ireland's own State-run RTE, too, a few pioneering programmes, notably Gay Byrne's *Late Late Show* (see p. 269), began to break the taboo of silence. Sometimes the result was near to farce. When in 1966 a woman confided to Byrne on screen that she had slept naked on her honeymoon, bishops preached sermons against this 'evil' programme and called for it to be taken off (the bishops nowadays keep more quiet).

As recently as 1984 the 'Granard affair' shocked the nation, revealing how some attitudes in rural Ireland were still locked in the past. A schoolgirl of fifteen, Anne Lovett, died alone in childbirth beside a statue of the Virgin, in a grotto near her home village of Granard, Co. Longford. It emerged that her parents, teachers and friends had all discussed the pregnancy, but none had tried to find her the care she needed, so great was the shame still attached locally to illegitimate birth. Gay Byrne then took up the case on his daily radio talk-show, inviting letters from women with parallel shocking experiences, and scores arrived. He devoted two hours of radio time to reading out extracts from them – stories of clandestine childbirth, clumsy self-abortion, brutal husbands or incestuous fathers. 'It was a relentless onslaught of terrible intimacies,' commented the *Irish Times*, 'a sort of secret history of modern Ireland . . . stories that had been bottled up and swallowed down.' It was the kind of suffering that had always been swept under the carpet in Ireland, but today it comes out in an avalanche. Even local papers are beginning to report such cases.

The long and tortuous battle for birth control has followed the same kind of path. A law of 1935 had banned all sale, import or manufacture of contraceptives, and this was strictly applied. But then in the 1960s a number of women began to use the pill, on doctors' advice, and this was allowed as a 'cycle regulator'. In the early 1970s, women's militant groups in Dublin started to press for real reform; once, for publicity, they flouted the law by bringing condoms *en masse* from Belfast in a special train. One of their leaders, the young senator Mary Robinson, put forward a reform Bill, which failed. But then in 1973 their cause received an unexpected boost from the crucial McGhee judgement. Mary McGhee, a wife and mother in Co. Dublin, had been fitted with a diaphragm by her doctor on health grounds, but the package that she ordered by post from England was seized by Customs. The Supreme Court, however, ruled that the clause in the 1935 Act forbidding the import of contraceptives for private use was unconstitutional in terms of personal freedom. This decision set off Ireland's first major public debate on birth control, at a time when the Catholic countries of the Continent were fast liberalizing. Mary Robinson tried again, but again was defeated by the Dáil. However, the Church itself was now shifting its ground, in a statement conceding that Parliament should decide in the matter. So finally in 1979 Charles Haughey, then minister of health, pushed through a Family Planning Act that modestly allowed condoms, diaphragms and the pill to be sold in chemists' shops to married couples only, and on doctor's prescription. It was a historic breakthrough. Haughey described it as 'an Irish solution to an Irish problem' – a phrase that has since been applied to many an Irish compromise.

In 1985 the law was further liberalized, allowing chemists to sell condoms to anyone over eighteen, without prescription. The pill was still for married women only, for 'genuine family planning purposes', but some doctors would discreetly give it to unmarrieds too. In 1993, virtually all remaining curbs were removed, under new decrees: the condom is now quite freely available, for those who know where to look, and the pill can be issued to anyone, though it still needs a doctor's prescription, which for medical reasons is wise. A growing number of local doctors are ready to cooperate, but many still refuse, on moral grounds. Women wed or unwed can be fitted for a diaphragm at any of Ireland's ten family-planning clinics, which do a busy trade in the towns but are not so much in touch with the rural areas.

As for the simple condom, until 1993 its sale was restricted to the clinics and to chemists' shops. In the cities, many chemists were prepared to stock them, but in rural areas a majority refused, either on moral grounds, or under pressure from local opinion or from the priest. Customers also had to face the problem of confidentiality, in a rural Ireland so addicted to gossip – 'sure, d'you know, Mary O'Shea was in buying her rubbers today, and her husband away at sea and all,' a sales assistant might whisper. But at least the more liberal chemists would turn a blind eye to the rule banning the sale of condoms to under-eighteens.

In the late 1980s, with AIDS spreading in Ireland, and the number of teenage pregnancies also rising fast, the pressure groups stepped up their campaign for the removal of the last restrictions, notably on vending-machines. Civil disobedience came into vogue. In central Dublin, Richard Branson's Virgin Megastore invited the Irish Family Planning Association to open a condom counter amid its videos and computer games, in defiance of the law. This did brisk business. In 1991 it was given a £500 fine, which the U2 rock band gallantly paid for it, but it still did not close down. 'We are being penalized for helping with preventive health, and Ireland will be the laughing-stock of Europe,' said the IFPA's leader, Christine Donaghy; 'this is the only EC country that controls the import of condoms.' In 1992 the Irish Medical Organization, including all doctors, voted for the free sale of condoms. T-shirts appeared on Dublin streets, 'Wear a condom – just in Casey' (not that *he* did). And a nationwide campaign opened, to encourage pubs and discos to install vending-machines; within six months, 140 had done so, some of them in rural areas. Finally in 1993 the Government pushed a law through Parliament that removed the age limit and, with a few provisos, permitted vending-machines – despite warnings from some bishops that wider availability of condoms would 'give the appearance of approving abuse of God's gift of sexuality'. Today you can see piles of condoms in many Dublin shops. They and the pubs are supposed to apply for a licence, but not all bother, and an official blind eye is turned.

So the birth-control battle is virtually won. Sterilization, too, which the Catholic-run hospitals firmly opposed, is now becoming easier to obtain. An estimated 25 per cent of Irish adults today practise contraception, a figure below the EU average but increasing, and this is a major factor behind the fall in the birth rate (see p. 17). But especially in country areas there is still a good deal of fear and ignorance about sex, as well as a legacy of religious guilt-feelings even among non-believers; conversely, many practising Catholics simply reject the Church's teachings in this field.

Notably, there is still a lack of proper sex education in schools, which has made it harder to combat the spread of AIDS and of unwanted teenage pregnancies. Until not so long ago, sex education did not exist. Today, the Department of Education still has no firm policy, but leaves it up to each school and its principal, so the pattern varies. Church of Ireland schools teach the subject more than Catholic ones. In some cases, the priests running the school do not allow it at all, or only on their own terms (i.e. no mention of birth control). In others, a liberal lay principal may encourage teachers to explain about contraception and advise on 'safe' sex within a stable relationship. In this haphazard way, sex education is slowly making progress, sometimes with odd results. One ten-year-old came back from school and said, 'Mum, I saw a condominium lying in the road today. Teacher says if you wear one you'll never get ill.'

It was above all the growth of AIDS that in 1992–3 pushed the Government into freeing the sale of condoms. Before this, for years it had done little to combat the epidemic, and it seemed reluctant even to accept its existence in Ireland; relief work was left mainly to small, ill-funded voluntary agencies. Some hospitals would refuse to treat HIV-positive patients, or staff would abuse them. This may have been linked to the Irish horror of homosexuality (see below), even though the spread of AIDS in Ireland comes as much from drug abuse as from sex. In 1987 an Irish AIDS sufferer living in London told RTE television, 'In England I can get far better treatment than in Ireland, and people are far less judgemental. Here they seem to regard me as unclean.'

The virus has been spreading at the rate of some 27 per cent a year, and Ireland is roughly on the European average for it, with 1,450 verified HIV-positive sufferers in 1994 (the real figure is certainly far higher). In 1992 the Department of Health did start putting more money and effort into the fight against AIDS. But there is still much less of a public campaign of warnings and advice than, say, in Britain or France. The Church's stance against condoms makes it harder. And although public attitudes are changing, the disease still carries a strong stigma; sufferers often try to hide the nature of their disease for as long as possible. I knew a young Dubliner whose father refused ever to speak to him after he learned he was gay; later he died of AIDS in London, and only just before the end did he tell his mother the truth.

Condoms are not the only answer to AIDS, but their freer sale may help. Until now, although some schools teach about the use of condoms, officialdom has been reticent. An AIDS video produced in 1991 by the Department of Health, for schools and clubs, devoted almost all of its thirty-seven minutes to arguing that no sex (outside marriage) is the only safe sex, and spent just one minute on condoms as a protection. And the Church takes a stricter line. A radical Jesuit, Fr Paul Lavelle, wrote a book on AIDS advocating condoms, but the hierarchy then banned it. In my own talks with bishops, I found them remarkably knowledge-able about exactly why and how a condom is not perfectly safe, either against the AIDS virus or against pregnancy; they all used the same patter, and I felt that maybe they had all been given some crash course. Bishop Murphy of Cork assured me: 'No condom is totally safe, it will not check AIDS, the only safe way is chastity.' The auxiliary Bishop Desmond Williams of Dublin added: 'A condom can leak, and even the tiniest drop of sperm can cause conception, or spread the AIDS virus. And how could we possibly approve of use of condoms by homosexuals, since we disapprove of all homosexual conduct?'

Up until 1993, homosexual activity was a crime in Ireland, under a law imposed by the British in 1881 in the heyday of Victorian puritanism (it was used in 1895, in England, to convict that most famous of Irish gays, Oscar Wilde). In Britain itself the law was repealed in 1957, but in Catholic Ireland you could still in theory get life imprisonment for what the Act described as 'the abominable crime of buggery'. In practice, there was a degree of Irish tolerance and no one had actually been prosecuted for many years (except for a few cases of coercion of minors and, curiously, for one married man who in 1990–92 served two years in prison for having anal intercourse with his wife). Until the 1970s, the Gardai would scour Phoenix Park in Dublin after dark, or the Liffey quays, to pick upon male couples having anonymous sex, and would impose fines; but then they stopped.

Until ten or twenty years ago, it was virtually impossible to admit in public to being gay. But attitudes then began to mellow. One turning-point came in 1978, at the televised funeral of the leading actor/manager Micheál Mac Liammóir, when President Patrick Hillery crossed the grave to shake hands with the dead man's lover, the actor Hilton Edwards, and said, 'I'm sorry for your trouble, Hilton,' the traditional Irish condolence for a widow. Since then, homosexuals have been 'coming out' all over the place; by the late 1980s there were officially recognized gay and lesbian societies in the universities, and active gay support groups in the cities, doing work in the field of AIDS. In rural areas, homosexuals could still get insulted or ostracized, and might feel the need to be very discreet. But the pattern varied, and was changing. In the touristy village of Dromahair, near Sligo, in 1992 I met a debonair hotel-keeper who had just publicly celebrated his 'wedding' with his gay lover.

Homosexuals, however, still felt uneasy about living on the wrong side of the law. Its very existence, however harmless in practice, made them fearful of being open to blackmail threats, harassment or job discrimination, which did exist. So pressure grew for reform. The campaign was led by one of Ireland's most remarkable public figures, Senator David Norris, who is friendly with the Labour Party and a professor at Trinity, noted Joyce scholar and brilliant lecturer, as well as working tirelessly for many causes (such as Dublin conservation) and making no secret of his own gay private life. He fought for a change in the law, and for welfare rights for homosexuals. In 1980 he took his case to the Irish High Court, arguing that the ban infringed civil liberties: the judge accepted his evidence, but said that he had to rule against Norris because of the Christian nature of the Irish State. Then in 1988 Norris pleaded to the European Court of Human Rights in Strasbourg, and won; the court agreed that the 1861 law was in breach of the European Convention on Human Rights (which Ireland had signed) and demanded that it be reformed right away. For two years the Government maintained an embarrassed silence. Then in 1991 it promised the European Court that it would change the law soon. But there was still no action, until the promise was discreetly written into the Fianna Fáil/Labour programme.

As usual in such matters, the Government had been under strong rival pressures. Most of the media supported Senator Norris. But the Church, and the powerful lay lobbies, claimed not only that homosexuality was wrong, but that to decriminalize it would make it more widespread. And an opinion survey gave yet another instance of the Irish people wanting to have their moral cake and eat it, i.e. to keep the old ideals yet accept social change: a majority wanted tolerance for homosexuals, but did *not* want the 1861 Act abolished. So the law was neither enforced nor repealed, and as a result was made to look an ass, as liberal commentators pointed out. 'If only we could get rid of that law,' David Norris told me in 1992, 'it would enable homosexuals to live with more dignity, and would reduce the mental illness and alcoholism so common among them. At present, the hypocrisy on the subject encourages promiscuity. But at least the freeing of birth control is a step forward, for it introduces into Ireland at last the concept of sex for pleasure and cherishing, whereas the Church has always held that only sex with the possibility of conception is legitimate.'

With Norris's Labour Party now in the ruling coalition, the

Government finally fulfilled its promise, and in July 1993 a Bill decriminalizing gay practice was put before Parliament. It passed easily, without even a division, and with few voices raised against. Norris's normally vocal opponents in the Senate kept fairly quiet, as did the bishops. They accepted the absurdity of trying to keep a law that was not enforced, and they did not want to look like *eejits*. So homosexuality is now legal between consenting partners aged seventeen or over (in Britain the age limit was reduced in 1994 from twenty-one to eighteen). 'The new law is very satisfactory, just what I wanted, it gives full equality between gays and others,' Norris told me. The next step, as he and other human-rights activists point out, is to break down the social prejudices. This will take time. But the ending of the official ban will make it much easier to take action against job discrimination. Lesbianism, incidentally, was never under any legal prohibition: the old law did not mention it, for Victorian England liked to pretend it did not exist!

Abortion, the subject of two referendums since 1983, has aroused stronger passions and sharper debate than any other of these moral sexual issues, inevitably. The self-styled 'pro-life' lobby is very strong, vocal and well organized; the 'pro-choice' lobby is far smaller, but also militant. And most people simply do not want to see abortion legalized in Ireland. So the debate has centred on whether it should be allowed in certain extreme circumstances, and on the right to travel abroad for it, or to spread information about obtaining it abroad.

Abortion has long been illegal in Ireland. But in the early 1980s the feeling grew in 'pro-life' circles that this should be clearly written into the Constitution, in view of the spread of legalized abortion in neighbouring countries and the risk that Ireland might somehow be infected by this, or might suffer from some European Court judgement. So the pro-life lobby pressed for an Amendment to the Constitution, and in 1983 Garret FitzGerald, then Taoiseach and himself opposed to abortion, agreed to hold a referendum. A bizarre and arcane debate then broke out as to when a foetus became a foetus, with the 'pro-lifers' claiming that it was from the moment of conception; and the Church hierarchy backed this in a statement calling on the Irish people 'to witness before Europe . . . to the sacredness of all human life, from conception until death'. With Church approval, Parliament then produced a strictly worded constitutional Amendment: 'The State acknowledges the right to life of the unborn and, with due regard to the equal right to life of the mother, guarantees in its laws to respect, and, as far as practicable, by its laws to defend and vindicate that right.' Put to referendum, this Amendment was carried by roughly two-thirds to one-third of voters, though the turnout was only 55 per cent; and whereas rural Ireland voted massively 'yes', in Dublin the majority was very slim. On the equal right to life of mother and foetus, David Norris told me: 'I said in the Senate that I gave thanks to God that I was (a) not heterosexual, (b) not a woman, and (c) not married to any of the Fianna Fáil hypocrites. I would not like to be told, after thirty years of marriage and ten children, that I was valued at the same intensity as an embryo the size of the head of a match.'

The impact of the pro-lifers' referendum victory was to make it harder for family-planning centres to give any advice about getting abortions abroad. Any such publicity was now illegal. Women could travel discreetly to clinics in England, as many did: but without the right contacts they might find it hard to discover where to go. The main pro-life movement, the pugnacious Society for the Protection of the Unborn Child, led by housewives and a few Catholic lawyers and doctors, launched a crusade to see that the law was fully observed. SPUC would sometimes send spies into a family-planning centre, feigning pregnancy; if they were given advice on abortion abroad, they would then report it to the police, and at least two centres were thus forced to close. A watch was also kept on suspect imported publications. So magazines such as *Cosmopolitan* and *Elle*, not wanting to lose their Irish sales, printed special Irish editions with their pregnancy advisory sections blacked out; and in May 1992 an issue of the *Guardian* was banned because it carried a big advertisement for the Marie Stopes abortion clinic. TV and radio programmes could debate the abortion issue, but not give any practical details. University students would distribute leaflets with addresses and phone numbers of British clinics and advisory services, partly with the aim of provoking the law and winning publicity; in 1991 this was brought before the EC Court of Justice in Luxembourg, which upheld Irish law and ruled against the students, claiming that the ban on information was not against EC rules on free movement of services. Some students were fined, but their battle went on. Scrawled in the ladies' toilets of some Irish pubs you would find the word 'abortion' and a London telephone number.

In February 1992 the 'Miss X' crisis brought the abortion debate again into sharp focus, and provoked more changes in the law. The parents of a Dublin girl of fourteen (for her sake, her identity was never revealed) claimed that she had been raped by a family friend, and they took her to London for an abortion. At the same time they innocently told the police, in order to seek their advice over criminal proceedings against the rapist. The police informed the judiciary – and the Attorney-General, Harry Whelehan, a conservative, considered it his duty under the Constitution to issue an injunction preventing the girl from going to England. In fact she was already there: but her scared, law-abiding parents quietly brought her home, before the abortion had taken place. By now the deeply distressed girl was threatening suicide. But the judges of the High Court upheld the Attorney-General's decision, using the wording of the 1983 Amendment to claim that the risk of the girl killing herself was 'much less than the certainty that the unborn child's life would be terminated if the order was not made'.

There was a national uproar, on a scale not heard in Ireland for years; each day the newspapers devoted several pages to the crisis. While the Church kept a prudent silence, and the SPUC lobby warmly applauded the judges, the liberals went into battle. Even many people normally opposed to abortion expressed support for the girl in this case, and dismay at the High Court. Women's groups demonstrated outside public offices, with placards such as, 'This State does *not* own women's bodies' or, satirically, 'Ireland defends men's right to procreate by rape'. The rock singer Sinead O'Connor went to petition the Taoiseach, who saw her. And the liberal *Irish Times* thundered in a leader:

'What has been done to this Irish Republic, what sort of State has it become that, in 1992, its full panoply of authority, its police, its law officers, its courts, are mobilized to condemn a fourteen-year-old child to the ordeal of pregnancy and childbirth after rape at the hands of a "depraved and evil man"? With what are we now to compare ourselves? Ceausescu's Romania? The Ayatollahs' Iran? Algeria? There are similarities. The implications of Mr Justice Costello's judgement . . . may be little short of catastrophic for the health and safety of Irishwomen, for the very concept of individual bodily rights, for the role of the State as a protective and benign organism.' And the paper called on the Government, 'by way of legal change . . . to pull Irish society out of this descent into cruelty'.

Behind the emotional furore, the legal aspects of the debate centred on the interpretation of the 1983 Amendment, which said nothing about travelling abroad for an abortion, and was ambiguous as to what 'equal right to life' the mother might have, if hers was in danger (FitzGerald in 1983 had wanted a more liberal wording, which might have more explicitly permitted abortion in order to save the mother's life, but he was outmanoeuvred by hard-line elements in the Dáil). So for clarification Miss X's parents appealed to judges of the Supreme Court, who by four votes to one came out with an unexpected decision. It was thought they might rule in favour of freedom of travel to another EC state. But they rejected this option and instead decreed that, under the Amendment, abortion could be legal if there was a 'real and substantial risk' of the mother committing suicide. Liberals heaved a sigh of relief, and the girl discreetly went back to London for her abortion. The SPUC lobby and the Church were furious, and called for a new referendum to reverse the ugly precedent set by the court.

The next bizarre twist involved the referendum on the Maastricht Treaty, in June. Under pressure from the Church and the SPUC lobby, the Government during the 1991 negotiations on Maastricht had extracted from its EC partners a special protocol to the Treaty, whereby Ireland would be exempt from any possible EC moves to liberalize abortion, and could keep its own legislation intact. Then in the national debate in June, the real issues of Maastricht, so crucial for Ireland's future, became virtually swamped by a confused side-debate on this protocol and its implications – while the Danes and French in their referendums, and the British in their great parliamentary debate, were discussing sovereignty, federalism and a single currency, the Irish were still talking about abortion! The SPUC lobby argued that the Supreme Court decision, by 'legalizing abortion', would undermine the protocol, and so they urged a 'no' vote on Maastricht; the liberals, though wary about the protocol, were mostly in favour of Maastricht in itself, and they tended to vote 'yes'. But the real priority of the debate seemed to be reflected in the *Irish Times's* banner headline, on the morning after the Treaty had been approved by 69 to 31 per cent: 'Comprehensive "Yes" vote heavy blow to anti-abortion lobby'. Not exactly Delors's vision of Maastricht, nor even Thatcher's.

After the confusion caused by the 'Miss X' affair and the Supreme Court judgement, the Taoiseach, Albert Reynolds, felt obliged to hold another referendum on abortion. This was set for 25 November, and it made some concessions to the liberal position. Voters were invited to say 'yes' to three proposed additions to the 1983 Amendment. The first would guarantee freedom to travel abroad; the second would allow, with a few provisos, freedom of information 'relating to services lawfully available in another State' (in practice, Britain). Both these amendments were approved by some two-thirds of votes cast. The third proposed change related to the so-called 'substantive issue': it would make abortion legal if this were necessary to save the mother's life, though *not* if the risk were one of suicide. But this proposal was rejected by 1,079,000 votes to 572,000. Some liberals disliked it because it did not go far enough. Many other voters followed the hard Catholic line, that any abortion was wrong, and to introduce it even to save a woman with cancer could set a dangerous precedent.

However, with this negative vote they simply spoiled their own case, for the result was a return to the status quo ante – *including* the Supreme Court judgement on 'Miss X'. This meant that a court in the future could also rule, by precedent, that a suicide threat was a valid reason for allowing an abortion. The SPUC lobby were furious, but there was little they could do, save demand yet another referendum. On the right-to-travel issue, all was now clear. But on the third issue, that of free information, there was still some muddle, for the referendum text had stated that this would have to be enshrined in a new law, and typically the new Government then delayed on producing this Bill. There was intense lobbying behind the scenes. The SPUC lobby claimed that, without a law, information was not yet free, and they were glad when the Supreme Court refused to lift injunctions against two women's centres that had previously been giving information on abortion. However, the liberal-minded new minister for equality and law reform, Mervyn Taylor, who is a Labour TD, and Jewish, promised in July 1993 that a Bill would come in the next Dáil session and that the right to information did now clearly exist. Meanwhile, the liberal women's groups have been taking the referendum result at its word, knowing that there is now little danger of prosecution, even without a formal law. Details of the English clinics are now freely published; and the family-planning centres can now legally give 'non-directive counselling' to pregnant women on what abortion would involve.

Despite these advances, it remains highly improbable that abortion on demand will be legalized in Ireland for many years. According to an *Irish Times* poll in October 1993, only 24 per cent are against abortion under any circumstance, while 30 per cent would accept it if the mother's life were in physical danger (the referendum proposal) and 41 per cent if the danger were merely a suicide threat (the *de facto* present situation). That leaves the 'pro-choice' vote at under 5 per cent. Most Irish people still regard abortion with instinctive horror, and will usually retain this element of the Church's teaching even when they have abandoned others. Any woman active in the 'pro-choice' movement is likely to face career difficulties, as has happened to one of its leaders, Ruth Reddick, turned down for dozens of jobs although highly regarded in her own field of the arts. 'You know why we can't employ you,' she is told.

So no abortion, please, we're Irish – yet even SPUC hard-liners will turn a blind eye to English clinics doing the dirty work for Irish women. Maire Vernon, spokesperson of SPUC, a friendly mother of four in a Dublin suburb, told me: 'This is a free country, and we cannot ban travel. A woman wanting an abortion in England must be free to get it. But of course we try to dissuade. The best answer for unwanted pregnancies is adoption, that's the Church's view, and there's no shortage of couples wanting to adopt.' What about a woman who is going to give birth to a monster? – 'There are no monsters, only human beings. Handicapped foetuses should not be aborted.'

For some years, an estimated 6,000 to 7,000 women a year have been secretly taking the trail to England, telling maybe just a few intimate friends and probably not their parents. The cost of the operation, fare included, is around £500, so the customers are mainly middle-class: but a growing number are from the working-class, or from the rural West, where a bush telegraph of London addresses has long operated. A girl with initiative has usually been able to find out where to go. And the English clinics are extremely helpful, I was told – 'You just say you are ringing from Ireland, and they do all they can. Mostly they are staffed by Irish nurses, all sweet and kind, proferring cups of tea, all part of a big conspiracy of helpfulness.' One expert on these matters, an *Irish Times* journalist, said to me: 'I myself would like abortion legalized. But the present situation after all is liveable with, now we have the rights of travel and information. But sex education still needs to be improved. Yes, abortion probably won't come here for some years – but what about the new abortion pill, now being tried out in France and America? This can bring on a mild miscarriage and does not need a doctor's supervision. How could you prevent these being smuggled into Ireland? And where would that leave the law?'

In all these moral matters, not only abortion, the Irish generally find it easier to sanction individual 'transgressions' than to reform the law. Under the legacy of Catholic tradition, they still cling to certain moral ideals which they do not want to lose, such as the sanctity of marriage. And they think in terms of these ideals, rather than of what is practically needed for modern society. 'If my teenage daughter were pregnant, of course I would take her to London: but I would never vote to bring abortion to Ireland,' said a woman in a Dublin tennis club. The laws stay immutable, but the individual has licence – convenient if hypocritical. And to a non-Catholic it seems an inevitable by-product of Catholicism, whereby you can break God's law each week but then confess and be forgiven.

But is this a sound basis for society? In March 1992, at the St Patrick's Day Parade in Cork, the float of the Munster Gay and Lesbian Collective was warmly applauded by the crowd and then given a prize. This prompted the indomitable Mary Holland to write in her *Irish Times* editorial: 'It is beginning to seem that almost all of the laws which affect the majority of people at the most intimate levels of personal morality are held in open contempt . . . In this newspaper, senior politicians have explained how they obtained divorces abroad, in contravention of the constitutional ban, and have remarried. Anything, but anything goes just so long as we don't have to confront and deal with our own problems as adult citizens within our own independent State . . . If the laws relating to marriage, homosexuality, abortion, are so out of touch with the needs of society that the State allows them to be broken with impunity, how can it hope to encourage quite different attitudes of civic responsibility towards laws designed to stop people evading tax, or defrauding semi-State companies, or ripping off the welfare system . . .?' So that brings us to divorce.

Women win new rights – and is divorce now coming to the Ballroom of Romance?

Divorce, like birth control, is another case where legislation based on Church teaching has been overtaken by social and moral change, thus creating confusion and, many would say, hypocrisy. As I write in the summer of 1994, Ireland still has no legal divorce but an estimated 70,000 broken marriages. And many of these individuals are now openly but 'illicitly' cohabiting with a new partner, often with children too, just like a normal family. To a remarkable degree this is now socially accepted, even in pious villages, in the usual Irish easygoing spirit. Yet in the 1986 referendum, divorce reform was rejected by 63 per cent of the voters. However a new referendum, more carefully prepared, is now set for early in 1995, and this time the result is likely to be different.

Divorce had been legalized under British rule, and the Free State inherited this law, but it was then outlawed in 1925 by Cosgrave's conservative Government, under pressure from the Church. Marital breakdown in those days was usually hidden from sight – couples might hardly speak to each other but still cohabit – in a world so concerned with appearances and property. But later, as society changed, and as breakdowns became more frequent and more visible, so the demand for divorce reform grew. And in 1986 Garret FitzGerald, then Taoiseach and himself pro-reform, won the tacit support of the Fianna Fáil opposition for a referendum to introduce divorce on a limited scale: the marriage must be seen to have failed for at least five years, with no chance of reconciliation. At the start of the campaign, polls suggested that some 57 per cent of voters were in favour. But the Church weighed in heavily, denouncing the reform from its pulpits; and Fianna Fáil, concerned about its links with the Church and with its conservative rural electorate, also moved into opposition, breaking its pact with the Taoiseach. Party and clergy together began to stir up fears about inheritance, in a rural society that ever since the Land Acts had remained so attached to property. Rumours were spread that a divorced wife might be evicted from her home, or cut off without a penny if her husband remarried, or a farmer would be forced to divide up his land. 'It was an unscrupulous campaign,' FitzGerald said later. Support for his plan steadily waned, to yield a 63 per cent hostile vote. Conservatism and material fears – probably more than Christian moral values – had carried the day.

So Ireland has remained the only country in Europe without divorce, in a situation full of anomalies both legal and social. I could quote the example of a modest middle-class couple I know,

Maeve and Brian, living in 'illegal' bliss in a Dublin suburb. Brian separated some years ago from his wife, Maureen. Later he met Maeve, then aged twenty-nine and single, and they fell in love. Her family were horrified at her 'getting involved with a married man', even though he was long separated, and her father would not let him in the house; the local priest came to lecture her, 'You scarlet woman!' But they did set up house together and now have a daughter, Siobhan. Maeve has changed her name to her husband's by deed poll, which is quite easy; new local friends think they are man and wife, older friends know the truth but accept them readily, and the parents are now reconciled to it. They would love to get married if they could, for their situation does have drawbacks. If Brian died suddenly, Maureen could claim the home, which is in his name, and Maeve would have no right to it. She has little security in the event of his death, or of their relationship breaking up. If they both died in a crash, Maureen could claim custody of Siobhan. By going to live in England, they could get a divorce that would be valid in Ireland and Maureen would have to accept it: but it would require two years' residence.

Liaisons of this kind used to be severely frowned on; but gradually they have become more acceptable, even in rural areas, and in the cities they are now common. Priests, who used to fulminate, now more often turn a blind eye. But this personal tolerance does not always extend to officialdom. In Co. Wexford in the early 1980s, a teacher in a Catholic convent school, Eileen Flynn, was dismissed for living openly with a married man whose wife had left him; she took the case to court, but lost. This was hardly surprising, and in a convent school it might well be the same today. But an unmarried couple may even find it hard to obtain council housing. And regarding tax, pensions, family allowances and child custody there are all sorts of anomalies, for since there is no divorce legislation, there are no rules for dealing with these unofficial liaisons; a deserted wife with children may not find it easy to obtain adequate benefits. However, there are some signs of change: when awarding child custody the courts are now coming to accept the validity of a 'stable unmarried partnership', as they call it, and may prefer to place the child in the care of a parent who has found a new firm liaison rather than in that of one who is alone.

One extremely 'grey' legal area concerns foreign divorces. If you get married in Ireland and then divorced abroad, that divorce is normally valid under Irish law and you can remarry in Ireland. Many people do this. Once, on *The Late Late Show* (see p. 269), Gay Byrne's guests were the Irish rugby star Mick Doyle and his past and present wives, seen chatting cordially together about his divorce and remarriage in England, with the aim of showing up the silliness of some Irish fears. However, the legality depends on domicile. Irish law will accept a divorce that has been obtained genuinely in a country that insists on at least a year or two's proven domicile there, as Britain does. But there are agencies in Dublin that for a fee will fix up a quickie divorce by post from a country such as Haiti, without any domicile; or there are Irish who get the same kind of deal by going to Nevada. Then they find that the Irish courts, after verifying, will not accept it. But there is no hard-and-fast rule and matters can vary from court to court. Some 'fake' divorces get by, some genuine ones are contested; as there is no divorce legislation in Ireland, there can only be ad hoc solutions. One journalist told me she had easily got remarried in Dublin after an American divorce; but another woman, also first married in Ireland, said that it had taken her six months to ascertain that her New York divorce and remarriage were valid. And I heard this story from a couple in Cork, now cohabiting there: 'We both lived in France with French spouses, and we both got divorced there. Now we want to marry here, but it's taking months. It seems to depend on whom you are dealing with, for one court or department will interpret the law differently from another; we have children with us from our French marriages, and we find that a foreign divorce is recognized here for social security but not for tax. The basic trouble is that, since there's no divorce in Ireland, the law and the bureaucracy have no idea how to deal with foreign divorces or remarriage, they have no rules. It gets the lawyers screwed up and they try to avoid such cases.'

The Church itself plays no part in such legal tangles. In local life too, it now keeps a lower profile on matters of sexual morality. A sociologist told me this revealing tale from a village in Co. Sligo in the early 1950s: 'A young woman with two children had a husband who was an alcoholic and beat her up. Finally things got very bad and he left for England. A young labourer came in to help her with the farm, he began to live with her, they had a child. And no one said anything. The elderly parish priest never raised the issue publicly. Then a new young priest arrived: he took a harsh biblical view, preached at them from the altar, tried to get the man to leave. The reaction of the villagers was curious. As soon as all this was said openly, they sided with the priest, turned against the couple, and the young man had to leave. Once the matter had come into the public sphere, private tolerance ended and people followed the official Church line, even if they did not like it. Today, no local priest would be such an *eejit* as to speak out in that way. If he did, no one would pay much attention. That is the change.'

Today priests will generally allow unmarried couples to attend Mass, though not to take Communion; and many younger priests are privately in favour of divorce. But publicly the bishops still speak out against it with the voice of Rome, and politically they still wield much influence when it comes to reform. In Dublin, I talked privately with one intellectual priest, known for his open-mindedness, who surprised me with the severity of his view: 'My feeling is that the Church is right: divorce would lead to more harm than good. I'm in favour of legal separation, if for instance a wife is being beaten up. But divorce itself would lead to far more marriage breakups. Even if a young woman is deserted by her husband against her will, and is entirely blameless, she should *not* remarry abroad or have other liaisons, but remain celibate all her life. It is a sacrifice she must make for the greater good. I know that our rigidity about this makes us lose a lot of people, but we are right. See St Mark 10.10: "What God hath joined together, let no man put asunder."' He went on to justify the Church's own alternative of annulment, granted in cases when a marriage can be deemed never to have taken place, i.e. if a girl had been pushed into marriage against her will, or if one party was homosexual, or

199

immature at the time. 'Yes, I know we are accused of hypocrisy and casuistry, of getting round divorce by giving it another name: but we don't see it that way. The solution for a young deserted wife could be to seek an annulment: several couples in this parish have had them. It used to take ten years, but now it's just one or two.' A spouse with an annulment can then get remarried in church, but by law, it is the first marriage that remains in force. So you could have two different marriages at once, co-existing under the rules of Church and State. A very Irish form of bigamy.

The Church, however, knows that civil divorce will probably now come to Ireland – 'We wouldn't like it, we'd try to prevent it, but in the event we could live with it,' one bishop told me. For the referendum, originally planned for October 1994, the Church was planning to campaign less stridently than in 1986, and to leave the militant lay groups to make the running. The Government, on its side, has been preparing the ground more carefully than was done for the 1986 referendum. In 1992 it published a White Paper on marital breakdown, that set out to clarify issues concerning property rights, maintenance for separated wives, and recognition of foreign divorces. Then in 1993 it brought before parliament a Matrimonial Home Bill and a Family Law Bill, aimed at assuaging the fears of farmers' wives and others; this legislation would grant equal rights to husband and wife, and in the event of a breakdown the property would be split. The first of these Bills was delayed early in 1994 on a legal technicality. Then another legal problem delayed the holding of the divorce referendum itself, originally planned for October 1994, but now unlikely before early 1995.

Today all political parties are in favour of reform, sharing the view that it is time for Ireland to get in step with the rest of Europe. After all, several senior politicians, including Bertie Ahern of Fianna Fáil, minister of finance, themselves have well-publicized broken marriages and in some cases are living with other women. In mid-1993, opinion surveys were showing some 66 per cent of voters wanting to remove the ban on civil divorce. However, by October this figure had dropped to 60 per cent; among farmers, a majority were still hostile to reform. As I write, in the summer of 1994, divorce reform seems likely to be carried; but the conservative reflex could again win the day, as in 1986.

Women's advances towards equal rights in modern Ireland must be seen against the background of the very strange Irish marriage patterns in the period since the Famine. As I suggested earlier, the impact of the Famine was to make farmers and others fearful of producing large families which might lead to more starvation, worse poverty, and the destructive splitting-up of farm property between heirs. So, as there was no birth control, late marriage was encouraged, or no marriage. The statistics are remarkable. In the Ireland of 1900, some 30 per cent of men and 25 per cent of women never married, whereas in most of Western Europe the figure for both sexes was then about 10 per cent.★ The average age of marriage was 33 for men, 29 for women, about six years later than in most of Europe. Even in 1926, 80 per cent of men aged between 25 and 30 were still unwed, 62 per cent of those between 30 and 35, 50 per cent of the 35–40s. Perhaps most astonishing, whereas only 20 per cent of farm owners never got married, for farm labourers the figure was 41 per cent, and as high as *84 per cent* for 'relatives assisting on farms' – the younger sons and daughters who stayed around on the property all their lives, doing the menial work, often leading pathetic, unfulfilled lives. Without birth control, many poor people were terrified of the hardship of raising a large family, and this deterred them from marriage. It was not until the 1950s and '60s that marriages became more frequent, and on average earlier, and Ireland began to move towards the European norms.

This late-marriage syndrome had great impact on the position of Irishwomen at that time. As it was mostly the men who married so late, a woman frequently had a much older husband, who had spent his life under the influence of his mother and was still emotionally tied to her; so brides had classic mother-in-law problems, more than in most countries. Or else the husband

★ See *Understanding Contemporary Ireland*, pp. 103–4.

became a domineering patriarch. Yet marriage, maybe just because it was hard to achieve, was the prized goal for any woman, a social status symbol. Did not de Valera's Constitution of 1937 affirm that a woman's place was 'within the home', and did it not add that 'the State shall endeavour to ensure that mothers shall not be obliged by economic necessity to engage in labour to the neglect of their duties in the home'? It was often frowned on for a woman to go out to work, and even an educated one with a good job was expected to give it up on marriage. Inside the home, the wife had much influence; but it was the husband alone who took charge of the farm or other business. And in a macho society women were excluded from the life of sport and pubs; the saloon bar was for the men, while the tiny, alcove-like 'snug', still there in many pubs today, was for the women and the priest. This whole scenario could be pleasant for a woman in a good marriage, but terrible in a bad one. Wives were often subject to beatings-up or other violence, by husbands who had drowned their own melancholy and frustration in too much drink – and when an Irishman gets drunk, it's said, it is about his mother that he sings.

In country areas it could be hard for a woman to find a good man to marry. The strongest and most ambitious of them tended to emigrate, and she was left with the boasters and wastrels, or the mummy's boys who never really grew up. (Irishmen have long had a reputation for being poor at human relationships, especially with women of their own age; it has even been suggested that the cult of the Virgin Mary led men to idealize women as pure and remote, making it hard for them to adjust to real live female partners.) Or else a woman would sacrifice herself to stay single on the farm to look after an elderly parent. In short, women often had a poor deal. In a tight rural society, they had few opportunities to yield to the facile solace of *bovarysme*. So some got right out, to Dublin or London, like Edna O'Brien's 'country girls'.

Very significantly, this entire situation, the 'Ballroom of Romance' syndrome as I call it, has been a dominant theme of Irish literature in this century, at least of short stories and plays, almost all of them written by *men* – sympathetic studies of gentle, brave, loving women ruined by weak, repressed, despotic or otherwise inadequate men, or simply failing to find a suitable man. The classic of the genre is William Trevor's *The Ballroom of Romance*, about a farmer's daughter who dreams of romance, fails to win the one man she loves, grows older and lonely as she stays on the farm to care for her crippled, widowed father, wistfully frequents the dreary Saturday-night hops at the nearby dancehall, and finally settles for a fourth-rate marriage with one of the local lazy, bibulous good-for-nothings. Several other of Trevor's stories explore similar themes – for example, *The Wedding in the Garden, Virgins, Music*, and his sublime *Reading Turgenev*, about a simple country girl who marries a dreary, repressed, impotent shopkeeper, tries for romance elsewhere but fails, and gradually descends into a fantasy world and quiet madness. This *Madame Bovary* without the misogyny is a sorrowful indictment of the lack of sex education in 1950s Ireland, and of the inability of rural society to cope with sexual problems.

A remarkable number of Seán O'Faoláin's stories also deal, sometimes satirically, sometimes more poignantly, with these themes of the plight of women and male inadequacy. *Our Fearful Innocence*, rather like *Reading Turgenev*, tells movingly of a woman's desperate retreat into solitude, in face of her impotent husband; *Hymeneal*, set in suburban Dublin, relates another unhappy marriage, between a sensitive, long-suffering wife and her pig of a selfish husband; and *Foreign Affairs* is the sharp study of a thirty-year non-love affair between a warm, brilliant Jewess and her repressed, feeble admirer, both of them Irish diplomats. More recently, John McGahern's much-praised novel *Amongst Women* (1990), set in rural Roscommon some forty years ago, is about a boorish, domineering patriarch of the old school; his stoical wife and his daughters have their own strength, and they run the home, but he in part ruins their lives.

As for drama, three of Ireland's best-known plays also follow these themes: O'Casey's *Juno* is decidedly more admirable than her awful Paycock; Synge's *Playboy* is a boastful impostor, unworthy of the love of serious Pegeen, who falls for him for his charm and wit, but also because there's hardly anyone else around in the wilds of Mayo, except the mountainy men; and Friel's five young Donegal spinster sisters find dancing at Lughnasa little compensation for the emptiness of their lives, with no husbands, only a feckless lover. In Friel's story 'The Diviner', a dignified, hard-working Donegal woman is widowed by two awful husbands, the first a drunken brawler, the second just a drunk. The list is endless ... When I asked a woman writer, Edna O'Brien, brought up in the 1930s and '40s in rural Clare, whether these portraits of women's plight were accurate for that time, she said: 'Certainly. Women were superior to men, but victims; more intelligent, but emotionally crippled by these situations. And Irishmen, these writers at least, have felt touchy and guilty about it. Hence nearly all the writing on this theme has been by men.'

However, matters have changed since the days of *The Ballroom of Romance*, as women have emerged from much of their old subservient drudgery into the Mary Robinson era. Modernization of agriculture has weakened the old patriarchal families and reduced the need for women as farm workers; many have moved to the towns, where economic change has produced all sorts of new job outlets for them; usually they now have greater financial autonomy; and for a wife to have a job of her own has become more acceptable. The spread of birth control, and the impact of women's rights campaigns, have also made life easier. Marriages have grown more equal, even if some macho spirit still persists in rural areas.

William Trevor suggested to me, in 1992: 'That "*Ballroom*" scenario would be less likely today. The woman would have better prospects of finding a job in a nearby town, and maybe a suitable husband too. She would probably have sold the farm; fewer women today sacrifice themselves in that way for an elderly parent. I think that Irish men are changing, too, becoming less tied to mummy, better at treating their wives as equals.' John McGahern gave me a slightly different slant: 'My books are really about power and control in the family. As I see it, Ireland is a vast network of independent republics, each one a family, quarrelling internally but full of solidarity against the world. I don't really see women as martyrs or victims today. Family life is far less hermetic and oppressive than it used to be – we can thank the decline of

Church influence for that. Yes, marriages have become more equal, couples are closer to each other, they have less ignorance of each other's sexuality.' And Sylvia Meehan, a women's-rights leader and former head of the State-backed Employment Equality Agency, said to me: 'In the old days, the outward façade of a marriage was more important than the individual's welfare. If a woman was maltreated by her husband, as happened so often, she herself believed that she had to bear her cross in silence. Today, there is much more public sympathy for a woman who leaves a bad husband. She has more control over her own life and work – and my Agency helps.'

Far more women now take jobs outside the home when they can, often out of choice rather than economic need. The percentage of married women who work, though still below the EU average, has increased since 1961 from one in twenty to one in five, and the change is greatest among younger married women. This can be put down partly to better child care outside the home, and to smaller families. But it also results from a change in attitudes.

Until recently there were even some legal obstacles to women working. One notorious rule, in the spirit of the 1937 Constitution, obliged a woman in the civil service to give up her post on marriage. But this was dropped in 1977, partly as a result of Ireland's joining the European Community, which was to have a tonic effect on women's rights. Ireland at the time it joined was in clear default of EC legislation on a number of matters, including equal pay. In 1975 the minister of labour, Michael O'Leary (Labour), went to Brussels with the urgent backing of Irish employers, to plead for a special derogation on equal pay for women, claiming that it would force many firms to close. But he was forced to comply with Community rules. 'The EC has been excellent for Irishwomen,' said Frances Fitzgerald, former chairwoman of the Council for the Status of Women. 'Every time I have contact at European level, I come back refreshed. There's a real vision there, it helps us to feel we are not alone.'

The campaigners today feel that women's legislative battle is largely won and they now have much the same rights as in other countries (except of course for divorce and, from one viewpoint, abortion). But it does not always work out so well in practice: women may have equal pay for the same job, but they can still find it harder than a man to secure the better jobs, for male attitudes are slower to change. Women have been moving into senior positions, but slowly. Many diplomats and principals of schools are women, but only 5 per cent of top management in private firms or public offices; in the civil service, few reach the senior grades. An EC inquiry in 1992, for what it is worth, found that the Irish had least confidence in a woman's ability to do a professional job as well as a man. Asked whether a woman could be as good a surgeon, barrister, MP or train-driver as a man, only 51 per cent of the Irish sample said 'yes', 56 per cent of the Greek and Italian samples (second lowest), 68 per cent in the UK and 70 per cent in France. In politics, a number of women enter the Dáil: in the November 1992 election, the total of women TDs went up from 12 to 20, out of 166. In the cabinet then formed, two of the seventeen ministers were women.

Mary Robinson has been the strongest pioneer of women's advance in Ireland. Her election was a portent of this advance, and her Presidential influence is now pushing it further. She told me that when she visits schools, and asks girls what they want to be as grown-ups, even tots of four or five reply, 'I want to be President' – and that's new. As a lawyer, before her election, she won numerous cases of women's rights in the courts; now as President she tirelessly supports women's groups all over the island. These groups today are active and diverse, and you find them everywhere, even in small villages. Few of their leaders are militant feminists in the classic sense. But I find that Irish women in public life today have a quite daunting toughness, a sharp, realistic intelligence; they are the successors of the strong women of the farms, no longer suffering in silence. When it comes to defence of the old moral values, they are often the most conservative, but the younger ones can be more radical than the men. No longer stuck running the home, they have been the first to gain from Ireland's big advances in education since the 1960s.

Excellent education – but the Church now plays less part

The Irish at all levels have an eagerness for education. This is usually seen as the legacy of a peasant people's desire to seek an escape from poverty through self-improvement; and it can be dated back to the improvised 'hedge schools' of the eighteenth and early nineteenth centuries, where villagers would teach literacy and Irish history to their own children. Today, many parents are ready to help pay for their children's education. And as many as 80 per cent of teenagers, near to the highest EU level, stay on at school till the end of the secondary cycle at seventeen or eighteen.

Another key factor in Irish education is the major role of the Churches in the running of schools. It is here that the organic link between Church and State in Ireland is most evident, but today this is much contested, and changes are under way. The State supervises education and it pays for all schools (except the private ones), but individually the schools have long been owned and run by the Catholic Church, or by the Protestant Churches, or by local bodies. The teaching is mostly very good, but the Catholic Church in particular has tended to use the schools as its prime terrain for imbuing young minds with its own ethos. Today this direct influence has been waning, as more and more lay teachers, including principals, take over from the dwindling ranks of monks and nuns, and as more lay people are appointed to school boards. The Government now has plans to secularize still further. Some Church leaders accept the changes, while others fight to keep as much control as they can.

The British regime in the old days founded a few universities but did little for school education. It did however permit some Catholic religious orders, notably the Christian Brothers and the Sisters of Mercy, to open schools for poorer children. After 1921 the Free State Government proclaimed its ideal of making Ireland a great teaching nation, but in practice it put little money or effort into education, beyond the ill-judged campaign to restore the Irish language (see p. 291): by the 1960s, many schools were physically decrepit, the curriculum was severely out of date, and few children got beyond primary stage.

Then the Government finally accepted that if Ireland was to modernize its economy and society, education must be improved too. In the late 1960s a go-ahead minister of education, Donogh O'Malley of Fianna Fáil, carried through reforms that updated the curriculum, raised the minimum school-leaving age from fourteen to fifteen and, above all, introduced free secondary education – a crucial change in modern Ireland. New schools were built, older ones expanded, more teachers appointed, and education's share in the national budget was raised from just over 3 per cent in 1961 to 6·3 per cent by 1973. These changes were to make a big impact, as a new poorer class eagerly began to enter second-ary education, hitherto mainly a fee-paying middle-class preserve. But some social inequalities remained and still do so today (see below).

Except in the small private fee-paying sector, a school is run roughly as follows under the Church/State partnership system. The Department of Education sets the curriculum, pays the staff salaries and 85 per cent of the building and running costs; the parish provides the other 15 per cent. In a primary school, the manager is normally the parish priest, appointed by the local bishop, who is the school's patron and has a say in selecting staff. This pattern is now gradually changing, as management boards with some lay members play more part in the running of schools. But a State decree of 1971 is still in force that 'religion should permeate the whole school day'.

As for secondary schools, the majority are run by religious orders, under the same kind of State aegis – a few élitist ones by the Jesuits, the more ordinary ones by, with others, the Christian Brothers. This order has played a crucial role in Irish education, and many a writer has described his youthful years under the Brothers, with a mixture of affectionate respect and satiric fury. The order was founded in the early nineteenth century; then after the Famine it created many schools for the sons of the poor and became identified with the nationalist struggle. Today it has some eighty schools in Ireland. It has always taught its boys well in the classroom, but it has also driven them hard, even brutally, inculcating tough, manful attitudes, and preaching nationalism: in 1977 Conor Cruise O'Brien caused a stir by declaring in the Senate that the Brothers' schools were breeding-grounds for future IRA terrorists! Some convent schools have been almost as strict with girls (witness Edna O'Brien's sharp account of her schooldays in *The Country Girls*), but while the nuns have been rigid on sexual matters, they have often been quite feminist in urging their girls to go for their rights and get good jobs. And the Brothers' old severity has now softened considerably.

The past twenty years have seen gradual changes at both primary and secondary level, due above all to the decline in recruitment to the religious orders, at a time when the demand for teachers had been increasing. In secondary schools, the proportion of staff belonging to the orders has fallen from over 50 per cent in 1961 to some 12 per cent, while the rest are lay; at one convent school I visited in Galway, the principal was a nun but all but one of the rest of her staff of forty were lay. And whereas the Christian Brothers used to have some fifty new recruits a year, today it is four or five; several of their schools have closed. For some years the Church authorities tried at least to keep the principalships of schools in religious hands, but here too they are now losing ground and about one-third of principals are lay, owing to the lack of suitable religious candidates. And for school administration as opposed to pedagogy, whereas a school used to have a single manager, usually a local priest, chosen by the bishop, many of them now have a management board comprising some priests but also representatives of teachers, parents and local interests, and the bishop appoints only half of these. Most of these lay teachers and board members will probably be committed Christians. Even so, the changes have inevitably made the ethos of schools more secular, less evangelistic.

The Church itself has been divided about these changes. The hierarchy, resenting its loss of influence, has tended to oppose them. But some of the religious orders are not unhappy that their fall in numbers is forcing them to retrench. They feel that their historic mission, for which they started these schools long ago, is to help the poor; and now they want to get back into social work, 'closer to the daily needs of the poor and away from the ivory tower of school administration – let the State look after that,' I was told by Brother Pat Collings, principal of the Christian Brothers' Synge Street School in central Dublin. It is the same spirit that has taken many nuns out of convent teaching and into the slums, or has sent priests into the Third World. This Synge Street School, with 950 pupils, has some famous old boys, including Gay Byrne, Éamonn Andrews and Liam Cosgrave; but its buildings are gloomy and shabby and its facilities poor, without even a canteen (staff and pupils bring sandwiches). Of the staff of thirty-five, only four are Brothers – 'We are less clerical than before, but still totally Christian,' said Collings, below portraits of the Pope smiling down from the walls.

Schools provide two to four hours' religious education a week. As to whether a lay teacher is expected to be a practising Catholic, the pattern today varies from school to school. Brother Collings said, 'Here at Synge Street we insist on it. And anyway I don't think a non-believer would be happy in our atmosphere.' In primary schools, the hierarchy has long expected all the teachers to be convinced Catholics, but in schools with a lay principal matters can be fairly easygoing. One factor is that at primary level a teacher handles all subjects, including religion, and all are expected to prepare the pupils for sacraments; a non-believer can ask to be excused these duties, but it may not be easy. At secondary level, religion, like history or physics, is taught by specialists and most staff are not involved. Formerly a candidate even for a secondary post was scrutinized on his or her beliefs, but today very often no questions are asked, and the job goes to the best applicant. Or else an agnostic, when interviewed for the job, will cynically claim to be a believer and later just keep quiet – like paying lip-service to Communism in the old East German schools.

Even in rural primary schools, the old-style pious local teacher, on whom the Church could depend, is today becoming less common; many of the younger ones are more radical, unionized, critical of Church influence. The powerful primary-teachers' union, the Irish National Teachers' Organization, is not ideologically anticlerical in the French sense; but it tends to contest the hierarchy and the religious orders qua employers, and it disputes their right to select staff on religious grounds. In 1965, it made efforts to back John McGahern, when he was summarily dismissed from his teaching post after the publication of his anticlerical novel *The Dark* (see p. 238).

There are also quite a number of Protestant schools, playing an important role; in fact, they contain some 11 per cent of all Irish pupils, although only 3 per cent of the population is Protestant. They have long enjoyed a certain kudos, especially with the middle class; many parents of Catholic background, who have found their own schools too rigid or too churchy, have preferred to send their children to these schools, where the ethos tends to be more liberal and less sectarian. And the Church of Ireland keenly supports its schools, as the prime remaining bastions of its influence in Ireland. I visited one fee-paying girls' primary-cum-secondary school, Rathdown, just east of Dublin. The facilities were mediocre, as usual in Irish schools, but the atmosphere was pleasant, and I heard from parents that teaching is excellent. Stella Mew, the impressive lay principal, told me: 'Our board of governors are all Protestant, but lay, and ecclesiastical influence is minimal. I myself am a committed Christian. The school is partly modelled on the British system, with prefects, and "houses" that compete. In pre-Vatican II days, the Archbishop of Dublin preached sermons against us, as against Trinity, but that's all ended. Half our pupils are from Catholic homes, and I get on well with the local Catholic clergy.'

Not satisfied with this Protestant alternative, in the 1970s a few groups of parents began to campaign for the creation of schools unattached to any Church; they argued that parents should have this choice. They even felt that such schools might be able to set an example to the North (see p. 422). So a handful of these so-called 'multi-denominational' schools have been set up since 1976. The initiative has come from parents, who in most cases have paid for the buildings, but the schools are now Government-funded in the usual way and are part of the State system. The Churches,

Protestants included, were at first opposed to this intrusion into their own domain, but they now generally accept the new schools, whose syllabus does include some religious instruction of a multidenominational kind. The parents involved tend to be liberal-minded or lapsed Catholics, plus a few Protestants. The initial project was a primary school in the well-to-do east Dublin suburb of Dalkey – pleasant modern buildings and a rather Montessori atmosphere. 'We have no morning prayers here,' said the principal, 'but I go to lunch with the Catholic bishop, and one of his priests comes here to give catechism to his own flock.' Other schools have since opened. But they are all at primary level, and there are still only twelve of them. So the venture is a limited one and is not expected to spread very far – especially now that so many Catholic schools are becoming more secular.

Far more numerous, and more important for the future, are the 'community schools' that have also developed since the 1970s; they are taking the place of former vocational technical schools and now number about seventy. All are owned and run by the State and are essentially secular, though the religious orders are invited to play some part in management. At one such school in working-class north Dublin, I found most of the board of management to be delegates of teachers, parents and the State, with just two appointees of the Jesuits and Sisters of Mercy. Religious influence was slight, and religious education was voluntary. But the ambience was somewhat utilitarian, like many an urban comprehensive in Britain.

Today there is a debate in Ireland on how far this trend of secularization should be encouraged. Even some priests argue that the Church should mostly pull out of education and devote itself to pastoral and social work. But the vast majority still consider it important that the Catholic ethos should retain its influence in the teaching of subjects such as history and civics, let alone sex. As for parents, the community schools may be attractive in the cities, but in country areas the old Catholic tradition keeps much of its appeal. And surveys show that the majority of Irish parents still want their children to have a Christian-based education. Even many of those critical of Church dogma are ready to admire the huge and devoted contribution of the religious orders to Irish education, ever since the Famine. I met a group of young women teachers at a convent school in Galway: 'We are all liberals,' one said, 'not especially Catholic. But we do feel that these Church schools have a moral force, a sense of tradition, character and purpose, that is lacking in the new community ones, rather more utilitarian.'

In this situation, the Government is hesitant to abolish the official policy phrase that 'religion should permeate the whole school day'. It is under pressure to do so, from the teachers' unions and from non-religious parents. But it does not want to offend other parents, nor to provoke the Church when it needs its acquiescence on more important matters, such as divorce and overall educational reform. In 1992 the Government put forward a Green Paper full of reform proposals; and during 1993 the Fianna Fáil/Labour coalition extensively consulted teachers, parents and the Churches about these – more than can be said for the Tories in Britain. The result was due to form a White Paper in 1994, perhaps to be framed as a Bill a year or so later, in the usual leisurely Irish manner. The new minister of education, Ms Niamh Bhreathnach, is the first ever in this post from the secular-minded Labour Party, and she is concerned to give official structural form to the ad hoc secular trends of recent years.

The White Paper, which was due to appear in September 1994, is likely to propose, in effect, that the roles both of Church and State be scaled down. It would set up a new intermediary tier of local education authorities, rather as in Britain, to take charge of schools in each area; these bodies would include some Church representatives, but would not *be* the Churches, as now. The Department of Education, too, would hand over some powers to these bodies, and would confine itself to overall policy-making and funding. Within each school, the role of boards of managements would be strengthened, and each would probably consist of delegates of staff, parents and Churches, in three equal shares. So the bishops would cease to control local schools so directly, but would still play a part. In 1993–4, during the great national debate on these proposals, the Catholic Church at first demanded to retain majority representation on the boards. The Church of Ireland was even more reserved, for schools are its last real channel of influence in the Republic; its leaders pointed out that, having so many pupils who were Catholic, they were already de facto pluralist and did not need reform. However, by early 1994 it appeared that all the Churches would in the end cede to the White Paper's proposals. In any event, this new deal need not mean the end of Christian influence in schools. A Christian Brothers school, for example, with the vast majority of its teachers and parents actively Catholic, will still teach those values. Schools will become less ecclesiastical, but can remain Christian, if that is what most parents want.

There is also a debate on the cost of education. The regular State-funded schools are free, save that parents are generally asked to make a modest voluntary contribution of about £50 a year. A few other schools are purely private, charging high fees, as in Britain. And some Protestant ones are in between, receiving State grants but also charging fees on a means-test basis. Rathdown, for example, offers some bursaries for poorer pupils but expects others to pay around £1,200 a year. Of the exclusive purely private schools, some of the best Catholic ones are run by the Jesuits — notably Clongowes Wood College, the famous boarding-school in Co. Kildare that had such a traumatic effect on James Joyce, as he described it in *Portrait of the Artist as a Young Man*. Its Protestant counterpart, less academically distinguished, is St Columba's College, just south of Dublin. Founded in 1843 for the sons of the Protestant landed gentry, it is still run on the lines of an English public boarding-school, but today it has girls as well as boys, day pupils as well as boarders, and 40 per cent of its pupils are Catholic, mostly the children of professional people, businessmen and big farmers.

The Irish, as I have said, are ambitious for education. Not only will many middle-class parents make sacrifices to pay for schooling, but some farmers in remote areas will bear the cost of sending their children away to secondary school rather than have them stay and help on the farm; and in all classes parents will put money into university education, which in Ireland tends to be far from free (see below). One sociologist emphasized the element of national pride in this cachet put on education: 'People seem to feel that it's a way of exploiting the key Irish resource of intelligence and imagination, of enabling Ireland to prove its worth as a modern state and valorize its potential.' Maybe this relates to the pride the Irish still feel in their missionary Dark Ages role as 'the island of saints and scholars'.

Then in the nineteenth century the peasants embraced education as one of the few possible routes of escape from their poverty. Some villages created their own local 'hedge-schools', as depicted in Brian Friel's play *Translations*, in which a Donegal schoolmaster teaches Latin and Greek through Irish (intended by Friel as a metaphor). The rural eagerness continues even today; remarkably, the poorer counties of the West, such as Kerry and Mayo, have the highest proportions of young people entering universities – 30 to 33 per cent of the age group, compared with Dublin's 19 per cent. And in Ireland as a whole some 80 per cent of pupils, against 48 per cent in England and Wales, stay on at school till seventeen or eighteen to take the Leaving Certificate, equivalent to English A-levels. By no means all then go on to university, but some take vocational courses. It is true that many stay on simply to avoid unemployment and are even encouraged by their teachers to do so. Many also realize that, if they are going to need to emigrate, it would be wise to take a good education with them.

Irish experts claim also that the quality of the classroom education is unusually high, but this is not easy to assess. They tend to take as yardsticks the countries they know best, England and the United States, where standards in State schools are certainly much lower than in Ireland. Whether Irish quality is higher than in Scotland, France or Germany is less certain, but it could be comparable. The basics of literacy and numeracy are taught well, and this is appreciated by foreign investors (see p. 74). At secondary level, the emphasis tends to be academic rather than modern and technical, but Ireland avoids the early specialization found in England; pupils get a broad general education, and for the Leaving Certificate they sit from five to seven main subjects, usually including mathematics, history, and a foreign language – plus Irish, which most of them dislike, apart from those in the burgeoning new Irish-language schools (see p. 293).

After the reforms of the 1960s, Governments poured money into education. Universities and technical colleges were enabled to expand, from a total of 21,000 students in 1965 to over 78,000 today, embracing over 35 per cent of the age group, technical colleges included. As a result Ireland today is producing far more graduates than its economy strictly needs, and many are obliged to seek jobs abroad. So the Government is sometimes accused of using Irish public money to train young people who then go to help other countries. The official answer to this, given to me by several educators and economists, is threefold. First, it actually costs the State less to pay for a student at college than to have him or her idle on the dole. Secondly, many of these emigrant graduates then acquire useful skills abroad, which they can use for Ireland if they later return home (see p. 309). And thirdly, is not a university education about developing the full personality, not just training for the market-place?

Yet there are others who argue that Irish education is still too academic, and that if the technical side were more developed, then it might be easier to create more jobs. Ireland has nothing like the German apprenticeship system (see p. 83); moreover, white-collar jobs have tended to carry higher prestige than technical ones, among school-leavers and graduates. Despite progress in scientific and technical education since the 1970s, the 1992 Green Paper has now urged that more be done. Classical humanism versus modern technology in education – it is a familiar issue in many countries today.

And so is the issue of equal opportunity. The reforms of the late 1960s may have opened up secondary education to many who previously could not afford it, but subsequent expansion of the universities has benefited mainly the middle class. University entrance is decided on a points system related to Leaving Certificate marks, rather as in Britain; each university fixes its total intake per faculty, then accepts those with the most points. It is all highly competitive, 'an annual obsession of the middle classes', as someone put it; but at least it is done impartially, without any of the cronyism common in Ireland. However, workers' children play an inadequate part in this marathon. First, the urban working class does not yet fully share the thirst for education of other classes, or at least it shyly feels that a university milieu is not within its own culture. So it holds back – 'You go and get a job! – what do you need a degree for?' is still a common parental attitude in north Dublin. Secondly, the Government's largesse over education has waned in recent years; it expects most parents to pay some share of the cost of higher education, and the grants awarded on a means-test basis have been growing fewer and slimmer. Many workers' families thus feel they cannot afford university. The Provost of Trinity, Dr Thomas Mitchell, explained to me: 'Government policy is for a third of our revenue to come from parents; the average annual tuition fee is £1,500, out of a cost to us of £4,500. But only 30 per cent of students are on grants, and this figure has been declining. The system is too inflexible, it takes no account of special cases, of the really bright kid from a poor home who needs help. So of course our universities have few working-class students.'

The Republic of Ireland has seven main centres of university education. Trinity College in central Dublin, Protestant in origin, is the distinguished doyen, just over 400 years old. Its main rival is University College, Dublin, founded in 1854; the University Colleges in Cork and Galway were also founded around that time, and since 1908 these three have been grouped to form the National University of Ireland. St Patrick's College, Maynooth, west of Dublin, created back in 1795 as a seminary for the Catholic clergy (see p. 171), is also now part of the NUI. Two much newer ventures, both slanted towards business, science and technology, are Dublin City University and the dynamic and high-powered University of Limerick, American-influenced. All these universities are autonomous but depend on Government funding; Church influence is slight (except of course at Maynooth) and is not an issue. There are also various regional technical colleges and specialized institutes.

Trinity and the NUI colleges, all founded under English rule, are far closer to English than to Continental universities, alike in their ambience, looks and structures. The venerable Victorian campuses of Cork, Galway and Maynooth would not be out of place on the English scene. With student numbers restricted as in England, access to professors is fairly easy, also informal in the Irish manner, and the human scale is preserved; in addition, as in Britain and far more than on the Continent, there is plenty of both sport and social and cultural club activity. One UCD student told me he belonged to fourteen clubs. It is all a far cry from even such illustrious *almae matres* as Göttingen, Grenoble or Bologna, today little more than overswollen student broiler houses.★ Small wonder that Erasmus students from the Continent adore coming to study in Ireland (see p. 333).

The English connection still shines bright at Trinity College, Dublin, even if it is today more Irish than it used to be. Originally intended as the first college of a University of Dublin (but a second was never built), TCD was founded in 1592 by Queen Elizabeth in order to entice back the Irish from seeking higher education in France, Italy and Spain, 'whereby they have become infected by popery'. Though never formally a Protestant university, it always had a strong Protestant ethos, as well as being consciously modelled on Oxford and Cambridge. And the roll-call of its alumni is illustrious, including Swift, Congreve, Burke, Berkeley, Wilde, Wolfe Tone, Synge and Samuel Beckett. After independence it went through a bleak period, since it was identified with the former British rulers. Yet even in the 1920s some 20 per cent of its students were Catholic.

TCD had long been very popular with British students, since it was a nice place, and relatively easy to get into, especially after the hierarchy's ban on Catholics enrolling, which began in 1875 and was reinforced in 1944 (see p. 178). In the 1960s some 40 per cent of its intake was from the United Kingdom, including many Protestants from the North; there was also a large contingent from around the world. Then in 1970 the hierarchy's ban was lifted; and

---

★ See my books *France Today* and *Germany and the Germans*.

after this, with a growing demand among the Irish for higher education, the TCD authorities under government pressure began a policy of giving priority to Irish students. Today the British component has fallen to below 2 per cent; and the intake from Northern Ireland has dropped to around 2·5 per cent, partly because the Troubles have made Ulster Protestants less keen to go to Dublin. There has also, alas, been a cut-back in the numbers of foreign students who used to add such variety and vitality to TCD (three present Malaysian cabinet ministers are alumni). They still come from the Third World and from Europe, but in far fewer numbers. Trinity today is entirely non-denominational; some 90 per cent of its students are from a Catholic background, and it now has its first Catholic Provost since (briefly) James II. In short, it has moved closer to the mainstream of Irish education, and become less of a strange half-English anomaly.

Yet much of its old Oxbridge legacy survives, in its rituals, its distinguished scholarship, and in its close links with British universities. There is communal dining in a great hall, with dons at high table and grace in Latin; and lots of cricket, unusual in Ireland. Pass through the massive grey Palladian portals in the heart of old Dublin, and you are in a vast series of quadrangles in a jumble of styles, like some larger-scale counterpart of Trinity, Cambridge, but less elegant. Here, and spilling out into the streets around, some 9,800 students spend an overcrowded but intense and sociable existence, full of debates, parties, pranks; some 650 live inside college, the rest out in digs and hostels. At the 400th anniversary celebrations in 1992, there was a ball for 10,000 people in huge marquees on the sports grounds. One summer night, as a professor and I sat on the grass by the Pavilion Bar, amid the songful rugger bloods with their Guinnesses, he said, 'It's still great, this place, unique. But since the Catholic ban ended some of the excitement has gone; we're no longer beleaguered, we've merged into Ireland.'

Trinity is the most sought-after university, by Irish students. Of the others, University College, Dublin, was also once in the city centre, but its staff and 11,000 students now work out on a spacious modern campus in Dublin 4. A little less international than Trinity, and less academically renowned, it has always been a stronghold of the Catholic middle class. At Cork, the University College is compact, animated, cosy, popular with Europeans and graced by some famous professors such as Joseph Lee. University College, Galway, has rather dreary buildings but a vivacious and creative student life, and is an active centre of Gaelic studies. It used to be strongly geared to the humanities but is now developing its business and scientific side, too, influenced by its upstart new rival in the west, the University of Limerick. This paragon of hi-tech and modern business studies is a new departure on the Irish scene. It was the brainchild of Dr Edward Walsh, today its president, one of Ireland's most assertive and controversial figures, with sharp views on emigration (he's for it) and the Irish language (he's less keen). He also believes that the Irish universities are out of date and should be geared more closely to the modern economy. He spent some years in America, where he took his doctorate; then in his early thirties he founded at Limerick what was first an institute of technology and is now a full university.

It has a pleasant parkland setting beside the Shannon, just outside town – a handsome nineteenth-century mansion with modern steel-and-glass buildings attached, very compact. The entrepreneurial ambience is rather like that of a modern, well-run business, and the 6,000 students seem to enjoy this ethos. Following the model of some new US universities, much of their four-year course is interdisciplinary and based on continuous assessment; and one year is spent working on attachment in a firm, in Ireland or abroad. But the arts and humanities are not ignored: about a fifth of studies are in that field. The university is much in demand with school-leavers, enticed by its job-related approach. Its critics, however, find it too industry-geared and vocational; and some of them see Walsh himself as too much of a clever, high-handed Thatcherite. But he is confident of his own vision. 'Universities', he told me, 'must get back to their earliest medieval vocation of serving the community. In those days, in thirteenth-century Bologna for instance, this meant training priests, doctors and lawyers – the three strategic vocations of that time. Today we need to move closer to the market-place. Universities are there to respond to those ready to pay for a service, and I go along with that. Happily, we are making some impact, for the older universities have been moving in our direction.'

And so has the Government. As in Britain, the universities are self-governing in their courses and their teaching, but they depend on the State for most of their funding. So the Department of Education and the Higher Education Authority are able to put pressure on the universities to expand certain faculties and slim down or even close others. 'Alas,' said an arts professor I met at Cork, 'we may be autonomous but he who pays the piper calls the tune. The Department has become more utilitarian, it wants to see value for money from our training of students.' It is a familiar argument everywhere in Europe: are universities there for the sake of scholarship and personal enrichment, or to service the economy? Ireland still hopes to have it both ways, as it fights for its economy to keep pace with rising aspirations and new lifestyles.

Changing lifestyles: new sophisticated cooking, but the pubs are emptying

As in Britain, only some years later, and from a lower base, Irish lifestyles and consumer habits have changed considerably, under the impact of rising prosperity since the 1960s, and of foreign influences. Television and modern advertising have made their impact. The range of goods in the shops has widened, with the spread of the new Irish supermarket chains such as Dunne's and Quinnsworth. Even in Dublin, the clothes shops used to be poorly supplied with the latest styles, but now offer much the same variety as in a comparable British city: Laura Ashley and Marks & Spencer are on Grafton Street. Foreign holidays and dining-out have become a middle-class norm; tennis and golf have also grown in popularity, as witness the ring of new golf-courses around Dublin, not just for tourists. But the gulf between the very rich and the poor has, if anything, been increasing.

The Irish standard of living remains well below that of the rest of north-west Europe, as a few statistics can show (see also p. 68). Salaries are lower than in Britain, while the cost of living is some 20 per cent higher, mainly because of higher taxation and distribution costs. Petrol, cars, telephoning, and postage are all substantially more expensive; food is a little dearer, too, but clothes are at about the same prices. Only housing remains well below the inflated British level. The OECD Economic Survey for 1993 indicates how Ireland compares with some other countries (see table).

Ireland Compared with Four Other Countries

	Ireland	France	Portugal	Spain	UK
Annual private consumption per capita (in US$)	5,886	10,482	5,278	7,326	10,051
Passenger cars per 1,000 inhabitants	278	494	181	347	449
Telephones per 1,000 inhabitants	265	610	220	396	524
TV sets per 1,000 inhabitants	260	399	160	380	435

A handful of people are very rich, but even they do not flaunt their wealth publicly: this is not popular in Ireland's 'begrudging society' where success is more envied than admired. In the streets of Dublin there is far less sign of private wealth than, say, in London or Paris, where admittedly many of the richest people are foreigners. The middle classes live for the most part unostentatiously, in a modest comfort sometimes verging on a kind of genteel shabbiness. In their furnishings and décor they lack any great zest for the smart and stylish: their zest they reserve for other things, for convivial conversation, music, drama, and sports such as horse-riding. Pub-going is on the decline. But cuisine, never one of Ireland's stronger points, is now at last being taken more seriously.

Alike at home and in restaurants, patterns of eating have been changing for the better, if erratically. Until recently the picture was nearly everywhere dismal – the ubiquitous fry-up, the ubiquitous boiled spud and overcooked, soggy vegetables. Today a number of sophisticated restaurants have appeared; and in many shops the range of food has widened immensely, to include exotic foreign fruits, pastas, French cheeses, even herbs and spices. But the quality of the actual cooking generally lags far behind that of the produce – a judgement shared by the leading Dublin food writers John and Sally McKenna, who told me:

'Until around the 1960s, most people ate from a very small range of purely local fresh produce, mainly from the farms. Then came the consumer revolution, which brought a vast array of tinned, frozen and other processed foods into the supermarkets, not always with the best results. Today, amongst a minority at least, there's a swing back to the buying of quality foods in small speciality shops – the trend that we encourage. But the weak point of Irish food remains the cooking; there's little tradition of it, and it is slow to develop, save at the level of a few classy restaurants often with foreign chefs. Ireland can supply excellent ingredients, especially its fish, meat, poultry and dairy products: but then the food is just boiled or fried, with little seasoning, herbs or sauces, all dull and unimaginative. At most social levels, the fry-up remains the usual evening meal.' I agreed. In prosperous livestock-breeding country I visited one well-off farmer's family, with colour TV, videos, expensive new furniture, but the casual supper they invited me to share was the usual fry of bacon, sausages, black pudding, egg and chips, much the same as they had probably eaten at breakfast. Helpings are hefty in Ireland, but vegetables tend to be dreary and salads minimal. And the famous 'full Irish breakfast' has a predictable monotony, save in a few good hotels.

This situation is the legacy of the past, of a very poor people long colonized by a nation with no great culinary tradition either. The peasantry in the old days depended on the potato, which was frighteningly vulnerable to crop failure (witness the Famine), but in itself a wholesome diet with varied proteins. They also had some cereals, milk, eggs and occasional meat. The landed gentry fared more lavishly, with plenty of meat and game from their estate, but the cooking was no more inspired than in English country houses at that time.

More recently, change has come, especially to the towns, under the impact of EU trade, foreign holidays, TV cookery programmes, and generally wider horizons. In a supermarket in Sligo in 1992 I found mangoes, kumquats, ugli fruit, avocados, aubergines and the inevitable kiwis – unimaginable in a small town twenty years previously. In Dublin you can buy French croissants. The range of vegetables (see p. 111) has widened beyond the basic cabbage and carrots, and on a few dinner-tables and menus you might now find, say, courgettes and mange-touts, no longer always overcooked. And the Irish are starting to grow or import herbs, garlic and spices; some middle-class families now try them out in their own cooking, inspired by the food columns and cookbooks of writers such as Darina Allen, who will introduce, say, lamb with marjoram or a Sicilian pasta recipe. Or people will practise making the dishes they have enjoyed on foreign holidays, such as paella, moussaka or *coq au vin*. Wine today is found everywhere, though high taxes make it even more expensive than it is in England. Twenty years ago, it was still something of a rarity in the remoter provinces; and as small shopkeepers or hoteliers knew little about it, you could sometimes find surprising bargains. In a Sligo village store in 1973, I spied a vintage claret on a top shelf: 'Sure now,' said the woman at the counter, 'that one's a bit old and dusty, I'll let you have it for half price.'

Dublin thirty years ago had only a tiny handful of good restaurants; today there are scores, many of them foreign. The range includes Chinese, Indian, Indonesian, Japanese, Lebanese, Moroccan, Russian and Thai. Sometimes the food or ambience is not too authentic: some Italian places could best be described as 'Irish-Italian', with service by motherly Irish ladies rather than zippy *camarieri*. But Dublin has some excellent, genuine French restaurants, with French chefs and waiters; and the food seldom follows *nouvelle cuisine* excesses, for the Irish expect large helpings. There are also good places to eat in and around Cork (with an annual gourmet festival in Kinsale). Some new hotels in the provinces offer fairly sophisticated modern cooking, foreign-influenced; others try for an originality that the chef can't manage, and flounder into pretentious absurdity, e.g. the haddock with banana and yoghurt dish I found in Co. Clare. A number of other restaurants concentrate more modestly on the slim repertoire of Irish or English dishes; Irish stew can be very tasty when made properly, so can carrageen-seaweed soup, or the boxty, an Irish potato pancake with meat fillings. The ubiquitous Irish soda bread is best when home-made; and Ireland produces a few excellent farmhouse cheeses.

It is Myrtle Allen, Darina's mother-in-law, who has probably done more than anyone to raise Irish food standards and stimulate interest in good food. Now aged around seventy, she is Ireland's best-known and best-loved chef. In 1947 she and her husband Ivan, both of them Quakers, he a gentleman farmer, bought Ballymaloe House, east of Cork, a handsome part-Georgian mansion with 400-acre farm attached. In 1964 they opened a restaurant there, then turned it into a very personal country hotel, hugely admired not only for its food but for what *The Good Hotel Guide* has called 'the special convivial quality of its hospitality'. Most of Myrtle's produce comes from the family's home farm and this has dictated the style and philosophy of her cooking; she believes in using very fresh first-class ingredients and cooking them simply but imaginatively, without frills, disdaining fancy sauces. Dishes might include cauliflower soup, roast pork with wild garlic, goose with apple stuffing. Some critics, myself included, have found the results a little too bland; but what she does, she does perfectly, propelled by a hard-work ethic that may spring from her Quaker ethos. One of her six children married Darina, who now runs a well-known cookery school near the hotel. Together, the Allens' articles, books, lectures and TV work have had a major influence – on a certain public and on other restaurateurs. Ballymaloe has been the prototype and inspiration of the new style of Irish country hotel, usually a converted stately mansion, maybe run by its original landed-gentry owners (see p. 326); today there are scores of them, all tending to serve much the same kind of discreet 'country house' cooking (e.g. game terrine, poached salmon, casserole of pork), sometimes excellent, sometimes rather dull.

For years Myrtle Allen has crusaded against the threat to good produce, in Ireland as elsewhere, from mass production and other modern trends – what she calls 'this constant pressure, pressure, pressure for cheaper, poor-quality food'. She founded the Irish branch of Eurotoques, the association of leading chefs such as Paul Bocuse who share her views. She has given loud voice to the fears that modern methods of farming and processing could spoil flavour and quality; she has spoken up against the supermarkets' buying practices, and has fought (with some success) against the 'absurd' EU hygiene regulations that have risked putting them out of business. She holds that traditional ways are best – but more expensive, so 'people must be ready to pay more for good food'. Of course she is called an élitist. By 1993 the set dinner at Ballymaloe was £30.

She is also a keen Irish patriot. She has gone often on food promotions abroad, for example to Brussels and New York, to help Irish exports. In 1981–5 she even ran a restaurant in central Paris that was owned by friends; she would bring over Irish lamb and bacon, Irish cream, cheese and brown flour, to provide Irish dishes that proved popular with Parisians at least as novelties (notably at *le brunch du dimanche*). Allen is hugely proud of Irish farm produce, which in the right hands (such as hers) can certainly lead to fine results. In effect she has been creating a new style of Irish farm-based country cooking, simple but flavoursome, quite distinct from the French. But in other hands than hers, alike in restaurants and homes, the produce is seldom handled with such finesse: Ireland is still awash with soggy vegetables and frizzled chops. And although standards are slowly rising, with new foreign influences, there are contrary pressures too; Allen fears that improvements in cooking are possibly outweighed by the decline in the quality of mass ingredients. 'For exciting little dinners, things are getting better, but for everyday eating, the worse trend is winning,' she said – the same kind of polarization as in France today, despite its very different tradition.

As in Britain, the middle classes take their evening meal somewhat later than the lower-income groups with their early suppers. Dublin yuppies and others now give the same kind of cosy little dinner parties as in London; wine is normally served, even though it is highly taxed. But at all social levels the hospitable Irish can display a true Irish casualness about the way they entertain. You may not actually be invited to a meal; you may be just asked round, then food appears. Once I had an appointment with a professor in his home, at 6 p.m.: he was late, so I was put in the sitting-room, where his wife plied me with tea, then whiskey, then said, 'Oh, we've some spaghetti bolognaise, why not have that while you wait?' – so I ate a huge plateful on my lap. That would not happen in France, where you get a big dinner at eight, or nothing. At the same time, the vogue for dining out in good restaurants developed fast during the booming 1970s and 1980s, owing not only to rising prosperity but to changing social mores. Young executives, who previously might have spent a whole evening drinking in pubs, are now more likely to go for a meal in a bistro, and probably end up spending less. Hence the crisis today in the pub world.

The pub has long been a great Irish institution, lovingly chronicled by writers. It is seen as a place where all classes rub shoulders democratically, however smartly or roughly they may be dressed, and where any stranger can join in the 'crack' around the bar. German visitors especially love these pubs, for the first-name no-introductions informality that they much more seldom find at home. And Dublin still nurtures a whole cult of its famous pubs, such as Mulligan's of Poulbeg Street, where Brendan Behan used to drink, and Doheny and Nesbitt, where TDs and media folk gather. There's a role in pubs even for the solitary drinker, whom the humorist Flann O'Brien may have had in mind in his well-known line, 'The pint of plain: your only man', i.e. the notion that only a glass of beer gives reliable comfort – in this case 'plain' porter (stout), still the king of Irish drinks.

There has however been a darker side to this full-blooded tradition of gregarious boozing. In the countryside especially, the pub was the breeding-ground of chronic male drunkenness, leading maybe to brawls, wife-bashings, ruined health. Drink was cheap, and in the evenings there was little else to do. In a macho spirit, men would gather in groups at the bars, where the incessant buying of rounds was a convivial custom but could lead to them drinking more than they intended. The Church tried to make younger people sign the pledge, but not often with much success. And there were simply too many pubs: many villages in the west had one for every twenty or thirty people. But today there is less heavy drinking in pubs – and a consequent drop in public drunkenness and violence.

Official Irish drinking statistics are very curious. According to one set of figures produced by the United Nations, the Irish spend a far higher percentage of their disposable income on alcohol than any other EU nation – and this may have helped to sustain their popular boozy image. But on closer inspection it emerges that national criteria vary; while official Irish consumer statistics put drinking in pubs under 'alcohol', in most other countries it is classified under 'entertainment' or 'restaurant going'. So Ireland is not really so out of line. In fact other statistics, produced by Euromonitor, a marketing body, suggest that the Irish have the *lowest* per capita consumption of alcohol of any EU state except Greece and Italy. In Britain it is 20 per cent higher, in Germany 60 per cent. These statistics may seem just as surprising as the UN ones. One explanation is that as many as 26 per cent of Irish people do not drink alcohol at all (the Church still has an influence here), whereas some others, mainly men, drink heavily. What's more, far more of the drinking takes place in pubs rather than in homes than in most countries, hence it is more conspicuous.

In any case, alcoholic drinking has recently been on the decline. As in many other European countries, consumption rose steadily during the 1960s, largely as a result of increased prosperity, to reach a peak in the mid-1970s. It then levelled off, and in the 1980s it fell substantially, before again levelling off. There are several likely reasons for the fall – among them, better education, public health campaigns, the spread of television and other rival entertainments, maybe the rise of the middle-class dining-out vogue, and certainly the fact that women are today going to pubs much more. They go in the company of men, so there is less all-male macho-type drinking than before (much of it is now linked to sporting events, a booze-up after a victory or defeat). Probably more important, the Government has increased the taxes on alcoholic drinks, pushing up their prices much faster than the rate of inflation; and it has imposed stricter penalties on driving after drinking, an important deterrent in rural areas dependent on the car. Many people have thus been taking to soft drinks. Stout, above all Guinness, remains the most popular drink in Irish pubs: but today its sales are almost equalled by the lighter lager or pils, brewed in Ireland under licence from Carlsberg, Heineken and others (Smethwick's, now part of the Guinness group, brews Harp lager – if you can't beat 'em, join 'em). As in most other non-wine-producing countries, sales of imported wines have risen sharply, with prosperity: but in Ireland in volume terms they equal only 6 per cent of sales of beer. Sales of fruit juices have risen sharply too, and of mineral water, notably Ireland's best-known brand, the sparkling Ballygowan from Co. Limerick, now much drunk by younger writers who want to avoid Brendan Behan's fate (see p. 236). I note also that the Irish of all classes drink alcohol at home during the day less than they used to, or than I had expected. When visiting people at home, I would be offered wine or beer with a meal, but at other times tea, or coffee (usually awful). Those who gave me hard drink in the afternoon were generally bishops.*

The result of the decline in heavy drinking is that many pubs today are on hard times; the lucky ones in tourist areas can at least hope to make profits in summer, but almost half of Irish pubs run at a loss. Many in fact are run as secondary operations by people who have another business, maybe a local shop or a farm; but they

---

* Irish whiskeys of course remain popular, Paddy, Jameson and the rest. And so, in a few back rooms in a few areas, does illicitly distilled poteen, a traditional Irish fire-water made from potatoes. It was outlawed by the British in 1831 (they thought it made the Irish even more unruly) and has stayed so ever since. Some bold characters still distil it secretly, up in the wilds of the West; and it sells readily on the black market, for about £7 or £8 a bottle, while legal spirits cost some £13. But Garda patrols obtain scores of convictions a year, and fines are upwards of £1,000. This 'quare stuff' is really no more harmful than many imported spirits, and there is some demand for its ban to be lifted. But with teenage alcoholism growing, this is not likely to happen.

do not want to close or sell, often for reasons of family tradition. So there are still far too many pubs; in one Co. Limerick village with 200 people, I counted five. A few are picturesque and full of character, but most are just gloomy, and to my mind depressing. Empty much of the day, they may possibly fill up late, for Irish villagers today tend to stay at home much of the evening, maybe glued to the box, then go round to the local for a quick one soon before it closes (and perhaps stay on in a back room for the thrill of illicit drinking after closing time at 11·30 or so, with the Gardai conniving).

The more enterprising pubs are now trying to woo customers by other means. As in England, in towns they can often do a good lunchtime trade by laying on food. Or in the evenings they turn to live music of various kinds, or other diversions (most of the sessions of traditional Irish music are held in pubs, see p. 281). The owner of the lively Hooded Cloak pub in Macroom, near Cork, told me: 'People do more of their drinking at home nowadays, owing to the drink-and-drive problem, and because off-licence prices are so much cheaper. They have become far more selective about their pub-going. Twenty years ago, every Friday and Saturday night was very busy here. But now they won't come unless they think they are getting value for money, so we have to entice them with other things than just drink. I now lay on Irish music, fashion shows, bridge parties, even plays. People want a *show*. So we have to keep working at it.'

Adults may be drinking less, but there has been a disturbing rise of alcoholism and heavy drinking among teenagers, especially working-class girls. Young people drink at home, or out in the fields, or even in pubs despite the ban on serving alcohol to under-eighteens. It is a phenomenon linked to the rise of urban petty crime and drugs, and to the malaise caused by high unemployment. Many out-of-work teenagers who live at home, and are fed by their parents, spend a sizeable part of their dole money on drink.

Extreme rural poverty may have declined in Ireland, but in the cities the gulf between the lifestyles of rich and poor is flagrant – you have only to contrast the easy life of the smarter Dublin suburbs with the inner-city slums and the desolate outer housing estates of Tallaght or Ballymun. Here many inhabitants are emigrants from the farms who have lost their old rural community values, severe but safe, and they feel adrift in the big city. These areas tend to be the breeding-grounds of drug abuse and vandalism. Drugs made their entry fairly late into Ireland but then spread fast; the number of addicts treated at the main Dublin drugs advisory centre rose nearly fourfold in 1979–83. Dermot Bolger, with a touch of Irish hype, suggested to me that 'Dublin then suddenly became the heroin capital of Europe, and the police were unable to cope'. He luridly described Dublin drug-trafficking in his novel *The Journey Home* (see pp. 247–9), while others have claimed that the city now has a heroin problem proportionately as great as New York's.

Muggings, housebreakings and car thefts have also increased. Dublin used to be such a safe city apart from the odd drunken brawl; today it is becoming more like Rome, a place where women do not care to walk alone after dark in the murkier suburbs, or where people will not leave their cars in some streets overnight. 'These tensions are putting the old Irish chummy solidarity under strain,' one Trinity professor suggested to me. 'The Irish used to feel that in a way they were all friends. But now the growth of crime creates a new mistrust, and the growth of urban inequality creates new begrudgery.' Equally there has been an increase in homelessness, women's poverty, teenagers running away from home. And the official welfare services, though generous in their own way, are ill geared towards dealing with these new kinds of social problem.

The Welfare State came late to Ireland. It was not until 1946 that de Valera created government health and social-welfare departments, and until the 1970s these were poorly funded. But today Ireland has rather good health and social services for a country of its level of prosperity. Within the social-security system, medical attention is free for poorer people, while the better-off make some payments; some hospitals are run by the State, many others by the Churches, but with State funding. Medical care has improved enormously since forty or so years ago, when country doctors would travel out in the night to help women in childbirth in remote cottages; today the mothers all go to maternity wards. And benefits for the elderly, the chronically sick and the unemployed are at reasonable levels.

There are however some lacunae in the welfare system, and one concerns family law and child care. Until the 1970s, family policy was defined mainly by the Church, which held that this was no business of the State (hence the famous defeat of Noel Browne's mother-and-child scheme in 1951, see pp. 159–60). Today the State does play more part, but there has been little change in the well-intentioned laws protecting family privacy; thus, for instance, if there is evidence of a child being maltreated by parents, the police or social workers possess far less right to intervene than in Britain. And although Governments are full of bold rhetoric about the importance of the family, they are reluctant to take any responsibility. Child benefits are among the lowest in the EU, leading to many reported cases of child poverty. And there are no public nursery schools; the Government argues that children are better at home, and this accords with the Church's ethos, that a woman should stay at home to look after the kids. Church pressures, still quite strong, thus chime with State parsimony.

Another lacuna concerns State support for the homeless and destitute. 'Because the State does so little, voluntary or unofficial bodies have to step in,' was a refrain I heard constantly. A surprising number of these bodies are funded by the EU, such as Combat Poverty. Others are run by active Christians, not so much by the Church itself as by dedicated individuals, such as 'Sister Stan' (see p. 165) and the Rev. Peter McVerry. In Waterford, I found a Franciscan priest providing homes for the elderly – 'It's all part of liberation theology' – with some government funding. In Dublin, Sister Stan's agency, Focus Point, tries to find homes for the destitute of all kinds, such as deserted wives with children, who are poorly catered for by the State. The agency's task is made harder by recent cutbacks in State funding for new social housing. As a result, Dublin Corporation is building far fewer homes than ten years ago and the shortage is growing.

The new coalition Government promised to remedy matters, but has been very slow to act.

Perhaps the most impressive of the welfare pioneers is Peter McVerry, the tall, good-looking Jesuit, Clongowes-educated, who since 1983 has run a hostel for delinquent teenagers, aged twelve to sixteen, on the fourth floor of a tower block in the slum district of Ballymun. The kids tend to be noisy and destructive, and the neighbours have repeatedly tried to get the hostel removed; but he has held out. He told me: 'These are very damaged kids, from bad families; the kind who would always be last in the queue for jobs, or it's hard to find schools who will take them. Many have run away from home, or they are delinquents who have been caught for shoplifting, drug-pushing or robbing cars. They would have been sent to detention centres, but I think it is better to keep them within the community: society should try to help such kids. And with rising unemployment the problem is getting worse.

'The authorities', he went on, 'have simply buried their heads in the sand about the problem, and the social services are disastrous. The Government has spent £17 million on doing up the Taoiseach's office, so money *is* available; but homeless children are a low priority. The advantage of Ireland is that at least I have easy access to the minister of health, he's a decent fellow, he tries to do his best, but the Health Board officials con him into believing that I'm exaggerating the problem – although there are hundreds of kids that need our help, many sleeping under the stars. The Health Board, it's true, has now opened one hostel for homeless girls, some of them teenage prostitutes; and it does give some funds to hostels run by voluntary bodies such as Focus Point. But it's all very erratic. What we need is proper purpose-built hostels: but the Corporation won't provide the sites, it is scared about its voters.' He summed up: 'Above all, I'm running a political pressure-group to try to get the State to act, to take responsibility for these children and enact new legislation. That's why the Health Board is against me. But the diocese is in favour of my work, and the Jesuit Order backs me fully.'

Bishop Desmond Williams, one of the five auxiliary bishops of Dublin, is also active in work for the poor. He runs food centres for drop-outs in his diocese, and will even provide shelter in his own home for teenage 'travellers'. Formerly known as 'tinkers', the travellers are still a common feature of Ireland, and are ethnically quite distinct from Gypsies, despite their somewhat similar lifestyle. There are some 700 traveller families even within Dublin. Many still live in caravans, mostly on the edge of towns; but about half are now in houses, usually grouped in their own little ghettos. Some still earn a living from their traditional trade of doing odd jobs, or buying and selling second-hand goods. But many simply depend on the dole.

Very high unemployment is thought to be having a damaging effect on Irish social morale. 'It creates a listless, apathetic ambience,' says Bishop Williams, 'and it's hard for teenagers to push themselves into the work ethic if they see no signs of it around. In one road of thirty houses near here, no one gets up before nine. A few of the more energetic ones do put their enforced leisure to good use, by doing voluntary work for the community, running clubs and so on; but they are a minority.' Most older people just kill time, maybe going into the public parks or libraries; younger ones watch videos or stay in bed, demoralized. And some lose even the will to look for work. The basic benefit rate is about £60, rising to some £130 for a family with two children; as an ordinary unskilled job pays no more than this, some people prefer to remain on the dole – 'The State is simply subsidizing idleness,' was the sharp comment of one critic of the system. Some people look for work abroad, but this has become harder to find. A few think of going to live in the country, where the quality of life can be higher and living costs lower than in Dublin (see p. 148).

The State spends large sums on unemployment benefits, also on the income supports for small farmers and a range of weekly social-assistance payments for the really needy. Altogether some 35 per cent of the population are dependent on social welfare, but often without having the dignity of an occupation. Through this kind of direct aid, the State is sincerely endeavouring to stave off serious poverty. But the result today is inevitable cut-backs in other fields, such as housing and education. Hence the constant cry from economists that Ireland is living above its means.

7

THE CELTIC VITALITY OF A POPULIST CULTURE

Ireland has long been a major exporter of its people and its culture – the ancient scholar-monks who helped to civilize the Continent, the folk musicians who went to America, or writers like Shaw and Wilde who settled in England. And today, in a new way, this cultural export drive continues, as witness the successes abroad of Irish rock groups or folk-singers such as U2 or Christie Moore, the plays of Brian Friel, the films of Neil Jordan and Jim Sheridan, and countless new novels.

It is a truism to say that this small country has an astonishing level of cultural output, vitality and expressiveness. It may be a Celtic trait, or a manner of asserting national identity – the same kind of instinct to keep nationhood alive through culture that I found in the 1970s in an even smaller but equally proud country, Slovenia. Just as the Gaelic revival of the late nineteenth century, led by Yeats and other intellectuals, was in part a response to British rule, so today's very different cultural revival, more populist, more diffuse, is in some sense an Irish reaction against pervasive Anglo-American commercial influences. Hence the renaissance of traditional music; the spread of schools where the teaching is in Irish; and the wave of younger writers who reject old-style nationalism but readily admit, 'I feel very Irish,' and whose writings spontaneously express their Irishness. Roddy Doyle is an example.

The cultural scene today, whether folk-based or modern, does tend to be populist rather than highbrow, and somewhat inward-looking. There is not so much standard European classical culture on offer, maybe because the bourgeois audience for it is so much

235

smaller than, say, in France or Britain; sometimes amid the explosive Irish rhythms I did find myself longing for a little more Mozart. Nor (*pace Finnegans Wake*) do the Irish much favour the avant-garde. Yet there are pockets of highbrow intellectualism, as witness the rarefied, very 'European' novels of John Banville, or the cerebral battle, quite Parisian in its acerbity, that broke out in 1992 between those rival literary pundits, Edna Longley and Séamus Deane. Literature and theatre remain the dominant arts in this land of witty talkers and racy story-tellers. It is not a land with much visual tradition, though today its visual arts scene is at last becoming livelier. Its cinema too is flowering, with foreign help. And Irish television since the 1960s has played an important radical role in society, thanks to the provocative, taboo-breaking chat-shows pioneered by the mighty Gay Byrne and others.

Much of the best new writing and theatre has been coming from the troubled North. Down in the Republic, apart from a new buzz in Galway the cultural scene of this centralized country remains heavily Dublin-focused. The city wears its fabled Joycean literary heritage a shade self-consciously, with an eye on the tourist trade; and visitors can find the intense and compact little world of its cultural élites tiresomely self-absorbed. 'Dublin is a secret society,' commented the young writer Ferdia Mac Anna, 'with its own warmth and tolerance, yet bitchy, back-biting, full of wit and coded language, an intimate world hard to share with outsiders.' But I forgive a lot to a town that puts posters of modern-poetry quotations in its suburban trains. And there are still masses of writers being busily creative, eagerly wooed by London and New York publishers, often winning prizes abroad (the 1993 Booker, for example, went to Doyle). They all know each other, they meet constantly in each other's homes, but less often in pubs than in the old boozy Brendan Behan days; as a result, maybe more good real writing is being done today. The young novelist Dermot Bolger said to me: 'The old pub society among writers was stultifying. Heavy drinking killed Behan, and we younger writers are avoiding that path. We are known as the Ballygowan generation' (after the mineral water).

The Irish may be rightly proud of their culture, yet State

patronage for the arts has always been niggardly, so that most of the support has had to come from rich individuals, or from a few generous firms such as Guinness. In a country far from wealthy, Governments have preferred to put their priorities elsewhere, on helping industry and education. In fact the Irish Arts Council was not created until 1973 and its budget remains modest, £11·5 million for 1993: even Tory-ruled Britain, no paragon in this field, has spent a larger share of GDP on official patronage. When in 1991 it was Dublin's turn to be European City of Culture, State backing for this year-long festival was much lower than it had been for Glasgow in 1990, in fact just about as feeble as for Athens and Florence, and one official claimed, 'Dublin is so cultured already that we hardly need to help it.' Other Irish towns are even worse starved of Government largesse (see p. 262).

Whatever his other shortcomings, the Irish politician to have done most for culture has probably been Charles Haughey. He is no lover of intellectuals, but has a genuine feeling for the arts. In 1982, as Taoiseach, he set up Aosdana ('The Wise People'), an academy of some 150 creative artists and writers who are each eligible for a modest official stipend of about £6,000 a year, if their other earnings are below a certain level. Many creative people have benefited. It was also Haughey, as minister of finance in 1969, who instituted the scheme whereby earnings on creative work are free from income tax, for anyone living in Ireland, Irish or foreign. This tax haven has drawn a number of foreign writers and artists, for example Frederic Forsyth, to settle in Ireland at least for a few years.

Puritan censorship is now almost gone

Today, a serious writer can live and be published freely in Ireland. But it was not always so. Earlier this century, Joyce and others were prompted to emigrate by the narrow puritanical ambience that left Ireland intellectually isolated from the world in the years after independence; and this was soon made worse by a stern moral censorship. In 1926, with the active backing of the Church, the Government set up a Committee of Enquiry on Evil Literature, which paved the way for the notorious Censorship of Publications Act of 1929, directed against anything judged to be 'indecent or obscene'. It was supposed to be aimed mainly at pornographic magazines, or works dealing with birth control, rather than at real literature. But the 1,200 books banned outright during the 1930s included some of literary merit, if they touched on topics such as homosexuality, or were judged to be blasphemous. Even a novel as innocent as Kate O'Brien's *The Land of Spices* was outlawed for just one sentence about a homosexual affair. Acting very often on complaints from individual zealots, the Censorship Board banned books by George Orwell, Aldous Huxley, Bertrand Russell, and by Irish writers such as Seán O'Faoláin and Brendan Behan (*Borstal Boy*), but not Joyce.★ Serious authors came to expect this fate, even to be proud of it, as Benedict Kiely said: 'You'd be damned near ashamed if you weren't banned . . . The only badge of honour you got in the old days was to be called "indecent" or "obscene".' Readers had to buy their copies of the wicked books in Britain or the North, then smuggle them through the customs.

In 1940 Seán O'Faoláin began a concerted campaign against the censorship laws through the pages of his influential magazine *The Bell*, and this gradually stimulated a public debate. But in the 1960s several serious writers were still being penalized. In 1965 John McGahern's second novel, *The Dark*, was banned, an admittedly outspoken book, anticlerical, that had the word 'fuck' on the first page and a description of a boy masturbating: McGahern was

---

★ Curiously, neither *Ulysses* nor any other of Joyce's works were ever formally banned in Ireland, even when *Ulysses* could not be published in Britain or the United States. The original Paris edition was not widely on sale, but it could be imported; the Censorship Board does not take action on a book unless the public lodges protests, and this did not happen in Joyce's case, perhaps because he was known to be an Irish genius. However, the Church sometimes did its own censorship. At Clongowes College (see p. 214), which Joyce described so sharply in *Portrait of the Artist as a Young Man*, the Jesuits in charge would sometimes confiscate pupils' copies, even as late as the 1960s, and his name could not be spoken. Today his picture hangs in the school, and the book is on the State examinations syllabus.

sacked from his job in a Church-run school and went to live in London. As for Edna O'Brien, '*The Country Girls* [1960] and five of my other early novels were banned,' she told me. 'I was made to feel a leper in my native Clare village, where the parish priest burned some of the books. But today all is changed and I'm admired and idolized in Clare.' By the 1960s there was growing pressure to ease the censorship, even from a few liberal-minded clergy; Irish society was by now opening out to the modern world, and the frank TV programmes and films available to viewers via the BBC were beginning to make nonsense of the restrictions on books. So finally in 1967 the Government produced legislation that modified the rules somewhat curiously: any banned book could now be removed from the Index after a period of twelve years. Thus in one fell swoop some 5,000 titles were reprieved, including works by Joyce and others, and a sorry chapter in Irish cultural history was brought virtually to an end.

Today the Censorship Board still exists but it keeps a lower profile, and no worthwhile book by an Irish writer has been banned for over fifteen years; the recent novels of Dermot Bolger, for instance, contain lurid sex descriptions that could never have been published thirty years ago. The Board's main concern today is with visually 'obscene' material. Few liberals object to its policy of keeping crude porn magazines out of Ireland (even *Playboy* is excluded); but there was a fuss recently when it banned Thames & Hudson's illustrated *Erotic Art of India*. Also contestable is the continued banning of some educational books that treat sexual matters explicitly, such as Alex Comfort's *The Joy of Sex*. However, even before the 1992 referendum, novels dealing with abortion could be published, so long as they did not give practical advice.

The 1992 Act dealt solely with publications: other arts and media have never been subject to formal censorship. However, in a few extreme cases the authorities have taken action. In the theatre, the main *cause célèbre* concerned the 1957 Dublin production of Tennessee Williams's *The Rose Tattoo*, whose producer, Alan Simpson, was arrested and charged with 'presenting for gain an indecent and profane performance'. This charge was later quashed by a district court, but the play itself was taken off. Apart from this, the theatre has been little afflicted by censorship; even back in 1955 Cyril Cusack was able to stage Seán O'Casey's anticlerical play *The Bishop's Bonfire* for five weeks, though a production of *'Bloomsday'*, a dramatized version of *Ulysses*, was prevented by the Archbishop of Dublin. In television, RTE is today just about as liberal as the BBC or ITV. In the cinema, films are occasionally banned – recently, Ken Russell's *Whore*, and the Hollywood movie *Bad Lieutenant* for its scene of the rape of a Catholic nun in church. Scorsese's *The Last Temptation of Christ* was permitted, but only with a preface by the director explaining that the film was not based on the Gospels but on some Greek book. In cases like these involving religion, the Church will sometimes put pressure behind the scenes, and is able to brandish a clause in the 1937 Constitution that makes blasphemy a punishable offence. But the main thrust of censorship has always been against sex, notably homosexuality; here, as over birth control, the Church has now tacitly backed down and accepted that the battle is lost.

Ireland today is one of the very few democracies that still has a law permitting censorship of books; the Censorship Board can still get them banned for up to twelve years, and a handful of foreign authors are still on this index. But gone are the days when many Irish novels could be published and sold only abroad. And this new freedom has possibly helped to enliven today's vigorous literary scene – unless one is to take the opposite view that creativity flourishes best under oppression, and that Joyce, O'Faoláin and others might never have written so well, had they not been inspired to rebel against a certain Ireland and its ethos.

Dublin's new-wave novelists, Derry's poets and playwrights

Whence comes this exceptional Irish gift for literature and language, this facility with words and stories both spoken and written? Maybe it relates to the Celtic imagination – to the old isolation and poverty of a peasant race who came to people their majestic landscape with spirits, ghosts and mythical heroes, and to weave tales around them for telling by the firesides on winter nights; the Celts of Wales and Brittany have similar traditions, a similar if lesser eloquence. The old Irish language contains a richness and idiomatic vividness which have infiltrated the English that the Irish speak, lending it qualities absent from standard English. And many people with little formal education will often possess a rich and wide vocabulary, a sense of anecdote, wit, and quirky phrasing. The Irish playwrights, Synge, O'Casey and others, have caught this well. It is part of the heritage of any Irish writer.

As I suggested earlier, it is also true that literature tends to enjoy a special prominence, as a focus of national identity, in a colonial or post-colonial society. The philosopher Richard Kearney has pointed out that the Gaelic revival of the Yeats period helped to create a nationalist/rural literary tradition, with books relating to the countryside and the old Irish values; and this was later balanced by a modernist/urban/realist tradition, deriving from Joyce and O'Casey (Joyce, for all his innovative style, was a great realist). These two traditions continue today, even if much of the writing on rural themes is no longer noticeably nationalist.

In the first decades after independence, not only did the censorship deter many writers from dealing with the very personal worlds of adolescence, love and marriage, but the new full Irish nationhood drew them to concentrate primarily on themes of Irishness and the Irish experience. The influential Cork novelist Daniel Corkery had pronounced that Irish literature, to be considered truly Irish, must deal with three themes: the land, religion and nationalism. And as if in response to this, leading writers such as O'Flaherty, O'Faoláin, Frank O'Connor, Mary Lavin and Patrick Kavanagh wrote above all about being Irish in rural or small-town Ireland. O'Flaherty was something of an ardent nationalist whereas O'Faoláin, O'Connor and Kavanagh focused attention on the narrow, repressed mediocrity of provincial Ireland, the reality behind the de Valera ideals. But all wrote on these very 'Irish' themes, rather than more universal ones.

Most of these writers and some later ones too, notably William Trevor, have excelled above all in the short story. In fact, the novel as a major literary form came relatively late to Ireland. Its early practitioners tended to be women of the Anglo-Irish gentry who had the leisure for it – Maria Edgeworth, Somerville and Ross, and later Molly Keane and Elizabeth Bowen – and only with Joyce was the long narrative novel fully established. Why this Irish preference for the short story? Two standard explanations are usually given. The first, surely true, is that it springs from folk culture, from the strong Irish oral tradition of the local *seanchaí* or *seannachie* (storyteller). Second, that Ireland had no indigenous urban bourgeoisie or stratified provincial society to provide the material that inspired the great nineteenth-century novels of England, France and Russia. William Trevor told me that he shared both views: 'I certainly feel more at home myself with the short story, I think my stories are better than my novels. It's something to do with the *seanchaí* tradition, yes, the Irish love of anecdote. Also with the fact that when the novel arrived, Ireland wasn't ready for it; the civilized writing and reading of novels of the Balzac or Trollope kind was alien in this uneasy, still largely peasant society. And while the Irish are witty and expressive, they lack the intellectual stamina for the long, philosophical, analytical novel of the Thomas Mann kind. They soon run out of steam: you see it even in their football techniques!' From another writer I heard a more quirky explanation: 'It's the influence of weekly confession before Mass, which rubs out all sins and so you have to start again. No plot can last longer than a week.'

In the 1960s, new young writers began to reject the 'Irishness' of the O'Flaherty generation and to turn back to more universal themes of private human experience. They were helped by the new liberal climate and by the waning of censorship, even if at first some of them fell foul of it. Edna O'Brien, Trevor and McGahern were the forerunners. O'Brien's *The Country Girls* may not be a 'great' novel, but it was something of a breakthrough in Irish fiction, the first time that a woman writer had dealt so candidly with adolescent female sexuality, in a setting of rural bigotry. 'I'm interested in love, not in what it is to be Irish,' she told me, 'and I write about the human condition, not about Ireland. The main influence on me has been Chekhov, and my style is partly modelled on his.' Trevor, whose best stories are nearly all about sensitive provincial misfits, yearning for fulfilment, spoke to me similarly: 'I have a nostalgia for the Ireland of my youth, but I don't really think of myself as an "Irish" writer. Stories like *Reading Turgenev* could be set in any rural society, such as France: I was trying to say something about the position of women in those days in that kind of narrow milieu, not about Ireland.' Indeed, that story's heroine is a nicer Emma Bovary.

As for John McGahern, unlike Trevor and O'Brien who have moved to England, he has returned to live in his *pays* of remote rural Leitrim, where his father was a police sergeant. There he set what is probably his best novel, *Amongst Women* (1990), an austere but compassionate study of a stubborn old patriarch farmer and his tender–tyrannical relations with his wife and daughters, in the 1950s. McGahern is a modest, gentle, quietly witty man. As we drank in his local pub at Mohill, Co. Leitrim, he told me of his view of Ireland as a network of independent republics, each one a family (see p. 204): 'My novels are about power and control within the family. It is a universal theme, which applies to many societies, and *Amongst Women* has been popular in France. If I use a Leitrim setting, it's because this is the place I know and can describe best.' But this seems a shade disingenuous. The human themes of these writers may indeed be universal; but this does not prevent the settings, and the particular nature of family and social life, from being vividly and identifiably Irish – and that is part of the strength of these books. No one could be more Irish than the old republican farmer in *Amongst Women*, proud of his land, endlessly telling his rosaries, cursing and protecting his daughters. All these three novelists have been writing about the remembered rural Ireland of their childhood, and it belongs to them as surely as Normandy does to Flaubert or Dorset to Hardy.

These writers are all realists of everyday life, easy to read. A novelist of a very different kind, a unique figure in Ireland today, is John Banville. He is much more intellectual, and his work is full of metaphor and complex ideas, written in an ultra-fastidious aesthetic style. Some of his books are set in Ireland, but the best are those that probe deep into the minds of great European

243

scientists and mathematicians, notably Copernicus and Kepler; in fact, though he lives in Dublin and is literary editor of the *Irish Times*, Banville sees himself as essentially a European writer, and his work may have more in common with experimental French fiction than with Irish realism. For my own taste, his books are too fanciful and overwrought, but critics consider him Ireland's greatest living novelist, and at least it is unusual and refreshing to find a Dublin intellectual so involved in Europe! He is no sufferer of fools gladly, and there are those who personally find him arrogant, prickly, and too clever by half. Certainly he likes to speak his mind. He told a television interviewer: 'The artist's only responsibility is to create masterpieces, he has *no* duty to society. I wanted to get away from "Irish" themes or from having to comment on Ireland today. People regard my books as Gothic extravaganzas, but I see them as realism; one has only to go down the street to see how full of Gothic extravagance life is. I think of my novels as sonnet sequences, and I may spend up to a year writing the first paragraph.'

At the end of 1980s there burst upon the scene the so-called 'new urban working–class realists', an assortment of gifted young writers very Irish in their eloquence and sensibility, but also very modern. They have caused quite a stir. The best-known names are Dermot Bolger, Roddy Doyle, and Ferdia Mac Anna, their self-appointed spokesman; Sarah Berkeley, Katie O'Donovan and Michael O'Loughlin are amongst the others, with Joseph O'Connor and Colm Tóibín on the sidelines. Many of them have gravitated around the Raven Arts Press, the pioneering little publishing firm which Bolger runs from a tiny flat above an off-licence in a workaday district of North Dublin.

Not all of these writers are in fact working-class (Mac Anna's father was an Abbey Theatre director) and not all are full-blown realists: Bolger's poetical, allegorical treatment of Dublin is a world away from Doyle's racy comic repartee. But what most of them have in common is a rejection alike of the novel of rural life, the 'Dublin 4' novel of bourgeois manners, and the so-called 'literary' novel (i.e. Banville, even Joyce): they see themselves as very different from the older McGahern generation, and as giving expression to the new world of the poorer suburbs and 'the harsh realities of modern urban disillusionment', in Mac Anna's phrase. He told me: 'We are in revolt against the snobbish Dublin literary establishment, and they don't like us either, they consider us non-literary.' In his apocalyptic article 'The Dublin Renaissance' for the *Irish Review* of spring 1991, he wrote of these mould-breakers:

'They saw Dublin not as some ancient colonial backwater full of larger-than life "characters" boozing their heads off in stage-Irish pubs, but as a troubled modern entity, plagued by drugs, unemployment, high taxes and emigration. No city of the "Rare Ould Times" here. Instead, Bolger and O'Loughlin painted a portrait of a Dublin that was being choked by the modern world, its youth in turmoil and its older citizens crippled by despair . . . Theirs is a literary landscape dominated by neon-lit amusement arcades, four-in-one cinema complexes, greasy chippers, garish video bars and dingy basement flats where lives of poverty, violence and squalor are played out to a soundtrack of rock music and TV babble. Anyone expecting a Dublin of garrulous chancers and Joycean characters will be either disappointed or shocked – or both.'

Many Irish critics, however, point out that these writers are not making so radical a break with the past as they might think: they owe quite a debt to Joyce's own urban realism, even if they have shifted the milieu out to the suburbs and down the social scale a notch or two. But like so many Irish writers of the past sixty years, they have felt inhibited by the giant shadow of Joyce. Neil Jordan, now in his mid-forties, who wrote some excellent novels and stories ('Night in Tunisia', etc) before turning to film-making, has said, 'Every Irish writer has to devise his or her own stratagem to avoid the crippling influence of Joyce. My ultimate stratagem was to start writing films instead.' Or to quote again the ever-pungent Mac Anna: 'There was a major myth inhibiting Dublin's artistic and literary development. The myth's name was James Joyce and it made writers feel that anything that could or should have been written about Dublin had already been penned by the man himself . . . [who] had hijacked the city and imprisoned it in his writing . . . In short, he intimidated the bejazus out of the

Dublin writers of the sixties, seventies and eighties . . . *Ulysses*, you could say, is a nightmare from which Dublin is trying to awake . . . Perhaps it is no coincidence that nowadays most Dubliners choose not to read *Ulysses*, just as most Irish Catholics choose not to read the Bible. It saves all the hassle.'

Mac Anna is an amusing bloke who works as an RTE television producer and has made comic films based on Shakespeare, with such titles as *Hamlet and Her Brothers*. He wrote a short, moving book about his recovery from cancer, *Bald Head*, then made his name with *The Last of the High Kings*, a satiric semi-autobiographical novel that led to comparisons with Salinger – the enjoyable if rather too joky portrait of a crazy middle-class family in a Dublin suburb. Its teenage adolescent hero is torn between the old Irish nationalist world represented by his over-the-top pro-IRA mother, and the new Anglo-American pop and rock culture that he shares with his friends. 'The two are not incompatible and one can have both,' Mac Anna told me; 'I am not one of those who see Irish culture as under some sinister threat from modern pop culture, for this too is Ireland.' And if it is, then maybe the exuberant young 'soul' musicians of Doyle's *The Commitments* are an illustration of it.

Roddy Doyle's best-selling novels are very much a celebration of the North Dublin working class, but he himself is lower-middle-class by background. For fourteen years, until 1993, he taught in a community school in the suburb of Kilbarrack, the 'Barrytown' of his books – the rows of little houses where unwed Sharon Rabbitte giggled through her pregnancy in *The Snapper*, the tower block beside fields where Jimmy Rabbitte Jnr watched a horse being taken up in the lift in *The Commitments*. This book sold little at first, but was then boosted to fame and fortune by Alan Parker's smash-hit film version. There followed two other sagas of the Rabbitte family, *The Snapper* and *The Van*, and then *Paddy Clarke Ha Ha Ha*, an acute portrait of life as seen by a ten-year-old, with brilliantly authentic dialogue and a sad undercurrent of marital breakup (it won the 1993 Booker Prize). Doyle's books have very little narrative or physical description but plenty of quick-fire demotic dialogue – a technique that has its limitations and makes them read a bit like film scripts. In fact, some critics have unkindly suggested that this is what he must have had in mind, for two of his books have made fine films. Doyle explained to me: 'I'm not interested in what things or people look like, I see life in terms of dialogue, and I believe that people *are* their talk.' He is a quiet, polite, reflective man, not at all like his earthly boisterous characters with their endless expletives. He gives a warm, funny and affectionate picture of the North Dublin scene, and he captures well the gut vitality of the Irish. But it is all rather too rosy-tinted, even sentimental at times. It is hard to believe that a raped pregnant eighteen-year-old or out-of-work teenagers would take their plight quite so cheerfully: these books dwell little on the darker side of modern urban life, on the pain and anxiety suppressed behind the verbal euphoria. 'I'm an optimist,' says Roddy Doyle Ha Ha Ha. However, his TV Series *The Family* (1994), also set in North Dublin, finally revealed a more sombre vein.

If neither Doyle nor Mac Anna deal directly in their books with the 'harsh realities' that Mac Anna himself referred to, this is not true of some of the other young writers – and notably Dermot Bolger. Born a year later than Doyle, in 1959, and the son of a seaman, Bolger has spent his life amid the sprawling new North Dublin housing estates of Finglas (see p. 131), where he has set his lyrical yet baleful novels. Of the first two, *Night Shift* and *The Woman's Daughter*, the latter was an incantatory poetical study of incest and loneliness, switching to and fro in time, as a young girl tries to come to terms with her mysterious past and the desolating life of modern suburbia. Then in 1990 came his masterpiece, *The Journey Home*, the powerful story of a young man's odyssey through modern Dublin, across a landscape of political corruption, drugs, drunken parties, unemployment and oppressive office life, till finally he escapes to a rural refuge of older, wiser values. It is Bolger's vision of the eroding impact of the city on newcomers from the country, and the loss of an older, more dignified order, amid the wasteland of Euro-consumerism. *The Journey Home* has been one of the most talked-about of recent Irish novels, and it divided the critics. Some found it all too over-the-top, the panorama too bleakly pessimistic, the pleading too special, the lyricism too strained; and certainly the portrait of the evil Plunkett family of political tycoons, masters of corruption, cruelty and sexual depravity, strays blatantly into caricature. But despite its realistic settings, the novel is intended as epic allegory. Frank Delaney called it 'the most remarkable book' to come out of Ireland 'in the last fifteen or twenty years'; some other critics were equally full of praise, and I would agree. Its impact is hypnotic, terrific − a stunningly ambitious book whose excesses can be forgiven.

Bushy-bearded and bohemian, Bolger is a friendly, wistful, gentle character, quite unpretentious. He took me around Finglas, showing me the precise locations for the book, the tiny flat above a betting-shop that he had in mind as his hero's 'pad', the assertive dual-carriageways that cut off the new housing from the farmland just beyond. In print, he is ferocious against much in modern Ireland; he is also in revolt against the Dublin literary establishment. But in their style and approach his books are much less 'anti-literary' than, say, Doyle's. The poetic effects, the sense of poetic myth, are literary; and though he repudiates nationalism, his yearning for older, uncorrupted non-urban values brings him back in a way to the Yeats tradition. As he told me, this was inspired by a bizarre early influence on him: when he was fifteen he ran away from home and by chance met an elderly lady of the Anglo-Irish gentry, the astonishing Sheila Fitzgerald, a kind of female guru or wise hippy, full of freethinking ecological sanity, living alone in a caravan in the West. It was she who first introduced him to books and ideas, befriended him and encouraged him to write. Later, he put her into *The Journey Home* ('She is the only real person in the book'), as the wise old lady in a caravan near Sligo who protects and comforts his hero Hano after his flight from the awful city. Bolger sent me to see her − and so in 1992 I found her still living alone in her caravan, a tiny, frail but chirpy 88-year-old, amid a colony of hippy artists beside a building-site near Wexford. Such is Ireland.

Bolger summed up his views on the book: 'I see *The Journey Home* as a kind of a fable, as psychic history of Dublin in the 1980s. People call it a political novel, which certainly it is in the sense that it pinpoints abuses in modern Irish society, including political corruption. But it has nothing in common with the old nationalist political literature. Nationalism and "Irishness" do not interest me – even if my books *are* very much about Ireland. And what is Irishness anyway? A novel set on a Finglas motorway is every bit as Irish as one set in Connemara featuring some half-mad priest. Or as *Dancing at Lughnasa*.'

These varied new authors may not be to all tastes. But they give proof of the ongoing vitality of Irish writing today. Most of them seem obsessed with Dublin life, maybe too much so. Bolger's Raven Arts Press has published a whole book, *Invisible Dublin*, made up of essays by new writers about their home suburbs, including Doyle on Kilbarrack, Mac Anna on Howth, O'Loughlin on Glasnevin Cemetery, Bolger's sister June Considine on Finglas – but not a word about Dublin 4 or smart Killiney. At least it makes a change from all the Joycean nostalgia about St Stephen's Green.

A few other writers live out in the provinces, for example John McGahern in his native Leitrim, the playwright John B. Keane in his native Kerry, Brian Friel in Donegal near his native Derry. But more of them have emigrated, in the old tradition. Despite the waning of the old intolerant climate, they can still find this the best way of preserving their inspiration to write about Ireland – like Joyce himself, who said, 'The shortest way to Tara is via the mail-boat to Holyhead.' Wilde and Shaw, both Anglo-Irish Protestants, moved early to England. Samuel Beckett, also a Protestant, moved to Paris. In more recent times, the Belfast-born novelist Brian Moore emigrated to Canada, and William Trevor to England at the age of thirty-two. 'I might never have written a word, had I not left,' he told me in his quiet Devon home; 'I love Ireland, but I'd be too pressurized there by local society, people are all on the top of each other wanting to know your business. Here in England one can be more private.' Edna O'Brien, who lives in Chelsea, said much the same: 'People say to me, "How can you write about Ireland if you don't live there?", and I say, "How could I write about it if I *did* live there?" The Irish are too gossipy, curious, gregarious. If I lived in a house like this in Dublin, they'd be knocking at the door all the time. But I still go back often to my roots in Clare; they nourish me, unlike London, which I don't like.'

Indeed nowadays, with air travel, television work and greater affluence, the old definitive emigration of the Joycean kind has turned to something more like commuting. The novelist and film-writer Shane Connaughton divides his time between Kentish Town and a house near Dublin; the young Joseph O'Connor (brother of Sinead), author of an excellent first novel about the London pop scene, *Cowboys and Indians*, is similarly at home in both cities, while Colm Tóibín has lived in Barcelona, the setting for his novel *South*. And Séamus Heaney's part-time professorships at Harvard and Oxford woo him away from his Dublin 4 seaside home.

Heaney is the best-known living poet of a nation that takes its poetry seriously and gives its poets a high profile; some of them become household names. The Irish buy more poetry books per capita than any other English-speaking country and recently a cottage industry has developed of tiny firms turning out slim volumes of verse; a new one appears almost every week. Many of the writers are women, turning to private themes of love, family or nature; satire and social comment are rarer. In summer, poetry festivals are popular, such as the annual Merriman summer school in Clare (see p. 299), and the famous Yeats Summer School in Sligo, where the Irish sociably rub shoulders with American college girls, earnest Japanese, and German scholars explaining why Yeats contested Rilke's view of death.

It is the abiding prestige and charisma of Yeats, great nationalist public figure as well as inspiring, ever-quotable poet, that has done much to maintain so high a status for poetry in Ireland – even if hardly any of today's verse comes anywhere near to his own level of terrible beauty. In the generation after his, the dominant figure was Patrick Kavanagh, a wonderful lyricist with a strong social compassion, whose masterpiece *The Great Hunger* (1942), set in his homeland of Co. Monaghan, told of the dreary and frustrated lives of the poor farmers of that time. Of Kavanagh's contemporaries, probably the best poet was Austin Clarke. They have been followed more recently by Thomas Kinsella, John Montague, Paul Durcan and others, plus a number of good poets from the North (see below) including Heaney. Kinsella, born in 1928 into a working-class Dublin home, wrote some excellent early poetry about his boyhood there; he has since moved into a more obscure and experimental mode, becoming something of a poet's poet, but he keeps his following. He now lives and teaches in Philadelphia – another voluntary semi-exile. Paul Durcan, born 1944, is a self-styled public poet who believes in writing verse on public topical themes, rather in the manner of Allen Ginsberg, and he turns out a poem a day. Raw, direct, often very funny, his work is derided as too journalistic by some critics, but he is the best-selling Irish poet today, after Heaney.

Seamus Heaney has become a cult figure with a large worldwide reputation, now contested by some critics. Personally he is a delightful, warm teddy-bear of a man, and an urbane and gifted speaker. He was born in 1929 in Co. Londonderry, son of a Catholic farmer; and his earlier poems, in the much praised *Death of a Naturalist* volume, tenderly evoke his boyhood there, the life of the farm, the closeness to nature and its changing moods; some critics have raised comparisons with Wordsworth. Since then, moving to Belfast, Dublin and America, Heaney seems to have been groping for other themes, not always so fruitfully. His verse has become more spare, cool and astringent, no longer so lyrical and seldom very quotable. Some poems express his pained bewilderment at the violence in his troubled homeland, his political concern at odds with his artist's hesitancy to become too closely involved, as in the enigmatic lines:

> I am neither internee nor informer
> An inner émigré, grown long-haired
> And thoughtful; a wood-kerne
> Escaped from the massacre . . .

Heaney was taken up by the London critics and media, then by the American ones, and was idolized into an icon. Since 1984 he has held the prestigious Boylston professorship at Harvard, and in 1989 he won the chair of poetry at Oxford. Robert Lowell called him the 'the best Irish poet since Yeats', and for Professor John Carey of Oxford he is simply 'the greatest living poet'. Of the ten books written about him, only two have been by Irish writers: but now just a few Dublin critics have begun to question his reputation and the reasons for it. One of them described his verse as hard to penetrate, unmusical, and therefore seldom quoted. It has also been suggested, probably with some truth, that 'the Northern Ireland factor' is at the root of the Anglo-American cult of Heaney. In other words, his warm personal qualities, his charms as a speaker, the appeal of his early verse, have all swelled his reputation; but so has his role as the foremost poetic voice from the tragic North. The media always love a war poet, even one so discreet and oblique as Heaney.

Much more direct and memorable verse came, in pre-Troubles days, from a greater Ulster poet, Louis MacNeice, born in Belfast in 1907. He was a Protestant, and spent most of his life in England. But he always felt close to his Irish roots, and he retained an exasperated, critical affection for his native land – as witness this famous passage from *Autumn Journal* (1938), four lines of which I quoted right at the start of this book:

> Why should I want to go back
>   To you, Ireland, my Ireland?
> The blots on the page are so black
>   That they cannot be covered with shamrock.
> I hate your grandiose airs,
>   Your sob-stuff, your laugh and your swagger,
> Your assumption that everyone cares
>   Who is king of your castle.
> Castles are out of date,
>   The tide flows round the children's sandy fancy;
> Put up what flag you like, it is too late
>   To save your soul with bunting.
> *Odi atque amo* . . .

Northern Ireland has produced a remarkable number of good writers in the past fifty or so years. Among poets, Derek Mahon, Paul Muldoon, Michael Longley and Tom Paulin, as well as

Heaney. Among playwrights, Frank McGuinness (born in Donegal) and Ann Devlin, as well as Brian Friel. Among novelists, Benedict Kiely and Brian Moore. Jennifer Johnston is a Protestant Dubliner who has moved to the North, now living with her husband outside Derry; and while many of her novels deal with the decline of the Anglo-Irish gentry in the South, she has also explored the impact of the Troubles, for example in *Shadows on Our Skin*, set in Derry.

Several of these writers have taken the reverse route, away from the North, to settle either abroad or in the Republic (Heaney, Mahon, Kiely and the poet and critic Séamus Deane). But whether they go or stay, many are still vexed by the dilemma of whether they have some moral duty to write about the North's conflict, or can honourably ignore it and withdraw into other themes – into what Mahon has called his 'palace of porcelain'. If they ignore the conflict, might they be accused of cowardice and irresponsibility? But if they write about it too readily, might they appear to be opportunistically exploiting dramatic, saleable material? – in an Ulster where, in the nationalist poet Paul Muldoon's witty phrase, life is 'nasty, British and short'. Some writers hesitate because, amid the North's strong tribal pressures, they do not want to be sucked into becoming mere mouthpieces for one side or the other; whatever their private loyalties, they want to keep an artistic independence. This may explain why there is not more direct writing about the Troubles.

However, matters may be changing with a younger generation: Belfast's enterprising Blackstaff Press recently published a 346-page anthology of poems on the Troubles. And several good new writers have been appearing on the quite lively Belfast cultural scene (see p. 435). Among them, Robert McLiam Wilson went to England and wrote a very stylish novel, *Ripley Bogle*, about being a down-and-out in London. I met him at a literary party in Belfast, where his vision of his native land had a touch of MacNeice: 'I have the perfect credit card, I'm a West Belfast Catholic. But I'm fed up with the Irish, north and south – with their obsessive navel-gazing, sectarianism, distortions of the truth. So I left for England, studied at Cambridge, wrote two novels *not* about Ireland. But now here I am, back again, and I *am* working on a novel set in Belfast. So you see.'

The major intellectual venture in the North in recent years has been the pro-nationalist Field Day operation, based in Derry. This was founded in 1980 by Brian Friel and the Belfast actor Stephen Rea; the poets Heaney, Paulin and Seamus Deane joined too, and the musician David Hammond, all forming a knot of close friends. Field Day began excitingly as a small radical theatre company, putting on plays in Derry and other local towns and taking them to Belfast and Dublin; it premièred some interesting new Irish plays, notably Friel's *Translations*. Then it turned also to publishing, with a series of pamphlets on political and social issues that aimed to look at the North's problem in fresh ways, from a standpoint of moderate nationalism. 'This aroused a lot of hostility,' Professor Deane told me; 'some people called us old-style out-of-date nationalists, others even dubbed us the cultural avant-garde of the IRA, which was nonsense.'

The group's next project was the highly ambitious *Field Day Anthology of Irish Writing*, edited by Deane – a 4,000-page work that embraced writing of every kind across 1,500 years, forming a kind of parallel history of Ireland. Appearing in 1991, it at once drew a sharp critical broadside from an intellectual of Protestant origin, the acerbic Edna Longley of Queen's University (wife of the gentler Michael Longley, see p. 436). She charged the anthology with excessive nationalism, while Dublin feminists joined the fray to accuse it also of sexism, pointing out that it had no women on its 21-member editorial board, and claiming that modern women writers were shockingly under-represented in its pages. There followed a resounding public duel between Longley and Deane, mirroring the Protestant/Catholic tensions of the North. 'Edna's a suffragette, too aggressive and a bit paranoid,' said one Field Day member. 'We ourselves hardly care what she says. But it's true that we should have had some women on board.' So Field Day set about making amends, with an extra volume edited just by women, and including just women writers.

It was the noisiest Irish literary row for many years. By the time it subsided, Field Day had run into worse difficulties, for other reasons. The quality of its new plays and productions was falling off; and the business-minded Friel seemed to be losing interest in the venture he had created. In 1990 he gave *Dancing at Lughnasa* to the Abbey Theatre in Dublin for its initial production, because he knew they could do it better; it was the first time in ten years that a new Friel play had not been premièred by Field Day, and it caused a rift between him and Stephen Rea. By 1993, with the Arts Councils of Belfast and Dublin withdrawing their support, Field Day's whole future was in doubt. Despite a certain cliquey élitism, it had been a valuable venture; but its distinguished leaders had better fish to fry. Rea himself had just won international stardom from his role in Neil Jordan's film *The Crying Game*.

Brian Friel, Ireland's major living playwright, is seen by many critics as the equal of Synge or O'Casey. Although he is politically committed and his plays deal with social themes, he is himself a very private man, rarely giving interviews or making public statements; and so he can be assessed only via his work, which can be enigmatic, even contradictory. He was born in Omagh, Co. Tyrone, the son of a teacher; the family then moved to Derry, where he attended the same Catholic college as John Hume, and like Hume was moulded by the political tensions of Derry at that time and the nationalist hatreds of Unionist injustice (see p. 380). Friel went to Maynooth College to prepare to be a priest, but gave it up after two and a half years, describing it later as 'an awful experience, it nearly drove me cracked' (priests do not emerge in a good light in his plays). He turned to writing short stories, then plays, which now number sixteen. He lives quietly by the sea at Moville, Co. Donegal, across the border from Derry, and has set many of his plays in his adored Donegal.

In one of his rare comments on his own work, Friel has said that his plays are concerned with 'man in society, in conflict with community, government, academy, church, family – and essentially in conflict with himself'. One could add that while some of his plays are set in the past, it is a mythical rather than a realistic past (e.g. *Translations*), and that he uses the past to illumine the present. Like so many Irish writers, he is concerned with the impact of history; but also with the power of myth and of

255

language. This 'private man with a public message' is exploring the condition of Ireland; and the themes that re-emerge are those of emigration, loneliness, the breakdown of authority, the individual dislocated from family or society, generally in the setting of remote rural communities – the imaginary Donegal village of Ballybeg that he uses again and again.

It was *Philadelphia Here I Come* (1964) that first made his name: theatrically powerful and original, full of flashing eloquence, it is the study of a young man driven to emigrate by the impossibilities of communicating with his psychically paralysed father. 'The horrifyingly stupefied condition of the Irish social and political world which it also revealed was treated almost as a foil to the brilliant chat of Gar O'Donnell' (the hero), Séamus Deane has written. There followed two plays dealing indirectly with the Troubles, which drew accusations from some English and American critics that Friel was being sympathetic to the IRA. But he then disconcerted them by turning to a completely non-political theme for *Faith Healer* (1979), which many consider his greatest play; composed of four monologues, it is a tragedy about a miracle healer.

Translations (1980), also greatly admired, is a kind of parable set in the Donegal of the 1830s, where a hedge-school teacher fluent in Latin and Greek is trying to come to terms with the pragmatic English occupying forces. Its themes are the death of the Irish language at that time, the eternal misunderstandings between the Irish and the English, and generally the failure of language to provide real communication. Lastly, *Dancing at Lughnasa* is slighter and less intellectually complex than his earlier masterpieces, but is perhaps his warmest and most enjoyable play, and has proved his biggest popular success around the world. Its five Donegal sisters of the 1930s, their dreams, their unfulfilled hopes, their courage, their wild dancing, provided audiences with the most vivid theatrical image of rural Ireland since Synge's *Playboy*. And the initial Dublin production of 1990 did at least something to restore the ailing fortunes of the Abbey Theatre.

The Abbey and Gate theatres – and new playboys in the Western world

Quite a high proportion of the best playwrights of the British Isles have come from Ireland – starting with Congreve and Farquhar in Restoration times, then moving on via Goldsmith and Sheridan to Wilde and Shaw, all of them Protestants who later settled in England. Dublin's own native theatre did not begin to flourish until early this century, with the founding of the Abbey Theatre and the plays of Yeats and Synge. Since then it has produced O'Casey and the maverick Brendan Behan, true Dubliners; Samuel Beckett, also Dublin-born, preferred to live in Paris and even wrote in French, but the Irish claim him as their own. And so on to the present day, and the work of Friel, Tom Murphy, Frank McGuinness and others.

This is the background to the Irish theatre's continued vitality today. Dublin may not be a major city for art or classical music, but it is very much a theatre city, with a big annual drama festival. Not only are the best new Irish plays seen around the world, but some of the Dublin productions are exported too, to London, New York or elsewhere – 'The English language is a big bonus for us, for example we're taking our *Godot* to Chicago,' said the Gate's director, Michael Colgan.

Dubliners take theatre seriously. If some new Irish play is a hit or a flop, or divides the critics, it is the talk of town more than in a larger city such as London. This reflects the cultural intimacy of Dublin, just as the vigour of the dialogue and acting reflects the Irish gift for language. And yet, by many modern European standards, this remains a very traditional theatre in its *mise-en-scène*. Its accent is on literary texts, ideas, poetry, strong acting, not on visual flourishes; and the clever innovative styles of French or German directors, such as Patrice Chereau or Peter Zadek, have had even less influence in Dublin than in London. Neither producers nor audiences care for the avant-garde. This has the advantage that the text is not mauled about but done straight and given its proper priority. No question, as in Zadek's *Othello* in Hamburg, of presenting Desdemona as a prostitute in a bikini – Synge's

Pegeen would never be treated like that! And yet, there are times when I have found myself wishing for a little more visual enchantment.

The scene is still dominated by the two main rival theatres, the Abbey and the Gate, with their different traditions. The Abbey was founded by Yeats and Lady Gregory, in the full flush of the Gaelic revival, to give a voice to an Irish culture which they felt was under-represented; and its prime mission has always been to present new Irish plays. Its première of Synge's *Playboy of the Western World*, in 1907, caused a famous riot. The Gate Theatre was created later, in 1928, by Micheál Mac Liammóir and Hilton Edwards, with the aim of introducing foreign work such as Ibsen's or Chekhov's to Dublin. With plays written in English, the Gate for example might concentrate on an Anglo-Irish writer such as Wilde, the Abbey on the Dublin vernacular of O'Casey. This, and the very public gay relationship of Mac Liammóir and Edwards, caused the two theatres to be called Sodom and Begorrah. Today, their distinct roles persist, with the nuance that the once-illustrious Abbey has run into trouble, while the Gate is flowering and probably has the higher standards of the two.

The Abbey, a rather ugly theatre in a drab area off O'Connell Street, has an Arts Council annual grant of some £2 million, five times that of the Gate. It holds the rank of National Theatre, with two of its board members appointed by the Taoiseach, but this semi-official status may be a dubious advantage. Most of its permanent company of actors have safe salaried jobs for life, like civil servants. One critic made an unkind comparison with the GDR's Berliner Ensemble under Brecht's widow in the 1980s, suggesting that the Abbey had similarly become ossified by too much official reverence. This was too harsh, but certainly the Abbey recently has lacked a coherent vision and management policy, and since 1985 seven different people have held the post of artistic director. The most notable was Gary Hynes, a gifted young woman who had created the remarkable Druid Theatre in Galway (see below). She defied the Irish dislike of the avant-garde by directing a non-naturalistic *Plough and the Stars*, with all the actors shaven-headed. Some critics applauded this clever reworking of an Irish classic, unusual for the Abbey, but many Dubliners were shocked. Hynes had some successes, for example an excellent new work by Tom Murphy, *Conversations on a Homecoming*: but another new play, by the novelist John McGahern, was a failure. Hynes was regularly castigated by the media, and in 1993 she left the Abbey, to be succeeded by Patrick Mason, one of Ireland's very best directors. It would not be fair to say that the Abbey's recent record has been entirely negative: its *Dancing at Lughnasa* was a brilliant success, as was its *Hedda Gabler* with an Irish cast led by Fiona Shaw. But it seems to have lost some of its old flair for stimulating new work by younger Irish playwrights.

The Gate Theatre, newly refurbished, has been doing very well lately under its enterprising director, the suave Michael Colgan. Its 1991 and 1992 seasons included *Tartuffe*, *The Cherry Orchard* and Brian Friel's reworking of *A Month in the Country*, as well as a Beckett festival. Dublin has a variety of other theatres too, including a lively fringe. These are poorly subsidized by the Arts Council, which is generous only to the Abbey; but they somehow survive, with the help of good audiences. The Passion Machine, a sympathetic new shoestring venture in North Dublin, has presented high-spirited new comedies of local working-class life, some of them by Roddy Doyle. The Project, in Temple Bar, is another small fringe theatre giving a voice to new writers. Here in 1992 I saw *Digging for Fire* by the young Dublin playwright Declan Hughes, who co-founded the Rough Magic company. His excellent play, which later came to London, is about young middle-class Dubliners trying to come to terms with modern life; one of the characters has AIDS, and there is some explicit talk about oral sex. As often with Irish theatre, I was struck by the ebullient sparkle of the dialogue, so different from the more reserved Pinter/Ayckbourn style. The play's director, Lynne Parker, from Belfast, gave me a philosophy that seemed to fit in with Mac Anna's and Bolger's: 'We have put on Brecht, Arthur Miller, and various new plays about modern Irish realities. But we are against all those sentimental rural plays in a pseudo-Synge tradition, set in the past. That applies even to *Lughnasa*.'

Apart from Friel, Ireland's best living playwrights include the popular Hugh Leonard, and J. B. Keane, the Kerry chronicler of strong rural dramas (*The Field*, etc): both are now in their mid-sixties. Tom Murphy, author of *Whistle in the Dark* and *The Gigli Concert*, has made penetrating realistic studies of Irish small-town life and the impact of emigration. Of the newer playwrights, the best is Frank McGuinness, a Catholic from the North whose plays often bear on its problems. His remarkable *Behold the Sons of Ulster Marching Towards the Somme* explored the motives that led loyalist volunteers to go to fight for England, equating the Germans with the hated Fenians back home. *Carthaginians*, equally powerful, dealt with the Bloody Sunday massacre in Derry. Billy Roche's realistic dramas of life in his home town of Wexford also show an interesting fresh talent.

Irish audiences tend to prefer Irish plays on Irish subjects – no surprise, in this somewhat self-absorbed society. Foreign plays do less well, unless the production is unusually brilliant, as in the case of the Abbey's *Hedda Gabler*. 'We still need to know what it is to be Irish, and where we come from,' suggested one critic, 'hence the success of all these plays about our rural past, like *Lughnasa*.' In Galway, the director of the Druid Theatre, Macliosa Stafford, made me the same point more strongly: 'The burden of Ireland's tragic past is what makes our theatre so rich, it gives fire to our work. Look at plays like Tom Murphy's *Famine*, it was like the Holocaust. And to write on these themes is to liberate yourself from the past, to overcome it.'

The creation of Galway's Druid has been quite a landmark, in a Republic where twenty years ago there was virtually no theatre outside Dublin, save for occasional tours. The little company was founded in 1975 by two local university students, one of them Gary Hynes, and they began to perform fresh versions of the Irish classics, plus modern plays. 'We had no theatre background, we had never seen Siobhan McKenna in the great roles,' Hynes told me, 'so we came to it all pure. When we did Synge's *Playboy*, we were very aware of our closeness to its setting, out there in the "Western world", and this helped us to get deep inside it. Without being avant-garde, we did some reinterpretation – for instance we played the Widow Quin as a young woman, which added to the pathos.' The Dublin critics at first ignored the Druid. But then in 1980 it took its *Playboy* to the Edinburgh Festival, where it won a prize, so Dublin sat up and took notice; and today it has quite a generous Arts Council grant, though it still performs in a converted warehouse, with no proper theatre. After Hynes left for the Abbey, Stafford took over, also steeped in the Gaelic west, a true Druid you might say, but internationally minded, too. 'We have just done a new Polish play on a rural theme, with a director from Poland,' he told me, 'but we transferred the setting and dialect to the west of Ireland, so as to help people to relate. I'm very interested in east European drama, we've done an Irish première of Vaclav Havel, and I certainly agree that the Dublin theatre is too Ireland-geared, too US- and UK-geared as well. But here we also do new Irish plays, by Murphy, McGuinness and others.' So the Druid, out in the romantic West beside the Gaeltacht, has today taken over something of the Abbey's role as a breeding-ground of Irish creativity. It is all quite exciting, in this small town that even has two other theatres.

There are now stirrings in just a few other towns, too, after a bleak period. Until the 1960s Ireland still had the so-called 'fit-ups', little groups of travelling players who would pitch their tent in some village or small town and offer rough-and-ready Shakespeare to the locals – as portrayed in the Hollywood film *The Playboys*, scripted by Shane Connaughton from memories of his Cavan boyhood. But the fit-ups were killed off by television, and for years there was nothing but theatrical wasteland in the counties that had inspired the dramas of Synge, Yeats, Keane, Friel and others. In the 1980s however, prompted by the success of the Druid, one regular company opened in Sligo and another in Waterford, the enterprising Red Kettle. Its young manager, T. V. Honan, told me: 'While the staid old Theatre Royal just does amateur and touring shows, *we* have introduced live professional theatre to this town. We have put on locally written plays about local life, for example one set in a jute factory, and these have been popular. We have also done everything from *Aeschylus* to *What the Butler Saw*, plus an American play about

Nazi persecution of homosexuals which our Irish audience found relevant.'

In the little Mayo town of Ballina, where Mary Robinson comes from, I found a great surprise – two highbrow Parisian actors, Pierre and Yvette Campos, he formerly with the Théâtre National Populaire, now running a modest company that performs in schools, discos, hotels. I was told locally that its standards are quite high. 'We came here on holiday, loved it, decided to stay, and started this venture in 1987,' said the Camposes. 'We can hardly make a living from our plays, so we claim support from the dole like small farmers. But we enjoy our work – even if local audiences are as conservative as in small French towns forty years ago. When we put on a feminist play with bawdy language and a wrestling-match between a man and a woman, people stayed away in droves. We have also done Molière, Cocteau and Ionesco. People of course prefer Irish rural comedies. But we refuse to pander too much to their taste, for we feel a sense of mission to bring real culture here.' Very Parisian – but also a plus for the new EU spirit of cultural exchange.

There is no regular theatre company in Limerick, nor even in Cork, whose current cultural crisis typifies the neglect of the arts in the provinces by State officialdom. The Arts Council is heavily Dublin-focused, and though it has been prompted into aiding the Druid Theatre, it pays little more than lip-service to any real policy of decentralization. Witness the sorry saga of the Cork ballet, in a city which has quite a musical tradition. A German family called Fleischmann settled there in the late nineteenth century, invited by the bishop to help improve church music, which they did. They also founded a choral society, a choral festival and symphony orchestra; and in the 1940s they encouraged a local dancer, Joan Denise Moriarty, to create a ballet school and *corps de ballet*, which in 1971 became the Irish National Ballet. It was Ireland's only ballet company, and it won State support and recognition. But by the late 1980s Dr Moriarty and Professor Aloys Fleischmann were both very old, and the company's audiences were falling off. The Arts Council abruptly cut off its subsidy, claiming that its policy was too highbrow. In reality, the

Council's board felt that Cork was the wrong place for a national ballet, which ought to be in Dublin; they were also under pressure from Taoiseach Haughey, the enemy of Cork (see p. 136). So the ballet, starved of funds, was forced to close. This broke Moriarty's heart, and she died in 1992. And the touchy people of Cork were left feeling bitterly that they had yet again been snubbed by Haughey and the Dublin centralizers. Nor has any new national ballet company yet been created in Dublin (though in 1994 the Arts Council began to discuss the matter).

Cork has other cultural problems, too. Its revered Opera House, no longer used for professional opera, has declined into a venue for a mixed assortment of local amateur shows, routine touring drama companies, plus a few saucy offerings such as male strippers. The City Corporation provides a subsidy, but neither city nor State will put up the money needed to restore it to its proper use, nor can they agree on what should be done. And since Fleischmann's death in 1993, the future of the symphony orchestra, an amateur body of fair quality, is also in doubt. But there is still plenty of other amateur musical activity, plus an art gallery, some small summer arts festivals, and two or three little theatres used for amateur or touring shows. This university city has large potential audiences for the arts: but neither the City Corporation, starved of funds, nor the Arts Council, aloof in Dublin, seems prepared to provide the help needed, in an age when culture cannot easily exist without subsidy. It is a disgrace for the Republic's proud Second City.

Dublin in the eighteenth century was quite an important musical centre, where Handel held the world première of the *Messiah* in 1842. Today that classical legacy finds echoes in the annual Wexford Opera Festival, a smart social event to which the Dublin 4 *beau monde* comes down in special trains, as to Glyndebourne. There are also opera seasons in Dublin, and concerts by the RTE's two orchestras. But classical music is not the Irish forte. This songful and musical nation prefers to put the accent on its own traditional music (see p. 277).

Creating an authentic Irish cinema

In the much younger world of cinema, Ireland has virtually no tradition of its own. And until recently it did little more than provide the scenic locations and folksy subject-matter for commercial films by visiting Hollywood or British directors, supplying world audiences with a saleably cosy view of Irishness. Thus David Lean set his blockbusting *Ryan's Daughter* on the Kerry coast, while John Ford portrayed a kind of never-never-land Ireland in *The Quiet Man*, a romantic comedy starring John Wayne. But not all foreigners' work was like this. On a much more serious level, John Huston's marvellous little film of Joyce's *The Dead*, although made in a studio in America, was authentic in its Joycean atmosphere. Then a very different Dublin appeared in the recent film versions of two of Roddy Doyle's novels, made by English directors – Alan Parker's *The Commitments* and Stephen Frears's *The Snapper*. Shot in real Dublin locations with real Dublin actors, these films did authentically capture a certain Dublin working-class exuberance. But their portrait was even more indulgent and rosy-tinted than in Doyle's books.

In an expensive medium like cinema, it may not be surprising that so small a country has never developed a native industry. The Government hitherto has shown only erratic interest; in 1981 it set up the Irish Film Board to develop the industry, then closed it down in 1987 as it was losing money. It has since created the Irish Film Centre, which opened in 1992 in Dublin's Temple Bar – in itself a worthwhile venture that may well help to stimulate film culture, but is not the same as financial aid. And hard-pressed Irish television (see below) has never had the funds to sponsor feature films as Channel 4 does in Britain. So young would-be film-makers have tended to go and work abroad. However, in 1993 the new Fianna Fáil/Labour coalition created a new Film Board, under the talented Leila Doolan, and promised enough funding to give it some teeth. She was given a modest £2·37 million budget for 1994, to be used for stimulating new production.

Even before this, just a few Irish directors had finally managed to find foreign financial backers to make real Irish films in Ireland: 'Green Grow the Rushes' was the euphoric heading of an article in the London *Independent* of February 1991, heralding what its author called 'a bit of a boomlet', as several promising new Irish films appeared in quick succession, including Jim Sheridan's *My Left Foot*, Neil Jordan's *The Miracle*, and Thaddeus O'Sullivan's *December Bride*.

For relatively low-budget and serious films of this kind, the producers have generally turned to Britain for their funding – Channel 4 and Granada TV have both been helpful – rather than to some Hollywood company that might try to impose its own stars and production values. Sheridan told me: 'Hollywood would never even have looked at a script for *My Left Foot* – what, a movie about a severely disabled person! Maybe it's just as well, for they might well have spoilt it.' And when Hollywood does get involved, the results can be all too predictable, as with *The Playboys*. This film was written by the excellent Shane Connaughton, who co-scripted *My Left Foot* and has published evocative novels about the rural Cavan of his boyhood. He and the director Gillies Mackinnon put themselves in the Samuel Goldwyn Company's hands for *The Playboys*, a romantic rustic drama which they set and shot in Connaughton's native village. The 1950s period detail was good. But, under the Goldwyn influence, plenty of cliché'd melodrama and Oirish whimsy crept in, slanted at the American market. 'Ireland is a place – at least in the movies – where more local colour is produced than can be consumed domestically,' was the wry comment of one London film critic; 'the blarney quotient of *The Playboys* is medium to high.'

The outstanding talent of the new Irish cinema is Neil Jordan's, but there are other names to watch as well. Their films are disparate, dealing with universal themes of childhood, rural pride and poverty, suffering, even terrorism. *My Left Foot* was based on Christie Brown's celebrated account of his Dublin working-class childhood as a victim of cerebral palsy, and how he taught himself to write with the toes of one foot. The film was faithful to the book, save that it made Brown's tortured diction easier to follow than it had been in real life. It was dominated by the hypnotic performance of Daniel Day-Lewis, who has some Irish roots, and for it he justly won an Oscar. It was a moving and powerful film, well directed by Jim Sheridan. But he then did less great things with *The Field*, taken from John B. Keane's play on the very Irish theme of an old farmer's ferocious attachment to his land, in 1930s Kerry. Here Sheridan attempted an epic grandeur which toppled over into the banal and heavy-handed. In 1993 he made *In the Name of the Father*, a study of the 'Guildford Four' wrongly convicted of pub bombings, with Day-Lewis in the role of Gerry Conlon. It won good reviews as a piece of film-making, but was criticized by some in Britain for being too sympathetic to the republicans, and in Ireland for distorting parts of the real story. To finance his films, Sheridan turned to Granada TV, while Channel 4 provided the modest budget needed for *December Bride*, an impressive first feature by the Dublin-born director Thaddeus O'Sullivan. This was an austere but luminous portrait of the lives of an isolated group of poor Protestant farmers in Co. Down, earlier this century; it gave a superb part to the wonderful Saskia Reeves as the patient, dignified farm-girl who lives with two brothers in a *ménage-à-trois*.

Neil Jordan, born in Sligo in 1950, started out as the promising writer of some good stories and novels, before moving into cinema almost by accident: he worked with John Boorman, then was backed by Channel 4 to make *Angel*, a strikingly original film set amid the Troubles in Belfast. Jordan is a darkly handsome and even romantic figure, cultivating a brooding, Byronic, angst-ridden persona. He is an intellectual, influenced by Buñuel and the French *nouveau roman*, and his stylized films are full of surreal touches; but he also has a yen for making big popular movies. The *Irish Times* quoted him as saying, 'My brain is not suited to speaking to a wide popular audience.' But to me he said, as we sat in his lovely house above the sea at Killiney Bay: 'I make two kinds of films, so-called "art" and so-called "big" ones, and I'm happy with both. I don't want to make just low-budget movies, it's like working in miniature: I want a big canvas, too.' Yet to my mind the two low-budget, very personal films he had made in his own Ireland, *Angel* and *The Miracle*, are superior to his bigger ones made abroad.

After *Angel* he went to England to film *The Company of Wolves*, a kind of werewolf-meets-Red-Riding-Hood fantasy, and the much-praised *Mona Lisa*, a thriller set in a milieu of high-class call-girls and pimps. He then made some disappointing commercial movies in America, but returned to Ireland for *The Miracle*, a delightful offbeat fable set by the sea at Bray, near Dublin. It had an Oedipus plot (enigmatic sexuality is a theme recurrent in Jordan's work), but was also a fresh, poetic picture of adolescence, with a lovely surreal climax where circus animals escape and an elephant invades a tiny church. Channel 4 put up much of the money, as they did again for his next film, *The Crying Game*, a stylish thriller set partly in the North but mainly in a stylized London, about an IRA volunteer drawn into a web of romance, mystery and violence. It was a critical success in Britain and America, though I myself found it contrived and wilfully sensationalist. The transexual/transvestite twist in the plot seemed gratuitous; and so did the bloody terrorist climax, bereft of any insights into IRA motives and feelings. Yet Jordan has called this 'the most Irish film I've done'. His is a huge talent. But as with many directors, his complex ideas and personal art do not sit easily with box-office compromise.

This is the problem for Irish cinema as a whole. Will its best talent join the usual diaspora? Is it to be just a terrain for Hollywood-style versions of Irishness? Or, helped by sympathetic British funding, will its directors remain to make true, modest, personal *films d'auteur*, reflecting a real Irish culture?

Television as social catalyst – thanks to Gay Byrne

In television as in cinema, this small English-speaking country has problems of how to combat Anglo-American hegemony and preserve a national identity – especially as most Irish homes can so easily pick up the nearby BBC and ITV stations. When the State television service was set up in 1962, relatively late, it was given the mission of creating an Irish cultural voice that could offset these Anglo–American influences, at a time when British TV was becoming widely viewed in the Dublin area. And this role it has fulfilled quite well. Despite limited funding, it produces a remarkable amount of lively television (along with a lot of trash); and it is Irish home-made programmes that are the most popular with viewers, even in areas that have access to the British channels too. Radio Telefís Éireann, State-owned but autonomous rather like the BBC, has two television networks and two radio networks, plus a local radio service in Irish (see p. 301). RTE is financed partly by advertising, but there is no separate commercial television as in Britain.

Along with this formal cultural role, the RTE has performed another one, too, less deliberate, more spontaneous and probably more important – that of catalyst of social change and pioneer of free, open debate, in a society previously gripped by taboos of silence. In the early 1960s, Ireland was still a very enclosed, tight little place, where criticisms of the power of the Church, for example, or the ban on divorce, or the sacred cows of nationalism, were rarely aired in public – and certainly not on State radio, which before 1962 was directly controlled by civil servants and followed a cautious Reithian code of conduct, carefully excluding all unorthodox material. But when the RTE was born, with a law guaranteeing its editorial independence, a new wave of television broadcasters set about breaking down the old taboos. The changes in Ireland at that period, towards a more open, frank and modern society, would in time have happened anyway; but television certainly hastened the process.

As Ireland had no TV expertise of its own, the new RTE hired producers and journalists from outside, from the British and American networks, many of them Irish émigrés glad to come back home. These young turks did not feel bound by the old moral constraints of radio, or were not even aware of them; and so they began doing what they considered normal, though for Ireland it was most abnormal. The boldest and brightest star of this media revolution was the young Gay Byrne, who was to become much the most influential broadcaster in Ireland and a national figure of the first rank – as he still is today. With his two-hour television talk show, *The Late Late Show*, and his radio phone-in programme, he developed into a kind of conduit for the thoughts and feelings of the nation, a mirror of its conscience.

Born in Dublin in 1934, the son of a manual worker, Byrne worked first for Granada TV in England as a newscaster and interviewer. Then when the RTE's new controllers felt the need for a talk show in 1962, Byrne was brought in to host it. As there were too few celebrities visiting Dublin for the usual star-interview show, a more original formula was chosen for *The Late Late Show*: a few celebrity items would mix in with variety, music *and* discussion of topical issues. As with *TW3* in Britain at the same period, this mixing of genres was possible in those pioneering days, as it might not be today. But it was met with indignation: for years, politicians, bishops and others would protest, 'The show must decide whether it is light entertainment or current affairs, and stop frivolously confusing the two.' But the formula was popular with the public, and was kept.

Worse indignation was caused by the topical discussions. In contrast to the tight-lipped old radio service, Byrne would fill the studio with guests discussing taboo topics such as marital breakup, homosexuality, atheism, or whether the Irish language had any real value. An English feminist was brought in to talk about abortion. And the bishops for the first time found their authority questioned in public (see p. 159). Byrne's gleeful *glasnost* delighted many viewers, but it shocked others; voices in high places would call for 'this dirty, evil show' to be taken off. But the RTE's Board courageously backed Byrne and rarely tried to curb him; as the show went out live, it could not be censored. For many years it was top of the Irish ratings, and in 1994 it was still on the air, with Byrne still in charge as both presenter and producer.

Since 1971 he has had his own two-hour radio show too. Here, with material of a more private nature, and using a more soothing, intimate style, he has become a kind of national agony aunt, as gently he talks to the listeners, mostly women, who phone in with intimate personal details they might normally tell no one: witness the famous 'Granard' broadcast in 1984 (see p. 181), after an unwed girl had died alone in childbirth. Women adore Byrne. And thus, in an age when Church confession has been in steady decline, he has become a new kind of public father confessor. He is not an intellectual, but a practising Catholic of humble background and average views, who instinctively feels close to ordinary people and is able to give them a voice. This, plus his huge capacity for self-discipline and hard work, has been a large part of his strength. And curiously he has never seen himself as a crusader for free debate or liberal causes. During my own talk with him, he said, 'From the start I was purely a showbiz man, not really interested in politics. If I have staged provocative debates, it has been mainly in the interests of a lively show, and not through any mission to reform society.' So he is that rarity, a conservative who has promoted radical change.

On the screen, the suavely debonair manner, the cool self-confidence linked to a probing mind, are the stock-in-trade of any good chat-show host. But Byrne's approach is more unusual. And audiences watch fascinated as his clever interviewing leads people to reveal unexpected truths, or simply make fools of themselves. 'Gaybo', as he is called, remains an actor at heart, and his show has always been a kind of circus, tabloid in style even when being serious. He will prance around, using funny voices, wearing comic hats, making much use of his rapturous studio audience: a pop group might be followed by Gay teasing an old granny up from Galway, then by a hard-hitting talk on birth control. There are also freebies for the audience, and quiz prizes with blatant commercial plugs – much too much so. The famous guests are expected to enter into the zany spirit of the show, and Byrne may well get some august statesman to sing a little song. He selects his guests mainly for their entertainment value, with little regard for their high office. No wonder that politicians have often feared or disliked him.

Byrne has always turned down offers to move to the larger stage of Britain or America, including one from the BBC to succeed Éamonn Andrews. He has preferred to stay in his own homeland, where he can remain king. By the early 1990s he was

270

the longest-surviving host of the world's longest-running live chat show. But today the show has been losing much of its old sparkle, and its ratings have been slipping. It is hardly surprising. Byrne has probably been at it too long, and the hard-hitting talk no longer startles, for Irish society has changed and there are now other RTE programmes just as outspoken. But his legacy has been extraordinary. Surely in no other country has a broadcaster played so dominant a role and for so long. Probably it could not have happened in a much larger society or a less self-absorbed one; or in one less in need of some kind of confessional guide through a period of bewildering moral and social change.

The Late Late Show led the way into a liberation that has since been followed by other producers, and today almost anything goes on RTE. Various programmes deal frankly with drugs, AIDS, birth control and abortion – 'There's almost *too* much discussion of these things, we've grown obsessed,' complained one senior editor. On satire shows, I have seen skits on de Valera, that national icon, and even on nuns buying condoms. Feature films are shown uncut, though sexy or violent ones are generally kept away from family viewing hours. The RTE's liberal policy sometimes comes under fire from lay moralist pressure groups, or from some Church leaders, but the Government itself does not intervene.

Irish television is full of talent, and for a country of this size its record is remarkable, even though quality has suffered recently from budget cut-backs. *Nighthawks* is a clever and lively regular programme for young people. There are also two good 'soap' series: *Glenroe*, with a rural setting, and *Fair City*, about middle-class Dubliners on a housing estate, complete with illegitimate children and marital breakdowns. Lack of money makes it hard to do full-scale drama or feature filming, save when co-productions can be arranged, as in the case of *The Treaty*, an ambitious 'docu-drama' about the 1921 period, made in partnership with London's Thames Television. There have been co-productions also with French, German and American companies. The news bulletins are skilfully done, though the slant may be somewhat insular, again partly for money reasons; on the big foreign subjects, it is hard to compete with the much larger British networks. Documentaries can be excellent, for example one I saw on victims of violence in the North. But the funding for them has been reduced, and today the accent is more on studio discussions, which at least can exploit the Irish flair for lively talk. These debates, including Gay Byrne's, tend to be much lengthier and more rambling than British television would allow, but this is a deliberate choice, and Irish audiences accept it. There is a strange informal intimacy about Irish television, relating maybe to the size of the country, also to the Irish love of being personal and gossipy, even with strangers. It makes every studio chat seem like a family occasion.

In the ratings for the two RTE networks, the most popular programmes are Irish-made, usually led by *Glenroe*, with *The Late Late Show* coming second or third; the only imported programme that gets regularly into the top ten is *Coronation Street*. 'Yes, I suppose it shows once again that the Irish are a bit self-absorbed, but also that they have a strong sense of community,' said one RTE executive. About 25 per cent of viewers, mainly in the south-west, can pick up only the RTE; the others have access to BBC and ITV as well, either direct or by cable, and in these areas the audience share-out between the RTE and British networks is roughly fifty-fifty. Many people turn to BBC or ITV for news or sport, or feature films or big dramas. The RTE feels the competition intensely, and this has led to a ratings battle which has certainly harmed the cultural quality of its output. Today there are fewer serious programmes than twenty years ago, and rather more quizzes, imported serials, and what one disillusioned producer called 'silly imitations of British television – a great pity, for we have the talent to do better'.

One aspect of this problem is the RTE's relations with the Government, which are good politically, less so financially. The law that created the RTE, back in the golden Lemass era, granted it an editorial autonomy which it has always guarded jealously. As with the BBC, although the members of its Board are appointed by the Government they are not politicians but come widely from the professions, even from within RTE ranks (Gay Byrne is one of them). They can protect the RTE from official pressures, but they also interfere little in day-to-day programme-making. And this system has generally worked smoothly, save for a period in the early 1970s when the RTE, rather like the BBC, was not yet sure how to cover the Troubles in the North and made mistakes. At one point the Government sacked its entire Board, accusing it of giving too much publicity to the IRA. But the Government since then has been careful to respect the RTE's autonomy, even when programmes are critical – as happened often when Haughey was Taoiseach, for he was no darling of liberal broadcasters. He in turn never hid his dislike of the RTE, which he felt was biased against him (much as Thatcher had felt about the BBC). There was not much he could do against it politically, but he did have another weapon: finance. The RTE's budget comes roughly half from advertising, and half from the licence-fee revenue, which is channelled to it via the Government. And in 1991 Haughey made a cut-back of some 20 per cent in its funds from this source. Whether or not he was being vindictive, RTE executives were furious, as I heard from Joe Mulholland, head of news and current affairs: 'With a reduced budget, we have no choice but to cut down on our serious expensive film-making and rely more on cheap imports, such as American serials. The Government in the Lemass era gave us this role of being the cultural voice of Ireland, but its cuts are now having precisely the opposite effect.'

The RTE today is also fearful that the Government might sanction a third network, purely private and commercial. Soundings were made for this in the early 1990s, but adequate financial backing was not found, to the RTE's relief. However, the lobby for a commercial channel is still alive, and has political allies. Its opponents wield the powerful argument that three networks would be too many for a country as small as Ireland, especially in the present economic climate. There would simply not be the advertising, which already is barely enough for the needs of the RTE and of Ireland's struggling newspapers.

Of the Republic's four main morning dailies (three in Dublin, one in Cork), by far the best is the *Irish Times*, which has a smallish circulation (94,000) but enjoys much the same kind of position as

Le Monde in France as a great liberal voice, the paper that all the intelligentsia read. It was founded in 1859 by an Englishman, Major Lawrence Knox, and for many years was a Protestant paper, speaking for the Anglo-Irish minority. Since the 1960s, with the opening up of Irish society, it has come to reflect the views of the liberal urban middle class, and it now has a liberal Catholic editor, Conor Brady; but it remains imbued with a certain Protestant free-thinking ethos, and some of its staff are still Protestant (see p. 177). Since 1974 it has been controlled by a non-profit-making trust, with a charter that commands it to be 'independent of all interests, religious, commercial or political'. So it is non-aligned. But it has often been harshly critical of Fianna Fáil-led Governments and the Catholic hierarchy, and has taken a crusading liberal line on the moral issues (see p. 190). It has quite good foreign coverage and some excellent columnists, notably Mary Holland, Nuala O'Faoláin, Fintain O'Toole and Dick Walshe. The elegance and wit of their writing contrasts with the paper's dingy, money-starved offices, which only in 1992 were beginning to be modernized.

The *Times*'s main rival, the *Irish Independent* (sales 150,000), is owned mainly by the business magnate Tony O'Reilly.* It is more popular in style, and geared more towards small-town and country people. But it is less conservative than it used to be and has some good writers. One star feature is its gossip column, written by the famous Terry Keane; she is known to *le tout Dublin* as the friend of Charlie Haughey. The third daily, the *Irish Press*, was founded by de Valera and is still somewhat nationalist in tone; it is in decline, with sales down to about 60,000. There is also the *Cork Examiner*, worthy, dull and very provincial. In addition, the main British papers sell widely in the Republic; in fact, among dailies the top seller after the *Irish Independent* is not the *Irish Times* but the *Daily Mirror*. With their much bigger resources, these papers can offer far more lavish features and, in the case of the

---

* See p. 79. O'Reilly has also been trying to build up a newspaper empire abroad. In 1994 he fought with the Mirror Group to win control of the *Independent* and *Independent on Sunday* in London. But although he secured a 30 per cent stake, the Mirror Group eventually won majority control.

qualities, much fuller world coverage. And so, in the Press as in television, cinema and the pop-music scene, the Irish feel the need to struggle against Anglo-American domination. Hence the stress they put on their own culture, their music, their Gaelic sports, their language.

8

PROMOTING THE ESSENCE OF THE IRISH CULTURAL TRADITION

Over the past thirty or forty years, fears have often been voiced that Ireland's own traditions and identity might be swamped by the inrush of Anglo-American popular culture. When this enclosed society began to open to the world in the Lemass era, it led to important material and social changes, new lifestyles, new outside influences notably via television. 'In fact we are going through a deep and far-reaching cultural revolution,' wrote the psychology professor E. F. O'Doherty in 1963. 'One cannot radically change the material culture and hope to preserve all the rest intact.' In other words, he and others felt that it would not be easy for the Irish to have their cake and eat it, as they wished – to embrace modernism yet retain their own culture, in face of the mass commercial pressures from the two English-speaking giants on either side. The Irish did not even have the language barrier that gives some protection to other small European countries.

Since then, the Irish have been trying hard, and with partial success, to preserve or even revive their own culture, in the three areas where it is most distinctively Irish: music, sport, and language. These will be the subject of this chapter. The revival of traditional music has been striking, and has even led to an Irish rock move-ment that has spread round the world, via the success of U2 and other groups. The Irish games of hurling and Gaelic football are still very popular, though challenged by the rise of international soccer. And the ancient Irish language is enjoying a kind of revival too, in some circles, despite the dominance of English. All this, together with the success abroad of Irish novels, poetry, plays and films, has given the Irish a greater cultural self-confidence; and the

Anglo-American 'threat' is now less of an issue than twenty or thirty years ago. But there remains a debate on how far it makes practical sense to revive the obscure Irish language, in today's Europe; and another debate on whether legitimate national cultural pride can be separated from a narrower political nationalism.

The music revival: from Sean Nós *and The Chieftains to U2's world conquest*

The Irish went out and rescued and rediscovered their music in the 1950s and 1960s, at a time when this precious tradition appeared to be in decline, under threat from the modern changes in society. Since then the revival has gathered pace, and today the music is everywhere – fiddlers in village pubs, solo singers of sad ancient airs, stout matrons gathering for bouncy *céilí* dances; and scores of summer festivals large and small, such as the giant annual *fleadh* in Finsbury Park, London, which mixes folk balladeers like Christie Moore with the new Irish rock and pop scene of Bob Geldof and Sinead O'Connor.

Any listener to the music-making must sense that the Irish personality expresses itself through its music in a very special way. Some experts have referred to a mysterious, even spiritual quality in Irish traditional music, as if it were reflecting the collective experience of griefs and passions reaching far back into history. Certainly no other country in Europe has retained so rich and vigorous a tradition of this kind of music, orally transmitted and often performed by amateurs. The reasons may lie in history. One nationalist suggested to me that classical music never caught on widely in Ireland because it was an import of the colonizers; and whereas in other countries much of the folk music was later subsumed by classical music and thus distorted, in Ireland it was outlawed by the British after the sixteenth century and forced to go underground. This helped it to keep its purity. Like Irish Catholicism, it became a cherished expression of national identity.

The rhythms and scoring may seem simple and repetitive

compared with classical or 'art' music. But they have a tunefulness, a lyric quality, and a diversity of genres – the jigs and reels, *céilí* and set dances, the solo unaccompanied singing, the harp music, the instrumental bands, then the newer, reworked melodies of the 'Danny Boy' kind, the tin-pan alley songs, and on to today's flowering of Irish rock.

The music's origins are mysterious and ancient: some scholars believe that the early dances of the rural West came from India and North Africa. Then in the seventeenth and eighteenth centuries Ireland was influenced by European baroque music and dances, hence the polkas and mazurkas still found today. In the Middle Ages, the bard was a figure of high social status in Ireland, an official poet-cum-musician, and this bardic tradition led to the special Irish genre of solo narrative singing known as *Sean Nós* (old style), still surviving today in a few places. In the old days, rural communities regularly made their own music for their entertainment, both singing and dancing. In summer, they would use the roads as dance-floors – hence the popular tradition of 'dancing at the crossroads' which de Valera took as an image of his ideal of a pure, innocent Ireland. And when the Irish emigrated to America in the nineteenth century, they took their music with them (see p. 307) – to the Appalachian mountains and other rural areas, where Country and Western today bears a clear Irish influence.

However, back in Ireland itself, by around the 1950s the tradition had grown stale and the Irish were beginning to desert their own music, especially in the cities. They now had other distractions. Local 'ballrooms of romance' with their waltzes and foxtrots were in vogue; pop music was just arriving, to entice the young away; English television was providing glossier entertainments than *Sean Nós*; and heavy emigration left fewer young people on the farms to whom the oral traditions could be handed on. What's more, *carpets* were coming in. 'In my childhood in Clare in the 1950s,' one woman told me, 'forty or fifty of us would hold *céilí* dances on the stone floor of our big family kitchen on Saturday nights – it was lovely. But then as my parents grew more prosperous they carpeted the whole house. And you can't do Irish dancing on a carpet.' Perhaps the growth of rural traffic was upsetting the crossroads dancing, too.

It was around the same time that a number of musicians, disturbed by these trends, began to take action. In 1951 they formed an association called Comhaltas Ceoltóirí Éireann (CCE: Irish Music Movement), which pledged itself to restore and develop traditional music, also the Irish language; and it set about organizing festivals and music classes. Its influence gradually spread, and by the early sixties there was an explosion of music in Ireland. Many new professional groups were formed. One was The Chieftains, born in 1962 and still active today, which superbly performs traditional music on traditional instruments; another, also very authentic, was The Dubliners, a long-bearded ballad group. CCE today is a large organization, to which most local amateur music bodies are affiliated. Its leadership gets criticized for its assertive nationalism (see below), but there is no doubt of the key role it played in turning the tide in the 1950s. 'We arrived in the nick of time to save Irish music. Another ten years, and it might have been too late – the pop and rock movement could have killed it,' the CCE's president, Labhrás Ó Murchú (Laurence Murphy), told me.

There were other influences, too, in this musical revolution, and one of them came from America – as described by Nuala O'Connor in her book *Bringing It All Back Home*, which in 1991 accompanied a superb BBC TV series about the Irish music. The early emigration that brought its music across the Atlantic had gradually spawned a flourishing Irish music industry in New York and other towns, some of it phoney (the tin-pan alley creations) but some genuine. And when in the 1950s music in Ireland began to revive, a few of these Irish Americans felt drawn to go back and work in their own culture, 'bringing it all back home'. Notably, the three Clancy brothers had left Co. Tipperary as poor emigrants in 1947, and later began giving folk-song concerts in New York. After a few years they were doing well, and in 1961 they started to make tours back in Ireland, where they had a big success and played a key part in the folk-music revival. Pete Seeger was an influence on them, and they in turn influenced Bob

Dylan. So Irish music and the new American folk movement, which itself had Irish elements, made an impact on each other.

Irish musical experts consider that O'Connor's book overplayed the role of America in the Irish revival, apart from the Clancys. However, they would all endorse her glowing assessment of the great Seán Ó Riada (1931–71), who did far more than any other individual to revitalize Irish music: 'He was a man for all seasons; a composer trained in the art music of Europe who immersed himself in the oral music tradition of Ireland. He was exercised all his life by the question of Irish cultural identity . . . He found new ways for the music to express itself: in orchestral settings, film programme music, and liturgical and choral singing. Guided by his vision, traditional music changed radically, and became access-ible to a modern Irish audience.' So, while CCE supplied the organization, Ó Riada gave the inspiration and the intellectual framework. He was a jazz pianist, a composer of modern quasi-serial music, and a teacher at University College, Cork. He also threw himself passionately into Irish music, formed a successful band of traditional musicians, and influenced The Chieftains and other groups. Expertly he orchestrated and scored whole areas of orally transmitted music that were lying half-forgotten; and all musicians today acknowledge their huge debt to him. But he burnt himself out, dying at the age of forty.

From its earliest days the revival was greatly assisted by State radio, and then by RTE television, both of which still have regular programmes of Irish music. It has been helped also by the growth of modern tourism, bringing foreign audiences in summer, and by the rise in prosperity since the 1950s which has given more money and leisure for concert-going and record-buying. So, by a happy irony, the modern trends which in the 1950s seemed to be a threat to traditional music have finally proved its allies. The movement has spread abroad, and CCE now has branches in, for example, Tokyo, Luxembourg and Sardinia, catering not only for Irish residents there but for foreigners interested in Irish culture. At home, CCE sponsors about forty-five annual music festivals (*fleadhanna*, plural of *fleadh*, pronounced 'flah'), embracing some 20,000 competitors in dance, song and instrumental playing.

The past few years have seen an increase in the popularity of *céilí* dancing, and especially of set dancing, by amateur enthusiasts who will meet once or twice a week in the back room of a pub, maybe with a teacher. The *céilí* (plural *céilthe*) is Scottish as much as Irish, and it means simply a party with music, where probably there is dancing to the tunes of jig, reel or hornpipe. *Céilí* bands were common in Ireland from early in the century, but nowadays the music may well be that of an accordion. These are group dances, varying in style from county to county, and curiously the best-known are named after local battles: 'The Walls of Limerick', 'The Siege of Ennis', 'The Bridge of Athlone'. But today most amateur groups prefer set dancing to *céilí* dancing. The former are performed in a circle by two or four couples, and they use polka rhythms as much as reels or jigs. Again, there are regional variations; many of the best Irish set dances come originally from Kerry.

Clare and Kerry have long been the heartlands of Irish music, but today it has spread everywhere. In Waterford, the big Metropole pub has live music every Monday. Here in one room I found a party of about twenty middle-aged couples doing energetic set dancing, to an accordion. It was lively, instructive, but not very aesthetic to watch. In the main lounge, however, a delightful *seisiun* (session) was in progress – about a dozen local amateur musicians, some of them bulky men with big beards, others with rough, dreamy Irish faces. There was an excellent girl violinist, a boy with a flute, and a handsome Oberammergau-looking type with a chiselled biblical beard, singing old ballads intently as if wrapped in a trance. This very informal regular *seisiun* had been started only two years ago, I was told; the members would turn up when they felt like it and perform just for the fun of it, with no payment save for a few free drinks.

Many pubs today have a weekly *seisiun* of this kind, with maybe just three or four musicians, or more. Some are held all the year, others only in the summer season; and the performers seldom get anything beyond a token fee (so much of the public music-making in Ireland is free that it undercuts the professional groups, who must often rely on foreign tours for their main earnings). The principal instrument is the fiddle, as the Irish call the violin; others are the flute, the tin whistle, and the *bodhran*, a small goatskin drum that is beaten with the knuckles or a stick. The Irish version of bagpipes, the *uilleann* (elbow) pipes, are more often played solo than as part of a band. As for that noblest of Irish instruments, the harp, its heyday ended in the eighteenth century and it is not so often heard nowadays: but it remains the official Irish emblem, on banknotes and documents. Seán Ó Riada did research into the harp music of the seventeenth and eighteenth centuries and tried to stimulate a revival, with some success. Some talented young players have now emerged, and there is an annual harp festival at the Co. Cavan home of the greatest Irish seventeenth-century harpist, Turlough Carolan.

Of the Irish music that one hears today, to tell which is authentically traditional, and which some more recent invention, is not always easy. Comhaltas Ceoltóirí Éireann's leaders, Labhrás Ó Murchú and his wife Una, see themselves as the sacred guardians of all that is true and pure in the traditional; and in 1991 they opened a new showcase for it in the ancient Tipperary town of Cashel, barely an hour's drive from Bunratty and its 'medieval' frolics, which Ó Murchú certainly does not see as true and pure. This handsome new Brú Ború centre, just below Cashel's half-ruined hilltop cathedral, has trained a team of thirty young local musicians who give concerts. Here I heard solo singing of ancient slow airs in Irish, telling of love and war, in the *Sean Nós* style – the true heart of the traditional. Then girls in bright green dresses danced jigs, also solo; and another girl played the harp. It was an impressive experience, but a bit solemn and reverential, like being in church.

Brú Ború puts its accent on older songs sung in Irish; but other CCE concerts may well feature early nineteenth-century ballads which are nearly all in English, for the Irish language was then declining fast. And this is where controversy begins. 'We see a close link between Ireland's music and its language,' Ó Murchú told me, 'and our role is to promote both: we get funding from the Department of the Gaeltacht' (see p. 296). Ó Murchú is a nationalist who believes in protecting Irish culture against outside influences, and has even upbraided the Arts Council for supporting 'foreign' art forms such as classical music! So in turn he gets criticized. 'He is using Irish music as a tool for his ideology,' said one Arts Council member, 'and he runs the CCE almost like a political party. They seem to be trying to preserve some romantic de Valera vision of an Ireland full of colleens dancing at the crossroads, with no urban unemployment or poverty – a bit escapist.' This is too harsh, and in fact Ó Murchú has modified his stance recently. But he remains a highly conservative figure. He has been president of CCE since 1968 and he runs it with a strong hand – a difficult man who has personality clashes with some other leaders of Irish music. Across the country, many local CCE leaders are also arch-conservatives, some of them active in the anti-abortion lobby. But others simply want to enjoy the music. No one denies that the CCE has done a fine job in promoting the music revival, and everyone wants this to continue. But not everyone wants the music to be dragged into politics, or into the moral debate.

The Chieftains, entirely non-political, has been the most success-ful of the traditional groups. Its leader, the piper Paddy Moloney, a charismatic figure on many a concert platform, gave me his own story: 'I was born in North Dublin in 1938, but I was marked above all by my childhood visits to Co. Laois, where my grand-father was a fiddler, and the warm, old-style music parties in his house inspired me to be a musician. Then I met Garech Browne, a cousin of the Guinnesses [see p. 324], who formed a record company for me; he produced my first record, and encouraged me to form The Chieftains, in 1962. I also worked with Seán Ó Riada, and we have remained faithful to his model. We are the only group with the complete range of Irish instruments.' The Chieftains have taken their music as far afield as China.

The boom in folk and ballad singing has taken various forms, some more traditional than others. Christie Moore is today the most popular Irish folk-singer, with a huge repertoire both Irish and foreign, and a rich, haunting voice; he is somewhat political, but not in the nationalist CCE sense, more in the socially commit-ted manner of Bob Dylan. De Dannan, a successful Galway-based band, uses traditional dance music as its core but mixes it with some non-Irish genres, including its own adaptations of the Beatles, Bach and black gospel music; for this it has been criticized by some Irish purists.

Many of the best-loved songs and ballads that one hears in Ireland, and thinks of as 'typically Irish', are not in fact Irish traditional. It is a question of the melodic style of the song, more than of its date or origins. Some of these songs came in from England or Scotland centuries ago, or they were Anglo-Irish products, or popular compositions of Thomas Moore in the early nineteenth century or Percy French at the end of the century. I am thinking of songs like 'The Mountains of Mourne', or Moore's 'Believe Me If All Those Endearing Young Charms'. Go to one of the medieval banquets at Bunratty Castle, Co. Clare, and you will find awful food, jokey merrymaking, and lyrical singing by lovely Irish voices. You will probably hear 'Tabhair dom do Lámh' ('Give Me Your Hand'), an authentic old Irish melody composed by a blind harpist in the seventeenth century. You will also hear other songs very beautiful but less traditional, such as 'The Kerry Dances', written in 1890, and inevitably 'Danny Boy' ('The Londonderry Air'), which is based on an old air but has more recent words by an American. To my untutored mind, many of the songs of this kind do retain some kind of emotional Irish flavour, and the purists might be wrong to reject them just because they do not fit into the traditional canon. They are surely in a different league from the tin-pan alley commercial products of the turn-of-the-century Irish in New York – quaint or sentimental numbers such as 'Mother Machree' or 'When Irish Eyes are Smiling'.

In the newer world of rock and pop, the Irish contribution over the past twenty years has been formidable. It could be that the innate Irish genius for popular music has played some part: certainly some of the early Irish rock bands in the 1970s were directly influenced by traditional music, or they even began as traditional players, then moved to rock. The Horslips, a middle-class, educated group, performed a mixture of traditional, folk and rock that proved very seductive, and they are credited with having pioneered so-called Celtic Rock. Similarly The Saw Doctors, based in Galway, create rock and pop music that reflects their native West. The Pogues, very popular today, began as rebellious modern-style balladeers before the rock element took over. Even Van Morrison, essentially a rock musician, produces work clearly influenced by his Celtic origins in Belfast.

As for today's biggest names, Sinead O'Connor and U2, here the influences are not so clear. O'Connor, with her shaven head and waif-like Joan-at-the-stake persona, has been a star since she was nineteen. She likes to provoke, as when she tore up a picture of the Pope in front of thirty million American TV viewers and called the Catholic Church 'an evil empire built on lies'. She claims to dislike modern Irish society, and most critics would say they find no Celtic influences in her singing. Others suggest that there is none the less something Irish about her directness, emotionalism and intensity.

Equally in the case of U2, the Irishness lies if anywhere in the expression rather than the music. This group has been described as 'Ireland's major cultural phenomenon today' and for the past few years it has been the world's most prominent rock band. It has been on the cover of *Time* ('Rock's Hottest Ticket'), and its albums sell up to 14 million each. The four members were all still at school together in Dublin when they formed their group, in 1977, and they quickly acquired a clever and civilized young manager, Paul McGuinness, who has played a key part in their success. They are socially committed on the Christian Left, their songs deal with imperialism, war, human rights and drugs as well as more personal themes, and their powerful impact comes from this as well as from the loud, passionate voice of their lead singer Bono (Paul Hewson). He has said that, at school, 'I rebelled against being Irish, I rebelled against speaking the Irish language, Irish culture . . .' But now, as quoted in *Bringing It All Back Home*, he takes a different view: 'I think there's an Irishness to what U2 do; I'm not quite sure what it is. I think it's something to do with the romantic spirit of the words I write, but also of the melodies that Edge makes on the guitar . . .' Irish musical experts, however, claim to find no traditional influences in the music itself, which is pure modern rock; but they will accept that the directness of style, the feelings, the concern for storytelling, are in some ways Irish.

Although so much of their work today is geared to America, the immensely rich U2 show their fidelity by still choosing to live in Ireland. In their head office, a converted banana warehouse by the Liffey, I went to see Paul McGuinness, Trinity philosophy graduate and respected Dublin public figure: 'The Irish now feel that rock and roll is fully part of their culture. I doubt that in many countries would the manager of a rock band be appointed to the Arts Council, as I have been.' What's more, the huge success abroad of U2, and of other musical groups, has helped to give the Irish a new self-confidence, and this spills over from culture into wider fields. As compared with even ten years ago, they now feel less threatened by Anglo-American popular culture, and more able to contribute to it creatively as equals. From London to New York, Hamburg to Tokyo, Irish musicians are hugely popular. Even the Eurovision song contest, which Ireland won three times running in 1992–4, bears witness to Irish prominence in popular music.

Gaelic sporting nationalists under threat from soccer

As with music, so with sport only more so, for it is so much more widely played: Ireland's uniqueness expresses itself through its own games of hurling and Gaelic football, seen as a crucial part of the national identity. Today they are menaced by the rise of soccer (Association Football), but they remain very popular, and are played on a strict amateur basis, with no professional teams. The intercounty matches draw big crowds in the towns (up to 60,000 at Croke Park stadium, Dublin), but the Gaelic heartland is the rural areas, where most villages and schools have their own teams. Such is the power of these games that politicians and Church leaders take good care to be involved: the Taoiseach or his ministers want to be seen at the big matches, where bishops officially preside. In the Christian Brothers' schools, priests traditionally have inculcated manliness through the Gaelic games, as English public schools did on the rugby field. Among other small nations, perhaps only the Basques have such an emotional attachment to their own sports.

The Irish games are fast and fast-scoring, excellent to play and to watch. Gaelic football, played fifteen-a-side, is a little like a cross between soccer and rugby, for the players can push or punch the ball (but not throw it). It is played also by the Irish in Britain and the US, while Australian football, invented by Irish immigrants, has quite similar rules. As for hurling, Ireland's official national game, it has ancient roots: there are references to it in pre-Christian writings, and many of the legendary heroes were expert hurlers. Like hockey, it is played with a stick; but this is more like a big club, brandished aloft more wildly than in hockey, and the ball can also be used with the hand. Camogie is a gentler version of the game, for girls. Gaelic football is played all over Ireland, including the North (see p. 432), while the stronghold of hurling is the south-west, notably Co. Tipperary. Intercounty matches at Croke Park are festive occasions, as fans flock in from the country, wearing coloured hats and waving flags. But hooliganism is rare.

In this sport-mad country, soccer and rugby football are also played eagerly. As in England, rugby is mainly a middle-class sport, except in Co. Limerick, where it is more democratic. It was the game of the Anglo-Irish, and in private Protestant schools today it generally replaces the Gaelic games. Soccer is played professionally as well as by amateurs; and especially as a spectator sport it has been making great advances recently, owing to the impact of international matches screened on British television, and to the successes of Ireland's own team in the 1990 World Cup and other contests. But this rise of an 'alien' sport has been causing alarm to the guardians of the sacred flame of Ireland's own games, the huge and awesome Gaelic Athletic Association (GAA). It is quite a crisis.

The GAA is a kind of sporting equivalent of Comhaltas Ceoltóirí Éireann, but is even more nationalistic and far more influential. Well-organized, wealthy and State-funded, with some 800,000 members, it has been described as the most powerful body in Ireland after the Catholic Church. It was founded in 1884, around the same time as the Gaelic League, with the aim of promoting and protecting the Gaelic games (the British had once tried to ban hurling). Today the GAA still sees itself as a patriotic defender of the national faith: 'These games are more than just sport, they are part of the fabric of the nation, an essential expression of our Irish identity, like our language,' said one official, who went on to remind me that thirteen people had been shot by British troops during a match at Croke Park in 1920.

Such was the GAA's hatred of 'foreign' games that, after independence, it imposed a ban on its members playing soccer or rugby. Any who did so were expelled from GAA teams. This ban had no legal force, but it could amount to social ostracism in rural areas. The ban was lifted in 1971. But today, in face of the rise of soccer, the GAA remains stubbornly on the defensive. In 1991, its board refused to allow Dublin's Gaelic football club to arrange a joint fixture with a local soccer club, whereby two matches of the two kinds of football would be played on the same non-GAA ground on the same afternoon. This the GAA saw as sacrilege. Nor will it let Croke Park be used for soccer or rugby matches, even though for commercial reasons it readily hires out the stadium for pop concerts or other such shows. 'Why should we help our opponents?' is the official view.

As Ireland opens out to Europe, so the growing internationalization of sport has been drawing the Irish towards other games. The first influence was via television, as the major soccer matches screened by BBC and ITV became widely viewed. Then, under the management of the English soccer champion Jackie Charlton, Ireland's own team moved into the top world class, and even reached the quarter-finals in the World Cup in Italy in 1990; jubilant crowds welcomed it home in triumph to Dublin, as if it had actually won the cup. For the 1994 World Cup, the Irish team, amazingly, was the only one of the five from the British Isles to qualify for the final run-offs in the United States. This kind of success adds to the local prestige of soccer, which is now becoming widely played as well as watched, especially in the towns; at many schools which had always put the accent on Gaelic games, the boys are now more interested in playing soccer, and some urban schools even find it hard to get good Gaelic teams together.

So the Irish have taken over yet another English invention, and on current form are proving better at it than their old colonizers. But this is little solace to the GAA's leaders, who are worried. The *Irish Times* has accused them of pursuing a narrow nationalism, unworthy of the excellent games they seek to promote; others, too, see them as clinging with defensive arrogance to a siege mentality, in face of the challenge of soccer, which they ought to accept more gracefully. Yet they are showing enough confidence to be now building a new £35-million stadium at Croke Park, which will increase seating capacity from the present 64,000 to 80,000. They are probably justified, for the Gaelic games, despite the advance of soccer, will continue to play an important part in Irish life. And as they struggle to hold their ground, so the ancient Irish language is fighting to reassert itself against an earlier and far more powerful English import.

The fight for the Irish language: waning of the Gaeltacht, but a new vogue in the towns

The Irish are in a dilemma about the future of their own ancient language, which in some respects continues to die out, but in others is today making a modest comeback. Nearly everyone at least pays lip-service to the view that it must be preserved, as a national cultural asset, even a key to the Irish identity. But not so many are prepared to do much about this, when it is so much simpler to talk English. And how in practical terms it can coexist with English in daily use is a matter of some debate – and of politics, as an assertive nationalistic language lobby fights to keep the Government to its formal promises: '*Déanfaidh an Bord an Ghaeilge, agus go háirithe a húsáid mar theanga bheo agus mar ghnáthmheán cumarsáide, a chur chun cinn,'* runs the Act of Parliament calling for Irish to be promoted as a living language in daily use.

Whereas 12 per cent of the Welsh in Wales use Welsh as their daily first language, in Ireland the figure for Irish is little more than 1 per cent; and in the Irish-speaking enclaves of the rural West, the 'Gaeltacht', it is still steadily declining, in face of English. But in the cities, the picture is different. There, a growing minority of parents are now voluntarily sending their children to new State-backed schools where the teaching is all in Irish; in some middle-class circles the use of Irish has become quite chic; poets write in it, Mary Robinson eagerly promotes it and speaks it publicly; the Government, under pressure from the language lobby, pours funds into it and in 1993 even promised to set up an Irish-language television service.

Popular attitudes are ambivalent. Everyone has to learn some Irish at school, but then as adults most of them never use it and they tend to forget it. Yet they still see it as part of their heritage, the essence of an ancient culture of which they are proud. Above all, it is a secret weapon that marks them out from the British and Americans, even more than Irish music or Gaelic games. I have met couples on holiday abroad who speak Irish together, if they can, to avoid being taken for English. And people are vaguely pleased that the Government still insists on Irish terms for all public titles – Taoiseach, Dáil, Bord Fáilte and so on – which give a comforting sense of national identity. But this is not the same as the practical use of the spoken language, when all the other pressures are to use English, and it is in some ways clearly an advantage to be part of the English-speaking world. Can an artificial urban revival, however sincere, really go very far? Some enthusiasts think that it can, and even talk of Ireland becoming a bilingual nation, like Canada. Others are more sceptical, or even ask, 'What's the point?'

This is a rich, expressive Celtic tongue, quite distinct from Welsh and Breton, which are more similar to each other. It was the daily language of Ireland until about the seventeenth century, when the colonizers began to impose English and the natives gradually went along with this, mostly for economic reasons: 'Irish does not sell the cow,' the saying went. As all official transactions were in English, and the British economy dominated the country, so the Irish turned to English, too. And this practical motivation grew stronger during the emigrations that followed the Famine, when families felt that it would be damaging to move to an anglophone country with nothing but Irish; some parents would even punish their children for speaking it. The new national school system also favoured English. So for all these reasons the language gradually declined; according to census records, by 1851 it was used by only 25 per cent of people, and in 1911 by only 12 per cent. So although British pressures were partly to blame, it was above all the Irish themselves who deserted their own language.

After independence, the official policy of restoration was badly applied and met with failure. The Gaelic League, founded in 1893, had given the political and cultural impetus for a revival of Irish; and in the 1920s this became the ideology of the rulers of the Free State, who set about Gaelicizing education. Everyone, including Cosgrave and de Valera, wanted the new Ireland to be fully Irish-speaking and believed that somehow within a few years a miracle would be wrought. Hundreds of new Irish classes and primary schools were set up, amid much enthusiasm: but the difficulties soon became clear. There was a serious lack of teachers; and as the parents spoke only English, their children found the experiment gratuitous and artificial. It was imposed autocratically, without any broader social vision (see pp. 27–8). And by the 1940s it was collapsing, with most schools reverting to English as their main teaching vehicle. Yet the language was still lurking somewhere in the national psyche, as Seán O'Faoláin wrote eloquently in his brilliant book *The Irish* in 1947: 'It has now gone underground. It is, so to speak, being forgotten consciously. It nevertheless beats like a great earth-throb in the subconscious of the race. The Irish language is thus become the runic language of modern Ireland. Even though only a dwindling few think overtly in it all of us can, through it, touch, however dimly, a buried part of ourselves of which we are normally unaware. Through Gaelic we remember ancestrally – are again made very old and very young.'

The position today is equivocal. The 1937 Constitution, still in force, declares that Irish is 'the first official language' of the State, while English is merely 'a second official language' and 'the language of everyday use'. The Irish themselves smile at this absurdity, which is one of the various institutionalized myths surviving from the 1921 period and few politicians would dare to tamper with it. Fianna Fáil in particular, the foremost party of patriotism, makes obeisance to the ideal by declaring that its aim is 'to promote and restore the spoken use of the Irish language' (in Albert Reynolds's recent words). So the Government does quite a lot. It funds official promotional bodies such as Bord na Gaeilge (the Gaelic Board). It pays for a national radio network in Irish, for Irish classes in schools, and for summer holidays for city children in the rural Gaeltacht. What's more, all official signs and notices must be in both languages, e.g. 'exit/*isteach*, Post Office/ *Oifig an Phoist*, women/*mna*' (on toilets), however unnecessary this may seem. And public figures are expected to begin and end any speech with a few phrases in Irish, the ritual *cúpla focal*. All this is easily accepted, for people like having an Irish language, even if few are ready to help by learning it properly. According to surveys, the numbers answering 'yes' to the question 'Do you speak Irish?' have risen since 1961 from 27 to 31 per cent. But it could be that the real figure has dropped, whereas it is now simply more modish to say that you can speak it.

It is in education that matters are most paradoxical. The radical policy of the 1920s may have failed, but its legacy today is that all children must still learn some Irish in class, save in private schools that get no State aid. Until 1973, at least a pass mark in Irish was obligatory for the school leaving certificate (the equivalent of English A-levels) and for civil-service entry. But these rules were widely unpopular, and were dropped by a Fine Gael-led Government. Today, pupils still have to sit Irish for these exams, but it does not matter if they fail – 'a typical Irish fudge,' was one teacher's comment.

Children at primary level often enjoy their Irish lessons, which today are taught in a lively, expressive way with playlets, songs, dances, and few set texts. But at secondary level it is different: as exam pressures mount, most pupils find the Irish classes boring and irrelevant, as compared with French or German, which at least can be useful for getting jobs. Most of the set texts seem to them remote and archaic, e.g. the legendary Peig Sayers's writings about her simple life on the Blasket Islands, off the Kerry coast, a century ago. 'Irish is the subject we all like least,' said a bright seventeen-year-old I met in Galway, and at other secondary schools I heard much the same. 'Irish is our Cinderella here,' said the principal of one large semi-private college in Dublin, 'and frankly it's hard to find a reason for doing it, at a time when we're trying to strengthen our role in Europe, not fall off the edge of it. The kids at senior level are not interested. Most of them would drop Irish tomorrow, if they didn't have to sit it nominally at least for their exams.'

On the other hand, the most startling development of recent years has been the rapid rise in the number of State-backed schools that do all their main teaching in Irish, with English used hardly at all. This is not a scheme imposed by the Government, as in the 1920s: it came first from local parent demand, and then received State funding. Schools of this kind had been dwindling away, except in the rural Gaeltacht areas, but since 1972 the total of Irish-language primary schools outside the Gaeltacht has risen from 11 to 80, while that of secondary schools has risen since 1980 from 8 to 20, nearly all of them in urban areas. At primary level, and outside the Gaeltacht, these schools now comprise 2·31 per cent of all Irish pupils, against 0·58 per cent in 1972. So the numbers are still modest. But this is not just a middle-class trend: many of these schools are in working-class areas, even in the poor North Dublin slum district of Ballymun (see p. 129). Some parents are propelled by a measure of patriotic idealism: 'We are not ourselves Irish-speakers,' said one middle-class couple, 'but Ireland's language is a defence against its being swamped by Anglo-American culture, that's why we send our children to one of these Irish schools.' Many other parents choose them simply because they see them as better than the English-language ones. They tend to be newer, better-funded, and with smaller classes; the teachers are more motivated, the parents likewise. And the children seem to go along with being the guinea-pigs of this venture. They are taught Irish much better than in the other secondary schools; and they have more incentive, since they sit nearly all of their exam papers in Irish.

In the West Dublin suburb of Clondalkin, which is mixed middle and working class, Coláiste Chilliain (Killian's College) was opened in 1984 and now has 445 pupils, aged up to eighteen, who use textbooks in Irish for their history, geography, physics, etc., and have English classes for just three hours a week. The headmaster, Proinnsias Ó hAilín, told me: 'The pressures on them to speak English outside school are enormous, and only about 15 per cent come from Irish-speaking homes. So in school we have to be strict; they must speak Irish among themselves, and anyone caught talking English is gently punished.' Modern foreign languages are taught by the direct method.

One criticism made of these schools is that they could be distracting young people from learning 'useful' modern European languages, just when Ireland needs them. But the Irish-language lobby claims that the opposite is true. It cites the common educational view that to grow up bilingual, or to learn a second language well, is to cross a psychological barrier that then makes it easier to learn a third, fourth or fifth; and they point to multilingual countries like Switzerland that turn out far better linguists than monolingual Britain. Probably this view is correct. At all events, in modern languages as in most other subjects, these schools have better-than-average examination results. In sum, they are a success, and have even become a kind of status symbol for some parents. So there is this polarization in Irish education today, between an eager minority who take Irish seriously, and a majority who do their best to neglect it.

At tertiary level, the colleges of the National University, UCC, UCD and UCG, all require some nominal Irish for admission. But Trinity has never done so. It is optional also for the new business-geared University of Limerick whose president, the abrasive Dr Edward Walsh (see p. 220), has strong views on compulsory Irish, as he told me: 'I suffered from it in 1972, when for a chair related to nuclear physics I had to sit one paper in Irish; and I failed to get the job just because my Irish was so poor. It was victimization. Ireland used to lose many good scientists in that way – crazy! Fortunately, it happens much less today, and examiners have grown more reasonable. But I still think it is wrong to stuff compulsory Irish down pupils' throats. The language is a valuable part of our culture and should be kept alive – but only for those – maybe 10 or 15 per cent – who really want to learn and use it and will do so joyously.'

Another key question is whether the new rise of Irish in the towns can possibly compensate for its continued decline in its 'core areas' of the rural Gaeltacht ('Gaelic entity'). This is the collective name for certain officially designated areas that are supposedly still Irish-speaking and are now carefully subsidized and cherished by the Government – a bit like Indian reservations, you might say. Most are in the farther parts of the West, very scenic but today deprived and depopulating (see p. 107). Because they were so remote, they held on to their language when the rest of Ireland moved to English; and some are still heartlands of what is left of the old Irish folk culture. The biggest areas are in Donegal and in Galway, including the Aran Islands, that mysterious focus of folk tradition; others are in parts of Mayo, Kerry, Co. Cork, and elsewhere.

The Galway Gaeltacht comprises all of southern Connemara, where narrow bumpy roads lead from one little whitewashed village to another, through a rough landscape of green hills, bogs and little lakes, past a straggling coast of deep inlets and tiny rocky islands. All the road signs are just in Irish. Here one night I attended a *Sean Nós* festival in a crowded village pub at Carraroe – local people all talking Irish, singing in turn their solo ballads, semi-improvised, with strange, almost oriental rhythms. There were microphones, videos and girls in jeans; yet in some ways the scene might have been a century ago. I felt in the presence of an alien culture, so different from the world of modern Dublin; and I asked myself whether *this* was the true Ireland, or something today irrelevant to it. I also felt it was sad that the English and

Irish had long ago conspired to marginalize this beautiful Celtic language.

The total population of the Gaeltacht areas is 83,000, of whom nearly all can speak Irish but only about 30,000 use it as their daily first language. Some émigrés from the Gaeltacht return to it later to build retirement homes; and to obtain the grants available, a few of them cleverly pretend to be native Irish speakers when they are not. But it is mainly because of the young people that Irish is declining in these areas. The schools are nearly all Irish-language; but they do not carry the same cachet as in Dublin, and under modern influences such as television the children increasingly turn to English out of class. As emigration persists, so the old prejudice against Irish persists, too, among parents who feel that their children should concentrate on English, if they must go away to Dublin or abroad in search of a job. It is the same Irish drama as in the old days, now hitting the Gaeltacht much later.

The Government's policies for helping the Gaeltacht can be contradictory. Its agencies there have a dual function, (a) to preserve the language, and (b) to promote the economy of these hard-hit areas: but the second tends to militate against the first, for the more the areas are developed, the more their inhabitants are likely to give up speaking Irish. The economic agency, Udarás na Gaeltachta, has scored a few modest successes in attracting new small-scale industries, and tourism; and this has helped to check the fall in population. But it involves bringing in outside managers, technicians, hoteliers, tourists and others, who may benefit the economy but are not going to help the language. Even the civil servants and technocrats, sent in so busily from Dublin to improve the infrastructure and run the public services, are seldom Irish speakers – to the indignation of the officers of the language agency, Bord na Gaeilge, one of whom told me straight-faced, 'Alas, the Government seems to think that the job of Telecom Éireann is to build TV cable links, not to promote Irish.' So the purity of the Gaeltacht is being steadily diluted. Of the two priorities, linguistic and economic, there is no doubt that the local people prefer the latter, if they have to choose; and the Government tacitly agrees. After all, jobs come first. It tries to keep the semblance of an Irish-speaking area by insisting that all public signs are just in Irish; but this can be confusing for tourists, who are often given maps and brochures just in English. How are they to work out that the signpost to An Cheathru Rua refers to the Carraroe on the map?

Close beside the Connemara Gaeltacht stands the booming cultural city of Galway (see p. 140), where matters are rather different. Galway today sees itself as the Gaelic capital of Ireland, and has been filling up with intellectual enthusiasts similar to those who have been leading the language revival in Dublin. Irish is often heard in its streets; it has a flourishing little Irish-language theatre; its chamber of commerce is promoting the notion of a 'bilingual city'; at the university, where all the signs are in Irish, many students take Irish as a main subject and eminent scholars teach Gaelic studies. On one wall I read the graffito, 'We own this country, so why are we still speaking English?' All these idealists feel nourished by the nearby Gaeltacht, and they make pilgrimages there to drink at the fountains of its culture, attending its summer courses and festivals, talking Irish with its 'authentic' country people. So there's an eloquently ironic contrast between these struggling rural communities, more concerned with modern progress than folk culture, and the educated new urban champions of Irish who do not want them to let that culture die.

The population of the Gaeltacht areas had been falling for many years, but is now more or less stabilized. Even so, with the changes in agriculture their economic destiny looks uncertain. And the local future of the language seems even more precarious. 'People here in the Gaeltacht feel a strong tug of historical fatalism about Irish,' said one teacher; 'we think the tide is against us, we are a fragile last outpost on the fringe of the Atlantic, all will be lost.' Many experts believe that Irish is bound to go on dwindling away in these regions. But if soon there is no more Gaeltacht 'core area' where the language stays in traditional daily use, can this really be compensated by a semi-artificial renaissance in the towns? It is the same problem as in many regions of Europe today, such as Brittany.

★

Irish is a rich but difficult language with a curious word order and a complex grammar, full of inflexions. Over the years it has been much infiltrated by English, but in turn it has influenced the kind of English that the Irish speak. J. M. Synge at the turn of the century made a study of the speech rhythms and colloquialisms used by country people speaking English in some parts of Ireland, and he wove these into the wonderfully poetic text of his plays. In *The Playboy of the Western World*, set in Mayo, Christy says to Pegeen: 'Isn't there the light of seven heavens in your heart alone, the way you'll be an angel's lamp to me from this out, and I abroad in the darkness, spearing salmons in the Owen or the Carrowmore?'

Today in country areas you can still hear old Irish-derived idioms and phrases, even if the English spoken has been drawing steadily closer to 'English' English under modern influences such as television. 'And', 'after' and 'himself' are still used in curious ways – 'Sure and it's himself I'm after seeing in the pub, and he promising never to drink again,' i.e., 'I've just seen him in the pub, though he promised never to drink again.' In urban middle-class circles, the English used today is hardly any different from London English: but the Irish still cherish a few special words of their own, many of them taken from their own language – 'crack' for 'gregarious fun' (from the Irish *craic*), 'sláinte' for 'cheers', 'fáilte' for 'welcome', and 'eejit' for 'silly fool', which is probably a corruption of 'idiot'. Some words have even crept into English English: I was assured that 'smashing' (to mean 'superb') derives from the Irish *is maith é sin*, meaning 'that's good'.

In the Dublin world of the media and chattering classes, Irish has been creeping back into fashion, in a sort of way. Television comedians make jokes in it, some rock groups sing in it, advertisements use it – e.g. Bird's Eye's *Iasc* brand (Irish for 'fish'). These may be little more than gimmicks, but they reveal a more serious trend. The middle-class parents who send their children to Irish schools will now sometimes take the trouble to relearn it themselves (as Mary Robinson has been doing) and to speak it on occasions. And when they go abroad, it can be a useful badge of differentness. In a crowded Paris restaurant I met a Dublin couple who were talking English to their small children but Irish between themselves. Why, I asked? – 'Do you think we want to be taken for one of *your* lot?'

There is also a modest revival of writing in Irish, mainly poetry. Before the language went into eclipse in the nineteenth century, the last great Irish-language poets were Antoine Ó Reachtababhra (Anthony Raftery), the blind bard of Mayo, and Brian Mac Giolla Meidhre (Brian Merriman) of Clare, whose witty Rabelaisian saga *Cúirt an Mheádhon-Oídhche* ('The Midnight Court', 1780) has been widely translated. These poets are now in vogue: there's even an annual Merriman festival in Clare, very merry. When the Gaelic revival came in the late nineteenth century, although many of its leaders such as Yeats wrote in English, it also included some fine writers in Irish, such as Peader Ó Laoghaire and Máirtin Ó Cadhain; even Liam O'Flaherty wrote some stories in Irish. But then came another lean period. As books in Irish had such tiny sales, most good writers stuck to English, and the intelligentsia affected to despise those who preferred the native tongue. It is true that Behan first wrote *The Hostage* in Irish, in 1958. But the major influence on the current revival has been the great lyric poet Seán Ó Riordain (1916–77), a modernist somewhat like Eliot who brought Irish-language poetry out of an old-fashioned mode and gave it a contemporary voice.

The best and the best-known poet writing in Irish today is the astonishing Nuala Ní Dhomhnaill – not only a fine writer but an exuberant, warm and exotic personality, much loved. Born in 1952, the daughter of two doctors from Kerry, she was brought up bilingual; and her sexy, psychic and passionate verse is rooted in the songs and folklore of Kerry, to which she lends a modern tone – 'My poetic mode is in Irish, I could never write poetry in English,' she told me. With her flowing red hair, motherly figure, Jungian earth-mother persona and outspoken opinions, she cuts a striking figure on television and has become something of a cult in places like New York, 'where people treat me as a shaman, they want to touch me all the time, it's spooky'. This shaman is just about the most impressive and fascinating person I have met in Ireland, a mix of shrewd wisdom and visionary quirkiness. She lives with her Turkish husband and four children in a tiny Turkish-decorated house outside Dublin, where our talk ranged widely from politics to magic, women and language:

'English is a much more conceptual language than Irish, which can easily take in notions like magic spirits, fairies and "the other world" [*An saol eile*]. All this may sound twee in English, but not in Irish. Yeats understood it. In the Kerry Gaeltacht they still believe in spirits, and many of the old cabals and *piseoga* [superstitions] vaguely survive. But under the impact of rational Englishness they have been repressed, which is dangerous. It can lead to anorexia and other illnesses . . .

'On today's moral issues, I'm a liberal: but the debate has become too polarized. The Marxist feminist lobby may be right about abortion, but it fails to understand the other side, the desire of ordinary people for mystery, magic, superstition in their lives. So because liberals pooh-pooh all this, it remains the monopoly of a reactionary Church, and for their magic and mystery people have to turn to the clerics, those octogenarian eunuchoid despots in skirts. Myself, I *love* moving statues and miracles, and I respect people's desire to believe in them. Intellectuals do wrong to reject this side of our nature.

'On the language issue, the Government is hypocritical. It pays lip-service to the revival, but does little to help it. Either it should see that everyone learns Irish properly, or else it should drop the pretence of its being the "first language", make it really voluntary, and stop vaguely believing in some holy spirit or tongues of flame that will somehow keep it alive. I agree that our self-absorbed Irish complex about "Irishness" – so tedious! – would be far less strong if we used our own national language like the Danes, or like Israel, which really did manage to impose Hebrew. It's a pity that Irish was pushed out in the old days – partly our own fault. Now it is too late to bring it back as a main language.'

President Mary Robinson's own enthusiasm for Irish has done much to encourage its revival, since her election. She has been relearning it, and she brings it widely into her speeches, not just as the ritual *cúpla focal* at the start. 'I can spend a whole day conversing in Irish with people in the Gaeltacht, where I get pleasure from hearing its lilting quality,' she told me. 'The language is very central to our sense of identity, in face of English. We need to capture the hearts and minds of our young people about this.' And one Gaelic leader, Professor Seán Ó Tuama, commented in the *Irish Times*: 'Her invitation to the nation to join with her in discovering the value and meaning of Irish in their lives is the most exciting boost the language restoration movement has received for many a long day.'

This diverse movement, the so-called language lobby, includes academics, journalists, politicians and other activists. Twenty years ago it was perceived as strongly nationalist in a political sense, with possible IRA links; and this served to discredit the Irish language in many people's eyes. Today, some of its leaders remain politically nationalist, such as Labhrás Ó Murchú of CCE, and Proinsias Mac Aonghusa, who when chairman of Bord na Gaeilge called on Catholics in West Belfast in 1992 to vote for Gerry Adams: this caused quite a furore. But today most members of the lobby are nationalists purely in a cultural sense. Many of them re-Gaelicize their names, turning Patrick Allen into Padraig O hAilin, or Frank McSweeney into Proinsias McSuibhne.

The lobby puts constant pressure on the Government, and in 1993 it won a small victory in its long crusade for a separate Irish TV channel. RTE since 1972 has run a national radio network in Irish, full of local gossip about farmers' doings in the Gaeltacht, with a small but loyal audience. RTE also screens some TV programmes in Irish, mostly cultural. Then in January 1993 the new Government promised that it would set up a third TV channel, broadcasting in Irish for two or three hours a day. But by early 1994 it was still not clear what the channel would show for the rest of the day, how it would be paid for, or when it would start up. Sceptics asked how this small, struggling country could afford the indulgence of a third channel, in the present economic climate; and they wondered how its audience could be other than minimal, in face of the spread of satellite TV and other pressures. The language lobby's reply is that, if most children dislike learning Irish in school, then some more attractive way must be found to sell them the language out of school – maybe including the dubbing into Irish of popular imported material. Not a Euro-Disney but an Eiro-Disney?

Yet the fundamental question remains: just how important is it that a small nation should try to preserve its own language, when the odds are so stacked against it? For some people, the issue is clear. One of Ireland's most respected Gaelic scholars, Dr Gearoid Ó Tuathaigh of University College, Galway, said to me, 'If you allowed Irish to go, you would close the door on a marvellous heritage, a crucial part of Irishness. And the Irish, those resilient survivors, would feel a great sense of failure.' For Proinsias Mac Aonghusa, 'The language is the most Irish thing we have, more than the Book of Kells.' And the historian Joseph Lee, also sympathetic to the cause, has written, 'It may be that there is an Irish emotional reality which is silenced in English.' But it can be argued, conversely, that if English had not become Ireland's first language, then the Irish could never have made their remarkable contribution to English literature, and would have lost the self-confidence that this has brought.

According to opinion surveys, and to my own impressions, the vast majority of Irish people do not want the language to die. But if there is no realistic prospect of its reaching parity with English, of Ireland becoming a bilingual nation like, say, Canada, then what practical applications in daily life can it possibly find? There are few clear answers. The Government is criticized from both sides, but what other policy could it reasonably pursue? Probably it should drop the fiction of Irish as the 'first language' of State. Arguably it should cease to make Irish lessons compulsory in ordinary schools, but this would cause a political storm that few ministers would want to risk. The other extreme, to insist that all pupils learn Irish fully and are properly examined in it, seems equally unfeasible. So maybe the best course is to go on backing the spontaneous vogue for Irish-language schools and other cultural trends. But the children who come out of these schools, speaking Irish so well, then complain understandably that they can find few outlets for it in their work or leisure. To enforce a Gaelicization of public or business life would be impossible. So Irish in adult life is probably fated to remain a voluntary cultural asset, like the arts or sport, the language of those who really want it, maybe 10 per cent. After all, even Dr O Tuathaigh accepts that 'people can be non-Irish-speakers yet fully Irish, secure in their ethnicity', and Mary Robinson told me: 'It should be a choice. Nobody should feel less Irish if they do not speak Irish.'

The Irish look for foreign parallels that might help them in their dilemma. Some other small countries have held on to their language in face of mighty neighbours: Denmark vis-à-vis Germany, Finland vis-à-vis Russia. But they have not had the Irish experience of being colonized for so long by a powerful neighbour sharing a language with the Americans. Belgium and Canada are bilingual, Switzerland is multilingual; but these are the daily languages of substantial regions of these countries, whereas the Gaeltacht is so tiny, frail and scattered. In nations that are not sovereign, i.e. Wales, Brittany, the Basque country, language is often seen as a political weapon for survival and autonomy. Per Denez, a Breton nationalist and professor of Celtic languages at Rennes, told me he felt that independent Ireland today had little need for its own language, as compared with Brittany 'still struggling for its survival'. On the other hand, nationalism today is far more potent in Scotland, where hardly anyone speaks Gaelic, than in Wales with its many Welsh speakers: so there may not always be such a close link between language and national identity. As Irish is dissimilar from other Celtic tongues, it cannot gain much support from the success of Welsh, nor from Breton, which is also in danger of dying out. In short, there is no real foreign parallel to the dilemma of Irish, fighting on its own in a land that speaks English.

However, there are some who believe that European Union could be of help to Irish, paradox though this might seem. 'We are part of a Europe of cultural diversity, where other minority languages flourish,' Mary Robinson told me, 'and our Irish language and culture are our unique contribution to this Europe.' According to this view, which I heard from others too, just as EC membership has freed Ireland from economic and psychological over-dependence on Britain, so the new Europe can liberate Irish from its unequal face-to-face with English and bring it into a wider multilingual world, thus helping the Irish to accept the idea of bilingualism. The new links with Brittany are cited as an example. 'At first in the early 1970s', said Labhrás Ó Murchú, 'I was opposed to EC entry, I felt that our culture was still too fragile and would be swamped. But now I think I was wrong. I have seen what other countries do for their cultures and languages, and we have a lot to learn from them. Through the EC, other nations have become more aware of Ireland, and this helps our self-esteem.'

The music revival, the success abroad of Irish music groups, also helps the cultural self-confidence. At the head of bodies such as Bord na Gaeilge, CCE and the GAA, there may still be too many old-style nationalists, wanting to give their kind of slant to the cultural revival. But very few young people feel this way. They simply want to enjoy their Irishness and share it with others – in a wider world where the old Irish diaspora is finding a new role.

9

IRELAND AND THE WORLD: A
WIDENING OF HORIZONS

Ireland's relations with the outside world used to be almost
entirely focused on Britain, through the colonial link, and also on
the United States and Australia, through emigration. Today, EC
membership since 1973, and other changes, have brought important and growing new links with Europe, and have loosened the
old over-dependence on Britain. Ireland's active role in the United
Nations as well as in Europe, plus the influence of television,
foreign travel and greater education, have all served to broaden
the horizons of a once so enclosed and still self-preoccupied
society. This chapter looks at these changes – and at the impact
of mass emigration, which still haunts the Irish, even though its
nature has greatly altered in recent years.

The diaspora: emigrants become commuters

The Irish diaspora is phenomenal: since the mid nineteenth century,
Ireland has produced far more emigrants than many countries
with ten times its population. A few statistics can set the scene.
Between 1846 and 1921 some four million people left, and a
further two million by the 1960s. Today as many as 44 million
Americans claim at least some Irish blood and 11 million of these
are of pure Irish descent, according to census returns; among
Australians, nearly 30 per cent have Irish roots, making this the
most 'Irish' country outside Ireland. And by the 1920s, 43 per cent
of those born in Ireland were living elsewhere, as compared with

figures of 14.8 per cent for Norway and 14.1 per cent for Scotland, other countries with strong emigration. Today the exodus has slowed: but over a third of Irish-born people are still living abroad.

The trauma of emigration has profoundly marked the Irish psyche. In the Famine period of the 1840s, people emigrated for sheer physical survival, to avoid death by starvation or disease. Later they left mainly to escape rural poverty, in this Catholic land of large families. Most went reluctantly but some more readily, to seek wider opportunities. Today, the emigration has changed its nature: most of it is now from the towns and the educated classes, and is prompted less by dire poverty than by unemployment and rising aspirations. Many young people go planning to return after a few years. But the pain of separation continues: most families have some members living abroad, above all in England. And some poorer people still keep memories alive, orally transmitted, of relatives who left in the Famine or after. It is a tragedy not yet fully wiped from the heart.

Attitudes to emigration have always varied. For some people it has seemed positive, a chance to escape from a backward, stifling society into a better life, maybe even to bring their foreign skills back to Ireland one day. Joyce and some other writers left because Ireland was too narrow for them; only as exiles were they able to fulfil themselves. And today the Irish remain vaguely proud of the impact that their small country has been able to make on the world, through its emigrants – proud of the John F. Kennedys and Tony O'Reillys. And yet, for most Irish people over the past 150 years, emigration has seemed little more than a necessary evil, not only breaking up families and creating the anguish of exile, but depriving Ireland of so much of its skill and talent, possibly impeding economic growth. Governments since independence have frequently been criticized for policies that have failed to check the exodus. And Irish literature is full of nostalgic tales of exiles yearning for the Ould Country yet unable or unwilling to return; witness George Moore's *Home Sickness* (1902), about a successful New York barman who goes eagerly back on a visit to the Co. Cork village of his youth, but soon becomes horrified by its sloth, poverty and priest-ridden ignorance, drops his plan to resettle there, and returns to the Bowery where, trapped between two cultures, he continues to brood about the blue Irish hills and the girl he left behind. In those days, most Irish exiles could not afford to make a return visit, save maybe once or twice in a lifetime. But today, with better transport and more money, they come back regularly. And so, as emigrants become commuters, the pain of exile lessens – a major change of the past decades.

There was some emigration in the early nineteenth century, but it did not become a mass movement until the Famine period. According to Cecil Woodham-Smith's classic study of the Famine, *The Great Hunger*, over a million people then moved to Britain, and another million or so went to North America, crossing the ocean in the overcrowded, pest-ridden 'coffin ships' where many perished *en route*. But most survived, and by 1850 some 26 per cent of New York's population was Irish-born, while by 1855 the United States had 1·5 million people of Irish birth. This transatlantic exodus continued up to the late 1920s. Many of these new Irish Americans acquired an energy and sense of ambition that had eluded them in stagnating Ireland, and a few became rich and successful. But the majority stayed in menial jobs. Generally unskilled, unused to urban life, maybe speaking no English, they were despised and humiliated by the WASPs of that era; and the dread phrase 'No Irish Need Apply' appeared on many a job notice. It was an amazingly youthful exodus: of those who left Ireland between 1852 and 1921, over 50 per cent were aged between fifteen and twenty-four. And after about 1900, women emigrants outnumbered men. Daughters, more than sons, recoiled at the prospect of a life of subordinate drudgery on a small farm. It has even been suggested that, from the 1920s onwards, some of them were lured by the glamour of Hollywood movies to seek a new world.

Starting in the late 1920s, several new factors have now changed the nature and pattern of emigration. The first was the Great Depression, which reduced the American job market and led US Governments to impose much harsher curbs on immigration. The results were dramatic. Whereas in 1876–1925 ten times more Irish had settled in the USA than in Britain, after the Depression the picture was almost reversed. And this became a permanent change, as the American restrictions continued while Britain kept an open door to the Irish; during the 1980s, over two-thirds of all Irish emigrants went to Britain, and just 14 per cent to the USA. Irish quotas for US entry have today been extended, under the 'Morrison visa' scheme (see below): but they are still quite tight.

The second factor, more recent, is that the average emigrant is today much more educated than before, and many are well-qualified graduates. This reflects changes in society. Secondary or higher education now embraces far more young people than it did forty years ago (see p. 208); changes in farming have reduced the surplus population on the land, so there are fewer rural would-be emigrants; and unemployment has risen hugely in the towns, at all social levels. Whereas in the 1950s some 75 per cent of emigrants were rural, and mostly unskilled, today 75 per cent are from urban backgrounds – a huge change. Plenty of emigrants are still from the poorest classes. But the long-term unemployed or the really poor are now less likely to leave, for social welfare has improved in Ireland while in Britain under Thatcher it was cut back. So the jobless today have more incentive to stay in their Irish home setting.

Emigration is thus no longer the same desperate, coercive solution as in the old days. A new educated class is now leaving, not quite so desperately, yet not always gladly. Some young people go to seek training and experience abroad, and plan to return after a few years – but often they do not do so. Others leave because they cannot find suitable jobs in Ireland, or are not satisfied with their jobs; many graduates have been forced to take work well below their qualification (e.g. as waiters or barmen), or they find they can earn far more money abroad, where the salaries are higher and the income tax lower. In London I met a man from Mayo, youngest son of a farming family of eight, five of whom had emigrated. Despite a postgraduate degree from UCG, he could not find suitable work in his western homeland. So he moved to London, where he ran a welfare agency – and after ten years he finally managed to get back to Galway with a good job in industry. He was one of the luckier ones.

During Britain's boom years of the 1980s when skilled jobs were easy to find, thousands of young engineers, doctors, accountants, computer analysts and others moved across the Irish Sea. Over a third of those graduating in 1987 and 1988 went abroad; and in the 1980s the lure of London stole almost every architect qualifying at UCD. So this whole trend has raised again the issue of the brain drain, a stormy topic since the 1920s. Why, it is asked, is poor Ireland paying expensively to train graduates who then sell their skills to the service of richer countries? Some experts, notably the controversial Dr Edward Walsh of Limerick, argue that this kind of emigration does have its uses: it enables graduates to gain high-technology expertise which they cannot find in Ireland, and if they then come back home, this can be valuable. It can even help investment: witness the American microchip firm Intel, which in 1992 decided to build a plant in Ireland when it found it could hire 150 Irish engineers eager to return from Germany (see p. 75). But many émigrés do not return; and most economists will argue that overall the brain drain is damaging to Ireland. Under its new EU aid package, the Government is now using some Social Fund money to subsidize higher education; it argues that this is only fair, seeing that other EU members, notably Britain, benefit from it.

The third new factor has been the turning of emigration into a kind of commuting, less permanent than before, less like exile. The rise of affluence and of cheaper air transport, plus the switch of the main destination from America to nearby Britain, have all meant that emigrants are now far more likely to make return visits quite often. In the old days, there were poignant scenes at the railway stations of the rural West, as sons and daughters left for America, perhaps never to be seen again; and even from Britain they might not be back for many months. Today, Mayo's new Knock airport is busy with Irish coming home for weekends maybe ten times a year; and a Dublin–London air fare can cost less than a day's wages, say £40. Emigration has become more experimental, mobile, even in some cases seasonal: a worker may go to Canada for a summer job, then on to Bavaria for another in winter. I met one young graduate who had spent a year in Australia, then two years back in Dublin, and was just off to a job in London, planning to return. All this makes emigration more endurable, even fun, but of course it depends on the vagaries of the job markets, in a time of recession. The Irish are beginning to settle in towns like Paris and Munich (see pp. 334–5), but the Continent's share of Irish emigration remains small, a bare 6 per cent of the total, despite the growing links with Europe.

Finally, a fourth factor: the repeated cyclical changes in emigration since the 1960s, including a new homecoming trend. During the 1950s and early 1960s emigration was still at a high level, for the Irish economy was stagnating while Britain and other countries were enjoying the post-war boom; over half of those who left school in the early 1950s had emigrated by 1961, a terrifying figure. But then came the impact of the Lemass policy of growth, followed by some recession in Britain in the 1970s, and the picture changed radically. So many émigrés returned to live in Ireland that during the 1970s there was a net inflow of some 12,000 a year – the first time since 1930, and only the second since the Famine, that more Irish had come home than had left. 'Emigration used to haunt my parents' generation, but in my own age group none of my family had to leave,' said one young worker. And the population not only stopped declining but rose faster than anywhere else in Western Europe.

However, in the 1980s the exodus began again, for the British and Irish economies were once again desynchronized. While Ireland ran into trouble, Britain recovered and moved ahead; so the Irish net outflow totalled 130,000 for 1983–8, the great era of the yuppie exodus to London. But then the cycle took yet another twist, as Britain and the United States went into recession in the early 1990s. The Irish again began to return home, and the net annual outflow fell sharply in 1990–91 from 31,000 to just 1,000. Jobs in Britain became much harder to find in the building and retail sectors, and in graduate areas too: I even met an *architect* who went home to Dublin! Unemployment in Ireland was rising too – 'But if we're going to be on the dole, frankly we'd rather stay in our own country where the quality of life is better and our families can help us,' said one young UCD graduate. Many graduates do still go to try their luck abroad, and young people from the farms, too, but the hard cases of the urban working-class unemployed will now more often stay at home on welfare, creating social problems.

Emigration is likely to remain a feature of Irish life for many years. If the falling birth rate or other factors do finally lead to a major drop in unemployment, then of course the pressures to leave will decline too. But so long as the economies of Britain and other western countries are buoyant, there will always be plenty of young Irish seeking to explore this wider world, outside their tight little island. This is healthy and positive in many ways – so long as they can go willingly, without economic coercion, and can return to jobs in Ireland if and when they wish. This is still not the case – even if the old nineteenth-century sufferings are no more than a nasty tribal memory.

There remains the much-debated issue of whether heavy emigration has done economic or emotional damage to Ireland. Professor Joseph Lee has written that in the Victorian era the 'possessing classes' encouraged the exodus, for they feared that a surplus poverty-bound population could create unrest and threaten their privileges. So a conservative landowning culture was strengthened that gave little scope for investment or risk-taking, and this made the more able or ambitious all the readier to leave. In this century, too, Ireland has continued to export much of its best talent. Moreover, the escape-hole of emigration has reduced internal pressures for change, for restive would-be reformers might be told, 'If you don't like it here, why don't you leave?' Or they would just get too frustrated, and go. It reminds me of the old East Germany under Communism.

Emigration has been fuelled by Irish love–hate feelings for their own country – more love than hate, but a love frequently tinged with irritation and pessimism. Brian Friel has explored this brilliantly in *Philadelphia Here I Come*, whose young hero is emigrating not so much for economic reasons as through despair at his non-relationship with his emotionally paralysed father, and at the narrow, trivial Donegal society around him – and this plight becomes a metaphor for the paralysis of Ireland, as Friel sees it. That play was written in the early 1960s. Today, as Irish society liberalizes, as family ties become easier, as birth control and even divorce (maybe) come in, as the repressive hold of the Church weakens, so the like of Friel's Gar O'Donnell may find less emotional temptation to leave the island. But among émigrés today you can still find echoes of these attitudes. A bright girl from a village in Co. Monaghan, now working in a bank in London, told me: 'I hate that old-fashioned sentimental national-ism, that SPUC morality, that prying gossip. Yet I'm glad to be Irish, and I miss Ireland. So what do I do?' It is the dilemma of many of the young Irish in Britain today.

The Irish in Britain and America – and what's left of the Anglo-Irish gentry

The Irish emigrants to Britain in the nineteenth and early twentieth centuries came mostly by boat to Liverpool or Glasgow, and they settled first in those areas, and around Manchester. The majority took menial jobs as unskilled labourers, and were seldom made very welcome. 'No Irish Need Apply' notices went up, as in America. This pattern continued up until the 1960s, as new waves of migrants arrived. During World War Two, many came over to work in the munitions factories of the old British enemy – from Mayo, for example, as John Healy wrote, 'they went out in train loads to send back hated John Bull's lovely pounds' to their families at home. They would much rather have gone to America, had it been possible, but even British war work was better than none.

Today, although many of the Irish in Britain remain near the bottom of the social pile, a number have proved upwardly mobile and have done well, if less spectacularly so than in America. One example: Tom Beisty, from a small farm in Mayo, came over in 1961 at the age of sixteen to follow an elder brother. He took a job as a building labourer, worked furiously, showed flair, started his own little construction firm in north London, and in the boom years built it into a business with a £5 million annual turnover. That would hardly be possible in today's harsher climate. But even today some three-quarters of Britain's building trade is owned by Irish or people with Irish roots – 'It's just that we've had more incentive than the British to work hard and succeed,' said Beisty. In the 1960s, the new, more educated kind of emigrant began to arrive in greater numbers: many of the girls were nurses or secretaries, the men were in the professions, and many made straight for the booming London area. So today, with the industrial decline of Clydeside and Lancashire, with the growth of air transport and the rise of this new-style emigrant, fewer people now arrive by boat in the north-west, and more come direct to southern England, above all to London, where Irish accents mix with the Euro-Afro-Asian babel.

It is hard to give a reliable figure for the number of Irish in Britain, for citizenship is not the sole criterion. Some four to five million are said to have at least one Irish grandparent, which would make them automatically eligible for Irish citizenship if they wished it. But of the Irish living in Britain today, only about 650,000 were born in the Republic, and only about 590,000 have Irish citizenship. Some Irish take British citizenship, if they are going to stay. But this brings them few extra benefits, for under an agreement reached between the two Governments at the time of independence, the Irish in Britain have virtually the same rights as the British. They can vote, they can come and go as they please, without passports, and they have full rights to employment and social welfare. Other EU citizens have now won some of these same advantages, at least regarding work, welfare and free movement – but the Irish got there first, by special privilege. This freedom is in some ways an asset, but it can make the Irish less inclined to integrate socially into British life. Many therefore go on feeling they are outsiders.

Theirs is a very diversified community. It has no strong political lobby as in the United States, but there are lots of Irish activities – big social-cum-cultural centres in London's Camden Town and in

Liverpool; scores of Irish pubs; branches of the GAA for Irish
sport and of the CCE for traditional music; and a huge annual
outdoor *fleadh* in Finsbury Park, London, claiming to be the
biggest Irish popular music event in the world. Here with 30,000
others in 1992 I stood in the mud to listen to The Chieftains,
Christie Moore, Bob Geldof, The Saw Doctors. In London,
people from Cork and Kerry tend to live in the Camden Town
area, those from Galway and Mayo in Kilburn or Cricklewood.
At the London Mayo Association's Christmas dinner in Willesden,
I was told there are more Mayo people in London than in Mayo
itself – just as Paris has more Aveyronnais than there are in the
Aveyron. Yet for all the outward chumminess of the Irish, theirs
in Britain is an atomized society, with less solidarity than among
the Pakistanis or Chinese; and many immigrants have little contact
with other Irish groups or activities.

It is the middle-class and professional people who tend to be the
best adapted and best accepted. Some of them contribute their
Irish eloquence to the media scene, such as broadcasters Frank
Delaney and Terry Wogan, both Irish-born. A number of pop
stars choose to live in England, too, for example Van Morrison
and The Pogues; and numerous writers, not only veterans like
Edna O'Brien but young novelists, second-generation Irish, such
as Bridget O'Connor. In university circles, Irish studies have been
expanding: there is a thriving centre at Liverpool, while Oxford
recently created a chair of Irish History and gave it to the young
and powerfully omniscient Roy Foster, born in Waterford.

The attitudes of the Irish to living in Britain are equivocal,
unsurprisingly (see p. 7). One exuberant friend of my wife said:
'When people here ask me how it is that I'm so *very* friendly,
outgoing and direct, I say, "It's because I'm Irish," and they say,
"Oh yes, of *course*." If I went back to Dublin I'd find ten thousand
women just like me – it would be boring. Here in London I can
capitalize on my Irishness.' Most Irish, however, find that they are
more popular on the Continent than in Britain (see below). They
enjoy London's cosmopolitanism, the tolerance and lack of nosi-
ness; but they share the general foreign view of the southern
English middle class as too uptight and standoffish ('tepidly

emotionless,' said Edna O'Brien), and to this they add the usual Irish complex about their former colonizers, whom they often find patronizing – 'In the tube, when people hear my Irish accent, they snigger and I feel awkward,' said one girl, with an unnecessary touch of paranoia, I felt. Nearly all Irish say that with their own real English friends they get on well, but they still do not feel at home in England. They are treated neither as foreigners nor as quite native. They think of going home, but the longer they stay, the more they may feel they are 'growing out of Ireland, so cosy but so provincial', as one man put it. Many stay firstly for economic reasons. 'After getting a degree at an Irish technical college,' said one young man of twenty-three, 'I'm now earning £20,000 a year here in London as a civil engineer. In Ireland, I would find it hard to get any such job; and if I did, it would pay only half that, and be far more highly taxed. That's why I'm still here. But I miss the warmth of Ireland.'

At working-class level, today there are far fewer of the old rough navvies from the rural West whom the English, rightly or wrongly, used to despise as violent drunkards. Plenty of Irish still come as manual workers, but they are now of a different kind, less coarse and hard-drinking, less uneducated, for Ireland itself has changed. Some of them helped to build the Channel Tunnel; today they work on motorways and other sites – if they can find the jobs in these difficult days. They are respected as harder workers than the British, and some of them earn up to £600 or £800 a week. The *Independent* quoted one worker from Donegal, who plays golf and drinks wine: 'When we're in the bar and we're all having a singsong, some of these English lads will ask us why we sing so much. So I ask them for a song and you get these blank faces . . . I tell them that they need the Irish to fill in the silences left by the English.' They claim to get on quite well with the English, especially with people in the north country whose culture and warm temperament seem closer to their own than Londoners'. But of course they feel homesick for Ireland.

The pattern is still very varied. Many of the young migrants of the 1950s and '60s, now middle-aged, have never really settled in. One expert on the Irish in Britain, Father Bobby Gilmore, gave me a dour assessment: 'There is still this ideology of return, they think they are going to go back one day, but they leave it too late. There was a ballad by a man who lived in Kilburn, "It's a long, long way from Clare, and it's further every year . . ." Yet their hearts are still there in the West, they never settle here fully: it's amazing how few of them open bank accounts. They live in a kind of limbo, dreaming nostalgically of the Ireland of their boyhood, not realizing how much it has changed. But for the second generation, born here, it can be different: they do develop an identity with Britain.' But even the newer emigrants are still bringing with them their Irish temperament, their songful, chummy sociability that can hide an inner melancholy. According to recent surveys, of all ethnic or national groups in Britain the Irish die youngest, have the second highest suicide rate and the highest rate of entry to psychiatric hospitals. The only reason the experts can suggest for this is that they miss Ireland's very special social life and are often lonely. Of the new young arrivals, most find their feet but many do not. In 1991, almost one-third of single homeless people in Greater London were found to be Irish – the same problem that Dr Éamonn Casey found when he co-founded Shelter in the 1960s (see p. 167). Today, various voluntary Irish agencies in Britain are trying to help these newcomers, and the Irish Government subsidizes them. But emigration still has its darker side.

Daily relations with the British may have improved since the bad old days, but there is one new and troubling problem: the IRA. Some stupider British think of Ireland solely in terms of the IRA and know nothing else; they may even confuse North with South. So, however unfairly, the waves of bombings since the 1970s have created among some people a generalized anger against the Irish, and perfectly innocent Irish will sometimes catch the rough side of a British tongue, maybe a crude insult in a pub or train. This induces some people to disguise their Irish identity in public, notably in working-class areas, or otherwise to keep a low profile. Since the start of the Troubles, the St Patrick's Day parades in British cities have become very modest, low-key affairs, as compared with their lavish New York equivalent. And although there may be very little active support for the IRA among the Irish in Britain, the recent distortions of justice, the Birmingham Six or Guildford Four affairs and the rest (see p. 366), have lent some sneaking sympathy for the bombers. The Prevention of Terrorism Act, introduced in the 1970s to help the police fight the IRA, gives them special powers to question or detain suspects for up to seven days, and has obliged Britain to abstain from the European Convention on Human Rights. The powers are used almost entirely against the Irish, of South or North, and it has prompted the bitter jest that a suspect 'is innocent until proven Irish'. It is not a problem facing the Irish in the United States.

The Irish community in America is a vast subject, outside the scope of this book. The Irish there have assimilated much more fully than in Britain, and a number have made their way to the top, both in politics and business. That says something about the nature of American society, and about the thrusting ambition concealed within many an easygoing Irish heart. Presidents Kennedy, Nixon and Reagan all had Irish roots. Tony O'Reilly (see p. 79), the best-known Irish-American business leader, may live in Pittsburgh but he still has close links with Ireland. Another tycoon, Tom Flatley, left his Mayo home village in 1958 with just $25, worked as a plumber in Boston, and gradually built up a diversified business empire that today employs 6,000; he himself is said to be worth $700 million.

Immigration quotas have remained a major issue, since the depression of the 1930s. The Immigration Act of 1965 reduced the official Irish entry to some 1,000 a year, but this simply prompted a stream of illegal immigrants; Irish visitors would go over on tourist visas and then just stay. It was nothing compared with the wetback influx from Mexico, but it annoyed the authorities. Then in 1987 Congressman Brian Donnelly from Boston arranged a scheme whereby the Irish were given a special extra immigration quota for three years. After this expired, another Irish-American anxious to help the Irish, Congressman Bruce Morrison, pushed through the 1990 Immigration Act, which extended the so-called 'Morrison visas' for a further three-year period, ending September

1994. This scheme gave the Irish a quota of some 16,000 immigration visas a year, representing 40 per cent of the total allocation offered to thirty-four countries – a remarkable act of favouritism, showing once again the power of the Irish-American lobby. The visas have been awarded on a lottery basis by a computer, and their main aim has been to regularize the status of the illegal residents; some 80 per cent of the new visas have gone to them. But they must first go back to Ireland to collect them from the US embassy there, and must prove that they have a secure job in the United States. By 1993 the number of 'illegals' had been thus reduced to an estimated 40,000, and new tourist visas were being issued more warily. Several tourist applications by young single people, unemployed in Ireland, were turned down.

Even so, there are still plenty of students who manage to visit the United States each summer and find casual jobs. New York and Boston still exert a mythical sway on the Irish imagination, and America is still seen as glamorous, if less so than in the old days. For language reasons, and also because of the strong Irish/American connection, most young people still feel more at home there than on the Continent – the writer Ferdia Mac Anna, who sees modern American culture as part of his own culture, is a case in point (see p. 246). Academics, even poets, still go far more readily on exchanges to the USA than to Europe. Ireland and America may be so different, yet it is the Irish more than most peoples who have made America what it is; maybe it provides expression to another side of their own nature, which cannot so easily come to fruition in Ireland itself.

There is however a darker side to this picture: the failure of so many Irish-Americans to understand the realities of Northern Ireland. Many still see it as a colonial situation, with the British as the oppressors. Local support for the MacBride principles (see p. 403) is one part of the problem, but far worse is the material help given to the IRA by the infamous Noraid organization. One of its leaders, the veteran Michael Flannery, an IRA gun-runner in the 1970s, was until 1989 the Grand Master of the St Patrick's Day parade in New York – despite many protests. Noraid is run largely by Irish-American businessmen with pro-IRA views. It raises funds that ostensibly are for IRA prisoners and other victims of British 'injustice', but in practice some of this money finds its way to paying for terrorism. To some degree, this lobby remains one of the obstacles to peace in Ulster.

On a happier note, one facet of Ireland's American link is the current boom in so-called 'ethnic tourism'. Many Irish-Americans today go on holiday in Ireland to seek out their roots. The numbers are growing, for attitudes to having Irish blood have been changing in the USA, Australia and elsewhere. In the old days, the children of the refugees from famine and poverty would often try to hide or forget their humble origins, as they built up a new life in a new world. But today's generations feel no such shame; amongst rich people it is now quite fashionable to boast a forebear from a Connemara cottage, or even one who came to Australia as a convict. Grace Kelly helped to set this trend in 1961, with her much-publicized visit to her grandfather's former farmstead in Mayo.

This ethnic tourism today accounts for quite a slice of Ireland's holiday traffic, and is much encouraged by the authorities. They have been setting up a network of new family history centres, one in each county, with computerized indexes of old parish registers and land valuations, sometimes dating back centuries. You pay a nominal fee for an initial inquiry, then more for a fuller investigation. Or you can hire the services of a genealogical research firm, such as the one which dug up Ronald Reagan's peasant roots for him in Co. Tipperary. This could be wiser than trying to do the documentary research yourself, for some old records are in Latin, or else the handwriting can be a nightmare – 'After his fourteenth marriage in the day, and the same number of drinks, a priest's writing gets undecipherable,' I was told. In 1992 the tourist boards of both South and North staged a month-long Homecoming Festival, to entice more of the diaspora to explore their origins, thus helping Irish tourism. It was a nationwide explosion of clan rallies and cultural events, plus banquets, *Céilthe*, hurling matches, genealogical seminars and tours of historic sites. At Dromahair, Co. Leitrim, seat of the O'Rourke chieftains since pre-Norman times, some 12,000 O'Rourkes around the globe were sent invitations to a clan rally: 'We'll show them their spiritual home amid these O'Rourke ruins, we'll deluge them with O'Rourke folklore,' said the joky local organizer, Patrick O'Rourke.

Why do people want to seek their roots? 'It can be the sheer romance of it,' said a genealogist at one of the new centres. 'After we have done the archive work for them, they then get quite hooked on the real fieldwork, ferreting round local pubs for oldies who might remember great-uncle Seamus. One woman left for the US as a child in the 1920s, where she lost all contact with her Irish family; she was amazed to find she still had half-sisters alive in Clare.' While family pride and affection, or sheer curiosity, are the commonest motives for the quest, just a few people come seeking a long-lost heir on whom to bestow a legacy; or, conversely, they come armed with a legal brief, to establish a claim to some property (as in *The Field*, cf. p. 108). Today another practical motive is appearing, too: if you can prove that any grandparent was born in Ireland, you are able to claim Irish nationality, and a number of Americans, Australians and others now see this as a way of gaining a foothold in the EU, either for a work permit or the right to open a business.

I decided to test the new services by using my own case history. My father's father, from a Protestant family, migrated from Co. Waterford to Surrey in the 1880s, as a young doctor. So I went to the lively Waterford heritage centre, buzzing with computers, where a local historian, Julian Walton, dug out the documents. He told me about the Reverend S. B. Ardagh, who in 1854 was 'set on by a Popish mob' near Waterford, before emigrating to Canada. Walton took me to the little parish church at Kilmeadan where my great-uncle Robert lies buried; and to the old millhouse by a stream where my grandfather was born. His family, cotton-millers, owned it till the 1920s. It then fell into decline. But I was happy to find that it has now been acquired by a wealthy Chinese doctor, who has renovated it and filled it with his sumptuous collection of oriental art treasures. He proudly showed me round. The Ardagh ghosts, I felt, were in safe hands.

My family were probably Norman-Welsh in origin and came over to Ireland with Henry II, in 1171. In 1272 an Arthur Ardagh was captain of Dublin Castle; in 1346 another Arthur Ardagh commanded the bodyguard of the Black Prince at Crécy, and was later made Governor of Ireland. In short, we were firmly in the colonizers' camp, and so we embraced Protestantism at the Reformation. How we acquired our very Irish name (it means 'high place') is not clear; probably it came from the Welsh. There is a village of Ardagh in Co. Limerick, where the celebrated Ardagh Chalice (now in Dublin's National Museum) was found in a field in 1868. But although Ardagh is common as a place-name in Ireland, it is rare as a family name. And after their notable start in the Middle Ages, the Ardaghs by the 1900s had settled for the more modest life of local mill-owners. They were only very minor members of the so-called Ascendancy, and in no sense a part of the real Anglo-Irish landed gentry.

Today there are still just a few of these grand old landowning families left in Ireland – picturesque characters on the fringe of modern Irish life, struggling to keep up their stately homes. Most of them had come from England in earlier centuries, and they formed a major part of the Ascendancy, the ruling class in colonial days. Although they were nearly all Protestant and loyal to the Crown, these 'Anglo-Irish', as they came to be known, thought of themselves as Irish. Yet they benefited hugely from British rule, which enabled them to acquire their wealth and build their fine houses. Some of them treated their tenant farmers quite well. But many were thoughtless and heartless, wrapped up in their own world of hunting, dancing and tennis-parties, as depicted so vividly in the novels of Molly Keane (*Good Behaviour*, etc.) and Elizabeth Bowen (*The Last September*, etc.). In the years after 1916 these families became obvious targets for IRA fury, and many of their 'big houses' were burned down – some 200 in 1920–23 alone, out of a total of 2,000 or so.* Later, many other grand houses were

---

* These details and some others I have taken from Mark Bence-Jones's excellent book, *Twilight of the Ascendancy* (1987).

demolished after their owners had sold or abandoned them, including the Bowen family's Bowens' Court, in Co. Cork, and Lady Gregory's Coole Park, in Co. Galway, so much loved by Yeats. And in the years after independence, most of the Protestant ruling and landed classes moved away from an Ireland where they no longer felt welcome (see p. 176). In Co. Clare, the number of Ascendancy families dropped from around eighty in 1919 to ten by the early 1930s.

Today only about thirty major houses survive intact with their family portraits and original furnishings. Lord Longford's eldest son, the writer Thomas Pakenham, told me that of some one hundred 'gentry' houses in Co. Westmeath in 1921, only two are still lived in by the same families. One is his own, the seventeenth-century Tullynally Castle, where he spends part of the year. Many stately homes have been turned into schools, institutions or hotels; in some cases, the original owners now run them as private hotels, to make ends meet. Some other families make a living from farming, but find upkeep of these big houses very hard: one hears of stories of upper floors being steadily evacuated, through lack of money to pay for repairs to leaking roofs. Some houses are still inhabited but crumbling, others are empty and derelict. You see them everywhere, in this land where ruins are dubious pleasures.

The surviving Ascendancy families today play virtually no part in political life. They have not shown much eagerness to do so, but nor have they exactly been encouraged by the Irish. Some have gone into business, and some are active in conservationist causes, but many of those I met seemed to distance themselves from the affairs of modern Ireland, and just a few felt there was still some animosity against them. They are charming anomalies in today's State, these survivors of a past era. Very few have Irish accents; and they appear quite distinct from other Irish, more reserved, though hospitable – in fact, more like their English upper-class equivalents, but even more eccentric and markedly less well off. Some of their best-known figures – the Guinnesses, the Knight of Glin, Lady Mountcharles, Viscount Gormanston and others – form a firm little exclusive social circle. The famous Kildare Street Club, busy social centre of Ascendancy life in the old days, still exists but has moved to new premises on St Stephen's Green and has merged with another club. I found the food poor but the claret good, and the gloomy ambience that of a Pall Mall club on an off night. Today the members tend to be diplomats or businessmen rather than Anglo-Irish gentry. Irish politicians do not join: they have never been made welcome.

Desmond Guinness and the Knight of Glin have taken the lead in campaigning to rescue what is left of the heritage of fine old houses. Guinness founded the Irish Georgian Society, which raises funds to buy and restore old buildings of that period. It has done some good work, including the recent acquisition of Castletown House, a massive Georgian mansion near Dublin. But the Irish Government has not been very helpful. As the Knight of Glin has said, 'There is still a perceivable folk memory of distaste for great houses as an alleged symbol of greed'; therefore to provide tax relief for their owners to restore them is hardly seen as a vote-winner. Nor does Ireland's modest National Trust, An Taisce, have the funds or the brief to buy up threatened buildings, as in Britain. However, as in the case of Georgian Dublin (see p. 127), there are now signs of an official change of heart. In 1988 the Government set up a National Heritage Council, one of whose tasks is to fund architectural restoration. It now recognizes that Ireland's stately homes, whether symbols of past greed or not, are an important part of the national cultural heritage and worth preserving. They can even help tourism. So grants for repairs or improvements are now sometimes given to owners who will open their stately homes to the public. But there are still some cynics who claim that the Knight and his friends might not be entirely disinterested in calling for funds that would help to raise the value of their own properties.

He is a curious and controversial personality, this Desmond Fitz-Gerald (*sic*), Knight of Glin, whose family came over with the Normans in the twelfth century. They have resided ever since on the south shore of the Shannon estuary, where their handsome eighteenth-century Glin Castle was beautifully restored recently by 'Knightie' (as he is known). The 200-acre home farm, relic of a much vaster estate, does not bring in enough money, so the

Knight takes in lodgers, mostly rich Americans, at £100 per head per night for dinner, bed and breakfast; notices in the bedrooms urge guests also to leave a tip for the staff, and to remember to turn out the lights. Is not £100 rather a lot? – well, sometimes the Knight and his wife graciously dine with their guests (but sometimes not, depending a bit on *la tête du client*). He has written, 'As A. L. Rowse has noted, the land-owning "Ascendancy" may have been politically corrupt, but they built beautifully with their ill-gotten gains,' and the Knight is himself a serious authority on their art and architecture, the author of several books. But he is in a dilemma, for he is also agent in Ireland for Christie's, where his duty is to find precious antiques and furniture which can be auctioned – and most probably sold abroad. So much for preserving the Irish heritage?

His friend Desmond Guinness, a great-grandson of the first Lord Iveagh and son of the late Lord Moyne, is a leading member of the large Guinness family. Originally from Co. Down, they were pre-Norman Irish but later became Protestant, and their brewing business dates from 1759. Today the family own very few of its shares (see p. 78), but it has brought them the wealth that they still enjoy. Desmond lives in Leixlip Castle, Co. Kildare, which he has restored with great taste; a half-brother lives in another country house nearby, where he farms. They are a very hospitable, unpretentious, somewhat bohemian family, with a fondness for whimsy, jokes and rough old clothes. Desmond has a passion for distinguished old houses but dislikes that black creamy porter.

A cousin, Garech Browne, is one of Ireland's most amusing and stylish eccentrics, in a land that is full of them, and a noted collector of modern art. He lives at Luggala, a neo-Gothic lodge tucked into a lonely valley in the Wicklow Mountains where his mother, a Guinness heiress, used to hold famous bohemian literary parties for Brendan Behan and his likes. Garech himself is married to an Indian princess, who is sometimes around. He was asleep when I arrived as agreed at 7 p.m., but eventually he woke up and remembered who I was. He is a short, elf-like man in his fifties, with a bald head, a massive straggly beard, and a disarmingly direct manner. 'I am now going to tell you *all*, I can open the key to *any door* for you,' he said; he then showed me round his house, a rabbit-warren of messily elegant little rooms in period style, with brocades everywhere, Lucien Freud et al. on the walls, and Susan Hampshire coming to lunch tomorrow. Browne may seem a jester, but is also a very serious man who has done a great deal to promote modern arts and traditional culture in Ireland. In 1959 he founded Claddagh Records, which has since helped to bring fame to many Irish musicians, notably The Chieftains – 'I didn't just help to create them, I *did* create them.' He said I must hear some records, but he had no player in the house, so he took me into his old Mercedes where, shivering under the starry March night, we listened to cassettes of glorious Irish folk music on its radio. I went home very happy.

Another intriguing Anglo-Irish experience is to visit the stately neoclassical Lissadell House, in Co. Sligo, still the home of the Gore-Booth family. Yeats used to come here, to visit the two remarkable Gore-Booth sisters, Eva the poetess and Connie (Countess Markiewicz, wife of a Polish artist), who was a leader of the 1916 uprising and in 1918 became the first woman ever to be elected to the British House of Commons. Yeats wrote:

> The light of evening, Lissadell,
> Great windows open to the south,
> Two girls in silk kimonos, both
> Beautiful, one a gazelle . . .

On my last visit, their niece Aideen Gore-Booth, in her sprightly seventies, was still showing guests around (the house is open to the public). We sat in the 'Glory Hole', the room with the 'great windows' where Yeats lectured the girls about Irish poetry – and where Aideen was highly critical to me of Aunt Connie's 'wasteful' nationalist violence. The family went through a bad period in the 1960s and '70s, when its 3,000-acre estate became bankrupt, faced a court injunction, and narrowly escaped being sold off. Today the Gore-Booths are still poor, but they have survived. Theirs is a strange, melancholy house, more than a little run to seed, cluttered with bric-à-brac and family memorabilia (including photos of two brothers killed in World War Two), and full of Ascendancy ghosts.

Some families have adapted more successfully, either as gentlemen farmers, or by turning their homes into very personal country-house hotels which they run themselves. Sandy and Deborah Perceval, a few miles south from Lissadell, do both at once. His forebears came from England in the seventeenth century and by marriage acquired the estate of Temple House, which they later rebuilt as a big Georgian mansion (beside the ruins of a thirteenth-century castle of the Knights Templar). Here the Percevals are typical of the Anglo-Irish gentry, who welcome their paying guests like friends and try to make them forget they are in a hotel – but they don't overdo it. You eat communally round a big table; Deb cooks, cordon-bleu style; you can go coarse fishing or boating on the lake. Some bedrooms are huge; one, known as 'the half-acre', was slept in by Haughey when Taoiseach. Sandy, affable and cultured, takes his guests in summer to local musical pubs, where he plays the spoons. He is something of a Green, proud to show visitors the organic farm on his 1,000-acre estate. And he is a working farmer. On my last visit, he had just been up all night lambing. Some of his young staff are German; and in winter he holds shooting parties, often for French guests. So remote Sligo, like the rest of Ireland, is developing closer European links.

Ireland in the new Europe: Erasmus students, Irish pubs in Paris, happy German settlers

'So you come from *Europe!*' said an elderly Dublin lady to my German wife, as if it were another planet. Closely involved with Britain for so long, then with the United States, the Irish had long tended to ignore the Continent. But then came the European Community, which has been a success for Ireland; through it, the Irish have slowly been developing new links, human and cultural as well as economic, with this strange planet Europe. Some examples: the Irish population of Paris has grown amazingly since the mid-1970s, from 500 to some 8,000; over 100 Irish towns and villages are now actively twinned with Breton ones; students go on the new Erasmus exchanges, and graduates find jobs with Siemens, Philips and other big firms. Of course these travellers are an untypical few; amongst the average Irish, ignorance of Europe is still great, and ability to speak its languages, though improving, is even worse than in Britain. Yet there is little of the actual hostility found in Britain. A pro-Europe rhetoric, woolly but not insincere, pervades public speeches.

'Through Europe, Ireland is achieving a new modern identity, a means of escape from its old backwardness, its parochialism and over-dependence on Britain,' says that passionate Euro-idealist, Professor Richard Kearney. He and others stress that Ireland did have its own early links with the Continent, before it was an English colony. They point to the sixth- to eighth-century missionaries who left 'the island of saints and scholars' to spread culture and Christianity. Then in the sixteenth to eighteenth centuries many Irish fled to the Catholic countries of Europe to escape persecution at home; Irish seminaries were set up there; Irish soldiers fought in the armies of France, Spain and Austria; more recently, Joyce chose Paris for his voluntary exile, and Beckett too, who even wrote in French. But, compared to the bear-hug of England, did these links really add up to much? From the ending of the anti-Catholic laws in 1829, up until the 1970s, this 'offshore island of an offshore island' remained peripheral to the culture and way of life of the Continent, starved of its richness; as Patrick Kavanagh wrote in his poem *Lough Derg* in the 1940s, it was 'all Ireland that froze for want of Europe'.

The Common Market then produced the thaw. The Irish saw what benefits it could bring, and in their 1972 referendum they voted 'yes' to joining, by 83 per cent. Garret FitzGerald, who became foreign minister in 1973, was the enlightened pro-European who set Ireland on the path of being an active and positive member of the Community – 'He succeeded in making London look peripheral to Europe, while Dublin was metropolitan,' wrote his friend and admirer, Roy Jenkins. Haughey then took over the same policy, even declaring in 1990, with typical Haughey hype, that the EC was 'the greatest force for good that the world has ever known'. Ireland's struggling farmers might not put it quite like that, today. But the EC (EU) has always been supported by all the main political parties, and has never proved the same divisive issue as in Britain. And Ireland has provided some excellent European leaders, notably Peter Sutherland and Ray McSharry as Commissioners in Brussels. The Irish have handled their six-monthly presidencies well, and are rightly proud of the reputation they have won as perhaps the most effective of smaller member States. It has brought Ireland an entirely new voice in the world.

Today the farmers and some others may be sceptical, but most people remain pro-European. The EC has helped Ireland more than most member States – in at least six specific ways. First, in economic terms, it has greatly reduced the over-dependence on the British market. Second, politically and psychologically, it has enabled the old unequal face-to-face relationship with Britain to change into a new, more relaxed partnership, within a wider club where both are equal members; and this has eased the old Irish complex about the English. Third, it has impelled Ireland to modernize socially, in certain areas: the ending of the ban on married women in the civil service, and the laws on equal pay for women, were both due to the EC (see p. 205). Fourth, it has obliged Ireland to improve its environmental policies. Fifth, whatever the problems today with the CAP, this farming country has benefited enormously from the EU's budgetary emphasis on agriculture. Last, Ireland through persistent lobbying has gained more from the lucrative new Structural Funds than the other poorer members: it has presented its case better than Greece or Portugal, and has gained some £7·2 billion from these funds for 1994–9. Sceptics point out that, if the EU provides them with such hand-outs, then of course the Irish are in favour of it; and some criticize the politicians for what one student called 'their non-stop begging-bowl approach – it's all take-take-take, so humiliating'. Garret FitzGerald admitted to me: 'Yes, for most people the EU *is* a matter of economic self-interest, not of idealism or emotion. The element of true idealism is small – but it's influential.'

These issues emerged during the referendum debate on the Maastricht Treaty, in June 1992. The Danes had just voted 'no'; Euro-scepticism was spreading across Europe; and there was no chance that the Irish would repeat their high 1972 'yes' vote. So the final 69 per cent vote was considered creditable. But the general quality of the debate was poor. It came just after the 'Miss X' abortion crisis, which many people found a more pressing issue than the complexities of Maastricht; and as there was even a link between abortion and the Treaty (see p. 191), much of the debate centred on this aspect, relegating to second place the real Maastricht questions of monetary union, pooled sovereignty and subsidiarity.

The 31 per cent of 'no' votes represented a mixture of views and interests. There were some farmers, inevitably; and there was the Left-wing protectionist lobby led by Raymond Crotty (see p. 88). Sinn Féin, which after all means 'ourselves alone', rallied the older nationalist voters, neutralists, some of them frankly xenophobic, who want the old-style nation-state. Some other groups also stood for neutralism, putting up warning posters of a uniformed colleen conscripted into a European Army. Or they voiced fears of Ireland losing its cultural identity within a capitalist Europe. The Dublin working class voted 'no' quite heavily, angry that the EC had failed to solve unemployment. And the Greens warned of an over-industrial, centralized Europe in which Ireland would become a marginal pleasure-ground for tourists, full of golf-courses for Germans – the vision evoked by Dermot Bolger in the final pages of *The Journey Home* (see p. 247). Against this, the majority of Irish voted for an EC whose grants were getting ever larger, and for a Maastricht Treaty which was maybe a fudge but better than nothing. I smiled at one view I heard from an UCD student: 'We like the EC because Thatcher doesn't. If Britain is against it, then it must be good.'

Public awareness of Europe has been growing, but variably. The business and industrial world was initially wary of the EC, but is now well disposed and has formed many new links abroad. Civil servants, normally so conservative a breed, are the ones who have changed most strikingly. Most of their foreign contacts used to be just with London, and they would even hold meetings with Treasury officials for advice on economic policy. But this Big Brother approach ended with the EC. Today, if a civil servant wants to consult, he will as readily ring up a colleague in Madrid or Copenhagen as one in London – an example of the waning of dependence on Britain. But how far this new openness is shared by the politicians themselves, despite their Euro-rhetoric, is not quite so certain. Ministers jet off to Brussels, but, as in other countries, in daily practice they are so absorbed by their own domestic power games that their prime focus remains national. Yet they value the EU. One of its charms for them is that, since nearly all EU aid is channelled via Dublin, by doling it out in their own constituencies they can win much electoral kudos.

The Press and media likewise are concerned mainly with Irish issues, to an extent with British ones, and with Europe for its own sake far less. RTE for example has a staff correspondent in London but none in Paris, Bonn, Moscow or even Washington; there is one in Brussels, where several newspapers also keep a staff reporter because of the importance of the EU to Ireland. The *Irish Times*, with limited resources, does try to give reasonable coverage of events in other European countries, and of course Irish papers cannot afford many foreign correspondents of their own. But it is a question of attitudes, not just of money. Few senior editors and journalists in Dublin show much real empathy with European countries, or knowledge of them, or speak a foreign language. Nor do they often put foreign news on their front pages, or among the lead stories in bulletins. If asked, they will say it is because the public are not so interested – but this alibi can be a self-fulfilling prophecy.

And are the public interested? Maybe a Briton has no right to cast stones from his glasshouse at Irish insularity, for the British are in some ways worse. But my own frank view is this: while the Irish see themselves as good Europeans and are full of goodwill towards Europe, they know very little about it, whereas the British on average know and understand it better, but are much more wary of it. Isolated for so long, the Irish still find it hard to relate to non–Anglo-Saxon cultures. When they meet people from the Continent, they usually show warmth towards them as individuals, in the Irish manner, but not much real interest in where they come from. The business and civil-service worlds may have evolved, but for most ordinary people, Britain, the familiar enemy, is still the everyday point of reference: they can reel off the names of British cabinet ministers, actors or suburbs, yet show extreme ignorance of the politics or culture even of France or Germany. In rural areas, people know all about the complexities of the CAP, as indeed they must, and they are very friendly to tourists, but they still see the Continent as somehow alien. A group from Co. Limerick, on their first-ever brief holiday trip to Paris, spent their one evening there eating Irish Stew in the Kitty O'Shea pub – a touching *mal du pays*. Even on a sophisticated cultural level, John Banville and Colm Tóibín are untypical as writers with a European dimension, whereas most new novels and plays remain within an old Irish mould (see pp. 249, 260), apart from forays into the British and American worlds; it is as if Joyce and Beckett, indeed Synge and George Moore, also French-influenced, were flukes who have left few successors. Lamenting this situation, Brian Fallon of the *Irish Times* wrote: 'Compared with the enormous publicity given yearly [in Ireland] to the Booker Prize, there is hardly a mention of the Prix Goncourt . . . In view of our now-official European status, it does seem ironic that culturally we have become almost a province of the English-speaking world . . . It is time to lean towards Europe once again.'

Perhaps I have been too hard. Europe is still so novel for the Irish. And indeed this whole picture is now changing, bit by bit. Just a few Irish people are today highly cosmopolitan, they speak languages, they travel, they have European friends – and this is not some social élite, for they include students and young workers, as well as businessmen, officials and academics. They are still a small minority, but their numbers are growing, notably among the young, as interest in Europe slowly widens.

A case in point is the learning of languages. The Irish have the reputation of being even worse linguists than the British and little better than the Americans, and this may well be true. Like Americans, most of them think they can always get by in English: Ray McSharry, when appointed a Commissioner in Brussels, said without embarrassment that he spoke no French, and I am told he still spoke rather little when he left. However, in educational and business circles today there is much talk about the need for more emphasis on modern languages; and the demand to learn them has been growing, notably since about 1988, when the '1992' single market appeared on the horizon. Unlike Ireland's own language, they are not taught in primary schools; even in secondary schools they are not strictly compulsory, though most children do learn at least one, and some schools insist on it. In the twelve-to-fifteen age group, the percentage of children learning French rose from 68·2 to 72·3 between 1975 and 1988, while the numbers taking German went up faster, from 6·6 to 10·6 per cent: German today is being pushed by the authorities, for commercial reasons, and from a low level it is slowly gaining ground (only 2·7 per cent take Spanish, and fewer still Italian). But few children reach much level of fluency, even though some universities insist on at least one language being included in the entrance examination.

It is partly due to pressure from the Irish language lobby, ever jealous and vigilant, that the Government still has not made foreign languages compulsory in schools, as they are throughout the rest of Europe. Does this mean that modern needs are being sacrificed on the altar of a nationalist ideal? There are many who think so. Certainly if French or German were taught at primary level, it might make a difference, and it seems absurd that they are not. On the other hand, there is evidence that pupils in the Irish-language schools, growing up bilingual, do in fact find it easier, not harder, to learn another language later (the 'psychological barrier' theory, see p. 294). So the language lobby is not alone to blame. At all events, in many of the better secondary schools, and in universities, enthusiasm for French and German is growing. One headmistress talked excitedly to me about her new pupil exchanges with German schools. And at Limerick's modern university some 600 students are taking the European-studies option, which includes languages.

The advent since 1987 of the EU's Erasmus exchange scheme has done much to Europeanize the ambience and the outlook of Irish universities. Everyone talks about it, quite eagerly. Under this scheme, selected students go to spend between three months and a year in a foreign university, with an EU grant; the run-up includes intensive language tuition. The numbers involved are not large, about 2,000 of Ireland's 70,000 students at any one time; but the impact is considerable. Not only is this student élite being turned towards Europe and away from its usual UK/US outlets; but the campuses of Cork, Galway and UCD are alive with the accents of, say, Tübingen or Salamanca, and enriched by these visitors. At University College, Cork, between 1988 and 1992 the number of foreign students rose from 170 to 550, of whom some 200 were with Erasmus; and 140 UCC students were on Erasmus exchanges at sixteen universities abroad.

If more foreign Erasmus students are drawn to Ireland than vice versa, it is for two evident reasons. First, the pull of the English language ('We have Flemish students here, but why should ours want to go to Leuven?' said one rare Erasmo-sceptic don at UCD). Second, the very different nature of nearly all Continental universities (see p. 218). Ireland's, like Britain's, are relatively intimate and human-scale, with smallish classes and lots of social and club life – so unlike the anonymous broiler-houses of Bochum, Bordeaux or Bologna, which has 55,000 students to UCC's 8,000. Of course the visitors are delighted, and there's the added romantic/touristic appeal of Ireland itself. However, the Irish students abroad are pleased with Erasmus, too. And I found the normally sceptical Joseph Lee of UCC quite lyrical about the benefits of the scheme: 'In Ireland there's a pro-Europe rhetoric by no means matched by reality – save at the level of this major development, the Erasmus programme, which is transforming my students' perspectives, giving them new attitudes. But its real effects will seep through only later. By the millennium, 10,000 Irish students will have spent up to a year in Europe, and some by then will be moving into key decision-making positions, since it is the more active and ambitious who opt for Erasmus. This could make a big difference to Ireland.'

★

Numbers of Irish today live and work on the Continent, where generally they feel that (a) they are more popular than the English, and (b) they are made more welcome than in England. 'In Bavaria, which I know well,' said one girl graduate, 'people at first assume that I'm English and are coolly polite. When they learn that I'm Irish, their faces light up and they shower me with hospitality.' I heard this kind of story often.

The United States may still be the more favoured destination for the Irish, if they can get in, but in recent years a significant minority of young workers, graduates and vacationing students have been exploring Europe. Big firms like Siemens and Philips would take whole airloads of graduates and train them; other young people would come to work on building-sites, or take casual summer jobs; and by 1991 there were said to be 6,000 Irish in Munich in summer. This migration has since declined, owing to recession in Germany and elsewhere, plus competition from the much larger East European influx. Yet there are still plenty of Irish in Germany, with some real Irish-owned pubs in Hamburg and Berlin. Some Irish build up close links with Germans, like the girl I quoted above, with a German boyfriend: most, however, tend to stick together, nostalgically singing their own songs in the beerhalls, seldom marrying Germans.

In France they integrate much better – especially in fellow-Celtic Brittany. 'I feel closer to the Bretons than to the Welsh or Scots,' I was told by Paddy Moloney, chief musician of The Chieftains. 'I have a cottage near Lorient, where I spend two months each year. Our two Celtic languages are very different – I just can't follow Breton – but much of the music is quite similar, and that above all is what draws me to Brittany. I hugely enjoy our common Celtic culture.' Moloney is not the only fan: since 1980 the number of Irish/Breton town-twinnings has increased from 10 to 102, including Cork/Rennes and Galway/Lorient, and Ireland has far more with Brittany than with the rest of the world put together. They have led to romances, even marriages. Many Irish also attend the big annual inter-Celtic arts festival in Lorient, or spend their holidays in Breton *gîtes*. All in all, the traffic makes good money for Brittany Ferries on its Cork–Roscoff route.

Though the common tongue of the exchanges tends to be English, some younger Irish now use their French; and the growing desire on both sides to improve their French or English is seen as one main reason for the recent boom in twinnings.

In Paris, the Irish community dates back a long way – at least to the founding of the Collège Irlandais in 1598, as a seminary for Irish priests. The buildings, in the rue des Irlandais near the Panthéon, are today used as an Irish cultural centre, with a church attached. In Joyce's day the Irish colony in Paris was tiny; and so it remained until the coming of the EC in the 1970s, when it began to grow fast, from about 500 to an estimated 8,000 today, far larger proportionately than the British or American colonies. To a striking degree it typifies the new-style educated emigrant. Just as remarkably, many of these Irish seem to be integrating socially with Parisians, in a city not exactly known for its warm embrace of outsiders.

According to a recent survey by Piaras Mac Einri of UCC, as many as 70 per cent of Irish male emigrants in Paris, and 51 per cent of women, are graduates; 29 per cent work in education, mostly teaching English. Of the rest, many of the girls are secretaries, nurses or au pairs, and both sexes work in banking, engineering, computer trades, etc.; they tend to be very popular with French employers. Over half of those surveyed said that at least half of their friends and social contacts were French, while 43 per cent said they often read French newspapers. Paris had not a single Irish pub in 1985, but now it has about fifteen; and whereas many of those in Britain, America or even Germany 'serve as a kind of Irish refuge from the alien world outside', in Paris they are equally full of French, and others. I myself have enjoyed their club-like quality, not often found in Paris bars: at Finnegans Wake, in the Latin Quarter, I met publican Johnny Granville from Kerry, an ex-engineer, presiding over a warmly informal scene, with an American writer holding a literary soirée in one room. So the Joyce/Hemingway tradition flickers on. But most Irish come to Paris in a business spirit: 'It's such an entrepreneurial city,' said one UCD graduate, 'and we respond to the challenge, work hard, and do well' – just like the Irish in America, in the old days.

Recession, however, as in Germany, has now sent some of them back home. As for the non-graduates, during the building of Euro-Disneyland about one-third of the thousands working on its site near Paris were Irish – the usual trade for poorer Irish emigrants. They too have now gone home.

Of the Europeans who settle in Ireland, there are few in the cities but plenty in the countryside. And it is the Germans, in their thousands, who provide the most remarkable phenomenon. They tend to be the kind of educated Germans who dislike many aspects of their own country; and they have looked to Ireland as a total contrast, a hoped-for utopia. They first arrived in some numbers in the 1960s, after Heinrich Böll had published his *Irische Tagesbuch* (Irish Journal), a warm philosophical record of the months he spent in Mayo and his love for the tolerant, wise and kindly Irish. It was written at a time of his own growing disillusion with the new materialist Germany; and it made much impact on others with his radical views, who grew tempted to follow in his Irish footsteps.

Today you find them all over the West, above all in Leitrim, Sligo, Mayo and Cork counties, in isolated villas, cottages or farmsteads. They will generally explain that they left Germany to escape its workaholic rat-race, its overcrowding, pollution, bureaucracy, *Ordnung*, conformity, *und so weiter*, and to seek a greener, emptier land with a slower, more easygoing tempo. Some have grown bored and gone back home, but others have found their ideal, more or less, and have settled. Some are retired people; a few are militant autarkic Greens; many make a living as organic farmers, artists, artisans, technicians, hoteliers, or by running small businesses. Sometimes they get criticized for putting up land prices: but at least, like other blow-ins, they have been helping to revivify dying country areas (see p. 119). And most of them, if they behave tactfully, are well liked and accepted.

Down a long winding lane in remote Co. Cavan, I went to see Michael and Silke Cropp, from Hamburg – he a burly, bearded Falstaffian character, very genial. In Germany, he said, they had promoted concert tours for Irish groups such as The Chieftains.

'We went on holiday in Ireland, fell in love with it, decided to settle here. We left Germany for all the usual Greenish reasons, but although we farm organically and live simply, we are not purist Greens; we even have a car. Mainly we breed goats and sell our goats' cheeses, which have won several prizes: I'm often on television, and I'm well known – "Oh, that crazy German with his goats". I adore the Irish, they're great crack, and I find it much easier to enjoy life in Ireland. Here, unlike in Germany, one's eccentricities are actually appreciated. We find that the Germans and Irish get on extremely well together, despite their opposite temperaments. What's more, as Ireland was neutral in the war, there's no residue of anti-German feeling, so we don't need to feel uneasy' – a point made to me on several occasions.

Some Germans however, less jovial than Cropp, are not made so welcome, if they behave in too assertively German a way over protecting their property. While the Irish are deeply attached to the land they own, they also have a strong tradition of public right of way; and this paradox the Germans do not always understand. They sometimes put up fences round their estates, as they would back home, thus blocking access to paths and woodlands that have always been common right of way. And the locals, not used to fences, get angry. The Germans do have law on their side, but not custom – and in Ireland, custom tends to come first. 'There's this rich retired businessman, prowling around his domain with Alsatians and a shotgun, firing in the air at "trespassers" – we call him "Hitler",' I was told by a woman in Clare. And sometimes the law, too, is broken; in one much-quoted case, a German built a house by the sea at Wicklow, put fences on either side down to the water, with 'No Entry' signs, thus blocking off the beach. He had to be told that in Ireland, unlike Germany, beaches are public property, by law. He then sold out. But my favourite story is of the German in a Sligo village who bought an old rectory and was annoyed by the noisy crows nesting in its trees, so he started shooting them. This infuriated the locals. A neighbour told me: 'I thought up the idea of telling him that the villagers believed the crows were the spirits of their ancestors. This really alarmed him, and he stopped.'

Some Germans in theory admire the laid-back, unbureaucratic Irish way of life, but then in practice their own disciplined, hard-working temperament rebels against it. One professional couple from Frankfurt told me: 'Ireland has been good to us, we love it here. You are accepted for what you are, not judged all the time as in Germany, and you can bend the rules.' But then they added: 'When it comes to work, the Irish are so slow and lackadaisical, with little sense of duty or discipline. We started a small business here, with a team of young girls. But in the end we gave it up.' This is not, however, the experience of most foreign investors in Ireland (see p. 74).

Then there are the hardline fanatical Greens, just a few of them. On a stony upland in Co. Roscommon, I met a youngish couple from Bavaria who were trying to eke a living from selling organic vegetables. 'In Germany', said the man, 'we took part in the anti-nuclear sit-ins, and we steadily grew more depressed at the failure of our crusades, and the growing pollution that was damaging our health. So we came here, and bought this strip of land. We try to be self-sufficient as far as we can, living from our own fruit and vegetables, buying little except cereals for our children, from health stores. We may now buy an electric car, also set up wind machines. I try to explain about ecology to the villagers, but few of them get the point.' His austerity and solemnity, his vision, his strong views, came as a striking contrast to the joky, tolerant Irish rural whimsy I had been hearing in these parts; and intellectually they were quite a breath of fresh air, though his ideas were hardly my own. Later I met some other Germans who knew this family: 'They are very extreme. They come preaching their Green gospel, telling the Irish what to do, so people turn against them. Various Greens come here with these ideas, with this feeling that they have to punish themselves for their previous materialistic life – so they move to these remote, harsh bits of land, with little but rocks, peat and rushes, and try to live. It's like the Old Testament! The Irish are so nice, so welcoming, yet from Germany they get these weirdos – it's a pity, tactless.' Many such Greens give up the struggle after a few years. Either they modify their purism and turn to a more normal type of small farming, taking the 'farmers' dole' as the Irish do, or else they go back home. Often it is wife or girlfriend who leaves first, finding this Utopia not much fun. Broken marriages are common.

Some other German settlers have done well in farming, making a real contribution to Irish agriculture; it was they, and the British, who introduced organic farming (see p. 112). The very business-like Joseph Finke, for example, produces flour, lamb and sheep's wool on his 230-acre organic farm in Tipperary, the largest in Ireland. He arrived in 1983, 'to escape the rat-race of an increasingly conservative Germany: I felt I must either become very radical, or leave. My wife and I are happy here in Ireland, and people appreciate what we do. We've taught them a lot.' This he seems able to do with more tact than most. 'I approve of this kind of German,' said an elderly farmer's wife in the area; 'they are teaching us how to grow foods purely and live simply, as we did before this modern supermarket binge came in.'

In a different vein, Peter Kern and Gisela Meyer, living in a simple cottage not far from Sligo, are also appreciated locally for the work they do. He is a gentle, wispy-bearded hippy who worked as a surveyor in Essen, then settled in Ireland for the usual reasons, where he taught himself a new trade: he now makes fancy coloured candles for the export market, some of them replicas of frothy glasses of Guinness, which go down well with Americans. Gisela, a dark, motherly type, used to run a pub in Bochum, then had an illness which was cured by homeopathy, so she turned to that. 'Here I have a practice in alternative medicine, accepted by the Irish authorities. I do homoeopathy, chiropractic, holistic healing – popular round here, partly because many local people still believe in the old folk cures and practise them. For example, if a child has whooping cough, you give some milk to a ferret to drink, the child then drinks the rest of the bowl and is cured. For another cure, a child is passed under the belly of a donkey. Or you must take a thread from your clothing, put it on a stone in one local graveyard, take an old thread which you will find tied to the stone, put this on the afflicted part of your body, e.g. a sprained ankle, and the pain will go. And in the graveyard at Dromahair, a priest lies buried who said before he died, "Take the soil from my grave for your cures." There are lots of little teaspoons round the grave, where the soil is always unusually damp. You must take a teaspoonful of the soil, and put it under your pillow for nine days. It is supposed to cure all sicknesses, and it *does*: I myself was relieved of migraine. My own work has some affinities with folk medicine.'

Lastly, there are some cases where European settlers or tourists have behaved even worse than the Germans who put fences round their property or shoot crows. Around 1990, British, Dutch and German drop-outs began invading west Cork and some other areas. They would messily set up home in caravans or converted buses, sometimes along scenic parts of the coast; and they would claim Irish unemployment benefits, which under EC law they had the right to do, for periods of up to six months. Local officials were angry: but it was pointed out that many Irish were drawing just the same benefits, in British or German cities. There was quite a crisis. But finally most of the drop-outs moved away.

More seriously, around the same time numbers of French, German and Dutch would arrive with apparent innocence on fishing holidays, but would then systematically plunder the lakes of their pike, put them into the freeze trailers they had brought with them, and take the fish back home, where they could fetch high prices. Some lakes were fished dry, and local people grew furious. So the law was changed, making it illegal to export more than three pike at a time. But first some local fishermen quietly took their own revenge. At night they would drive holes in the foreigners' boats, then pretend they knew nothing about it.

Such are the occasional travails of European tourism in green and gentle Ireland. But mostly the visitors behave well and are liked, for themselves as well as the money they bring. Along with the CAP, they form a crucial part of rural Ireland's real direct contact with the big world outside.

A self-concerned society re-examines its neutrality

Active today in the United Nations as well as in the European Union, Ireland has opened out considerably to the world in the past three or four decades. It has an open economy. A new individual mobility is replacing the old once-and-for-all emigration. And through foreign holidays, television and much else, the Irish have become more aware of the outside world. Yet they also remain so very self-preoccupied, more than the British – and I know many foreigners who agree with me. They are not at all xenophobic, but curiously self-conscious about being Irish: put them in some foreign context, and they will relate everything back to Ireland, as if reluctant to focus on other matters for their own sake.

I can best give a few tiny examples. When I suggested to a university teacher that the Irish media and public seemed little concerned with foreign affairs, she replied, 'Oh, no, we are very interested in the Middle East, for instance, because we have Irish UN troops in Lebanon.' And a local journalist said: 'We are concerned about the starvation in Somalia because of our own tribal memories of the Famine.' Fair enough; but I would prefer that they might also be worried about these problems for their own sake. And when I showed my book *France Today* to a professor, he first looked in the index to see if the Irish-owned Château Margaux vineyards were listed. I expressed surprise. 'From an Irish point of view, that is what is important to me,' he said. 'But I suppose you were writing from a general point of view.'

Maybe this self-referring vision is the result of a small island nation's age-old concern to protect its own identity. Also, Ireland's special internal problems have created a special political climate, where the major European trends such as the rise and fall of the Left have virtually passed it by (fortunately, some might say). I can quote another small but pertinent example, this time from a play, Declan Hughes's otherwise excellent *Digging for Fire* (1992). The heroine, a serious young Dublin graduate, says of a recent bleak period in her life: 'When did I fall asleep? Was it in 1987? And what has happened since? The death of Socialism? – but that was just images on a TV screen. More serious: *I voted Fianna Fáil! Yes I did!*' I gulped. For many Irish, the fall of the Berlin Wall, and all that, really did seem less relevant than what Haughey and co. were up to.

★

Ireland is a country that foreigners love to visit, and they are made welcome. Yet apart from the loners seeking rural peace, they are seldom drawn to live and work there. They still see it as remote, provincial, nor does the high unemployment make matters easier. Dublin may be evolving, but it remains probably the least cosmopolitan of EU capitals. During my time there, I came across remarkably few foreigners – far fewer than one would find in towns of comparable size such as Amsterdam or Stuttgart, even maybe Copenhagen. There are new influences such as foreign restaurants, but in the Italian ones, even in the Chinese, one is often served by Irish waitresses. Most of the foreigners in Dublin seem to be summer tourists, or students – the usual flocks of Japanese, plus a number of Spanish girls of good family, sent by their parents who feel that Catholic Ireland would be safer than wicked London.

There are far fewer brown or black faces even than in Belfast; lack of jobs, of course, keeps them out. So the Republic is spared the racial problems found in so much of Europe today (the Troubles in the North, you could say, are enough for one small island). The Irish are not racist, and they even feel some solidarity with the Third World, in part because of their shared colonial experience. In proportion to their means, they give more generously than other Europeans to overseas aid, notably to the Trocaire charity of the Church; and the international Band Aid campaign was the work of an Irishman, Bob Geldof. Through Irish Catholicism's strong missionary tradition, many of the priests and nuns in Ireland have returned from years of service in Third World countries, and their influence has added to the wider sense of solidarity. At present, the few coloured people in Ireland are well accepted (one TD is a South African Asian Muslim). But if Asiatics or Africans were ever to arrive in some numbers, would the Irish remain so tolerant? As yet they have no experience of living in a multiracial society.

It is at the level of Government foreign policy that Ireland has changed most radically since the old insular de Valera days, thanks to the work of a few leaders of broad vision, such as Seán Lemass and Garret FitzGerald. Ireland did not join the United Nations until 1955, but since then it has played an active role, providing troops for several of the UN peacekeeping missions, notably in the Congo and Lebanon. In the UN it has taken an independent 'anti-imperialist' stance which has sometimes annoyed London or Washington, criticizing Britain over the Falklands war, complaining at US intervention in Central America, and distancing itself from both in the Gulf War. In Europe, its positive role ever since joining the EC needs no repeating. 'The more the Irish are involved in the outside world, the more it strengthens, not weakens, their own identity,' Garret FitzGerald has said, and many others in public life would agree. Some, such as the fervently pro-European Professor Richard Kearney of UCD, will argue that a Europe without frontiers, a Europe of the regions, offers Ireland the best chance to keep its own traditions and to fulfil its destiny, via a new interdependence. And a vanguard of younger people, still a minority, are discovering a new European identity that complements their Irish one – 'chinks of light in the old siege mentality', in the words of one girl.

The issue of sovereignty does not trouble the Irish greatly, save in the two contexts of neutrality and Northern Ireland. These are prime remaining questions, and they are connected. The Irish doctrine of neutrality derives from the 1921–2 events of partition and the civil war: these of course made them unwilling to join any military alliance with Britain, and they managed to stay out of World War Two. In 1994, Ireland was still the only EU country not to be a member of Nato (France is a member, if not a fully participating one). But times have been changing, with the end of the cold war, with the shift in the role of Nato, and the decision of the EU to consider setting up some defence system of its own. And in 1992 a muted debate began in Ireland as to whether its stance of neutrality was still valid. As a gesture, the Government began sending delegates with observer status to meetings of the Western European Union, though it claimed there was no question of becoming a full member of this Nato by-product. Most Irish people are still emotionally opposed to Ireland's joining a military alliance; and for it to attempt to do so might rekindle some of the passions of the civil war, as few politicians would wish. However, many Irish today argue that, in the new world context, to take part in some purely defensive system ought to be possible. Fine Gael is more in favour of this than either Labour or Fianna Fáil.

For the present, the debate seems somewhat theoretical; the issue will not really become urgent until the EU starts to decide on its planned defence system, in 1996. And by then, three other neutral countries, Austria, Finland and Sweden, may have joined. The Irish position will depend largely on what kind of arrangement is worked out with them. If they become full members of a new EU defence system, it would be hard for the Irish to stay out, as the Government has indicated. But if they were to be allowed to keep some kind of neutral status, it could provide Ireland with an alibi for doing so too. Much could also depend on what happens in Northern Ireland. If that problem were to be solved in a manner leading one day to Irish unity, then the Republic's historical justification for neutrality could be undermined. In this, and in some other ways too, Ireland's future within an integrated Europe relates to the future of that tragic drama across the border.

10

NORTHERN IRELAND: A RESILIENT RESPONSE TO ABNORMALITY

I liked Northern Ireland much better than I expected. As with many people living in Britain, my mind over the years had been thoroughly turned off by the endless news items about terrorism: I did not relish having to explore this situation, and I thought I would find a dour, unhappy place, locked in a tedious and absurd conflict. Of course the conflict *is* archaic and the violence tragic, but a great deal else goes on in the North that is positive and fascinating. And the people are marvellous, second to none. So I would endorse the final phrase of Dervla Murphy's fine book, *A Place Apart*: 'The Northern Irish may not be comprehensible but they are very addictive.' They have a dynamism and a creative energy that contrasts with the far more laid-back ambience of the South (and I found many other visitors agreeing with me, even preferring to live in the North). After all, they do have the stimulus of a mind-concentrating challenge. They are even more warm and friendly than Southerners; and despite the local catchphrase, 'Whatever you say, say nothing,' I found them quite ready to talk freely – whether in the ghettos of West Belfast, the border farmlands of Fermanagh, or the schools and offices of Dungannon or Derry (see p. 378). Even the worst bigots at least very often have charm, plying you with tea or whiskey as they blithely parade frightful prejudices as undeniable facts. So you have to disentangle truth from fantasy: 'Only believe half of what anyone tells you – and that includes me,' is another local quip.

Americans, British and others often suppose that all life in the North is lived under the shadow of the terrorism. It isn't so. Most of the killings are confined to a few trouble spots in particular areas; elsewhere, there may be an occasional sudden bomb blast, but so there is in Britain. In most ways, the daily life of work and pleasure goes on with surprising normality; or at least people have grown used to the obvious outward abnormalities, the armed military patrols and the segregated housing. Northerners' humour and resilience have borne them through more than twenty-five years of the so-called 'Troubles'. And so they have come to terms with a wearying situation that their politicians seem unable to resolve – an outdated sectarian confrontation that is less about religion than nationality, territory and political power, laced with sheer gang warfare. Today Northerners travel abroad a good deal and theirs is less of a parochial 'place apart' than it used to be; but, understandably, they are still obsessively concerned with their great central problem, which is the single focus of this chapter, too.

For a visitor, meeting strangers casually, it is often hard to tell who is Catholic, who Protestant; and it's tactless to ask. You cannot tell by a person's looks or dress, nor by variations of accent, which relate more to social class or region. In conversation, Northerners can identify each other by where they went to school, maybe by where they live, or by their names: a Cathal O'Donnell is far more likely to be a Catholic than a Malcolm Stuart. But even this can be deceptive; there was a tribe of loyalist assassins called Murphy. Catholics, being Irish, tend to be more musical, loquacious and fun-loving, Protestants more worthy and righteous, but sometimes more verbally aggressive, too. And they have different names for Ireland and for Britain. Protestants will refer to Britain as 'the mainland', the North as 'the province'; Catholics talk about 'the six counties', 'the twenty-six counties', 'the thirty-two counties', implying a common Irishness, anathema to loyalists. Both sides speak of 'Ulster', but inaccurately, for three of the counties of that ancient province are in the Republic (Donegal, Cavan, Monaghan). The Protestants' insulting nickname for a Catholic is 'Taig'; the reverse, a bit less insulting, is 'Prod'. (One choice example of loyalist graffiti: 'Don't be vague, kill a Taig.')

Broadly speaking, the terms Protestant/Unionist/loyalist are synonymous, as are Catholic/nationalist/republican, but with nuances in both cases. Nearly all Protestants are politically Unionist, but many can be very moderate, whereas 'loyalism' (to the Crown) implies something more hard-line and anti-Irish. Likewise, 'nationalist' means feeling Irish and wanting a United Ireland; 'republican' is a fiercer variant of this, implying support for Sinn Féin and maybe the IRA. In this chapter, I use 'Protestant' and 'Catholic' as shorthand for the two communities (even if many Sinn Féin supporters, for instance, are so lapsed as to be atheist). Almost all Catholics are Irish nationalist in broad sympathy, but, significantly, a large number of them today do not want to become part of the Republic just yet.

Benevolent direct rule, wary political stalemate

It was in 1919 that Winston Churchill wrote his much-quoted lines about the imperviousness of Ulster to the 'violent and tremendous changes' caused in the world by the 1914–18 war: 'As the deluge subsides and the waters fall we see the dreary steeples of Fermanagh and Tyrone emerging once again. The integrity of their quarrel is one of the few institutions that have been left unaltered in the cataclysm which has swept the world.' That still rings as true today. And for centuries this quarrel has marked the history of Ulster and its violent conflicts. The key episode was the 'plantation' period of the seventeenth century: in order to strengthen its hold over the province, the Government in London brought in thousands of settlers from England and especially Scotland, and gave them land taken from its Irish owners. The sense of injustice remains to this day, among a people with long tribal memories. Some Catholic farmers still speak of their Protestant neighbours owning land 'stolen' from them nearly four centuries ago. These settlements gradually gave Ulster its Protestant majority. Then in the nineteenth century this was the one part of Ireland to be heavily industrialized: big British-owned firms were set up in Belfast, notably Harland & Wolff, which became the world's largest shipyard. So when the rest of Ireland won its independence in 1921, the North with its Protestant majority chose to remain under the Crown. Britain found itself retaining the most wealthy and industrial part of the island.

After partition, the locally elected Government of the North enjoyed quite a degree of autonomy. It had its own parliament, in a neoclassical palace specially built for it out in the middle-class eastern suburbs of Belfast, next to the neo-Gothic Stormont Castle, the administrative centre (today 'Stormont' is still the everyday term for official rule in the North). With some two-thirds of the population, plus a first-past-the-post electoral system, the Protestants and their Unionist Party were able to hold a huge majority in parliament, and they used their power arrogantly. Catholics were excluded from the best jobs, the best higher education, most council housing; flagrant gerrymandering swelled that majority further, and enabled Unionists to dominate nearly all local councils. It is true that the Catholics themselves may have been partly to blame for this overall situation, for few of them tried to cooperate in making the new State work; and the Church insisted on segregated education.

However, by the 1960s, Stormont had embarked on an economic policy of developing the Protestant heartlands in the east of the province, and neglecting the more Catholic areas to the west of the river Bann; nearly all new industry, and new motorways, were located in the east around Belfast, the 'new town' of Craigavon was built in Co. Down (it later became a monstrous white elephant), and a new university was put in loyalist Coleraine to the detriment of a small existing college in Derry. But despite this varied discrimination, there was little open unrest in the North before 1968, and little violence apart from sporadic murders by an IRA strongly committed to ending partition. Individual relations between Catholics and Protestants, living all mixed up together, remained surprisingly smooth, on the whole.

By the late 1960s, however, Catholic resentment was rising and in 1968 a civil-rights movement was formed, partly inspired by the events of 1968 on the Continent. The great civil-rights marches focused world attention on Ulster's injustices, but they also sparked off sectarian rioting. Urged by London to take action, the North's relatively liberal-minded prime minister of the day, Terence O'Neill, proposed a package of reforms to help the Catholics, but this simply alarmed his own supporters, such as the Reverend Ian Paisley, who denounced him as a traitor. In 1969 the mob riots grew worse, in the slums of West Belfast and the Bogside area of Derry. Stormont, unable to cope, called upon London to send the British Army into the streets, and over the next three years Britain steadily increased its control over security policy. But the violence continued to escalate, as the Provisional IRA moved on to the offensive. During 1971, forty-eight British soldiers were killed, and on the 'Bloody Sunday' of 30 January 1972 the paratroopers finally reacted by killing thirteen unarmed civilians in Derry. In March, with matters now almost out of control, the Stormont Government of Brian Faulkner resigned and Britain was obliged to impose direct rule. William Whitelaw, the first secretary of state for the North, made commendable efforts to develop a power-sharing system that would involve Catholic as well as Protestant politicians. But this was boycotted by most Unionists, who refused to work with 'disloyal' nationalists; and so in 1974 direct rule was reimposed, this time more completely, and the Stormont parliament was abrogated.

Direct rule, never intended as more than a transient measure, has over the past twenty years brought tremendous advantages to the Catholic population and has answered many of the demands of the civil-rights marchers. It has freed the Catholics from the heavy hand of the Protestant majority and allowed them at last a better deal, under a relatively fair-minded British Government. After 1974, London abolished the old system of government; it set up its own administration in Stormont, created twenty-six new local district councils with extremely limited powers (but fairly elected under a new system of proportional representation), and itself took over responsibility for town planning, housing, health, education and much else. Public housing, which used to be given mainly to Protestants, was now allocated much more evenly. Catholic schools received better funding. A new official agency began to fight against the severe job discrimination. Today there are still sectors where Catholics are disadvantaged, but matters are far better than under the old Stormont regime, which most moderate Unionists will today admit was a disgrace to democracy. The power of the old Unionist politicians has been cut right back, and the real levers of patronage are now in the hands of the British civil servants in Stormont.

British conduct in Northern Ireland gets severely criticized, not always fairly. It is true that the behaviour of the Army and police can be stupid and short-sighted and sometimes cruel (see p. 366). But in social and economic matters the Government's record in redressing past injustices has been extremely positive. This is not a neocolonial situation, as many foreigners naïvely believe: the British imposed direct rule partly for security reasons, it is true, but also to help the Catholics against the majority, and this they have done. In the meantime, one loser has been local democracy, for although the North still sends its MPs to Westminster, and to Strasbourg, the elected councils have hardly any role (see p. 405). Local politicians, Unionists especially, complain of being 'colonized' by London. But until violence ends and a real political solution is found for the province, there is no alternative to direct rule.

Despite the social progress under direct rule, neither the political nor the military situation has changed fundamentally during these past twenty years. After reaching a peak in 1972, the level of violence then fell off and the street riots ended; but terrorism by both sides continued, remorselessly. Today the loyalists carry out more killings than the IRA, which concentrates on bomb attacks and murders of security personnel. In 1980–81, IRA prisoners' protests at their jail conditions led them into the notorious hunger strikes, from which ten of them died, including their leader, Bobby Sands; he was even elected a Sinn Féin MP in a by-election, while he was starving himself to death. The deaths had the effect, for a while at least, of increasing sympathy among nationalists for the IRA and its ally Sinn Féin. This was one factor that propelled the British Government into searching harder for a political solution and seeking the help of Dublin, and this resulted in the crucial Anglo-Irish Agreement of November 1985, negotiated and signed by Margaret Thatcher and Garret FitzGerald. Both governments agreed 'that any change in the status of Northern Ireland would only come about with the consent of a majority of [its] people'. But if this phrase reassured the Unionists a little, they were horrified by the clause that gave Dublin a consultative role in British policy for the North. The Unionists from then on began to fear that Britain was turning against them and might be planning a betrayal, so the Agreement subtly changed the climate in the North. Meanwhile, London continued its intermittent efforts to negotiate a proper political settlement. These led in 1991–92 to the first round-table talks, involving the Irish Government and all the main parties in the North except Sinn Féin (i.e. the two Unionist parties, the small centre Alliance Party, and the large moderate Catholic party, the SDLP). But the talks foundered on mutual intransigence, each side blaming the other. And so their ancient quarrel today preserves its fearsome integrity.

Today the Catholics are on the advance in the North, and the Protestants on the defensive, all along the line. Look at the population figures. Until not long ago, it was usually said that Protestants outnumbered Catholics by two to one: the 1926 census had put the latter at 33·7 per cent, and by 1971 the figure was still only 36·8 per cent. But then the 1991 census showed that out of a population of 1,573,000 the Catholics were at 41·4 per cent, the Protestants at 54 per cent, with 4 per cent 'other' or 'no religion'. The Catholics' increase has been due to their higher birthrate, and to a rise in Protestant emigration in face of an uncertain future. Today the Catholics' rate of advance is slowing, for their birth rate has begun to fall, as in the Republic. Even so, many loyalists remain frightened of being eventually outbred. And if the Protestant electorate were one day to fall below 50 per cent, this could change the political picture, for there would no longer be so much protection for the loyalists in the British promise that a united Ireland would not be imposed against the wishes of the majority. But any such change is many years away. And the argument assumes all Catholics voting for Irish unity, which is not the reality.

As Catholics grow in numbers and win more senior jobs, and as London deals directly with Dublin, so Protestant insecurity increases – and this explains the recent growth in terrorism by loyalist extremists. Rising unemployment has also worsened the morale of some Protestant working-class areas. The Catholics on the other hand, at least the middle class, have become markedly more assertive in social and community affairs. A new confident bourgeoisie socializes easily with the Protestants, enjoying the prosperity brought by direct rule and its generous funding. In the many new local cross-community ventures (see p. 410), it is the Catholics who make the running; they have caught the old Protestant work-ethic like the measles, as a new breed of Catholic entrepreneur emerges. 'Proactive' is their favourite catchword. And as one Catholic priest assured me, 'We know that time is on our side.'

In the better suburbs of Belfast, and in middle-class golf or bridge clubs around the province, the mixing is fairly easy. But elsewhere, above all in working-class districts, terrorist intimidation over the past twenty-five years has led to a segregation in housing, as people move out of mixed areas to the safety of their 'ghettos' (see p. 374). This is most noticeable in West Belfast, where the two sides live divided by high barriers euphemistically called 'peace lines'; in Derry, too, nearly all the Protestants have retreated to 'their' side of the river Foyle. And there has been a steady drift of Protestants into the eastern part of the province, away from the areas to the west, in Tyrone, Fermanagh and south Armagh, where the Catholics are in the majority. This kind of apartheid may help to reduce daily frictions, even violence: but it hardly promotes the togetherness needed to build a normal society. Added to it is the segregated education system, which is only slowly being modified by the growth of new integrated schools (see p. 422). All in all, most people from the two communities meet each other little, outside their workplaces, and they do not grow up together. Numerous local cross-community ventures, led by purposeful idealists and officially supported, are today working to bring people together across the sectarian divide; but they have to fight against an opposite trend of growing polarization. It is hard to tell which trend is winning. So daily life in the North has its abnormalities. And yet, for those in good jobs, it can be quite congenial.

It is not only these luckier ones who might find life harder, were it not for the money that the Government pours into the North. Special subsidies total over £2 billion a year, and public spending per head is some 50 per cent higher than the UK average. About half of the sum goes on security, the rest on top-ups to regular welfare payments, extra money for housing, education, etc., and special grants for farming and industry. The Troubles have clearly deterred much new investment, but this is not the only reason why the North's economy needs special support. Like the rest of Ireland, it is out on the periphery of the EU. And it has a legacy of older traditional industries now in decline. Belfast used to be one of the great industrial cities of the British Isles: but most of its old linen mills have now closed, and the once-mighty shipyards of Harland & Wolff now survive only with government subsidy, having seen their workforce reduced since 1976 from 11,000 to 2,400. All in all, it is little surprise that unemployment is well above the UK average – yet the picture is less bleak than it might be. In fact, thanks to Government efforts and the arrival of a number of new, modern firms, unemployment declined from a peak of 17·7 per cent in 1986 to around 13·3 per cent in 1994, compared with the UK figure of about 10 per cent; and the recession of the early 1990s hit the North less heavily than Britain itself. Even so, average earnings (welfare excluded) are only 85 per cent of the UK average, so the extra State benefits are much needed by poorer people.

Special funding for the North comes not only from the British Government but from the European Union (all of Ireland is covered by the EU's aid schemes for peripheral regions) and from the International Fund for Ireland. This body, funded mainly by the United States, also by Canada and some EU countries, was set up in 1986 to help areas affected by the Troubles, especially around the border. London's own direct aid also includes grants for new investment of up to 50 per cent of capital costs, and this has helped to attract a number of new firms recently, including foreign multinationals. They may be taking security risks; but they know that if they do get bombed (and this has seldom happened) they are fully compensated. And while the North may have obvious drawbacks, it does offer the assets of good communications and a skilled, well-educated workforce with an industrial tradition. In the past few years, several big American investors have settled or expanded in the Derry area (see p. 384); elsewhere, Daewoo, Electrolux and Michelin are active. One particular success is that of the French firm Montupet, maker of cylinder heads and other car components: it chose the North so as to be near to its main client, Ford, which has a plant there too. Montupet took over the West Belfast premises of the De Lorean car company, which collapsed in 1982 with debts of over £100 million – an ill-starred project mistakenly backed by the Government in the 1970s, in its anxiety to secure new industry.

Today much-bombed Belfast has the air of a city where business is booming, with imposing new shopping malls and new office building, helped along by urban development grants. The same picture is true in Derry and some other towns. But it is something of an artificial boom, depending heavily on official largesse. A Conservative Government, so opposed to high public spending in Britain itself, here in the North betrays its usual philosophy and is far more interventionist, lavishing money on health, environment, education and other services that on 'the mainland' groan under cut-backs. With direct rule, some 40 per cent of employees are in the public sector, twice the UK average. Private businesses, too, derive advantages from direct rule. They do not have to deal so much with local authorities, who can be difficult, but instead have easy access to a highly professional civil service, helpful and generous with its funding. And for those in good jobs, living standards are high, partly because housing is cheap. It may sound cynical, but as is often said, the North's middle classes have done well out of the conflict, save for those tiny few who have been its direct victims. But differences of class and income lie at the heart of the North's drama, for more even than in Britain this has been developing into a society of haves and have-nots. There are pockets of high chronic unemployment where despair and near-poverty do much to fuel the violence of both IRA and loyalists. And this compounds the difficulties of finding a political settlement.

The sectarian divide strongly dictates voting habits and thus the pattern of party politics. There is even less of a left/right colouring than in the South. Even within the secrecy of the ballot, people still stick to their tribal family, out of loyalty or else fear, and it is rare that a Catholic votes for a Unionist party, or a Protestant for the moderate nationalist SDLP. The only exception is provided by the small centre-focused Alliance Party, which claims roughly 50/50 Catholic/Protestant support and usually wins 7 or 8 per cent of the vote, rising to some 30 per cent in its heartland of Protestant middle-class East Belfast. But although the Alliance nobly tries to create some middle ground, it basically favours the Union with Britain and so is not quite neutral. Its Catholic voters, largely middle-class, tend to be those who think a united Ireland premature, or who want to take a liberal stance against sectarianism. Apart from this minority, even the most moderate of UUP or SDLP politicians, who might find almost total agreement on social and economic issues, still stare at each other stubbornly across the great divide when it comes to discussing the North's political future.

Of the two main Protestant groups, it was the Ulster Unionist Party that controlled Northern Ireland until 1972, and it remains much the larger of the two. Its rival, the Democratic Unionist Party, created by Ian Paisley in 1971, appeared to be catching up in the mid-1980s but has since fallen back. In the 1993 local elections it won 17 per cent of the vote, with the UUP at 29 per cent. But the DUP remains a force to be reckoned with, under its powerful demagogic leader. In its voters' make-up it is more down-to-earth and proletarian than the smoother UUP – as was suggested to me saltily by Sammy Wilson, a brash young DUP city councillor in Belfast who was lord mayor at the age of thirty-three: 'The UUP, when it was in power, sought to exclude people like me as much as it excluded nationalists, because I was from a working-class home and my father didn't own property. But the DUP then made it possible for the likes of me to enter politics. On social matters, we are a little to the left of the UUP, and as we are not an Establishment party, we have fewer restraints: we are readier to hold street protests, take the political fight outside parliament. Paisley has been thrown out of the House of Commons several times, and this style of leadership is our badge.' Under Paisley, the DUP is also more adamantly anti-nationalist than the UUP, less ready to accept power-sharing with the SDLP on local councils, or to allow compromises in talks on the North's constitutional future.

The Reverend Ian Paisley (see p. 419), who will be seventy in 1996, is regarded by many today as a waning force. But he does represent something real in the North, and like it or not he has managed to encapsulate many Protestant fears with his stridently negative stance – 'Ulster says no!' One writer, after spending ninety minutes at one of his Bible-bashing services, said, 'I knew that I had been in the presence of pure evil.' But others point out that in his North Antrim heartland, where he wins big majorities, he is a good constituency MP, ready to help all his electors whatever their religion. 'He is a schizo split six ways, two of them very decent people, two awful, two quite unpredictable,' was another comment I heard. He is certainly a grave hindrance towards a solution in the North. Yet he is also an astute, gifted man of some stature, charismatic in his way – different from the general run of second-raters at the head of the DUP.

One significant recent tendency has been for the Protestant professional, social and business élites to opt out of politics. In the old days, the Unionist Party was led by senior lawyers or industrial-ists, or by men from the landed gentry like Major James Chichester-Clark, now Lord Moyola. Today they find the physical risks too great, the rewards too small, and the political scope too restricted under direct rule. They prefer to stay in their own private spheres, making money. And the parties are run mostly by mediocrities with narrow vision and little flair for politics. This could be serious, for it deprives the Protestant community of the quality of leadership it needs for finding a settlement.

The Catholics are better served, for their élites have a more ambitious sense of public service. Their main group, the Social Democratic and Labour Party, was founded in 1970 by a brilliant young intellectual and civil-rights activist from Derry, John Hume, today the North's most powerful politician. He is a moody, abrasive, egotistical character, a bit like his fellow Catholic Social-ist, Jacques Delors, with whom he gets on well. Hume believes in consensus and partnership, but is a tough negotiator; and he brings a firm autocratic style to his leadership of the SDLP, which has been much more successful than the previous ill-organized national-ist parties and usually holds about 20 per cent of the total vote. As its name implies, it is social-democrat, and combines this with a moderate, pragmatic brand of nationalism; its constitution states that a united Ireland can be achieved only by consent, and Hume admits privately that this will take time.

While disagreeing about the North's political future, SDLP and UUP politicians frequently get on well together in local affairs and they share many common aims. At a European level, the same even applies to the province's three MEPs, Hume, Paisley and Jim Nicholson (Unionist), who lobby jointly in Brussels or Strasbourg for EC aid for the North. 'We get on well in this context, as there's so much common ground,' Hume told me. I ask if he could talk reasonably with his DUP arch-adversary. 'There are two Paisleys — it depends which one is in charge. But even when charming he's always negative. I said to him, "If the word *no* were taken out of the English language, you'd be speechless."'

The SDLP's main rivalry is with the much more radical nationalist party, Sinn Féin, close political ally of the IRA. The SDLP lives in constant fear of losing votes to Sinn Féin if it takes too moderate a stance either in the political talks or in local dealings with the Army and police: thus in many places the SDLP will refuse to liaise publicly with the RUC. Bigoted loyalists tend to lump SDLP and Sinn Féin together as stooges of the IRA, but this is inaccurate, for the SDLP genuinely repudiates violence as well as having a milder political approach. There is no love lost between them, as emerged clearly in the famous West Belfast constituency contest of the May 1992 general election, when Joe

Hendron of the SDLP, a much-liked local doctor with moderate, liberal views, managed to win the seat from Sinn Féin's tough president, Gerry Adams. Hendron was helped by the tactical voting of at least 1,000 Protestant voters, who took the rare step of deserting their allegiance in order to unseat Adams. He was Sinn Féin's only MP, and the party was furious. Accusing Hendron of campaign illegalities, it appealed to the electoral court to have his victory quashed, but lost. Amid the wrangling, Hendron in turn accused Sinn Féin of massive 'vote stealing' by personation – a practice that has long been common in the North (the Unionists and nationalists both used to do it). It is not difficult to forge a medical card or some other document used for identity when voting, and thus steal the vote of another elector. The authorities know that the abuse goes on, but have never been able to stop it. Sinn Féin are thought to practise it regularly, and Hendron told me he reckoned that in this case it had brought them over 2,000 illegal votes. This, in a British election for the Mother of Parliaments! I was reminded of vote-faking in Corsica, or in Latin American countries where 'whole cemeteries' are sometimes said to have voted for the ruling party.

Sinn Féin does not recognize British rule in the North, and at various periods in the past it has boycotted Westminster elections. When the IRA split in two in 1969 (see p. 43), Sinn Féin allied itself with the 'Provisionals', while the old 'Official' IRA turned into a separate left-wing political movement, now called the Workers' Party, which does poorly in elections. Since 1981, Sinn Féin has contested all elections in the North. Its vote reached a peak of 13·4 per cent in 1983, soon after the hunger strikes and when unemployment was at its worst. It then fell back to around 10 per cent, but today the party still has a very solid, loyal following; in the 1993 local elections, its score climbed back to 12·5 per cent and it became the party with the largest vote in Belfast, where it now has ten councillors; in his own constituency, Gerry Adams polls over 40 per cent.

The Sinn Féin vote is mainly working-class. It is fuelled by high unemployment, by hatred of the British presence in general and specifically by loathing of Army harassment (see p. 366). Many voters also remain nourished on an old romantic tradition of republicanism, going back to the 1916 and 1798 uprisings, and earlier. The party's leaders still subscribe to that tradition, too. But although they want the North to be united with the Catholic South, few of them are themselves actively Catholic; in fact, their party is hated by the Church hierarchy, it has a secular left-wing platform, and it would like a united Ireland to follow that path.

The Sinn Féin leaders I met reminded me in many ways of the old French Communists I used to know, somewhat ascetic and fanatical, yet personally affable, and strictly obedient to the party line in their conversation. In Derry's Bogside I talked with their chairperson, Mitchell McLaughlin, in a simple café a few yards from the memorial to those 'massacred' by the Army in 1972. I found many of his views perfectly plausible – if only they could have been abstracted from the support for terrorism, and shorn too of some dotty notions about why the British are still in Northern Ireland: 'We are not condoning violence any more than the Government and the other parties do, with their support for the Army's institutionalized violence. And it's not the Unionists who are our real enemy, but the British. *Their* presence here has created these barriers between the Irish people, who otherwise could get on well – and we do want the Protestants to remain in a united Ireland. So why do the English still occupy this part of Ireland? Maybe they fear they might lose Scotland and Wales next, if they pulled out. Certainly their Army gets very good training practice here, and Nato is keen for it to stay. Above all, the British Government has not yet caught up with the rest of the world; it is still locked in the cold war era, seeing the six counties as strategically important. This is the last colonial conflict left in Europe.' It could be retorted that Sinn Féin, too, remains locked in an earlier war era, that of the pre-1921 fight for independence, and is allowing the legacy of that colonial struggle to distort its view of today's scenario.

There are signs now of some shift in Sinn Féin thinking: instead of demanding immediate British withdrawal, some leaders are indicating that there might first have to be a period of peace. But the party remains closely linked to the IRA. Who calls the tune is not always clear, but most experts believe that the IRA leaders control Sinn Féin, more than vice versa. The strategy has long been a dual one, of political struggle plus armed struggle – in the famous words of one Sinn Féin official, 'the republican movement' would advance to power with 'the ballot paper in one hand, the Armalite in the other'. And by spring 1994, there was little sign of the IRA being ready for a cease-fire. The Armalite was still crackling away.

Terrorists and 'squaddies' in a vicious circle of brutality

Hardly a week passes without some new atrocity. At worst, it might be a massive bomb blast in a town centre; or IRA ambushers killing a carload of civilians for working for the security forces; or loyalist gunmen attacking a Belfast shop, murdering and maiming the innocent; or the hideous IRA practice of the 'human bomb', whereby a man they want to kill is strapped into a bomb-laden vehicle and forced to drive it against an Army checkpoint. Sometimes a wife and children will watch as their father is gunned down by intruders in his own home. Then there are other, less public, less widely reported practices, which add to the climate of fear in some areas – the protection rackets and extortions; the intimidations of people who won't pay up or are pressured to evacuate their homes; and the punishments of those who break the gunmen's law, such as the bullet in the knee ('kneecapping'), cruelly painful.

Their aims and tactics may differ, but the IRA and the loyalist paramilitaries are equally savage; the security forces, too, are far from blameless, with their sometimes brutal treatment of suspects. But it must be stressed that the violence varies enormously from area to area: parts of West and North Belfast, south Armagh and east Tyrone have long been battlegrounds, whereas Derry city has seen a virtual truce in recent years, and some rural areas have never known terrorism. But everywhere it remains as a dark shadow over the North, colouring the mood; and on any family it can strike blindly, unexpectedly. For example, in 1993 I met a middle-aged Catholic couple in Dungannon, Co. Tyrone, whose daughter, Julie Statham, a student at Queen's University, Belfast, had just committed suicide after her fiancé had been shot in his home by loyalist gunmen. 'Until this sudden tragedy came out of the blue', said the mother, a hospital nurse, 'our lives here had been entirely normal and happy, and we had never taken part in politics. I've had many letters of sympathy from local Protestants.'

The violence continues. But at least it has not been getting worse, in statistical terms. The darkest period was near the beginning of the Troubles, when in 1971–6 deaths averaged well over 200 a year, peaking at 460 in 1972. Since 1976 the annual total has seldom risen above 100 and has often been much less; if it has risen slightly since 1991, this has been due mainly to the increase in killings by loyalists, today outnumbering those by republicans (IRA and others). Of the 85 killings in 1993, 34 were attributable to republicans, 47 to loyalists. The milestone of 3,000 deaths since 1969 was reached in August 1992. Of these, an estimated 1,720 were killed by republicans, 780 by loyalists, 350 by the security forces and 150 unclassified. This is 3,000 deaths too many. Yet the violence does need to be put in perspective: even more people die in road accidents in the province each year, and there are fewer shootings in Belfast than in an American city such as Chicago. 'The violence is being contained,' government spokespersons claim. But it shows no sign of going away.

The nature of the problem, however, has changed over the years, as IRA policies have shifted and loyalist terrorism has grown. The old IRA split in two in 1969, and since then the 'Official' IRA, purely political, has steadily waned and has now virtually ceased to exist in the North; what we now mean by the IRA is the other half of that split, the Provisional IRA (the 'Provos'), an essentially military body, loosely allied to Sinn Féin. In the early years of the Troubles, it set about organizing the Catholic community into mass demonstrations, either peaceful or violent. But then it decided that these could be counter-productive, so this kind of street disorder is now rare. The IRA has also tended to abandon indiscriminate bombings that could lead to heavy civilian casualties.

So today its attacks are nearly always carefully targeted, against (a) buildings and property, and (b) those it sees as its enemies, mostly the security forces.

Thus during the early 1990s the IRA has pursued a strategy of letting off large bombs in the downtown areas of predominantly Protestant towns, such as Coleraine and Bangor, destroying shops and business premises. The centre of Belfast has also been hit: witness the bomb in May 1993 that injured 13 people and badly damaged the Grand Opera House. Nor have Britain's own cities been spared: in April 1993 a huge explosion on a Saturday in the City of London killed one person, injured 44, and caused damage put at more than £1 billion. Usually the IRA is careful to time the bombs to go off when such areas will be fairly empty, or at least to give advance warning: the IRA's leaders, whether prompted by conscience or not, realize that mass attacks on innocent civilians could alienate their own sympathizers. But there can be mistakes, for example if a warning is not properly given, as in the case of the bomb in March 1993 in a shopping centre in Warrington, Cheshire, that killed two children. These bomb campaigns are carefully political. Their aim, it appears, is to spread panic and indignation to the point where Britain is ready to think of withdrawal from Ulster. The cost of the damage falls on the British taxpayer, for the Government grants compensation, if not always to the full amount.

The IRA also targets those whom it regards as 'the agents of British imperialism' – the security forces themselves, civilians who work for them, and anyone such as a judge or senior civil servant. Several prominent people have been killed, including Lord Mountbatten and the Tory MP, Ian Gow. Usually these murders are committed outside Northern Ireland, for within it such people are heavily protected; but this did not prevent the then head of the civil service at Stormont, Sir Kenneth Bloomfield, from having his home bombed (he escaped). The IRA have also killed nearly a thousand members of the Army and the RUC, by bombing their barracks or checkpoints, ambushing patrols, or sniping at individuals off duty. More sinister, the IRA will sometimes turn its sights on the staff of any firm that does work for the security forces, or supplies them: thus in January 1992 seven building workers, all Protestant, died in an attack on their van in Co. Tyrone. The IRA and Sinn Féin regard the British and not the loyalists as their main enemy, and their overriding aim is simply to push them out. Direct attacks on Protestants not working for the British are quite rare.

The IRA today is a fairly small corps of a few hundred hard, experienced guerrillas with sophisticated weaponry. Yet many of them live family lives and even have regular jobs. In the 1970s they received arms and training from Gadafy's Libya; today their guns come from other sources, while most of their bombs are home-made, using chemicals from agricultural fertilizer. The IRA has also spawned rival splinter groups, even more ruthless – the Irish National Liberation Army and the Irish People's Liberation Organization.

The loyalist paramilitaries operate differently. Their attacks are much more random and untargeted – either acts of pure retaliation or sporadic sectarian killings of anyone with known republican sympathies. Sometimes they will simply burst into a shop or pub in a Catholic area and open fire. Unlike the IRA, these loyalists have no overall military strategy, save to fight back and to use terror to warn that Ulster must stay British. Most of them belong to two small terrorist bodies, the Ulster Freedom Fighters and the Ulster Volunteer Force, whose initials you see inscribed on murals in parts of Belfast. Both operate under the aegis of the Ulster Defence Association, an extremist movement that long remained legal, to the fury of nationalists, until 1992 when it was finally outlawed. Loyalist terrorism stayed at a fairly low level until 1985, when the Anglo-Irish Agreement sparked off Protestant fears. Since then, as Catholics in Ulster have become more assertive, and as Protestant insecurity has grown, so loyalist violence has developed as a spontaneous reflection of this, and today it accounts for more killings than does republican violence. These terrorists do mirror the fears of a section of the Protestant working class. But they are hard, vicious thugs, with the crudest political reasoning, and all Unionist politicians repudiate them.

The IRA, on the other hand, does keep some semblance of its

old political idealism. Together with Sinn Féin it still follows the dual strategy of seeking victory through violence and democratic means (the Armalite and the ballot box), and some of its fighters are university graduates with serious minds. It is also much closer to its own population than the UDA bodies are to theirs; in fact, it was a Unionist MP in Belfast who told me, 'The loyalist paramilitaries are parasites who extort from their own people, whereas the IRA in their way try to look after their community.' In some Catholic areas such as West Belfast, the IRA acts as a kind of moral police, with its own harsh justice. It will torture and shoot suspected police informers, but also kneecap drug-pushers, unauthorized racketeers or teenagers who vandalize homes or steal cars for joyrides. In Derry, a Catholic who had already been convicted by the courts for sex offences against children, but was on parole, was judged by the IRA to have been punished too lightly; so they shot him in both knees and left him to bleed to death. In short, the IRA tries to police its own areas, in a bid to keep the RUC out.

Since the start of the Troubles, the IRA and UDA alike have operated extortion and protection rackets of all kinds, as a form of fund-raising. In some cases, they even tacitly carve up the territory between them. In 1993 it was reckoned that more than £1 million a year was being extorted through these activities; and the Government has sometimes publicly appealed to businessmen to stop paying the protection money. The racketeers' favourite victims are building firms, which are relatively easy to hold to ransom; some insurance companies have suffered, too, but not so much the major shopping or manufacturing firms. One company received a 'receipt' for its donation, from a welfare agency. Protection money has also been extorted from Belfast drinking clubs, of both communities: recently the police were granted extra powers to investigate these clubs, and some twenty have now been closed down, so this particular racket has diminished.

In the 1970s and '80s there was regular extortion pressure against families, too. Agents would tour the housing estates, demanding contributions of, say, £5 weekly; those who refused to pay were threatened, and might find bricks hurled through their windows, or worse. The IRA has now largely stopped this practice; it prefers to extort from businesses rather than ordinary people. But the loyalist gangs still carry the collecting-box round some areas, demanding money from families and from local shops; those who refuse, or are late with their payments, may get a gift of a petrol bomb. 'The local people just can't stand this,' said one Unionist leader in North Belfast, 'and that is why so many Protestants are getting out of this area, to safer suburbs. It also explains why the loyalist paramilitaries are so much less popular with their own people than the IRA.'

Other intimidation has taken the form of trying to push people out of their homes; the paramilitaries regard this 'ethnic cleansing' as essential, if they are to control their own areas effectively. The loyalists have been especially ruthless against Catholic families. According to one official report, in 1969–72 some 60,000 people were forced to leave their homes, and 80 per cent of them were Catholics, driven out by the UDA. Today pressures of this kind are less common, for the segregation has been largely completed, at least in the more sensitive urban areas such as working-class Belfast. But threats still occur. A family may first receive an anonymous warning by telephone, then the children are harassed at school, or the father is beaten up in the street, or the house is vandalized. So the family leaves – and the police say that, sorry, they can do nothing.

The work of the security forces in the North, that fiercely controversial topic, involves collaboration between two very different bodies: the Army regiments brought over from Britain, and the local police, the Royal Ulster Constabulary. Soon after the start of the Troubles, the RUC was disarmed and the Army took over the main security effort. But then in 1976 the Government switched to a policy of 'Ulsterizing' the defence effort as far as possible, leaving the Army more free for tasks elsewhere. The Army presence has since been reduced from some 22,000 men to 11,000, while the RUC has been enlarged from 3,500 to about 8,000, plus 4,000 reserves; there is also a local Army regiment, the Royal Ulster Rangers (into which the Ulster Defence Regiment was merged in 1991). Army and RUC frequently operate together on patrols and searches, as can be seen at the numerous road checks around the province – the RUC in their sleek dark-green uniforms, looking controlled and serious; and the usually very young Army 'squaddies' in their helmets and battledress, wielding sub-machine-guns, often looking scared as much as scary. There is frequent friction between the two: the RUC tend to look down on the soldiers as being poorly trained and ill-suited to this kind of police work, which may be true.

The entire security operation is repeatedly criticized, not only by nationalists but by various politicians, journalists, international human-rights groups, and others. Alike in the North itself and in Britain, there have been the notorious cases of Army, police or detectives allegedly falsifying evidence or extracting false confessions, as witness the Birmingham Six scandal and others. The prison system has also been criticized, and the treatment of prisoners jailed for terrorist acts, though here conditions have now improved. But it is the routine daily operation in streets and homes that is probably the most counter-productive: in a word, Army and police may be trying to destroy the IRA, but they do it in a way that strengthens it.

In their daily security checks and searches in the North, Army and police behaviour can be extremely unjust *and* plain stupid. One hears repeated stories of men spreadeagled against walls and brutally searched, and of other rough, insulting interrogations of probably innocent people, mostly in the poorer Catholic areas. The saying goes that when the Army or RUC make a routine car check in Belfast, in the bourgeois Malone Road they will say, 'Excuse me, sir, would you mind if I looked in your boot?', while in the Falls Road it's, 'Open your fucking boot, you bastard, and quick'; one businessman told me that when he drove to work in his Mercedes he was never stopped, but once when he borrowed his son's battered old Mini, he was intercepted and questioned right away. And a girl in Co. Tyrone gave me this story: 'Two boys of seventeen here were arrested by the Army, after a riot. They were beaten up brutally, in a bid to extract confessions that they had been in the riot. One boy did break down and confess.

Later he joined the IRA to get his revenge.' Of course the Army and police have a difficult job to do, but if only they did it less roughly, they would antagonize the Catholics less, and produce fewer new recruits for the enemy they are trying to fight.

The RUC can behave badly too, but the Army are worst. These young squaddies and their NCOs tend to be clumsy, frightened, ill-educated, not adequately trained for the work they have to do, and poorly supervised by their officers, some of whom regard all young Catholics as potential IRA. Hence the excesses. But the pattern varies, and one radical Catholic said to me: 'I think that mostly the Army behave quite well, save for two regiments, the paratroopers and the Marines. They are assault troops and should not be here; they're like great rough Alsatian dogs.' Occasionally soldiers lose their discipline and go on the rampage, as happened in 1992 when paratroopers attacked staff and customers in pubs in Co. Tyrone, after a colleague had lost both legs in an IRA bomb attack; the officer in charge was suspended. Occasionally troops shoot innocent civilians by mistake. And their house searches are notorious: they will smash down front doors of homes to look for weapons, then not even offer an apology if they have been acting on a false tip-off.

A senior civil servant at Stormont, an Englishman, gave me his off-the-record view: 'We face a catch-22. In order to contain the paramilitaries, notably to stop them bringing bombs into city centres, we do need to keep a heavy military presence. We intend this to be reassuring to the entire peace-loving population, but alas it does tend to alienate the Catholics, who see us as one-sided. This is because we still consider the IRA our main enemy; it is the IRA that does the bombing, it is much larger and more organized that the loyalist groups, and it gets more support from its own population. So the searches and interrogations must go on – and the Army has been trained to do them brusquely. But I agree that this tough approach can produce a vicious circle, it brings new recruits to the IRA. We at Stormont try to explain this to the Army chiefs, but they are slow to get the point.' And it is exploited by Sinn Féin to sustain the argument that the security forces are conducting 'institutionalized violence'.

The authorities try to woo Catholics into sharing in the security effort: but here too there's a catch-22. Catholics are encouraged to join the RUC, but few will do so, for they know that it could turn them and their families into targets for IRA intimidation. So the RUC remains 92 per cent Protestant, and is thus perceived by Catholics as biased towards the loyalists – another vicious circle. There are occasional reports of collusion between the RUC and loyalist groups, even of a hard core of RUC militants who have organized loyalist paramilitaries to kill republicans; and a few other stories of SAS army units doing the same thing. Some RUC officers do not hide their strong loyalist sympathies; and there have been proven cases of IRA suspects, including girls, being hit on the head, kicked and obscenely insulted, during interrogations lasting several days, at the RUC's Castelreagh headquarters near Belfast, and elsewhere. Happily these incidents are rare, and usually the work of juniors. The RUC's more senior officers mostly have a good reputation: but, as with the Army, they do not always have perfect control over their lower ranks.

In their hunt for the terrorists, Army and police are always seeking for informers, and hundreds of arrests and weapon seizures have been made thanks to them. The military trucks in the streets display details of the 'confidential' telephone numbers that anyone can safely ring to pass information. But, in both communities, people who hate the paramilitaries still remain wary of informing on them, for they retain some irrational gut fear that somehow they might be found out. And even a suspected informer is liable to torture, then a bullet in the head.

The security forces' roughness springs in part from a deep frustration; they know who the leading terrorists are, even how to find them, but legally they cannot get them. Here they are now paying the price for their own past abuses, e.g. the Guildford Four, Birmingham Six and other cases, for new laws since 1992 now put much greater onus on Army or RUC to verify their evidence; and as the terrorists have become clever at hiding their tracks, the police rarely possess what they need to make an arrest. Sometimes an IRA outrage brings renewed calls for internment without trial; but this was a failure when used in the 1970s, and the Government remains wary of trying it again. Meanwhile, the slow battle goes on. The IRA stays set on a long war of attrition, though there are signs today that some at least of its leaders are beginning to weary of the struggle. But even if there were a cease-fire, racketeering and gangsterism would be likely to continue for some years. As with the Mafia, they have become a way of life, and of livelihood.

The impact of the terrorism on daily life varies greatly from area to area. Nearly everywhere, people have learned to live with it, and have even grown 'case-hardened'. In central Belfast, the bomb alerts, the ensuing road blocks and traffic jams, often caused by the IRA's deliberate false alarms, provoke irritation but not much more. In the bad areas, notably the working-class ghettos, the psychological impact is more harmful. Here the worst effect of violence is on the children, who grow up in this peculiar ambience and turn to vandalism as something normal; they are in danger of becoming the terrorists of tomorrow. In these areas, active adult sympathy for the IRA is put at around 20 per cent. But alike in the Catholic and Protestant ghettos, many of those who dislike the paramilitaries still look to them as a kind of insurance, a force that they might one day need to defend them against the other side, if the British were to leave. The well-known nationalist priest Denis Faul said to me, 'There'll be no peace until the Catholics say to the Provos, "We don't need you." But while the fear of the Orange rabble remains, they feel that only the IRA can protect them.' It is this that enables the gunmen to keep a certain hold over their communities.

That is one side of the picture. But there is more to the North than its violence. Travelling nowadays to middle-class South and Central Belfast, or to Derry reborn, or to a quiet scenic county such as Fermanagh – topics for the next three sections – one gains the impression also of a dynamic, prosperous province that is coping well with its troubles.

Belfast's double image: Malone Road versus Falls Road

When I drove into central Belfast one evening in 1973, it was like a ghost town; at 9 p.m. I could find nowhere to eat save one gallant little Chinese restaurant, almost empty; the opera house, and all the theatres save one, were shut and barred. Today, twenty years later, this central area has its share of good French restaurants, busy pubs and discos, theatres, glittering new shopping galleries. The Government has poured in money, and those in jobs have plenty to spend. Over in the western working-class ghettos, where unemployment is very high, the angry murals, the army patrols and the barricaded streets are sinister signs of the abnormality beneath the surface. But in other areas, life achieves a kind of normality. This resilient city has been struggling to escape from its former gloomy, unloved image, which no longer gives a fair picture. It is not a beautiful town, much of it is tatty and jumbled: but it has its own vibrancy, and it compares perfectly well with most industrial cities of northern England.

Like them, it was a phenomenon of Britain's nineteenth-century industrial greatness; in fact, in that period it was the fastest-growing town in the United Kingdom, with a population that increased tenfold in 1821–1911 to reach some 400,000, ahead of Dublin. It had the world's largest shipyard, Harland & Wolff, where the *Titanic* was built in 1911. These and other big firms were ruled by a confident Protestant élite, in a city that was said to be 'devoted to God and Mammon and not much else'. Then its industrial decline began with the slump of the 1920s, and continued through the 1950s and '60s when the shipyards and textile mills fell on bad times. Unemployment rose fast. On top of this came the Troubles, which deterred new investment and kept people away from the city centre at night, as random violence grew. Belfast was like a city under siege.

The first signs of its gradual recovery date from the late 1970s. First, as the security forces came to contain the violence better, people began to venture back into the central area, for entertainment and shopping. In 1979 the reopening of the restored Grand Opera House, today in active use, was a key symbolic event that

370

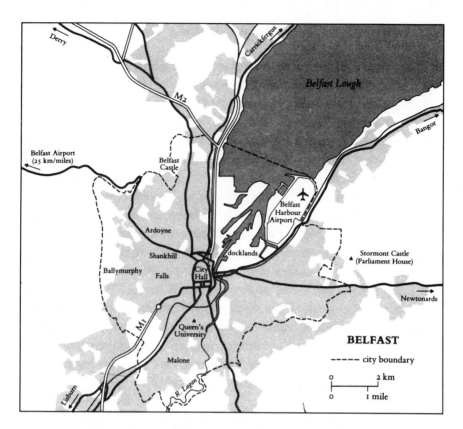

Map labels:
Derry, Carrickfergus, Belfast Lough, M2, Bangor, Belfast Airport (25 km/miles), Belfast Castle, Belfast Harbour Airport, Ardoyne, Shankhill, docklands, Stormont Castle (Parliament House), Ballymurphy, Falls, City Hall, Newtonards, M1, Queen's University, BELFAST, Malone, ----- city boundary, 0 2 km, 0 1 mile, R. Lagan, Lisburn

helped to rebuild confidence; other theatres followed, new shops and restaurants started to appear. Then, from the mid–1980s, the Government launched massive new injections of funds, in a bid to encourage new investment, promote urban renewal, and generally improve the city's image. Two junior ministers for Northern Ireland, Chris Patten and then Richard Needham, were especially active.

This policy has borne some fruit, but is criticized for its office-building programme, in a city where the Government, under direct rule, is by far the major employer. Its main offices are far out at Stormont, in the safety of the eastern suburbs. With the sensible aim of making them more accessible, the Government is today relocating many of them in downtown areas, where some 85 per cent of all new office space has been taken by the public sector. Developers have been encouraged to renovate old office buildings or pull them down and put up new blocks. But this has led to eyesores, and it has wasted public funds, for the demand was overestimated and many offices are now standing empty.

The policy of reviving commerce and business has been more successful. New firms of all kinds receive handsome development grants, with guarantees of compensation against bomb damage. As a result, central Belfast's shopping scene has been transformed, with the opening since 1989 of three big centres. The most glossy, Castle Court, with its cascading fountains and high, glass-roofed gallery, has been funded by the Bank of Japan and includes branches of Debenhams, Miss Selfridge, Benetton, Laura Ashley, Virgin, The Body Shop and other smart names. They are mostly doing well, but have led to the closure of a number of smaller, older shops nearby. Another new arcade has a branch of Bewley's, the famous Dublin coffee-shop; and a new Marks & Spencer has the sixth highest turnover of any of its UK stores. This part of the city centre, just north of the stately City Hall, has been transformed from near-dereliction into a pleasant, neatly paved pedestrian zone. The styles of urban design and of shopping-centre might seem outmoded in other West European cities, but in Belfast they come as invigorating novelties, tokens of a new normality. Meanwhile the city's development office has launched a well-funded PR campaign, 'Positively Belfast', with fireworks, hot-air balloons and big sporting events, and in 1991 it played host to the annual international Tall Ships race. 'We are steadily destroying the bad old image,' claimed an official.

Not that life is entirely normal. Bomb blasts still happen in downtown Belfast. Its premier hotel, the Europa, said to be Europe's most-often-bombed hotel outside Bosnia, was hit again by the IRA in May 1993. But the sporadic attacks have not put much of a damper on the lively nightlife scene that re-emerged in the 1980s. Belfast's so-called 'Golden Mile', a few garish streets of mostly down-market eateries, pubs and discos between the City Hall and the university, may not be nearly as golden as its name: but it's a world away from the dark silence I found there in 1973, and it secretes several excellent smart restaurants, often full, including the Michelin-starred Roscoff. The theatre, music and art-gallery scenes have become livelier, too. 'The city centre is neutral ground, unlike in Beirut,' said one pub-owner. 'Both communities can come here to relax, without the territorial tensions of working-class West Belfast.'

Nor is there much sign of these tensions in residential South Belfast, where Catholics and Protestants rub shoulders fairly easily. This Malone Road area, where mansions with gardens line leafy boulevards, looks indistinguishable from any well-to-do English suburb such as Edgbaston or Wimbledon. And in the smarter Protestant heartlands just outside the city – at Hillsborough to the south-west, or along the 'Gold Coast' by the sea around Bangor – lifestyles can be almost luxurious. Here you will see Mercedes and Jaguars on their way to the Royal Belfast Golf Club or the Royal Ulster Yacht Club, and mansions with private swimming-pools or tennis-courts. Many are the homes of senior civil servants posted from London under direct rule, or of the local Protestant professional and business élites. They have suffered little from recession, and they benefit from housing costs that are dramatically lower than in Britain. Thanks to the Troubles, prices never escalated as they did across the water; a four-bedroom detached house can go for £60,000, one-third of its English price, so the money saved on mortgages can be spent elsewhere. Golf-club and marina fees are much lower, too; and good secondary education is almost free, thanks to high school subsidies. So there is far more spending money, and higher living standards. What is more, out in these suburbs sectarian violence is rare, apart from the occasional IRA bomb in a shopping street at night. So, for a happy few, the quality of life can be rather good in the troubled North, as the blow-ins soon discover. A senior economist transferred from London said: 'People back in Britain are simply not aware of the advantages here, and of how Belfast has changed for the better. We arrived with such false preconceptions, but we found this a lovely place, with warm, friendly people. Daily life is *not* abnormal. And on my salary I reckon I'm 25 per cent better off than in Britain.'

The picture is so very different over in poorer West and North Belfast, where about 120,000 people live, one-third of the population of a city whose divide between rich and poor is more pronounced than in Britain. Unemployment, up to 80 per cent on some council estates, is compounded by violence and suspicion, in a tragedy that has its roots in the mid nineteenth century when Belfast industrialized so fast. In the Famine period, the growth of the linen industry drew hungry people in from the countryside, seeking work: Protestant peasants came down from Antrim in the North to settle in the Shankill Road area of West Belfast, while the adjacent Falls Road area filled up with Catholics moving in from Armagh and Tyrone. The first sectarian riots began in the 1850s.

A century later, while living standards had of course improved, much of the old back-to-back slum housing was still there, fearfully overcrowded; and jobs were growing scarcer. Some parts of West Belfast were solidly Catholic *or* Protestant, but others were more mixed, and in those days before the 'peace lines' there was intermingling: some Taigs would even attend Orange bonfires in July, or Prods would go to nationalist dances. But the slums and the poverty aggravated the latent sectarian tensions; and after the violence erupted in 1969, the migrations began, and the battles over territory, as Catholics and Protestants pushed each other out of 'their' areas (mostly it was the Prods who did the pushing). For several years, much of West Belfast was a battleground, with no-go areas where police and Army dared not enter – a scene vividly evoked by Dervla Murphy, the travel writer from the South, in her brilliant book on the North, *A Place Apart* (1978):

'Those ghettos really shattered me. Yet I have known far worse slums in Asia. But Belfast is in affluent Europe and why should large areas of it be swarming with undernourished wild children and knee-deep in stinking litter, and strewn with broken glass glinting in hot sun under a blue sky – all on a summer's day. So many bricked-up houses, reminding me of dead people with their eyes shut – some of them fine substantial buildings from which Protestants had had to flee in terror taking only their resentment with them. So many high brick, or corrugated iron, barricades between identical streets of little working-class homes, to prevent neighbours seeing and hearing each other, and so being provoked to hurt and kill each other.'

These barricades are the euphemistically named 'peace lines', some of them built in the 1970s, others added more recently. They were created by the authorities to seal off the rival areas, not so much to prevent daily frictions as to make it easier to control vandalism and killings by armed gangs after dark. And they have had some effect. Today, West Belfast is noticeably less horrific than Murphy found it, but still sinister and abnormal. It has been tidied up a little, the children are less wild and destructive: but there are still the empty bricked-up houses, still the decaying shop-façades, still the hideous fortified police stations and the high watch-towers above the zigzagging brick barriers – a smaller-scale, less absolute version of the Berlin Wall. On the Falls Road, the Sinn Féin office with its iron grille resembles an armed bunker; along the Shankill Road, where an IRA bomb attack killed ten in October 1993, many shops are closed. And everywhere, the patrols of squaddies with guns; everywhere, the angry graffiti and murals, colourful in their lurid pop-art styles. In the Crumlin Road, a UVF/UDA mural of black figures in stocking masks firing machine-guns. Scrawled slogans, 'Brits Out', 'Irish Out', 'Fuck the IRA', 'Brit murderers' – and, significantly, some UVF graffiti saying 'RUC scum'. In one loyalist street, the slogan 'No Pope Here', to which some wag has added, 'Lucky old Pope'.

The ghettoization has destroyed whole parishes. Ardoyne, a former Protestant parish within a Catholic area near the Crumlin Road, has virtually ceased to exist: its 800 families have left, its church has been burned, and Catholics have moved in. The ghetto apartheid may have helped to reduce casual violence, but it destroys social contact across the divide and thus hinders the work of reconciliation – a basic dilemma. Few people dare to go round the ends of the peace lines into each other's areas, even in daylight. And in places where there are no formal ghettos with peace lines, the sense of territory can be strong: this street is Catholic, that one is Protestant, and you stray from your own sector at your peril. In places, the 'frontiers' are marked by painted kerbstones, red-white-and-blue, green-white-and-gold.

The unpleasantness of life in the ghettos, where the paramilitaries rule, has been inciting many younger families to move out to freer, more normal parts of the city, better for their children. Young upwardly-mobile Catholics have been buying semi-detached villas in quiet parts of northern Belfast till now solidly Protestant; and the Protestants move out further still, into neighbouring towns. This, and industrial decline and slum clearance, go some way to explain the sharp fall in Belfast's population, from 450,000 to 330,000 since 1951.

The Government's economic effort for the city goes partly on trying to improve conditions in West Belfast. The old Stormont regime did little for housing, save to build some hideous high-density blocks at Divis, near the Falls Road: but the renewal programme since then, under direct rule, has been remarkable. Most of the old insanitary back-to-back slums have been pulled down; so has the ill-judged Divis complex. The newer housing, though simple, compares well with that of cities in Britain. The Government has also enticed some new light industries to settle in these areas – not an easy task – and it puts money into various job-creation and welfare schemes. In particular, it helps to fund cross-community ventures (i.e. involving Catholics and Protestants together), launched locally by urgent idealists crusading against poverty and sectarianism (see pp. 410–21).

The best known and most admired of them is Father Myles Kavanagh, a Passionist monk who runs a large business centre on the Crumlin Road, in a no man's land between two ghettos. It is in a former flax mill, where I went to see this breezy, blue-eyed pioneer in an Aran sweater, and he told me his story: 'After my monastery had been bombed by the UDA, I decided to try to help some of the young people in this very deprived area. In 1977 we made a study, which showed that out of a hundred boys who had left the local Catholic school, only twenty had jobs; the rest were on the streets or in prison, and *eleven* had been killed. I decided that reconciliation could come only through economic development: the two must go together. So I secured leave of absence from my Passionist order, and with friends I acquired this huge semi-derelict flax mill, where we set up the Flax Trust. Here we have gradually generated over seventy small separate businesses, now employing some 800 people. From the start we were cross-community – I was joined by a Presbyterian priest, Donald Frazer – and today the Catholic/Protestant mix here is about 60/40.

They get on perfectly well: in all this time, I have heard only one sectarian remark within these walls. And the paramilitaries leave us alone; they have never even made threats, they must know the fury it would cause. We also do social and welfare work, with our own youth clubs and a day-care centre for the elderly; we even take mixed groups of kids from both communities on holidays abroad [see pp. 413–14]. We try to reduce the old anger and despair, to generate hope, to create some future for these young people. It can be done.'

Somewhat similar work, on a smaller scale, is being done in the loyalist Shankill Road area by an impressive young working-class Protestant, Jackie Redpath. 'In these streets where I was brought up', he said, 'unemployment is still around 60 per cent. We have now set up a business and training centre here, with State backing, and we have secured £5 million of investment. We cooperate closely with the Catholics, Father Myles and others.' The Churches do indeed collaborate, with each other and with Stormont, on social and economic projects; and some politicians join in, across the divide. Dr Jo Hendron, the moderate SDLP MP for West Belfast, has good relations with Cecil Walker, the equally benign Ulster Unionist MP for North Belfast. 'We share common objectives,' said Walker, as he took me on a tour of the mixed Crumlin Road sector of his constituency, in his bullet-proof blue Sierra with two armed police drivers. Here there are no physical peace lines, but plenty of tensions. Walker showed me some new light factories built right on the sectarian divide, as a kind of buffer; the Catholic social hall where a few elderly Protestants still come to play Bingo; and bricked-up tenements abandoned by Catholics who have moved into a neat Protestant area just two streets away. 'Violence in Belfast is partly a matter of class,' he said. 'The middle classes have learned how to live together, but the working classes are still in the trenches.'

There are other men and women of good faith who are working, like Kavanagh and Redpath, to bring new jobs and a better harmony to these parts of Belfast. They are making some progress, slowly, and the example they set is important. But I should also mention another local leader, more controversial, who has a different outlook. Father Desmond Wilson is a kind of worker priest, an angry militant who lives in the desolate Catholic housing estate of Ballymurphy, amid ruined houses and IRA murals of gunmen proclaiming 'Our Day Will Come'. His political views are close to those of Sinn Féin, strong in his area; and his links with them do not endear him to Stormont, even though he is engaged in just the kind of community work that Stormont favours. For twenty years he has been working in adult education, to help the unemployed; near the Falls Road he has taken over Conway Mill, another disused flax factory, which he runs as a kind of cultural-cum-social centre, with classes, plays, discussions. The Government helped him for a while, then cut off his funds because of his alleged support for the IRA. About this and much else, including his Catholic Church, this priest expresses himself angrily: 'We try to bring the two communities together,' he told me, 'but Church and State both do their best to keep them apart – it's disgusting. The State has been deliberately starving West Belfast of jobs, and the greedy bishops have cynically accepted money from a Government which needs their help against Sinn Féin.' This turbulent priest used to be much respected among Belfast liberals, but he is now regarded as a bit absurd. Yet to his own people he remains a saviour – in these ghettos where life is harsher than amid the much gentler apartheid of Derry.

Derry's Phoenix-like revival – at a price

Derry is my favourite of all Irish towns. I like its looks and settings – the compact harmony of the ancient walled inner city, on its hill above the curving river Foyle. And I like its people – exceptionally warm, humorous, energetic and individual, buoyed up with pride in their town's distinguished history, bloody though some of it has been. 'Derry is different,' they claim – different in its approach to Ulster's problems, and different in its recent Phoenix-like rebirth, more remarkable than Belfast's. This has been helped by outside funding, also by dynamic local leadership

– from John Hume of the SDLP, a Derry man and its MP, and from the now legendary Paddy Doherty, a charismatic nationalist who has milked the funds of the hated British 'colonizers' to carry out the most impressive urban renewal effort in Ireland. A city centre that was smashed to bits in the violence of the early 1970s is now handsomely rebuilt and full of a busy new confidence.

There is, however, a darker side to this bright new coin: segregation. The violence of the 1970s caused the two populations to separate: Protestants moved *en masse* across the river, and today nearly all of them live on its east bank, whereas the city centre and the west-bank suburbs are solidly Catholic. The divide has at least been peaceful; today there is little terrorism or paramilitary pressure in Derry itself, where the IRA keeps a low profile and sectarian feeling is less strong than in Belfast. But although the two populations readily work together, they do not play or sing or even shop together. And the segregation is more complete than in Belfast, for it affects the middle as much as the working class. So this is a zestful but divided city. And most of the dynamic for renewal has come from the Catholic majority, while the Protestants feel somewhat left out.

The historical origins of this tribal rift are written vividly upon the town's urban geography – more than anywhere else in the North, people live amid the physical reminders of their past. Against a backdrop of the blue Donegal mountains across the border, the high city ramparts date from the start of the Plantations (1613–18) and have survived intact. Here I stood with my back to the old Protestant cathedral, beside Bishop's Gate where James II called upon the people to surrender in the great Siege of 1689. I looked down across the Bogside in the valley, with its angry nationalist murals, and across to a green hill by the border. 'That', said my guide, 'is where the Jacobite forces camped in the siege – and there just below us is where the British Army killed fourteen unarmed men on Bloody Sunday, 1972.' In Derry, history is multi-layered, interlocked, omnipresent. The old city used to be on an island formed by two arms of the Foyle: but the western arm dried up long ago, leaving just a bog – hence the name Bogside. This is a working-class Catholic area, much rebuilt since the 1969–72 riots. In the middle of its broad main road, the wall of one house has been bizarrely preserved, bearing the giant slogan, 'YOU ARE NOW ENTERING FREE DERRY' – a memorial to the years when the Bogside was a dangerous no-go area.

History, and politics, also explain the town's dual name. It was first built beside an oak-grove, which in Irish is *daire*: hence 'Derry'. Then in 1607, as the first English plantations here were funded by rich City of London merchants, the prefix was added which today is something of a political football. The SDLP-led town-cum-district council has formally changed the name back to Derry, but loyalists of course prefer 'Londonderry', and HMG still plays it that way too, so that road signs and State documents use this version. Londonderry is also still the name of the county. But locally the town is mostly known as Derry. Anyone using the longer name is probably very Orange.

At the time of the siege, this tiny city was a Protestant Williamite bastion. Then, from the mid nineteenth century, steady rural emigration from Donegal eventually produced a Catholic majority. But the Protestants still ruled: gerrymandering was such that in the 1967 local elections the Catholics, with 62 per cent of the voters, elected only eight of the twenty councillors, the rest were Unionist. The Protestants controlled housing and most jobs; and the old Stormont regime discriminated against Catholic Derry in several ways. It built a new university college in Coleraine that thwarted the growth of Derry's little Magee College (see p. 429), and it deterred new industry from settling in Co. Londonderry. So when the civil-rights movement emerged in 1968, Derry not surprisingly was one of its heartlands, the scene of some of its first and boldest marches. But this led in 1969–72 to repeated riots and violence, then to the British Army's overreaction on Bloody Sunday, and to a long campaign of IRA bombings of property in the 1970s. One-third of Derry's shops were burned out and closed, some 5,000 houses were wrecked or damaged. Morale was low, and around the world Derry had a black image. It was in this period that nearly all of the Protestant minority on the west bank moved across the river to the Waterside district, where they now have a majority and are well housed on neat new estates. A few of them left their homes under direct intimidation, others more freely but fearing for their safety. Of their original west bank population of 13,000, only about 10 per cent now remain, in this city of 80,000 people. But however humanly regrettable, the segregation has not hindered the economic resurgence of Derry; by reducing tensions, it may even have helped.

Today this indeed is a town reborn, an eye-opener to the visitor. Within the walled inner city, the streets have been rebuilt and new shopping centres opened, and scores of boutiques with quirky names like Toyology, Flip, The Whatnot, plus art galleries and a marvellous new history museum; the tourists, too, are coming back. Outside the town, new hi-tech industries have arrived, the airport has been enlarged, a new port is being built. Much of the impetus for all this came from John Hume, Derry's political heavyweight, who was born and bred in the town, and was a leader of its first civil-rights marches. He is a man with more vanity than charm; but he has terrific energy, persuasiveness and vision. As local MP and MEP, and the SDLP's leader, he has bludgeoned London, Brussels and the US-led International Fund for Ireland into giving extra support to a town with 24 per cent unemployment; and he has repeatedly toured America, to convince hard-headed tycoons that Derry's black image is now false and this is the place to invest.

Controversially, Hume has also promoted a species of power sharing (see p. 406) on the Derry district council (the town and its area), where the SDLP has a large overall majority. Though it need not do so, the party allows the mayoralty to rotate, so that in some years the post is held by an independent Unionist or even the DUP. In practical terms this may not mean much, for as in England a mayor is little more than a figurehead, and under direct rule a council has such limited powers, but Hume's gesture of cooperation has some symbolic importance. In effect he is using his home base of Derry as a showcase for his political programme of a Northern Ireland based on partnership. Some of his local opponents claim that this is a sham, for the mayor is merely a puppet of the SDLP; and in a sense this may be true. But Hume has imposed his ideas on the warier SDLP councillors, who in

1992 tried to block his choice of a Paisleyite as mayor, William Hay of the DUP. And Hume has tried to ensure that his policy is seen to work in the eyes of the world; he took Mayor Hay with him on a promotional tour of the United States.

The urban renewal in the city centre was helped by Hume, but has been due above all to the astonishing Paddy 'Bogside' Doherty. Slight, wiry, blue-eyed, now aged about seventy, father of thirteen, this hyper-energetic impresario won his nickname from his leadership role in calming the 1970s Bogside violence. A builder by trade, he then began training unemployed youths to work on new projects – 'It's the lack of jobs and responsibility that has fuelled the senseless violence,' he told me. This led to his creation in 1981 of the Inner City Trust, which has worked marvels in restoring the bombed and gutted old buildings, many of them Georgian. Doherty has sometimes had more than forty IRA ex-prisoners working on his sites. He has since gone ahead with larger projects – a replica of a medieval tower, a craft village, youth hostel, music centre, heritage centre. As he took me round, I was amazed at the number of bulldozers, cranes and men in safety helmets in so compact an area. One creation is an 'international reconciliation centre' that will, he says, 'provide a forum for people around the world involved in conflict. We have lived with it here for so long, we have plenty to teach about reconciliation.' Indeed – one of his own sons spent twelve years in prison for helping the IRA, while a son-in-law was killed *by* the IRA for allegedly helping the police.

Doherty the republican draws his funds for the ICT from where he can – the EU, the United States, Whitehall. 'I want the British *out* – but I *love* their money,' he said with a grin. 'My forebears here, the O'Doherty chieftains, spent centuries alternately fighting them and fraternizing; one O'Doherty was even knighted by Elizabeth. I continue that tradition.' Indeed he was on close terms with Richard Needham, who as a minister for Northern Ireland in 1985–91 warmly supported his work for Derry. Paddy is also on cordial terms with that eager environmentalist, Prince Charles, who has several times held dinners for him in England to meet American financiers and others, opening doors for new funds. When Charles said that he wanted to visit Doherty in Derry, he was told, 'Alas, impossible, Sir.' 'Why? – are you afraid I would be shot?' 'No,' said Paddy, 'but I would be – and you know by whom.'

The ICT's most spectacular creation is a convincing replica of an Irish medieval tower house, with tiny windows and looming stone battlements, on the site of a long-vanished castle of the O'Doherty chieftains, right by the ramparts. In its bowels is one of the best interpretative museums I have ever seen, opened in 1992 by Jacques Delors, none other. It has few original artefacts beyond a very ancient boat dug out from the Foyle, but it vividly links Derry's history with Ireland's, via wall displays, tableaux and nine videos, illustrating topics ranging from pre-Viking times to the Flight of the Earls, the Siege, the Famine, even the recent Bogside battles. There's a life-size tableau of the Apprentice Boys closing the gates at the start of the Siege. The museum's nationalist bias is restrained, and on the whole it achieves balance, even symbolically – the displays of the 1916–21 period have red-white-and-blue decorations on one side, green-white-and-gold ones on the other.

Next to the museum is another Doherty venture, the Craft Village, aimed mainly at tourists and opened in 1992 by President Mary Robinson. Various little cafés and shops, selling Irish souvenirs, local crafts and knitwear, are grouped around a neat patio; there's a French restaurant, Bon (*sic*) Cuisine, and an Irish one, Thran Maggie's. One plan is to try and persuade craftsmen to live and work here, but hardly any have arrived yet apart from one glass-maker. Up the hill, Doherty has completed lavish new premises for Derry's Heritage Centre, which like others in Ireland is now engaged in the new tourist business of wooing foreigners, mainly American, to seek out their roots. A number of them would be Dohertys, a common local name. Derry and Donegal were once the realms of the O'Doherty chieftains, Paddy's ancestors, and he recently organized a rally here of some 2,000 of his clan from around the world. Many were from families who had left in the Famine days when Derry was a major port for the emigration; and today a fine new bronze sculpture near the former harbour, of elderly parents saying adieu to their departing family, evokes that tragic episode. This, the museum, the ramparts and much else, are all on the city sightseeing trip offered to the tourists now returning to Derry: in 1993, two American tour operators put it back on to their Irish programme, after a gap of over twenty years.

Industry too is reviving, after a long, lean period. In the town are several hefty redbrick Victorian buildings, former shirt-factories that stand as souvenirs of the days when Derry was a major textile town; Karl Marx visited one of them, describing it in *Das Kapital* as an example of exploitation. Almost all of them closed long ago. And the more recent problem has been lack of work, not that of being forced to work too hard on minimal pay, as in Marx's day. The decline of the textile industry, plus Stormont's disdain for Derry, both served to push up unemployment, which in the 1950s and '60s reached 30 per cent. Then the new Stormont regime began to help; but at first in the violent 1970s it was far from easy to interest investors. Today the picture is brighter, with five large American firms active in the Derry area. Du Pont's synthetic-rubber plant employs some 1,200. Fruit of the Loom, the US leisurewear giant, has bought up one local clothing firm, McCarter, and now turns out nearly a million T-shirts a week, for EU markets; so the town's textile tradition has been renewed in a bright modern form – from sweatshops to sweatshirts. And Seagate, another American hi-tech firm, is building a plant to employ 500, after its vice-president had been lobbied by Hume in a bar in San Francisco.

'Yes, I won Seagate, I helped with Fruit of the Loom, I brought Marks & Spencer here, I got EC funding for the port, the airport, the new bridge,' I was told by this non-believer in mock modesty. But even Hume has not yet been able to pull unemployment below 24 per cent – a legacy of the past compounded by recession and Derry's difficult westerly position. However, Hume does seem able to persuade Americans that Derry would be a suitable springboard for their operations within the EU single market; and the town has secured more than its share of EU grants given to peripheral areas. Hence the impressive infrastructure – a new deep-water port at the mouth of the Foyle, an extension to the airport with an eye on London and the USA, and a handsome new curving suspension bridge over the river. In the town centre, a big new shopping centre has opened recently, and two others are being completed beside the river, one with Marks & Spencer as its anchor tenant. Is all this too ambitious? 'No,' I was assured by one Government official; 'Derry was neglected and under-utilized for too long. It can now resume its place as the commercial magnet for all western Ulster, including Donegal.'

Derry's two high-spired cathedrals confront each other across the ramparts and the lower Bogside. Up in the old town is the Protestant St Columb's (1628), named after Derry's saint. One of its souvenirs is a memorial to a nineteenth-century bishop's wife, Cecilia Alexander, who wrote such famous hymns as 'Once in Royal David's City'. Another, 'There is a Green Hill Far Away without a City Wall', she is said to have written beside the cathedral, gazing out over the city wall to the green hill above the Bogside. The Catholic cathedral, St Eugene's, is down within the Bogside. And one Sunday I went to services in both. St Eugene's was crammed full, with people moving in and out casually, lots of children, priests in red robes enacting high drama at the altar – I could have been in southern Italy. At St Columb's, the people were far fewer, they looked older and more bourgeois, with lots of ladies in hats, and they sat still, separated by high pew-backs – I could have been in Tunbridge Wells.

The two bishops, Edward Daly (Catholic) and James Mehaffey (Protestant), have a close personal friendship of Liverpudlian proportions. They make a point of regularly attending each other's cathedral services, of going together on city walkabouts and joint tours of the United States; they are both trustees of Doherty's ICT. This brave ecumenism has certainly helped to spur Derry's revival, and to lend the city a more reassuring image. It is actively supported by little groups of Christian community workers. But it is strongly opposed by the local Paisleyites of the DUP. And at the grass roots the majority of churchgoers on both sides are at best indifferent, in a city where, as throughout the North, the divide is essentially one of nationalism and politics, not religion. Protestants get along easily with Catholics in their workplaces, but their friends, shops, pubs, clubs, doctors, lawyers, are almost entirely Protestant, and the same is true of Catholics. The basic social problem has been anaesthetized, but not solved, in a town where the Catholics have the majority by some 70 to 30 per cent.

Beside the old bridge over the river is the new Statue of Reconciliation: two bronze male figures, ten feet high, stand either side of a stone chasm, holding out hands to each other, their fingers not quite touching. It is hardly yet a warm embrace. And many Protestants today still feel bitter about their migration across that river in the 1970s; they were not openly chased out of their own homes (save in a few cases), but they were no longer welcome. Many of them now cross over to the west bank for their work, but few go there for their leisure or even for shopping; they have their own venues on the east bank, or else they will make the thirty-mile journey to the Protestant towns along the coast, such as Coleraine. The pubs and restaurants of the old walled city are mainly used by Catholics at night – 'We just don't feel at ease among them, if we want to have fun with friends,' said one young Protestant factory worker. There does remain one Protestant enclave of working-class housing near the city centre, the Fountains district, tawdry and run-down, now due for demolition. A Protestant civic group is working to refurbish it, put in a new school, build it up again as a lively community; but it is not certain whether many Protestants will be enticed back there. The IRA may keep a low outward profile in Derry today, but people with relatives in the RUC do not feel safe living in a Catholic area. It is one reason why Protestants are still reluctant to go back to inhabit the west bank. And in the May 1993 local elections, the Protestants lost their last remaining councillor for a west-bank ward, making the segregation more complete than ever.

After the Protestants' long unjust dominance, the Catholics have been quietly redressing the balance. Today they control the district council and the ICT, and they take the lead in most community ventures and cultural events, such as the international arts festival held in 1992, the first since the Troubles. The Unionists always used to regard Derry's history as 'theirs', the celebrations of the Siege as theirs, marked by the Orange-style parades of the Apprentice Boys' society each July; but today, especially from Catholics, one hears much more talk of a sense of shared history – 'The Siege, even the plantations, are our heritage too,' said one SDLP man, 'and the new museum is there to prove it, dual tricolour pavings and all.'

Doherty builds his reconciliation centre, the bishops talk of fraternity, Hume extols partnership – but how much of it yet exists? The Catholics may run the show too assertively: but they have some cause to complain, as they do, that the Protestants are too reticent and will not accept the hand of partnership when it is offered, in all sorts of local ventures. It is the dilemma of all the North today (see pp. 414–16). The local DUP complains that 90 per cent of the ICT's staff of 350 are Catholic (see p. 405), but Doherty has asserted that Protestants have not taken up the posts offered them.

Not only has Derry made a huge step forward in recent years, but a growing minority of younger people are tiring of its old sectarian divisions, as witness the success of its new integrated schools (see p. 423). Across the divide, people are drawn together by a pride in their city, but it will take more time for the old suspicions to heal. 'One cannot say it aloud, but maybe the separation of the two populations is needed for a while, as part of the healing process,' said the Catholic auxiliary bishop, Francis Lagan. Is this realism, or a counsel of despair?

While Londonderry county has loyalist connections, Derry, so close to the Donegal border, is the most 'Irish' town in the North. In the Dungloe and Gweedor pubs, local amateurs play the fiddle, harp and bodhran, and sing folk ballads in Irish in their throaty accents – you might be in Galway or Kerry. Brian Friel and Seamus Heaney, those two most Irish of writers, are both from Derry, and here they founded the controversial Field Day theatre company, very intellectual/nationalist (see pp. 254–5). Many Derry people have Donegal roots, as you can tell from their names; and this is the natural capital of north-west Ireland, ten times the size of any town in Donegal. After a difficult time in the 1970s, people are again crossing the border in huge numbers for shopping and entertainment, as you can tell from the hordes of 'DL' cars in the streets. So this brings us to the strange question of Ireland's North/South border, so real and yet so unreal.

Along the strange border: smugglers, ethnic cleansers and a new luxury hotel

The entire North/South border, from Derry to Newry, is today one of the oddest in Europe, a mix of the totally invisible and the heavily fortified. On many roads there is no indication whatever of a frontier, and you can cross and recross quite unaware of it; even the customs posts have now gone, with the coming of the EC single market in 1993. But on some roads you are suddenly stopped short by one of those fearsome Army checkpoints, with steel barriers and battle-dressed squaddies holding machine-guns. It may be necessary. But it can be highly disconcerting to a foreign visitor, not the best welcome to the North.

Viewed historically this is an artificial border, splitting Ulster in two, dividing families, friends, communities, even slicing up some parishes and dioceses (one Church of Ireland diocese bestrides Co. Londonderry and Donegal). Today, seventy years after partition, many people still have close relatives just across the border. Or they live on one side, work on the other, and it all seems one country to them, save for a few matters such as tax and welfare payments – and the Army patrols. Mostly it is the Catholics who think like this, whereas for many loyalists the South is alien territory. But there are Protestants on the south side too: I met a vicar in Co. Leitrim whose parish spills over into Fermanagh, and I found a border village in Co. Cavan that has Orange parades in July.

Cross over from South to North, and you come to a land where the roads are generally much better, the houses and farms neater, the petrol and booze cheaper; in the South, the signposts are all in two languages (as in Wales), the letterboxes are green, the soldiers far less visible, the pubs more numerous and their crack more unrestrained. There are not many other outward differences. But dig deeper and you will meet the peculiar psychology of the border, or so I sensed as I criss-crossed along it from Co. Londonderry to Armagh – via smugglers' territory and the alleged 'ethnic cleansing' belt, across touristy lakeland Fermanagh with its blown-up bridges, past the domain of the amazing tycoon Sean Quinn, whose industrial and tourist empire bestrides the border, and so to notorious Crossmaglen, where the Army and IRA slog it out, each claiming to have 'sewn up' the other.

Smuggling has long been common along this border. In some places local people see it as a normal kind of activity, not disreputable, a way of getting even with the hated authorities. Much of the traffic, involving cattle, sheep and pigs, has been operated by local farmers either to take advantage of seasonal price fluctuations, or else, more daringly, to try to claim EC subsidies twice on the same animals, if they can be secretly moved across the border. (This kind of fraud is now in decline, owing to recent CAP changes.) Other smuggling has embraced petrol, diesel, alcoholic drinks, and electrical goods such as refrigerators, all of them made cheaper in the North by lower taxes and better distribution (see p. 66) or whenever the pound sterling has fallen in value against the punt. People from the South would load up the car in some Northern town, then drive back across minor roads where the customs posts were dozy or non-existent. Large-scale commercial smugglers of petrol and diesel have sometimes been caught and heavily fined, but the private small-scale freebooter has generally got away with it. Today, the EC single market has removed customs dues on goods such as drink, cars, electric durables; and VAT in the South has been brought down closer to UK levels. So in many sectors there is now much less incentive for smuggling. Petrol remains dearer in the South, but it is perfectly legal to go across to fill up your car, and the stations by the border do a brisk trade. By all accounts, the smuggling era is well past its prime. And one loser is the IRA, which is known to have drawn regular income from its role in this trafficking and attendant protection rackets.

According to British Army intelligence, the IRA throughout the Troubles has been trying to control this border as much as it can, for military, logistic, even political reasons. It brings in some arms and supplies from the South along these routes; its gunmen sometimes use the South as a bolt-hole; and there are some strips of border territory, notably in South Armagh, where it has even tried to gain a grip that would exclude the British. Hence the stories of what is nowadays called 'ethnic cleansing' – a campaign to drive Protestants out from these sensitive border areas. In a few cases, the IRA has picked off the single sons of older farmers; they then leave heartbroken, and no other Protestant will buy the farm, so it goes cheaply to Catholics. That at least is thought to have been IRA strategy, and sometimes it has worked. A number of Protestants have been intimidated into moving, and this has led to scares which the loyalist press in Belfast has exploited with stark articles below banner headlines, 'Ethnic Cleansing in Fermanagh'. 'It's a case of slow genocide, an attempt to roll back the border,' one Orange leader told me.

Today this is a clear exaggeration, according to all the local evidence. There were plenty of such killings in the 1970s and early 1980s, maybe 200 in Fermanagh alone, and many frightened Protestants left the border areas and have not returned. But today if people are murdered there by the IRA, it is generally because they are working for the RUC or the Army, and not through any systematic policy of 'cleansing'. Yet these murders, though less frequent, can still be horrific, especially since the introduction of the 'human bomb'. A farmer close to the border with Co. Monaghan told me in 1992: 'Last year the IRA took a Protestant suspected of working for the Army, smashed both his legs, made him drive his tractor with a fused bomb against an Army frontier checkpoint. The man was screaming. Someone heard him, managed to pull him off, and the bomb did not go off. The Army looked after the man for three months. Later, he saw one of the IRA men who had done the outrage, and shouted at me, "That's him!" But he was too terrified to give public evidence. So the Army could do nothing.'

The Army campaign against the IRA along the border causes various disruptions to civilian life. Local suspects may get their houses searched quite brutally, and under its 'Special Powers' the Army can do this without a warrant or prior notice – one woman came home to find an armed soldier sitting on her bed reading her letters. Not only are the concrete border checkpoints hideous and menacing (the Army says they are meant to be 'reassuring'), but the delays they cause can be tedious for motorists. You may have to wait in a queue at a red light, amid squaddies toting their machine-guns; and if a driver ahead is being searched and questioned, this can take several minutes. However, at many crossings the system has now been 'civilized', to the extent that suspect cars are shunted off to the side, to permit the main queue to go forward. And a notice proclaims, 'Sorry for any delay. Don't blame the security forces, blame the terrorists.' Even so, I have been left yet again with the feeling that the Army could do its necessary job more tactfully.

Local people have been angered even more by the Army's policy of blowing up road bridges or barricading the roads at many points along the border. Since the early 1970s, all seven roads linking Fermanagh to Leitrim have been thus blocked off: so people in the border villages of Garrison and Scribbagh have to make detours of over twenty miles, via Cavan or Donegal, to reach places in Leitrim a mere mile or two away. Here and to the east, around Clones, the inhabitants have often tried to reopen the roads themselves, but the Army has stopped them; they have sent petitions, but these fall on deaf ears in Belfast and Dublin, where 'this border area seems to be regarded as dangerous bandit country', I was told by a Leitrim farmer near Garrison, who added: 'The Army here lifted huge concrete blocks on to the roads with a helicopter. The villagers on both sides tried to remove them with drills and hammers, but it didn't work. So we are left isolated. Rossinver, just opposite Garrison, used to be such a lively place, but now it's dead.' At nearby Kiltyclogher, the road bridge over the river forming the border has been 'cratered', i.e. cut with a giant pothole, though a small footbridge has been allowed to stay. The Protestant church is on the South side, but most parishioners live across in the North. So for Sunday service the elderly ones without cars are driven to the footbridge, where the vicar's wife does a shuttle for them in her car. And at the hamlet of Aghalane, Co. Cavan, a handsome old bridge over the Woodford river, on what used to be the Dublin–Enniskillen main road, has been blown up; there's not even a footbridge. In this otherwise idyllic setting, neighbours in their charming thatched cottages look wistfully at each other, fifty metres apart: but they must drive many miles to meet. The scene gave me an uncanny sense of *déjà vu* – where had I seen just that? Answer, before November 1989, by the little river Werra dividing villages in Thuringia and Hessen, where my German wife and I have friends. At least, *that* far more terrible fortified border is no more.

Undeterred by these obstacles, a number of organizations in Fermanagh, and in Leitrim and Cavan in the South, are today eagerly engaged in cross-border development projects, economic and social. Fermanagh with its lakes and hills is not only a very scenic county, but also today most lively and active, with a good team of local officials. In the capital, Enniskillen, I met a group of mostly Catholic women who were leading the community effort (as in Derry and elsewhere, the impetus comes from the Catholics, while the Protestants are more reticent). I asked the reasons for their dynamism – 'It's women you're dealing with, John!' said one. They told me of the current efforts to develop this border area, with its small, struggling farms and lack of industry on top of its other problems; at Garrison, where the road ends in a crater, an old hotel bombed by the IRA is being rebuilt and a new cultural, social and commercial centre is under way. For these and other ventures, Fermanagh has secured a lavish array of international funding; the IFI alone has been backing 155 (*sic*) different projects, while the EU joins in via its Leader programme (see p. 116) and via Interreg, a fund that helps inter-regional border schemes from south Denmark to north Portugal. The proactive ladies of Enniskillen bombarded me with their acronyms and initials, the true jargon of the technocrat: 'Thanks to the IFI, DoE and ERDF, with help from INTERREG, this area has been earmarked an AONB, with AWTFs. CRISP, ACE, DENI and DANI help provide jobs for this ESA, while the SDLP and UUP are both helping.' In case you don't know, an AONB is an Area of Outstanding Natural Beauty.

Various community associations bring people together from North and South, for social and sporting events, child care, help for the aged, local-history studies, and much else. And there are joint economic projects, too. Most of the initiative, and the money, comes from better-funded Fermanagh; in the South, local people are also interested, but they get relatively little support from Dublin, and Leitrim and Cavan are anyway two of the poorest and most depopulated of Irish counties. One Fermanagh community worker put it bluntly: 'The Dublin Government uses its EU funding too much for local private business ventures, not community ones – it's the fault of the bad "clientelist" political system. Dublin may talk about rural development, but in practice it does little for a very deprived, isolated area like west Cavan; all the aid is going to Mayo and Galway. In the North, there is far more public funding and it's better spent. And the community spirit here is more dynamic'.

However, for one much-talked-about cross-border project the initiative has come mainly from Dublin. This is the reopening, for tourist purposes, of the old Ballimore & Ballyconnell Canal, which runs from south Fermanagh to the upper Shannon. It was first built back in 1860 to link the Erne and Shannon rivers for commercial shipping; then, ironically, the coming of the railways killed off most Irish waterway traffic and the 62-km canal was closed in 1869 after an absurdly short working life. During the next 120 years it quietly decayed, until in the 1980s the Irish Government drew up plans for its renovation (Haughey as Taoiseach promoted the idea), and work began in 1990. Funded largely by the EU and IFI, the project is being managed by the Irish State-owned electricity board; as almost all of the canal's length, and all but one of its sixteen locks, are in the South, the North is playing a minor role. At Ballyconnell, by the border in Co. Cavan, I found one lock being gracefully rebuilt in local stone: the aim is to preserve the canal's nineteenth-century picturesque character while adding modern gadgetry. 'All will be automatic,' said the electricity-board engineer in charge; 'No more wee man on site to operate the locks, you just press a button and slip in a smart card.' The canal plus the two rivers, 800 km in all, 'will form the longest inland waterway in Europe', I was confidently assured by various local people, whose Irish love of hyperbole overlooked the fact that the Danube is 2,850 km, the Rhine 1,320, the Loire 1,012.

The canal, reopened in May 1994, is expected to boost tourism in North and South. The many yacht-lovers who already take hired cabin cruisers along the Shannon, and others who do the same on Fermanagh's Lough Erne, will now be able to use the entire waterway, if they wish. Either side of Enniskillen the river Erne widens to form this beautiful lake, 70 km long and much liked by yachting tourists. Of those who hire its cruisers, a remarkable 60 per cent are German, 20 per cent Swiss, with a few British, Dutch, etc. Some boat marinas are virtual German enclaves. The Germans come looking for a slow, unregimented lifestyle they do not so readily find at home. But one boat-owner suggested another factor, too: 'People in Britain and Ireland, indeed in Belgium and Holland where BBC and ITV programmes are relayed, see the endless reports of violence in the North and so get a one-sided picture. The Germans don't get British TV and their own media cover these things very little. So they are not put off.'

Extra tourism is much needed in Fermanagh, where the violence has made it no easier to attract new investment, and the small farms are being hit by CAP reform, as in the South. So here too the farmers are being encouraged to diversify into 'agri-tourism' (see p. 115), by opening guest-houses or offering holidays on their land. And Fermanagh does have a tourist potential, not only for yachting, but for riding, golf, fishing, or hiking over the lovely hills – so long as the IRA keeps a low-enough profile. The notorious Enniskillen bomb blast of 1987, which killed eleven people at a memorial service, gave this graceful old town a black image from which it is only now emerging. Security measures are still tight; but the urban renewal is impressive, as in Derry. I especially liked the Buttermarket, a handsome old dairy, built in 1835 and then closed in 1940. It became derelict and was due to be demolished, but then the district council decided to restore it as a resource centre. Today around its neatly paved courtyard are sixteen craft workshops, all active, and a hi-tech centre with superfast faxes, EU-financed of course; craft festivals, with Irish dancing, are held in summer. Fermanagh, 55 per cent Catholic, had high emigration and a falling population until recently. But now, as in the South, the recession in England has been pulling people back to where they can at least spend their dole money in their own country among their own families. Hence the population has risen again, despite high local unemployment.

The one major recent job-creating investment in these parts has been the work of a local millionaire, Seán Quinn, a Citizen Kane figure with a giant success story. He began in the 1970s as a poor young man with a tiny 23-acre family farm, just inside Fermanagh by the border at Derrylin. He found gravel on his land and began to sell it for concrete, then to make concrete blocks himself. Finding a flair for business, he expanded fast, built factories for concrete, cement and roof tiles, all beside his old farm. Today he has an annual turnover of £45 million and eighty-five green lorries – plus a large new luxury hotel just across the border.

His factory complex stands alone by the border – a belching monstrosity below the grey gash of his limestone quarry on the hillside. There in his opulently furnished office I called on the man whom the Dublin writer Colm Tóibín had dubbed 'the great Thatcherite', gruff, dark and handsome, a former Gaelic football star. Like many a self-made tycoon, his reputation is that of a tough thruster, driving himself and others hard. I found him less awesome than I'd expected, despite his disconcerting start, 'Talking to John Ardagh is not the part of my business that I like most,' followed by some gratuitously unkind remarks about a manager he was about to sack.

Like Paddy Doherty in Derry, if in a different style, Quinn is a paragon of the North's new breed of Catholic entrepreneur. He is a nationalist who refuses to supply the Army with concrete ('One has to be prudent'); and the IRA seem to leave him alone, though there are rumours of protection money. Only some 10 per cent of his 320 staff are Protestant ('There aren't so many left, around here'). He commutes daily through the checkpoints from his home in Co. Cavan; once, when a soldier officiously stopped and searched him, Quinn knocked him flat – and got away with it. His next project is to build a wind-farm on the mountain at the border, with forty high towers providing energy for the Northern grid. 'It will be itself a tourist attraction,' he says, in retort to those now murmuring 'eyesore'.

I then drove over the border into Cavan, where on a rolling plateau near Ballyconnell I came upon Quinn's second marvel: the luxurious 144-bedroom Slieve Russell Hotel, opened in 1991. In Florida, a hotel of this size and style would go unremarked; for remotest rural Cavan, it is apocalyptic, and has become *the* social centre for the whole county and beyond. Quinn's gamble began when someone asked, 'How can we develop tourism in Cavan when it has virtually no hotels?' 'Right, I'll build one – a big one,' he replied. 'I needed to make a splash,' he explained to me, 'to make people curious as to why anyone should be so stupid as to build such a monster out in these wilds.' It has indeed been the talk of Ireland.

With a floodlit fountain in front and the Euro-flag flying, it blazes out into the night – a brash, ungainly building looking like some 1950s institution. 'We hired an architect, then sacked him and more or less built it ourselves,' says Quinn. It shows. The vast foyer is a riot of Roman pillars, made of concrete smoothed to look like marble. Nearly all the hotel is Quinn concrete – 'At least it won't burn down easily.' It may not be lovely, but it's impressive, with good food and amenities. My bedroom had three phones, two TVs, an outsize four-poster and a jacuzzi. The hotel's large, glamorous swimming-pool is the only one in the county. What's more, the public toilets have won top prize for Irish Super Loo of the Year; they are checked and cleaned hourly, on the dot ('I do not tolerate sloppiness').

The Slieve Russell has been a big success, locally and nationally. It may seem remote, but in fact is little over two hours' drive from either Belfast or Dublin. Haughey chose it for his official farewell lunch as Taoiseach, for 200 people; Mary Robinson has been to stay. Some 30 per cent of guests are from the North, which has no hotel anything like it; and foreign tourists are coming too, drawn by the excellent eighteen-hole golf course. The disco holding 1,000 is often packed; and many evening events are booked out months ahead. At one dinner-dance, I sat among the Cavan worthies, local farmers, shopkeepers, builders and their wives, all of them revelling in this opulent novelty that had descended magically in their midst. Writing in the *Independent on Sunday*, Colm Tóibín contrasted the Slieve Russell with nearby Hilton Park, the stately 'big house' of the Anglo-Irish Madden family, who now run it as a country hotel: 'After centuries of poverty, misery and revolt, this is rural Catholic Ireland declaring its right to build big houses too ... New money rises up in all its vulgarity just as the old world of landlords and privilege opens its doors to the outside world. Two Irelands within a few miles of each other.'

Close to Quinn's factory stands a famous curiosity: an old farm cottage that is actually dissected by the border. Its owners, now departed, could sleep in either State; their water supply was connected in the North, their electricity in the South. Here, driving up a side-track for a scenic view, I had an odd encounter: an Irish Army patrol was supervising the transfer of a load of explosives from a Co. Kildare lorry into a smaller van from the North. Was this the unearthing of some IRA cache? No. It was a routine shipment of dynamite for Quinn's quarry.

I drove east as far as South Armagh, a traditionally nationalist region which for some years has been the North's worst trouble-spot outside West and North Belfast. The IRA is strong. In reply, along the border with Louth and Monaghan the British Army has built an especially assertive series of fortresses and observation posts. Local resentment runs high.

The most notorious spot is Crossmaglen, a drab little border townlet that for years has encapsulated the bitterness of the Army/IRA struggle, and of hatreds and violence going far back into history. Rightly or wrongly, this area has always been seen as 'bandit country'; in the mid nineteenth century it had a dozen murders a year, mostly sectarian, and an old ditty runs, 'Between Carrickmacross and Crossmaglen / There are more rogues than honest men' (the accent is on the 'glen'). Banditry has become compounded with nationalism, in this former fiefdom of the O'Neills, long a breeding-ground of insurgents. And today Crossmaglen still sees itself as different from the rest of Northern Ireland: the local accent and temperament are closer to those of Monaghan, and the true local capital is not Newry in Armagh but Dundalk across in Louth. Before the Troubles came, all the links were there; and even today people will rather go shopping in Dundalk, even if goods are dearer.

This is the history of a town whose population is solidly nationalist, united in hatred of the British 'occupying' forces whose helicopters roar overhead and whose control posts crown the hills, like the local ancient ring-forts. Killings used to be daily affairs; today they are fewer, but 'Cross', as the locals call it, still wears a somewhat shell-shocked air. I found it a sad, run-down little place, with little of the usual spruceness of Northern towns. In the main square, where a score or so British soldiers have died, stands an IRA memorial 'to all those modest heroes who have suffered because of their passionate love for IRISH FREEDOM' (the Army does not try to remove it). I found all the public telephones broken; there were no restaurants, just two sleazy take-aways and some gloomy pubs, where I knew my voice would betray me. 'Fucking Brit,' a man mumbled into his Guinness. Somehow, normal life ticks over. I called on the Catholic priest, a mild little man who said that people had become hardened to the violence; he proudly showed me a video of one of the amateur operatic shows he had staged with out-of-work teenagers – 'We have to do something to keep up their morale.' Local people spoke to me affectionately of 'Cross', their home, as of some slightly handicapped child. They said they felt its grim image was unfair.

I went to see a local Sinn Féin councillor, Jim McAllister, a friendly, sympathetic, plausible man whose wife had just died of cancer. 'The Army claims it has South Armagh sewn up and the IRA cannot move. In fact it's the opposite: the IRA moves as it wants, while the Army and RUC cower inside their bases and have to be supplied by helicopter.' The Army can of course move freely when it chooses, but it's true that it does keep quite a low profile inside the town, for its own safety (just before my visit, another squaddie had been shot dead in the square). The British and the IRA wage a war of nerves. Right on the square is a grim fortified RUC lookout post, which gets bombed regularly; and behind it is the bunker-like RUC barracks with the Union Jack flying. Here in the 1970s the Army seized part of the town's Gaelic football field for a helicopter pad; it has since paid compensation, but still refuses to move out. This hardly wins over the population, nor do the house searches and bullyings of suspects. Once again, Army behaviour simply fuels sympathy for the IRA.

'The Army say they are here to keep the peace. But it's *they* who are breaking it. This place would be very peaceful without them: we get on fine with the few local Protestants,' said McAllister, faithful to the Sinn Féin line. He then spoke of older grievances: 'Why do you think this area is so poor? After partition, the British and the Unionists tried to keep it down. They would not bring in investment, or give grants to farms, because they wanted to force us to emigrate. They did not want prosperous Catholic communities in these border areas.' This is a widely shared local view, and as in Derry it has some element of truth. Today unemployment remains very high. But along all the border, and even here, London and Brussels are now deploying their armoury of grants. 'There are so many different EU funding schemes that we hardly know how to cope with them,' said the hopeful director of the town's new enterprise centre.

Crossmaglen is even beginning to think of tourism. One farmer has turned part of his land into a golf-course, now doing quite well, with 200 members. The boldest entrepreneur is Tony Hearty, a local man and former British Airports catering manager, who has a tiny jeweller's shop in town. Nearby he has converted a group of pretty eighteenth-century cottages into a 'Folk Craft Village' where on Sundays he holds jewellery and pottery sales and runs a tearoom with live Irish music. For all this he has won a tourist award in Belfast. He told me that he was now planning a much larger operation, a folk park with a barn theatre offering Irish banquets and musical shows – a sort of Bunratty. 'We have already been offered £90,000 by the IFI, nearly half of what we need. The American tour operators are showing interest; their customers are growing bored with Bunratty, etc., and would like something more novel and daring.' Such as the Army fortress very visible on the hill a mile away? 'No problem. Our reputation is most unfair. Here we have a sense of hospitality that is second to none. And lots of visitors prefer the North to the South. After all, we have to try harder.'

Job equality and power-sharing: an uphill battle against segregation

Crossmaglen may not be typical of the many local communities around the province where the real battle for hearts and minds is being fought. Here there are two contrasting trends – one towards greater segregation, the other towards more tolerance and contact – and it is hard to tell which is winning. Some people declare confidently, 'The middle ground is growing stronger,' others that 'the dynamic of the conflict is towards polarization'. This section will look at government efforts to end anti-Catholic discrimination in employment and to promote power-sharing on local councils. The next section will then look at the cross-community ventures of little groups and individuals who are trying to narrow the gulf; and at the equivocal role of the Churches, split between ecumenicism and Paisleyism.

It is in the field of public housing that direct rule has probably had the most success in redressing the injustices of the old Stormont regime. The old local councils, Unionist-led, used to allocate almost all housing to Protestants, and large Catholic families might have to stay for years on waiting-lists. After 1972 the Government took over this responsibility itself and has seen that the Catholics get their fair share. It has also poured money into slum clearance and rehousing programmes, which have borne good results in many towns, notably West Belfast. Even keen nationalists will today admit that Catholics are as well housed as Protestants on the public estates.

In the equally important field of job discrimination, the Government's efforts have been less radical, and progress has been slower. This is a complex problem, involving a mass of private firms as well as the public sector, and there has been a serious legacy of injustice to be cleared up, from the previous regime. Most big employers were Protestant, and they tended to hire Protestants, so Catholic unemployment was high. In a civil service loyal to a Unionist Government, Catholics were severely under-represented, especially in senior posts. But in a few cases this was their own doing, for some nationalists with good qualifications preferred not to work for a regime they hated politically, so they refused to accept jobs even when offered them. The few who went to work at Stormont Castle were disparagingly known as 'Castle Catholics' – collaborators!

An end to job discrimination was one of the major demands of the civil-rights marchers of the late 1960s. But only in 1976 did the Government set up its Fair Employment Agency, with the task of persuading employers to correct their biases; and only since 1990 has this agency been given adequate powers. Twenty years ago, the unemployment rate was 2·5 times higher among Catholics than Protestants; that figure is now down to 2·2, but this is no dramatic progress. In 1993, of the North's total of 14·2 per cent out of work, the Protestant figure was only 8 per cent, the Catholic 17·6 per cent. It is a pattern that varies from sector to sector. In Northern Ireland's largest industrial firm, Short Brothers, the aircraft makers, the percentage of Catholics in the workforce has been increased from 5 to 13 per cent since 1980. In the North's huge public sector, 35 per cent of all employees are now Catholic, which is little lower than their share of the adult population. But in the upper grades they still do less well. A 1990 survey of 9,200 senior jobs in eighty-seven public bodies found that 25 per cent were held by Catholics; in the main civil service, Catholics in senior grades have risen from 5 per cent to 17 per cent in the past twenty years. Nationalists complain that the Government could have done more to improve matters within its own civil-service ranks. Officials retort that all promotion has to be on merit, since 'reverse discrimination' (the appointment of 'token' Catholics for top jobs) is illegal: there are not enough highly qualified Catholics, and it takes time for good new middle-rank appointees to move into the upper ranks.

The same problems, plus others too, are to be found in the private sector. Catholic education has always put the stress on the arts and humanities, and on subjects such as law, rather than on science or mechanics. So there are many good lawyers, clerical workers and accountants, but fewer engineers or technicians. Some analysts have suggested that this relates to the Catholic ethos, more spiritual than practical. Whether this is so or not, firms have frequently pointed to a lack of qualified Catholic candidates for their technical jobs. But a more important cause of Catholic under-employment was that in the old days many big firms were deliberately located near to Protestant housing areas, such as East Belfast. Thirdly, the recession of recent years, causing a lack of new recruitment, has made it genuinely harder for employers to correct the balance in their workforce.

All this is true of Short Brothers, one of the world's oldest aircraft manufacturers, which in the 1930s moved from England to a site near the harbour in loyalist East Belfast. Its saga is interesting. Not only was the staff overwhelmingly Protestant, but in July there used to be Orange marches in the factory, with flags and banners, and in 1986 some Catholic workers were attacked. When the management then tried to ban the marches, it was met with a strike; but finally it got its way and today there are no more Orange emblems. Nationalized under Labour, Short's was privatized in 1989 and now belongs to the Quebec transport group, Bombardier (a Catholic family). The Fair Employment Agency has long tried to persuade Short's to employ more Catholics, and with modest success; under government pressure, the firm recently opened a second plant in south-west Belfast, near to the Catholic areas, and a recruitment office on 'neutral' ground in the city centre. In 1991 it created the post of Equal Opportunities Manager and gave it to a Catholic, Rory Galway. 'We have tried to change our recruitment practices,' he told me. 'Foremen used to say to their men, "We've twenty vacancies, tell your pals," but today it's done more fairly. Even so, it takes time to break down the old Catholic myth, "Short's is not for us, we never get promotion there," which deterred them even from applying. Today we are starting to get a good flow of Catholic applicants, and they are *not* worse at mechanics than the rest. From a low base of 5 per cent, we have pushed the Catholic workforce up to 13 per cent, but it's not easy to go fast in a time of redundancies – since 1991 we have shed 1,200 of our 9,000 staff. Of our thirteen senior posts filled locally, five are now held by Catholics – enough to satisfy the MacBride lobby.'

Short's sells to several US airlines and is a Boeing subcontractor, while Bombardier has been tendering for a big subway contract in New York. So the group is highly sensitive to US pressures against discrimination, centring on the 'MacBride principles'. The veteran republican and human-rights activist Seán MacBride, a 1930s IRA leader, former Irish foreign minister and Nobel Peace Prize winner, drew up a series of guidelines that he thought US investors in Northern Ireland should be obliged to observe; and this was taken up by several States, including New York, which passed laws forbidding their own State pension funds to invest in companies judged to be discriminating against Catholics in Northern Ireland. Individual firms, too, such as Ford, were directly lobbied by their pro-MacBride shareholders. This campaign continues today, and has even been making progress. It is well-intentioned, but naïve, and possibly dangerous. First, it has been exploited politically by the pro-IRA Noraid lobby (see p. 318), which has jumped on its bandwagon. Secondly, it could deter investors and thus be counter-productive. The British and US Governments, also John Hume, are opposed to the MacBride campaign and have been stressing its dangers. The British assert that their own fair employment legislation, now strengthened, renders the MacBride principles superfluous.

The Fair Employment Agency, set up in 1976, was a weak body, backed by ineffectual laws, as officials now readily admit. To speed up progress, the Government in 1989 brought in a stronger law, giving more power to the agency, today renamed the Fair Employment Commission. It now has the task of monitoring all firms with a staff of more than ten; they must submit annual reports on the presumed religious composition of their staff, and they face nominal fines if they refuse to do so. Some forty firms, mostly very small ones, have been fined so far – 'I find this monitoring most impertinent and distasteful,' said one Protestant director of a small company. But the commission still cannot force firms to employ any given number of Catholics. All it can do is urge them to take on more, indicate what it considers a fair percentage in their case (depending on location, etc.), and threaten the withholding of Government grants or public contracts if they fail to cooperate.

Another weapon of the new law is that tribunals have been set up to which individuals can appeal against discrimination. Several cases have been heard. A highly qualified Catholic nurse was awarded £30,000 by the Health Board, after she had complained to a tribunal about failure to short-list her for a senior post. And a public dispute has flared up recently about Queen's University, that former Protestant bastion (see p. 428). An FEA report in 1989 showed that only 21 per cent of its staff were Catholic, and in the clerical and administrative ranks the figure was 11 per cent. The overall percentage has since risen to 28 per cent. But in 1992 two Catholics claimed they had been discriminated against for jobs in the bursar's office, where *no* Catholic had ever been employed. The university settled out of court for £40,000 compensation, but refused to admit responsibility. This was one of the many cases where employers deny any deliberate discrimination, but blame their recruitment procedures. 'We don't want our scholarship to be upset by all this tedious ethnic bargaining,' said one professor at Queen's; 'the vice-chancellor is a decent Scot who finds the whole thing double-Dutch. He's besieged by pressures from nationalist papers with their endless stories, "Queen's isn't doing enough," and it wastes his time.'

Not all the discrimination is against Catholics, for they themselves are among the employers. In the building and catering trades, many little firms have long been Catholic-owned, and today a new breed of nationalist entrepreneur has been emerging in other fields too – witness Seán Quinn. Some have certainly been failing to comply with the new guidelines. Paddy Doherty, for example, has been accused of having a staff only 10 per cent Protestant on his Inner City Trust in Derry.

Wherever the blame lies, job segregation in the North is still considerable: a recent survey of 1,800 firms found that 267 of them had a workforce made up at least 95 per cent of one religion or the other. Many Catholics feel impatient that their unemployment level remains so much higher than the Protestants', and that their move into senior positions has not been faster. They argue that the Government could have done more, at least in its own public sector. And even the new stronger law still operates more by persuasion than by obligation. But probably this is necessary; to create quotas or other 'reverse discrimination' would be wrong. As it is, progress has been slow but steady, as Short's and other examples indicate, and this is likely to continue. Moreover, in the majority of firms, the fair employment issue is not one that clouds daily working relations. 'I just don't know the religion of most of my colleagues, it's something we hang up with our coats at the door on arrival,' said a technician in one modern hi-tech firm.

The Government has also been trying to build greater cross-community trust in local civic affairs – by encouraging power-sharing on the twenty-six district councils. This has borne fruit with many of them, even if it cannot add up to much when there is so little power to share; under the direct-rule system, a council is responsible for sport, culture, burials, garbage collection, tourist promotion and community relations, but little else, whereas key matters such as housing, education and town planning, locally run in Britain, are here run by the Government. Even car parks (or rather, *especially* car parks, easy terrorist targets) are in the hands of the Department of the Environment. The Government does have a duty to consult a council on roads and planning, but it keeps the last word. 'We're just a frustrated talk-shop, with no more power than a parish council,' said one DUP councillor in Belfast. But some others I met felt that even a limited talk-shop role might sometimes have political influence.

Within these strict parameters, the Government sees local power-sharing as a kind of testing-ground for a future Northern

Ireland political structure based on partnership: if it can be seen to work at this simple level, might it not also at a higher level? The SDLP broadly agrees with this approach, but the Unionists have inevitably been more cautious; and power-sharing has been tried out only by councils where the SDLP is strong. Generally, the system involves a rotation of mayors, as in Derry, or a kind of coalition, as in Dungannon. This is feasible, seeing that each main party on a council has a number of seats roughly equal to its voting strength: proportional representation, that taboo of domestic British politics, is accepted for local elections in Northern Ireland, so as to ensure that minority groups there do get a fair deal. Alike for Conservative and Labour Governments, this has marked quite a volte-face.

The Derry initiative, described earlier, is not the best example, for the SDLP there has an absolute majority and has no need to share; it simply allows others to hold the mayoralty, sometimes, and keeps the real power itself (such as it is). It is largely a symbolic gesture, though useful. More significant is the case of Dungannon district council, Co. Tyrone, in an area with a long background of sectarian hostility and a population roughly fifty-fifty. Until 1987 the council had a narrow Unionist majority, but the elections that year threw up a stalemate: 8 UUP, 3 DUP, 5 SDLP, 4 Sinn Féin, 2 independent nationalists, i.e. 11/11. Under the impulse of two moderate local leaders, Ken Maginnis, MP (UUP), and Vincent Currie (SDLP), it was agreed to try power-sharing. So the chairmanship and vice-chairmanship of the council (more important than the mayoralty) have since been held turn-by-turn every six months by the UUP, SDLP and independents: Sinn Féin has been excluded because of its 'failure to renounce violence', and the DUP has excluded itself from what it calls 'this mickey-mouse arrangement'.

In Dungannon's handsome new council offices, I discussed all this with Currie and the then chairman, Jim Hamilton of the UUP. The forceful and persuasive Currie did most of the talking (his brother Austin is a Fine Gael TD for Dublin): 'SDLP and UUP tend to agree on most local issues, though of course we disagree about the political future of the North and the Anglo/

Irish Agreement. Debate is sharp, but we have proved that we *can* cooperate on practical matters, and our gamble with power-sharing has paid off. We have managed to neutralize both the DUP and Sinn Féin. And the Government has rewarded us with some generous special funding, for a new hospital, leisure centre, etc., to the envy of some other councils which have failed to try out power-sharing. Our success is bound to influence Northern Ireland as a whole.' However, soon after we met, in the May 1993 local elections Sinn Féin won a seat from the SDLP, and Maginnis lost his own seat to a fellow UUP man. So power-sharing suffered a slight blow: but it still continues, for the basic 11/11 divide remains the same.

The good news from the 1993 local elections is that the number of councils involved in power-sharing has now gone up from eleven to fifteen out of the twenty-six. This has been due to SDLP progress, and to a greater readiness by some moderate UUP-led councils to try the scheme. But in their major eastern strongholds, the Unionists still do not share their power. In Belfast itself, the UUP, DUP and their allies have always held an absolute majority of seats, and have exploited this high-handedly, collaborating very little with the moderate Alliance Party and SDLP. Tensions on the council can run high, especially as Sinn Féin is so strong in Belfast. But as the city's Catholic population increases, so the Unionist majority has been declining, and after the May 1993 elections it stood at only three seats (UUP 15, DUP 9, other Unionist 3; Alliance 5; SDLP 9, Sinn Féin 10). Before long, the Unionists may be obliged to share some power even in Belfast.

Ventures such as Dungannon's will not solve the North's wider problems, but they certainly are valuable in areas like this where tribal animosities have deep roots. Around Dungannon, some Catholics still regard Protestants as holding land which the early plantation settlers 'robbed' from their ancestors four centuries ago. Nor have they forgotten the Unionist abuses of power in the years before direct rule. The Unionist-led county council was especially unjust over public housing, so it was no coincidence that the North's first civil-rights march took place here, in 1968. Since then, the Catholics have been moving on to the offensive, buying up a number of businesses, stores and big houses in a town where the wealth used to be almost entirely Protestant. Even so, one elderly liberal-minded Catholic I met gave me a sombre view of the local social scene today: 'In the 1950s, unfair though things were, there was much more social mixing than now between Catholics and Protestants. On the public housing estates, the segregation is now almost total. Some middle-class areas like ours are still mixed; but though we are on easy terms with our Protestant neighbours, there's an unseen barrier, it's not friendship, we do not visit each others' houses. At the golf club, it *is* very mixed; they even rotate the presidency, as in the council. But among the working-class young, it's still cowboys and Indians. Rival gangs emerge from the discos and throw stones and bottles at each other. Some discos and pubs are mixed, others segregated; and you know exactly which you must not enter. Yes, it could be worse – at least the killings are now fewer. But there seems no solution, just an accommodation. One has to accept it, but I hate it.'

It was never true that the two communities in the North were always at each other's throats, in the old days. There were political divisions, and tribal enmities, but individually most neighbours got on adequately. They would go to the same dances; there were even mixed marriages. In country areas, farmers would help each other, as often they still do. But the impact of the Troubles, with the rise of the paramilitaries, has now served to increase physical segregation, especially in the towns; people feel more secure if they are living amongst their own kind. A 1993 survey of district-council wards in the North showed that about half of the population today live in areas either more than 90 per cent Protestant or more than 90 per cent Catholic; since 1973, the number of these almost exclusively Protestant wards has risen from 56 to 115, and of Catholic ones from 43 to 120. In Belfast, 35 of its 51 wards are in these categories; here the districts near Stormont and the RUC headquarters, in East Belfast, are almost solidly Protestant, and of course this makes it harder to recruit more Catholics into the public services. Yet in many of the smaller towns of Down or

Antrim there is plenty of easy intermingling. So the pattern is extremely diverse, making it hard to generalize. In some places, the two communities mix socially hardly at all; in others, where the housing is more mixed, there is more interchange. But in conversation people usually take care to avoid the delicate topics of religion, politics and the Troubles – 'They'd far rather talk to me about golf and bridge, so boring,' a Catholic intellectual in Bangor said of his mainly Protestant neighbours.

It is surprising, in this situation, that the number of mixed marriages is fairly high and has even been increasing. There are few reliable statistics, but it is believed that some 11 per cent of all marriages in the North are cross-community. The figure varies from place to place – over 20 per cent in the middle-class areas south and east of Belfast or on the Antrim coast, but as little as 4 or 5 per cent in working-class districts, where the segregation is greater and paramilitary pressures are stronger. Occasionally in West Belfast a Catholic/Protestant couple will have their home fire-bombed, and in one case in 1991 a woman was murdered by loyalists for marrying a 'Taig'. But these incidents are rare. In the quieter areas, young Catholics and Protestants meet at their work, or in pubs or dancehalls, or in student circles; they fall in love, and are prepared to defy the old sectarian feudings, which they find ridiculous.

Until not long ago, most parents used to be horrified by such marriages and would often boycott the wedding. I met a Catholic woman in her fifties who had clandestinely married a work colleague, a Presbyterian, and she never met his father until twenty years later. But today, save in hard-line Paisleyite circles, religious intolerance of mixed marriages has greatly declined, and the Catholic Church notably is now taking a gentler line, as in other countries. The problem today is much less one of religious dogmatism than social sectarianism: it is this that makes young couples feel the need to be cautious. After the wedding, most of them tend to leave their home areas and move to new ground where they are not known. A great many go to live abroad, usually in Britain. Even so, the fact that many young middle-class couples do fall in love and marry across the divide shows how great is the potential for reconciliation in the North. More people in the working classes would do the same if they had more opportunities to meet. Once again, fear, not hatred, is the enemy.

The cross-community crusade faces loyalist reticence

All kinds of little 'cross-community' or 'reconciliation' groups are today busy all over the North, working to bring the two sides closer. The ghettoization makes their work harder, but it also provides a challenge; and they have been growing in numbers and activity. For example, they take mixed teenage groups from the Belfast slums on holidays abroad; or they stage joint peace rallies, or hold mixed sporting or cultural events, or run women's associations or job-creation centres. The Churches play some part, ecumenically: but most of the impulse has come from lay people, or from individual churchmen such as Father Myles Kavanagh in Belfast. Their work of course reaches only a small part of the population, and its impact is limited. It cannot take the place of a political settlement, though it might help to pave the way for one. And although it is warmly encouraged by the Government, even funded in some cases, it is not formally imposed from above but is a spontaneous, grass-roots trend.

The most-publicized venture has been the Peace Movement, founded in 1976 by a group of Belfast women in reaction to the killing of three children by a runaway IRA vehicle. The movement aroused much attention worldwide, but it was over-exploited by the media and mishandled by its own organizers, while some nationalists came to feel that it was being used by the British to promote their own policies. Today the movement still exists, but on the sidelines. The newer ventures tend to be more local, and they try to avoid too much media publicity, which they feel might provoke reprisals by the paramilitaries.

Whereas the Peace Movement is a kind of political lobby, the well-established Corrymeela Community on the Antrim coast is a reconciliation centre aimed at individuals and social groups. It was founded in 1965 by Ray Davey, a Presbyterian priest, who was soon joined by some Catholic priests. It is non-denominational, and the Churches officially play no direct part in what essentially is a large residential centre holding meetings and courses of all kinds, to spread the word of reconciliation. It stands high on the lovely Antrim cliffs by the sea near Ballycastle, a spacious modern group of white buildings, looking somewhat Scandinavian; the ambience is breezy and relaxed, with lots of young people about. At the time of my visit, there was a weekend meeting of couples in mixed marriages, and another of families of IRA and loyalist prisoners. One building offers temporary shelter to people under severe intimidation by terrorists. And mixed youth groups of all kinds are prominent among the 8,000 annual visitors. I was shown round by a member of staff, an enthusiastic young lay Catholic from Derry. 'When we hold a course for a youth group', he said, 'our first aim is to break down their inbred prejudices, get them to accept each other as human beings, see what they have in common. Some kids from poorer homes arrive with tragic prejudices; Protestants for example suppose that *all* Catholics are IRA killers with masks, or vice versa. But if we do our job properly, they leave with tears of friendship, exchanging addresses and vowing to keep in touch.' Whether they can do so, back in their home milieu, is often another matter. Corrymeela's influence is of course limited, and it has never managed to achieve the wider impact that it hoped. Some people dismiss it as 'too nicey-nicey'. But I was rather impressed, and within its limits it does good work. Funded mainly by private donations, also by Stormont, it is run as a kind of club, with members sharing the same vision and commitment: 'Corrymeela begins when you leave, it is to set you thinking' is its slogan. And it has many overseas links, for its ideal of reconciliation extends worldwide.

A cross-community venture of a different kind I found just six miles away: on some muddy playing fields outside Ballycastle, teams from Co. Antrim and Co. Galway were engaged in a mixed tournament of soccer, rugby *and* hurling – amazing! The local Moy District Council, which covers this part of Antrim, has a

Unionist majority, but a liberal one. And despite local DUP protests it had backed the local community-relations committee, under a Catholic chairman, to organize this sporting event with Ballynasloe, its little twin-town near Galway. Soccer is played by everyone, so it poses no problems: but rugby is a mainly Protestant game in the North, while hurling is so nationalist that most loyalists will come nowhere near it. Even in Ballinasloe, the local GAA was at first hostile to the venture. And in Antrim it was hard to persuade the football team of Bushmills, a loyalist fief, to play in the same event as Catholic hurlers. Finally however all agreed, and the three sets of matches took place together – marred only by a last-minute cancellation of the girls' basketball event, after the IRA's murder of three Protestants in the area two days earlier (such is local life). Anyway, in the driving rain a big group of us all watched the games, then moved to the clubhouse for beer, soup and sandwiches. All seemed friendly. Chris Craig, the chairman of the Moy community-relations committee, told me: 'We get along fine in this area, so long as we keep off politics and religion.' And a sturdy Protestant lady from the Bushmills whiskey distillery added, 'You can't solve the world's problems with a game of hurling, but you've got to start somewhere, haven't you?'

In the poorer ghettos of North and West Belfast, the problems of reconciliation are more intractable, but a number of pioneers are at work on them. Their most eye-catching project has been to take mixed groups of deprived thirteen-to-seventeen-year-olds on holidays to Holland, on the assumption that if these youngsters can be pulled right out of their own awful environment, and given a lovely time among friendly hosts, then they can get on together, Prod and Taig, as they could never do back home, and this unique experience might have some lasting impact on their lives. To an extent, this does happen. The scheme has been going on since the mid-1970s, and is today part-funded by the EU, and supported and organized by Dutch welfare groups. In 1993, nine groups of about twenty-four each went to Holland, and one to Sweden. Father Myles Kavanagh's staff (see p. 376) are among those involved in the scheme, and he told me: 'We try to target the tough, antisocial kids who could become the paramilitary leaders of tomorrow. Here, they either fight, or just don't meet. On neutral ground, they quickly form friendships.' The trips abroad have even led to some mixed marriages. But it does not always work out so well.

One of Kavanagh's associates is Seán Nellis, a Catholic ex-teacher living in North Belfast, near the infamous 'peace line' of Duncairn Gardens where sectarian killings have been rife. On one side of the road, the New Lodge area (Catholic); on the other, the Tiger Bay area (Protestant); and between them, tall metal gates and fences that are locked each evening to keep the murderous gangs apart. Before the barriers were put up, riots were frequent. Nellis showed me the New Lodge memorial: 'Seventy-five civilians have died here since 1969 . . . victims of UDA/British Army collusion . . . in the present phase of the struggle for Irish Freedom.' He took me into his tiny house, to his top-floor 'prayer room' with its kitschy statues and madonnas, and told me of his work: 'In 1980 I took to Holland a mixed group of forty, boys and girls, from New Lodge and Tiger Bay. It worked well. Even on the plane going out, Catholics and Protestants who had never met before began sitting together. With their Dutch hosts they stayed in pairs, one of each in a family. Eleven years later, I interviewed several of them, to ask what influence they felt the trip had made. Nearly all said it had changed them radically, they still spoke of it as the high point of their lives. It had led to several romances, plus two mixed marriages. One of these couples moved out of the area, for obvious reasons: not long ago, a Catholic living with a Protestant girl was shot dead here by the UVF. In 1991 I interviewed the New Lodge Group, but I didn't dare go into Tiger Bay, where there had just been two killings.' Nellis gave me the transcript of his New Lodge talks, of which these are extracts:

'In Holland we had the odd argument, stupid political ones to be honest with you, but we still were friends, the last night we had in Holland we were all crying and hugging each other . . .'
'Once you get outside Northern Ireland you leave the troubles behind. Me and Duncan, still to this day we're the best of mates. And for nearly a year after, I went out with Mandy from the

413

Bay.' 'It made you realize that Protestants aren't any different from Catholics. It was the only chance you can get to meet a different religion. I mean, you wouldn't walk up and down Duncairn Gardens and have a conversation with one of them . . .' And the return home: 'Once they hit Belfast and they started driving down and seeing the murals and the flags out again and the soldiers, and you went, Oh my God, here it goes again . . . it's back to normal.'

As Nellis emphasized, the lack of any 'neutral sanctuary' in Belfast, where they can meet regularly, is the biggest obstacle to the follow-up to these trips. Visiting each other's ghettos is awkward, even risky. The kids can meet downtown, but that is artificial. The trips abroad are splendid, but the money for them is limited, and they can reach only a small number. So what of the thousands of other teenagers in the deprived Belfast areas today? Nellis and his colleagues take groups of them on outings to the sea or mountains, or to nearby parks for picnics. It works best with the eleven-to-thirteen-year olds. 'With the older ones, if you take them abroad it's fine. But put them together for a day in the Belfast area, and they just attack each other. Yet I'm convinced that without our work, matters here would be worse.'

In other parts of the North, less fraught than the Belfast ghettos, a number of cross-community ventures for adults are integrated into daily life and work quite well. In rural Fermanagh, near the border, various mixed women's groups and welfare groups are active, and a new development association that has seven Catholics, five Protestants on its board. In Derry, Paddy Doherty has a kind of Don Camillo/Peppone rivalry with Glen Barr, a loyalist with a UDA political background who has now moved into community work and runs a training scheme and workshop involving Catholics and Protestants alike. Locally he is considered tough, arrogant and difficult, but is admired for his work. His is an unusual example of a Protestant taking the initiative for a local grass-roots cross-community scheme (Corrymeela is something different). In most other cases, it is Catholics who make the running, then try to involve the local Protestants, who prove reticent. And this is one of the North's great problems today – an aspect of the overall Protestant defensiveness in face of the onward march of the Catholics.

The reasons for this situation are complex. Many people would say that the Catholics, for so long the underdogs, have felt the need to club together, to take initiatives to improve their lot, and thus they see the benefit of community ventures; the Protestants, wealthier, more individualistic, have been less interested. Others suggest that Catholicism, more cohesive, church-centred and priest-led, is more conducive to community activity than Protestantism, more loose and diverse, and split up between several churches. This may be so, but curiously it is the opposite of the position in some countries; as I have often written apropos of France, the Catholic French are less clubby and community-self-help-minded than the Protestant English.

A third factor is the Anglo-Irish Agreement of 1985, which has added to Protestant fear and defensiveness. Some Protestants fear that the Catholics want to take control and are not sincere in seeking community partnership. This may be true of some republicans, but the majority of decent Catholics running the new ventures are genuine in wanting Protestants to take part, and are sorry when they do not. In Derry, Colm Kavanagh is a highly reconciliation-minded Catholic, married to the principal of the new integrated school (see p. 423). He runs a community project in a mixed part of the Waterside, and he told me: 'When I applied for an assistant, an excellent Protestant girl applied; but then she backed out when she found that ours was a Catholic-led organization. It is always hard to persuade Protestants to join us, so of course our project remains Catholic-led; that's a vicious circle. The Catholics here always want to innovate, the Protestants to keep things as they are. But I admit that sometimes we are tactless – and they perceive our Church as too authoritarian and expansionist. The Vatican's *Ne Temere* decree, obliging the children of mixed marriages to be brought up as Catholics, went down badly here with Protestants. Happily, today it is applied less rigidly and many priests turn a blind eye.'

This is close to the nub of the problem. As is so often said, loyalists in the North perceive Catholicism and popery as the enemy, whereas for the nationalists the enemy is not Protestantism but Britain and its Army. One professor of politics, from a Protestant background, gave me this astute analysis: 'Many loyalists tend to lump together the leftish atheist Sinn Féin and the pious churchgoing Catholics, stupidly confusing them as all "papists". Meanwhile the Catholics are propelled by the feeling that *they* have right on their side, in view of past injustices. At reconciliation discussions, there is often an onslaught of moral anger by Catholics, to which the Protestants simply have no reply. And yet, Protestant working-class people do not feel that *they* created these injustices: "No one ever told me that I was part of a privileged upper class," is a cry you hear from loyalist workers. Remember that the British settlement in Ireland was very different in North and South: the South was colonized mainly by the gentry, Ulster by the working class. These are the people today fighting to hold their ground – like the "poor whites" in colonial Rhodesia.' Or as an elderly loyalist labourer put it to me more pithily, 'As a boy on the Shankill Road, if I was a "first class citizen", I never knew it. I ran around with me arse out of me trousers, just like the bloody Taigs.'

These are the kind of loyalists who make up much of the rank-and-file of the so-called Orange Order (officially, the Loyal Orange Institution of Ireland), the mass movement whose influence remains one obstacle to a reasonable political compromise in the North. It dates from the 1790s, when it was created in Co. Armagh to help defend Protestant farmers against Catholic attackers. Dervla Murphy wrote in 1978 in *A Place Apart*, 'The Orange tradition is an uncouth mixture of ignorance, xenophobia, self-deception, suspicion, rabble-rousing, fear and aggression. Inevitably it produces a great deal of loutish behaviour, which its leaders seem unwilling or unable to correct. One example is the custom of calling a football "The Pope" and ritually kicking it around a field. Some outsiders find this funny but I am not amused. It is impossible to imagine, in the wildest corner of Ireland, groups of Catholic peasants having similar games with footballs named "Queen Elizabeth."' Murphy went on to pinpoint the anomaly of Orangeism being so fanatically devoted to Union with Britain yet so far removed from civilized, tolerant British values: 'An institution like the Orange Order is utterly foreign to the British way of life in the twentieth century – another Northern paradox, since the Orangeman is so deliriously proud of his Britishness.'

Her portrait, written in the mid-1970s, is today a shade too harsh. There is still plenty of extreme bigotry within Orange ranks, but the Institution itself is fairly respectable and serious. It is part of a worldwide Orange movement, with branches as far afield as Ghana and New Zealand, but only in Northern Ireland is it political, with loyalty to the Crown and the Union as its crucial tenet. It embraces all the Protestant churches (above all the Presbyterians), and its members must promise to promote the Protestant faith, hence no Catholic can join. With about 100,000 members, very few of them women, the Institution is organized on masonic lines, and is made up of some 1,350 separate lodges, grouped within a Grand Orange Lodge, under a Grand Master. But it claims to be 'less secretive than freemasonry, more like Rotary'. On top of its political and religious roles, it holds social and sporting events and does welfare work for its members – all very clannish. An Orangeman will generally choose a fellow-member as his doctor, solicitor or plumber. Most notoriously, the order organizes giant parades all over the North on 12 July, to celebrate the Battle of the Boyne victory over the Jacobites in 1690, and on 1 July, to mark the Battle of the Somme, 1916, when 5,000 Ulstermen died within twelve hours in defence of King and Empire. There are banners, bands and flags, and plenty of provocative anti-popery. Dervla Murphy tells the nice anecdote of an English visitor stumbling upon one parade, asking what was going on, and being told curtly, 'It's the Twailfth.' Yes, but what's it all about, he asked. 'Och away home and read your Bible, man!' he was told – as if such a great victory of 1690 was certain to be described in the Protestant Bible.

The raucous July parades give an ugly image of Orangeism and are much criticized. The rest of the year, the order keeps a low public profile. It used to be a high-level forum for the Protestant

Establishment: bishops, judges, professors and top industrialists would all belong and attend its meetings (the Earl of Enniskillen was one past Grand Master). Today, this intelligentsia has deserted the order, which is now more proletarian: but it remains influential, especially in rural areas. Many of its ordinary members are rough, ignorant bigots who represent the worst side of loyalism, and they can create a bad climate locally. But in its upper ranks the Loyal Institution itself is a responsible body, totally opposed to violence as a political weapon (unlike Sinn Féin), and I heard well of it from the gentle Church of Ireland Bishop of Derry, James Mehaffey: 'It is less of an evil influence than is said. If it weren't there, less desirable elements could take over the loyalist movement. It provides a peaceful focus for the Protestant community, and it firmly excludes the paramilitaries. But it is so opposed to ecumenicism that it does make our own work more difficult. That's its most negative side.'

Ecumenicism at the senior church level goes well, between Catholic and Church of Ireland leaders and some Presbyterians. The friendship of Bishops Mehaffey and Daly in Derry may be the star example. But the latter's namesake, Cardinal Cahal Daly, Primate of All Ireland, based in Armagh, is on warm terms with some Protestant leaders, including Dr John Dunlop, Moderator of the Presbyterian Church in 1993, who told me of the regular joint services that he holds with other clergy in his North Belfast middle-class parish – 'We go preaching in each other's churches.' And in South Belfast, Bishop Poyntz (C. of I.) spoke eagerly of the trip to the Taizé ecumenical centre in Burgundy that he organized in 1991 for thirty-three Protestants and thirty-three Catholics. All the Churches denounce violence, and they sometimes hold joint peace rallies and conferences.

All this is fine. But how far it percolates down to parish congregations is another matter. In the 1970s there was so much local hostility that clergy on friendly terms, visiting each other's homes or churches, felt the need to be furtive about it; some Protestant rectors or their children were even physically attacked or threatened by gangs of Orange youths. Today this has eased. The Vatican's move towards ecumenicism, ending the ban on

Catholics entering Protestant churches, has helped to produce a better climate; the only strong opposition now comes from a DUP/Orange fringe, and it is no longer violent. However, local ecumenical services and other meetings still tend to be poorly attended. Most parishioners remain indifferent, if not hostile; and many clergy still feel the need to be careful in promoting ecumenicism, for fear of alienating their congregations.

Of the main Protestant Churches, the Church of Ireland is strongest in the west and south of the province, and the Presbyterians in the north and east, notably in Antrim, opposite the Scottish coast; they are about equal in Belfast. These Presbyterians, mostly of Scottish origin, are far more rigorous and Calvinist in spirit than the more easygoing Anglicans of the Church of Ireland, often of English ancestry. And they tend to be much more wary of ecumenicism than either the Anglicans or Catholics; but this pattern can vary, for as in Scotland theirs is a very decentralized Church, where the ministers are elected by their congregations and the post of moderator rotates each year. 'The Presbyterians blow hot and cold,' said one Anglican bishop; 'one year, the moderator may be very open-minded, the next you might get a true bible-thumping evangelist who won't set foot in a Catholic church.' Ray Davey, who founded Corrymeela, and Donald Frazer, who worked closely with Father Myles Kavanagh, were both Presbyterians. But others can take the line, 'The differences between our Churches are fundamental, so ecumenicism is a dangerous illusion.'

As for the Reverend Ian Paisley, he is a different thing again. He has a Baptist background, and he founded his own Free Presbyterian Church in Belfast, which is unconnected with the older Presbyterians. 'Our relations with him are very conflictual,' Dr Dunlop told me; 'he constantly harasses us, tries to steal our members.' Paisley even walked out of the Orange Order too, in the 1970s, because he felt it was becoming too ecumenical! This bizarre fanatic still has plenty of political influence, as leader of the DUP. His religious influence is less, restricted to his own few thousand followers, some of whom attend his large, rather ugly modern church in South Belfast, the Martyrs Memorial, to hear his fire-breathing sermons. There I found plenty of elderly middle-class ladies in hats, plus some younger couples with puzzled-looking children. There was lots of singing of hymns with silly words, led by the Great Man up on the platform, booming away. His sermon itself was entirely unpolitical, all about sinners coming to God, old-fashioned Bible-bashing stuff. First had come a short political address, explaining why he had just walked out of the round-table talks with the Irish Government – 'I could not talk to those frightful foreigners, making wicked illegal claims to our territory,' and he promised to resist these claims 'in the cause of Jesus'. Even if there were no political context, one would still find his style and performance amazing, horrifying, with its brilliant but crazed oratory – the technique of alternate cries and whispers, the vehement hysterical voice shouting skywards at God as if expecting some immediate divine intervention.

To talk with, I found Paisley personally charming, and his views both distressing and predictable. I also met his daughter Rhonda, who shares his charm and, more or less, his political stance, but has, on many social and welfare matters, her own more liberal, compassionate outlook. She is an artist, and has also done excellent social work among deprived Belfast teenagers, Catholic as well as Protestant; until 1993 she was on the city council, as DUP spokesperson on women's issues. On abortion, she told me that she has an open mind, whereas her party and the Presbyterians are closer to the Catholic position. Because of this broad hostility, abortion has never been openly legalized as in Britain. But nor is it officially illegal, as in the Republic. It is in a grey area. Many women go off to Britain for abortions, as from Dublin; and a few doctors and hospitals in the North do discreetly perform the operation, though it is never talked about. 'The Government has quite enough other problems here,' said Ms Paisley, 'and it simply won't touch the issue of abortion reform until there's been an overall political settlement.'

The Catholic Church, as in the South, has been growing out of touch with many younger people on the moral issues: Cardinal Daly, though politically a liberal, is an orthodox conservative on these other matters. Moreover, as anywhere in Europe, parts of the working class and some of the middle class too, both Catholic and Protestant, are becoming dechristianized in their own lives. But this trend is masked by the political conflict, which helps to keep Ulster's churches full out of sectarian loyalty. According to one 1989 survey, weekly Church attendance among Catholics is 86 per cent, even higher than in the South (see p. 160); and among Protestants it is 44 per cent, much higher than in Britain. One Catholic priest, the radical Father Denis Faul, commented to me: 'Church influence may be waning here, but less than in the South. The Army in fact helps us. "Thank you for putting up road blocks near the churches," I said to them; "it makes people so angry that they go to Mass all the more."'

Many young people are agnostic, and the religious aspect of the conflict means little to them. Yet sectarian bigotry continues, as a blind rooted habit. Ventures such as Seán Nellis's Dutch trips, and Father Kavanagh's Trust, show that if only the young can be brought together, in the right environment, they can overcome their prejudices and get on well. But they have so few opportunities to meet as the housing segregation continues and nearly all schools remain segregated, too. One answer is to bring the Dutch trip experience into daily local life – and this can only be done through changes in education.

The hopeful pioneers of integrated schooling

When nearly all Protestant children go to one set of schools, and nearly all Catholics to another, it does not make bridging the North's gulf any easier. It is not so much that they are taught with great bias inside the classroom: most teachers today do a reasonably fair job, and are now obliged by law to follow a common curriculum. The problem is more that the children seldom meet those of the other community. Arguably this mattered less when housing was less segregated and they might at least play together in the streets and parks. But today this happens less. So the children imbibe their parents' prejudices, chant their anti-Taig or anti-Prod slogans, and get little chance of making friends across the divide. Hence the recent moves by some moderates, Government-backed, to open integrated schools or to start joint school activities. It cannot be a panacea for the North's problems. But as one mother in loyalist East Belfast said of her son's integrated school, 'It won't stop people killing each other today – but dear God, *our* own kids won't do that.'

The segregated schools are not the same for Catholics as for Protestants. In the 1930s the Unionists decided to go into the state system, so today nearly all Protestant children are at State schools operated by the Government. The Catholics have their own Church schools, many of them run by religious orders such as the Christian Brothers, as in the South. In the old days, these schools received poor public funding and complained of discrimination. Today they are fully paid for by the Government, like the State schools; yet the divide remains. I met a teacher in Catholic South Armagh, a lapsed Protestant with a lapsed Catholic wife, and he could get no job because there was no State school in the area and no Church school would employ him.

As with the somewhat similar new interdenominational schools in the South – but in the North they serve a sharper purpose – the initial move for integrated schools came from a few parents, wanting to offer an escape from sectarianism for their children. The first to be founded, in 1981, was Lagan College, east of Belfast; today it has 800 pupils, and a waiting-list. The Government at first was wary of the whole venture, but since 1990 it has swung wholeheartedly behind integrated schooling and now gives it priority funding. These are State schools, but ecumenical, with some simple religious education; the official guideline is that each should have a minimum of 40 per cent from each confession, alike among pupils and staff. Today there are twenty-one integrated schools, four secondary and the rest primary, with a total of some 4,000 pupils; but this is little more than 1 per cent of the school population. So the scheme is no runaway success; but it is growing quietly, with new schools opening each year. If parents have hesitated, it is less for sectarian or security reasons than educational ones, fearing to join an experiment that might not be as academically sound as the older one. But initial exam results have been good. Inevitably, most parents are middle-class: but the lower-income groups are now starting to show interest, too.

The Unionists have gone along with the new venture, but are not enthusiastic. As for the Catholic Church, it is openly hostile, but on religious, not sectarian grounds; as in the South, and indeed around the globe, it wants to retain full control over teaching of young Catholics in its own schools, where it can put across its own ethos and dogma. Although some bishops are now growing more flexible and will even visit the new schools, Cardinal Daly himself firmly lays down the line from Rome. The hierarchy even mounted a High Court action against the Government's support for integrated schools, but it failed. 'It is entirely wrong', one bishop told me, 'to make segregated education a scapegoat for the Troubles, as some people do; or to suggest that it's an obstacle to better community relations. We Catholics shall never give up our right to teach our spiritual message in our own schools. And anyway, Catholics are far more tolerant of Protestantism than vice versa.' I heard even sharper language from Father Faul, now a headmaster in Dungannon: 'You tell me these new schools could teach "common Christian values", but what are *they*? In an integrated school, that crucifix there on my wall wouldn't be allowed, nor that Irish cross, nor a statue of the Blessed Virgin. These to us are major things, and I don't believe in a lowest common denominator of religion.'

Yet much of the impetus for integrated schools has come from lay Catholics. In Derry, I visited a pair of such schools, one primary, one secondary, whose principals were both Catholic. In the primary school, Oakgrove, a class of six-year-olds in smart green jerseys were learning about 'Jesus, the sower'. 'We are a Christian ecumenical school,' said the principal; 'and our applicants are growing faster than we can cope with. Parents in socially segregated Derry clearly feel a need for us.' I talked to some parents, who said the school was becoming a forum for their own integration too, across the sectarian divide. One mother, not a

423

churchgoer, said she so hated sectarian schooling that she had educated her daughter herself, before Oakgrove opened. Then the little girl returned bewildered from this new school, saying, 'Mum, am I a Catholic or a Protestant?' The pupils are encouraged to talk openly about their different religions. One child, from a mixed marriage, with a Catholic mother, had said touchingly, 'Mummy, at my old State school I didn't dare talk about you, but here I talk about you all the time.'

Thus the old monoliths of sectarian education are slowly breaking down. A few schools are becoming semi-integrated spontaneously and unofficially, simply by accepting pupils from the other faith. Templemore, a State grammar school in Derry, is in what used to be a highly Protestant area. The Protestant families moved out across the river (see p. 379), and Catholic families moved in. So Catholics, despite some Church opposition, began to send their children to Templemore, which is now very mixed, an integrated school in all but name.

In middle-class South Belfast, one striking example is Methodist College, known by its nickname 'Methody', an illustrious grammar school founded in 1868 to train Methodist ministers but now entirely lay; private and partly fee-paying, it is regarded as one of the North's two best schools, and is also the largest, with 2,400 pupils. Until recently it was a preserve of the Protestant bourgeoisie, but today 20 per cent of its intake is Catholic. This is the new aspiring Catholic middle class of the Malone Road area, people who have done well from direct rule and are attracted to 'Methody' by its academic record – liberal or lapsed Catholics critical of their own system. And the pupils get on easily together – 'Most of them couldn't care less about the religious denominations of their friends,' said one teacher. Ian Paisley sent one of his sons to Methody, where the boy became firm friends with a nationalist. I spent an hour with a class of twelve lively sixth-formers, two of them Catholic – though in conversation it was not easy to spot the difference. Most of the Protestants said they felt British *and* Irish, which is not the usual loyalist line. One Catholic said, 'A united Ireland would be nice one day, but it's not yet realistic.'

Most of this class had already won places at good British

universities, including Cambridge. The teaching is excellent, yet the fees are very low, for Methody, like other non-State grammar schools, is heavily funded by a Government that pours money into education in the North. 'My children are getting an English-public-school-type education almost for free,' said one delighted parent, from London. But official largesse brings very uneven results, and it is often said that Northern Ireland has the best and worst education in the UK. The proportion of pupils passing A-levels is 20 per cent, compared with only 13 per cent in England, 10 per cent in Wales. But the proportion of children leaving school with no qualifications and poor literacy is also the UK's highest – a reflection of Ulster's basic problems.

The Government and the moderates have also been trying to fight sectarianism by introducing a common syllabus in schools, and by reducing bias in the teaching of history. In line with the recent reform in Britain which set up a 'national curriculum' for all State schools, Northern Ireland now has its own 'common curriculum', which since 1992 is compulsory in all State-aided schools, including the Catholic ones. All children up to sixteen must follow the same broad range of subjects. The new system incorporates a strategy developed in the mid-1980s called Education for Mutual Understanding (EMU, but not Maastricht's), whereby all subjects should be infused with 'the teaching of the value of cultural and religious diversity, and of appreciating other viewpoints'. One lovely example: a group of children was told, 'Now please retell the story of Little Red Riding Hood from the point of view of the wolf, stressing his sympathetic side.'

An important part of the new EMU is the teaching of Irish history. Here much is changing. It is sometimes supposed that until recently all Protestant pupils were given one version of history, all Catholics quite another; this was never really true, but certainly there were differences. The State schools taught just British and foreign history, including little bits of Irish history only when it was an integral part of Britain's own, e.g. Gladstone and Home Rule; teachers thought it inappropriate for their 'British' pupils to learn anything more. In the Catholic schools, many teachers supplied an emotive personal bias, but mostly they discouraged their pupils from taking Irish history options for A-levels, for they feared that their papers would be discriminated against by prejudiced examiners (Northern Ireland sits for the same O- and A-level boards as Britain, plus one of its own, which in those days was not always free from bias). So Irish history was little taught inside the classroom, at senior level. But outside it, children were fed with the potent popular myths, IRA or Orange, handed down orally or in crudely emotional little books that showed Cromwell or King Billy as either hero or villain. Kids thus grew up with, say, two very different pictures of the Battle of the Boyne.

After the Troubles began, attitudes among teachers and parents began to change, as David Harkness, professor of Irish history at Queen's, indicated to me: 'Moderate Unionists started to ask how this conflict had happened. They wanted a good solid objective picture of the past, and the feeling grew that if only both sides understood why they had then acted so badly, they might become more tolerant about the present.' Some excellent, fair-minded histories of the Ulster problem began to appear: J. C. Beckett had prepared the way with his *The Making of Modern Ireland* (1966), followed by A. T. Q. Stewart's *The Narrow Ground: The Roots of Conflict in Ulster* (1977) and now Jonathan Bardon's massive *History of Ulster* (1992); BBC Television, too, influenced the public with some powerful, objective programmes. Then in the 1980s this new stress on Ulster history was taken up by the Department of Education, in the context of EMU: today all schools are obliged to devote plenty of time to the subject, following the same syllabus. This seems to work fairly well, and serious classroom bias has declined. Professor Harkness spoke up for his profession: 'History teachers are professionals, they know how to separate objective historical truth from their personal political aspirations about the present. There is now just one way of teaching the Battle of the Boyne, which we put into its European context, often ignored till now. Many older Protestants just can't believe that King William had Papal backing.'

Under EMU, State and Catholic schools are encouraged to do

joint field projects: a mixed group might be set to study the impact of the Plantations in its area, or the Famine. 'The Catholic children', Jonathan Bardon told me, 'may discover with surprise that poor Protestants too were dying of starvation in their area.' The schools themselves tend to favour these projects, but inevitably there has been some opposition from parents and local politicians. Some parents, mostly rural loyalists, have objected to their children going off on mixed groups with Catholics; and at least one Unionist-led council passed a motion condemning this 'indoctrination'. The old sectarian myths of history, Orange or Republican, are still very much alive and will fade only slowly. 'People don't want their sustaining myths interfered with,' said Harkness; 'our job as historians is not to leave them out, but explain them.' And so, via history teaching as via integrated schooling, a new generation moves haltingly towards a better understanding.

Northern Ireland's universities consist of Queen's, Belfast, founded in 1845, and the much newer University of Ulster (1967), with campuses at Derry, Coleraine and Jordanstown (near Belfast). Higher education is not formally segregated as in the schools: but at Queen's in the old days the Protestant ethos dominated, and even a clever young Catholic might find it hard to gain admission. Since the 1970s, however, much has changed. First, the young Protestant middle class tends increasingly to go off to universities in Britain, where it can escape the tensions of the Troubles and probably find better career outlets. Far fewer Northern students today go to Trinity, Dublin (see p. 219), but some 40 per cent of them, i.e. a vast majority of the Protestant ones, now cross the water to 'the mainland', a ninefold increase since 1970. And their places on the North's own campuses are being taken by Catholics, of all social classes, now assertively aspiring to better careers. Whereas Catholic students used to be few at Queen's, they now make up over 50 per cent. Its teaching staff is still mostly Protestant, it is true, but that is partly because so many have come from Britain.

Queen's, near the centre of Belfast, has a handsome nucleus of 1840s 'Redbrick Tudor' buildings, typically British. Here groups of militant students have been tending to polarize the ambience – or so many teachers complain. The nationalists have won control of the Students' Union with its lively, messy premises, and have stuck up a slogan in Irish at the entrance, 'Fáilte go hAontas na Mac Léinn' – perfectly harmless, since all it means is 'Welcome to Queen's Students' Union'. But it is a symbolic gesture that annoys loyalist students. And the nationalists in turn are angry that the university still plays the National Anthem at its official ceremonies. A rare old dispute has been raging about all this.

Catholic and Protestant students at Queen's mix quite well superficially, but it seldom goes deep, and few serious friendships are made. 'Alas, our students seem to go through university unchanged in their relations with each other,' said one teacher of politics. This sectarianism is less acute in the science and arts faculties, where often there are love affairs and mixed marriages, but it can be quite marked in disciplines such as politics or sociology, perhaps inevitably. It is a very different picture from the gentler one at 'Methody', for several reasons. These students are older, more emancipated, more outspoken than the closeted and prudent pupils. And their backgrounds are often very different. While the élitist 'Methody' pupils may go on to Oxbridge or Edinburgh, Queen's has a sizeable intake of working-class students from nationalist areas.

A professor of politics introduced me to his seminar group, a rather solemn lot. None admitted to being Unionist, while several expressed bitterness against Britain and its Army. No one was hopeful of a solution. Their teacher said afterwards: 'They are just fed up with the situation. They have heard all the arguments so often, they take them for granted and think them hardly worthy of intellectual discussion. So I have an uphill task in my classes on Irish politics. I overheard one student say, "I was born and brought up on the Falls Road, so what can *he* teach me about Irish politics?" We on the staff do our best to teach an objective approach, and sometimes we succeed. But I must confess, I get fed up too. It is easier when we talk about Russian politics.'

At the three little colleges of the University of Ulster, life is more serene, less politicized. Of these, Magee College at Derry dates from the nineteenth century, those at Jordanstown and Coleraine from 1967. When in the mid-1960s the Stormont Government decided to create a new university, its initial plan was to build it at Coleraine, a loyalist town, and to phase out Magee. This was vehemently opposed by John Hume and other Derry leaders, who saw it as yet another act of discrimination by Stormont against the mainly Catholic region of Derry. Finally a compromise was reached and Magee was kept alive, but Coleraine has grown faster. Today both these colleges have large numbers of students from the Republic, who under EU rules have the same rights of entry as to the more overcrowded Irish universities. But although proud of being Irish they are not militantly nationalist. 'There is no sign of sectarian conflict here,' said a teacher on the tidy, spacious new campus at Coleraine, 'save for a few IRA graffiti in the toilets.' Coleraine even has a young Irish writer-in-residence, Cathal Ó Searcaigh from Donegal, who writes poetry in Irish – and he is teaching Irish to some of the Protestant students. In such a loyalist area, that would have been hard to imagine even twenty years ago. But the cultural scene in the North is changing, too.

Protestants learning Irish: towards a common Ulster culture?

The two communities are marked out by their culture, as well as by religion. The nationalists, or many of them, play Gaelic football or hurling, they sing Irish folk-songs, they are taught about Irish patriots such as Wolfe Tone, and a fair number of them speak Irish. The true loyalists reject all this. Yet, apart from the crude folklore of Orange marches, do they possess any distinctive culture of their own, as the Scots and Welsh so clearly do? Is there even some Ulster cultural identity, common to both sides? Do common roots exists, below the sectarian rift? These are questions in vogue today among Northern intellectuals, at debates and conferences where liberal speakers propose that Ulster's cultural diversity is an asset, and that the two communities must explore each other's cultures and seek out what they might have in common.

For the Catholics, the question of identity is simple. They feel Irish, sharing the richness of Irish culture with the people of the Republic. But where the Protestants belong is less evident. They claim to feel British, but then culturally Britain is so diverse. Some will even admit to feeling British within Ireland but Irish when they go abroad. Yet the vast majority of loyalists still define themselves as being, above all, *not* Irish, and they see Irish culture as no part of their own heritage. Until not long ago, everything Irish was firmly excluded from the Unionist-dominated Belfast cultural scene. Classical ballet and opera were presented, but never a concert of Irish music. And in the State schools no Irish literature was taught, not even Yeats. But today there are some signs of thaw. Just a few Protestants are beginning to learn Irish. And the Government has turned actively to supporting the Irish language and culture.

For the Catholics, their Irish language is one badge of their identity, as in the South. Over 20 per cent of them speak it well (9·5 per cent of the population, said the 1991 census). It is taught in many Catholic schools, even taken as a GCSE subject; there are also five all-Irish primary schools, like those in the Republic (see p. 293). Most Catholics would like to keep this trend purely cultural. However, in the past ten or fifteen years Sinn Féin has been seeking to exploit the Irish language and culture for its own political ends, as an arm of its republicanism: a Sinn Féin booklet, *Learning Irish*, even stated with extraordinary provocation, 'Every phrase you learn is a bullet in the armed struggle.' This was not exactly calculated to reduce loyalist suspicions of Irish, described dismissively by the Belfast DUP leader Sammy Wilson as 'leprechaun language'.

Other nationalists regret the Sinn Féin influence and are trying to promote their culture without political strings, and to involve Protestants in it. On the Falls Road in West Belfast, I visited the highly sympathetic Culturlann, an Irish cultural centre recently opened in a former Presbyterian church, of all places. It puts on plays, poetry readings, folk-songs, all in Irish; it teaches Irish music and dancing, and has an Irish bookshop. All the notices are in Irish. It also runs a modest radio station, and an Irish newspaper, *La* (Day). Some of the funding comes from the Arts Council and Stormont's community relations unit. Culturlann is admired for managing to stay out of politics, despite its Falls Road location: 'We distance ourselves from those who seek to make language a political issue,' one of the staff claimed to me. 'Irish culture should be for the whole community, and it's a pity that so many loyalists have this misconception, talking about "leprechaun language". Sinn Féin are partly to blame. Happily, a growing minority of Protestants now visit our plays and concerts – even here on the Falls Road!'

The change in official attitudes has been even more striking. The old Stormont was implacably hostile to Irish, and at one point tried to ban it from all schools. After 1972, the new regime at first did nothing; but since the development in the later 1980s of its new strategies for education and community relations, the Government has swung round to supporting Irish and now funds it to the tune of £1·2 million a year. In 1989 it played a part in setting up the Ultach Trust, which exists to promote the language and has a leading Unionist on its board. The head of Stormont's Community Relations Unit, Tony McCusker, told me: 'We wanted to find a way of supporting Irish that would not seem to Unionists as though we were backing militant republicanism. That's why we set up the trust – part of a move to pull the language out of a political context into a cultural one.' A pointer in this policy came in 1992 when the official ban on 'foreign' street-names was lifted, so a street can now bear dual names, English and Irish, as in the Republic. A citizen can even write letters to public offices in Irish, and will get an answer – but in English!

The BBC's attitudes to Irish culture underwent an equally remarkable change, somewhat sooner. Until the early 1970s the BBC in Northern Ireland reflected 'Britishness'; it was not so much biased towards loyalism as a voice of the London Establishment, and its locally made programmes had very little Irish content. After about 1973 this began to change, under a new Controller of the Belfast studios, the distinguished broadcaster Richard Francis. Arguing that the Catholic minority had a poor deal, he started to introduce Irish programmes. But of course there was local opposition. When a producer did a programme from Derry featuring a local choir singing in Irish, Unionist MPs protested in Parliament against 'this illegal broadcast in a foreign language' (a reference to a law dating from World War Two). And Tony McAuley, a senior BBC arts producer in Belfast, told me in 1993: 'In 1970 I was only the second local Catholic ever to be hired as a producer – I was in a tiny minority. Today the BBC staff is more evenly balanced, but I still get teased sometimes. I do regular programmes of Irish music, and a studio technician once put up a notice, "Taig-time with Tony" – a joke, but with serious overtones, as when people here speak derisively of "Fenian music", meaning all Irish music.' Today, as well as music and plays, the BBC has a daily radio programme in Irish, but not much on television. There are excellent, impartial documentaries on the North's problems (e.g. a recent series analysing the Fermanagh 'ethnic cleansing' issue). And there is regular live coverage of Gaelic games – to the indignation of some loyalists.

In fact, the North's cultural division spreads over into sport, and your religion can be noted by the games that you play. Rugby football, for instance, is almost exclusively a Protestant game in the North, but is also played widely in the South, by Catholics; as there is one all-Ireland team for rugby, it tends to be made up of Northern Protestants and Southern Catholics. Of the Gaelic games, hurling is not played much in the North, but Gaelic football is very popular (Co. Down won the Irish championship in 1992). Protestants do not play these games, and loyalist hatred of them can be such that Unionist-led councils have sometimes tried to prevent the GAA from getting land for its pitches. The GAA in turn has its own tough nationalist line (see p. 288): it will not allow Army or RUC personnel to attend its matches in uniform, nor to play in them. Soccer, widely played by both communities, is less controversial.

Sport is today seen as a means of promoting community relations: witness the twinning matches I attended. But although just a few local soccer teams are now mixed Catholic/Protestant, the vast majority are still either one or the other. And even soccer can present problems, as in the notorious case of Derry Football Club. In the early 1970s, during Derry's dark days, there were severe riots at some of its home matches, and Protestant teams from the North refused to go and play there. So Derry had no choice but to withdraw from the North's Irish League of football clubs. For some years it was in limbo, but finally it applied to join the Republic's League of Ireland and was accepted. So the club now plays just with the South.

As their insecurity about their long-term future grows, so the Protestants in the North are starting to look more closely at their traditions, and to ask who they really are and where they belong. It is a re-examining that began in intellectual circles and has now spread more widely. The Protestant settlers of the plantation period came mainly from Scotland, but also from England. And like many other colonizers, for example the South African Boers and the *pieds noirs* in Algeria, they did not bring very much culture with them; nor did they make any great efforts to develop one, being perhaps too busy with other, more practical matters. The Scots were puritanical Presbyterians, rather severe, upright and joyless, caring little for music, art or poetry, even refusing to have mirrors in their homes. So in the North it was the devil (as they saw it) who had all the best tunes – the Catholics, with their lively music and literature.

The loyalists of the north-east coast, around Belfast and in Co. Antrim, have always felt closely involved with south-west Scotland, which at one point is only thirteen miles away across the straits: Presbyterians even used to row across to worship in Scotland on Sundays. Dublin for them was another world. But even the Scottish settlers were a mixed bag. Some of them, curiously, were Catholics who had come over from a part of south-west Scotland never touched by the Reformation, and had settled in the beautiful Glens of Antrim, near the coast. Today the people of these glens are still solidly Catholic, but not nationalist – an intriguing example of the North's cultural complexity.

This complexity centres round the crucial question of *who* were Ulster's original inhabitants. The nationalists have always claimed that they, the Irish Gaels, were there first, while the Protestant planters were mere blow-ins from the seventeenth century; and this remains the basis of their case for a United Ireland. But it may not be so simple. Some historians today are restating the view that western Scotland was colonized in the fifth century AD by migrants from the ancient kingdom of Ulster, who brought their Gaelic language with them, and after this came endless toing and froing, of which the 'recent' Plantations were simply a final episode. A. T. Q. Stewart has written in his key book *The Narrow Ground*: 'The theory of a racial distinction between planter and "Gael", though it still dominates Irish thinking on the subject, can no longer be sustained ... We usually think of eastern Ulster as an extension of Scotland, but it is just as true that western Scotland was once an extension of the Ulster kingdom of Dalriada.'

These ideas are contested by some historians. But if they are true, they make the present conflict all the more absurd, or at least they shift its rationale. The argument can be used either way, to (a) undermine or (b) strengthen the loyalist position. Either it can show (a) that the Protestants have no reason to deny their Irishness, and in fact have some common identity with the nationalists; or else (b) that they are not blow-ins and have at least as much right as the Catholics to claim this as their original homeland. This is the argument exploited today by some loyalists, with the slogan, 'This ancient land is ours!' In East Belfast is a huge mural with a Union Jack and the words, 'Cuchulainn, ancient defender of Ulster from Irish attacks over 2,000 years ago' – a reference to the mythical Ulster hero who fought against the forces of Maeve, queen of Connaught.

Ulster's early history is in any case shrouded in myth and uncertainty, and it may not seem very relevant to today's problems. What is clear, as Stewart and others point out, is that there is no great difference racially between the two communities. As Stewart has written, when the settlers arrived after the Reformation, '... their religion was the barrier which cut them off from the native Irish and placed them permanently in a state of siege.

The gulf fixed between planter and Gael was the wider in that it resulted from the confrontation of extremes, of the Roman Church with the Calvinism of the Scottish lowlanders.' Today, the religious rift has softened, and the conflict has become more one of nationality, territory, and political power.

This leaves unresolved the question of whether Ulster culture today has any specific identity of its own, or consists of facets of Irish and British culture. A few Protestant intellectuals in Belfast, notably the lawyer David Trimble MP and the critic Edna Longley, are today asserting that there *is* an Ulster culture distinct from the Irish, and are harnessing the work of Ulster-born writers to build up the concept of an Ulster literary tradition. But this is not entirely convincing. Certainly Ulster has produced some notable writers, such as the Protestant-born poets Louis MacNeice and W. R. Rodgers, the novelist Brian Moore, and Catholics such as Brian Friel, Seamus Heaney and the critic Seamus Deane, with whom Edna Longley has clashed so sharply (see p. 254). But Ulster writers are so disparate, and so prone to emigrate, that it is hard to allow them any common identity; and the Catholic ones think of themselves as Irish. Belfast today does have quite a lively cultural scene, with plenty of art galleries, concerts, theatres, some good work by a breed of younger playwrights, and an excellent publishing firm, the Blackstaff Press. But it is hard to find a distinctively 'Ulster' flavour, in the way that Glasgow's vibrant scene asserts itself as unmistakably Scottish.

The other trend today is to stress the common Irishness of culture in the North – for example, in popular music, where the two traditions are interwoven. Many old melodies have two sets of words, one Irish, one English, indicating their common origins: there is a song about the Battle of the Boyne with both Orange and nationalist versions, while the North's best-known tune, 'The Londonderry Air', also has both English and Irish words. Some of the best performers of Irish music are in fact Northern Protestants. And a few Protestants are now beginning to accept that Irish music belongs to them too. This is part of a wider new trend, whereby a minority of Protestants are now ceasing to reject Irish culture out of hand. A few little groups of them, in Belfast and some rural areas, are starting to learn Irish. Newry council's Irish-language officer is a Protestant; and at one council meeting a Unionist stated that his great-grandfather had been an Irish speaker – unthinkable twenty years ago. These are straws in the wind of a clearly discernible change.

The best-known advocate of this movement is the poet Michael Longley. He has a different approach from his wife Edna, who is more Unionist. Longley, a charming, gentle, humorous man, is a Protestant born in Belfast of English parents; and he is one of the first Northern Protestant intellectuals to have become concerned with reconciling the two cultures. 'Although I am English in origin, I feel Irish,' he told me. 'But at school here thirty years ago, I was taught no Irish literature, art or music, and we sang English songs. Ulster's cultural apartheid is abnormal, and damaging to both communities. The trouble is that, while the Catholics have all Irish culture to fall back on, the Unionists have little culture of their own – and they tend to feel stranded, for they are not really British either. Happily, just a few of them are now at last turning to Irish culture as part of their own heritage. And if the Troubles are to be solved, it is important for Protestants and Catholics to make common cause in exploring their joint culture, which must be *Irish*.'

The future: 'Lord, make Ireland united, but not yet'

'Lord, give me chastity, but not yet,' wrote St Augustine, and that is how a great many Northern Catholics feel today about a United Ireland: 'Give us unity, but not yet.' Some 40 per cent of them, according to the surveys, want to remain under British rule, at least for the time being. It is a view shared even by the well-known radical priest Father Denis Faul (whom I quoted earlier), although he is a republican and in some ways sharply anti-British. 'I'm in touch with fellow-republicans,' he said, 'and none of us want the border removed just yet. Under direct rule, housing and education for Catholics have improved hugely; we now get better and freer welfare services and education than in the Republic. We have no allegiance whatever to the Queen, but we want to stay where the money is – and we consider that the British owe us this money, after the centuries they spent robbing and oppressing us! I hate the continuing job discrimination, and I loathe the Army's behaviour here. But I don't want the British to leave just yet: we need more time first for reconciliation. And things *are* improving here, slowly. The middle ground is getting stronger – that is the great reason for hope.'

Many others would say that the situation is improving in some ways, getting worse in others. The segregation continues, the violence and the political stalemate, too. But probably Father Faul is right to say that the middle ground is gaining. In schools, in town halls and in workplaces, there are more and more initiatives to heal the divide; and the younger generations especially have been growing less sectarian, more impatient with the absurdities of the conflict. But the politicians lag behind, failing to build on this mood and to make the compromises needed for a settlement. And the terrorist violence remains a demoralizing anxiety. Not only have loyalists recently stepped up their random killings, but the IRA have taken to massive bomb attacks in the downtown areas of Protestant towns; their strategy, it seems, is to provoke a loyalist backlash which could prompt a wearied British Government to start a withdrawal. For this is the paradox: while the IRA want the British out at all costs, many of their fellow-nationalists have other priorities.

The British Government receives endless criticism for its internal role in Northern Ireland, much of it unfair. In sum, its security record has been patchy, its social and economic record rather good, since 1972. The Army and RUC have at least prevented the violence from escalating out of hand, but their tactless brutalities have brought the IRA added support, thus spoiling their own policy of trying to isolate the terrorists from their population. Yet in other respects, direct rule has been beneficial. It has wiped out most of the injustices of the old Stormont regime, and has helped the Catholics towards greater equality, if not enough in terms of employment. Since the mid-1980s the Government has put its weight behind practical schemes for integration and community relations, which have begun to bear some fruit. And its economic support has prevented the Troubles from plunging the province into disaster. Several former ministers, and I would single out Richard Needham, under-secretary of state in 1985–90, are remembered warmly by both communities. One nationalist summed up for me what is quite a common view: 'Just as the British stand condemned by history for their past colonial record in Ireland, so history will show that, since 1972, they have done something here to make amends.'

Many decent people around the world persist in seeing this as a colonial problem. But today this is nonsense. Britain is no longer in the North for its own interests. The old strategic imperative, whereby Britain felt that it needed to stay in Ireland to guard its own back door, has steadily waned and is now dead. The economic interest has vanished too, for whereas the North's heavy industry and landed estates were once of value to Britain, today they are a liability. If Britain today remains in charge of the North, it is much more from a sense of duty. It imposed direct rule in part to help the Catholics (as well as to keep the peace), and now it feels some residual obligation to the harassed Protestants. It does not want to be seen to be giving in to terrorism; and above all it fears that a rapid withdrawal could lead to much worse violence. 'If the British pulled out fast, there'd be massacre,' John Hume, that moderate nationalist, said to me, 'so they must wait at least for a political agreement. But they would like to leave, if the conditions were right.' A Conservative Government would happily be rid of a problem that is expensive, invidious, and wasteful of British soldiers' lives; and a Labour Government would be even more impatient to withdraw. As for British public opinion, it is heartily fed up with the North, and many people even favour negotiating a settlement with the IRA. Politically this remains difficult. So for the time being Britain remains saddled with a situation that, after all, it has learned to live with.

SDLP and Unionists alike regard it as important to reach some settlement on the North's constitutional future that could end the

anomaly of direct rule and restore some kind of real local government, probably based on power-sharing. This could help towards
ending the violence; and it might be useless to wait first for the
violence itself to diminish. In 1991–2 the British Government
organized a series of round-table talks with all the main political
parties (except Sinn Féin) and the Republic's Government. That
the talks took place at all was an achievement, for it was the first
time that nationalists and Unionists had sat down face to face to
discuss their future; and it had not been easy to persuade Ian
Paisley to parley with Dublin politicians. But predictably the talks
then foundered on the refusal of either side to make real concessions
– 'The trouble with the North', said one exasperated observer, 'is
that it has no tradition of practical negotiation and compromise.
Politicians don't know how to do it, they just harangue each
other.' The Irish side refused to modify Articles 2 and 3 of the
Irish Constitution (see below), always a major stumbling-block;
and the Unionists rejected the kind of power-sharing proposed by
the SDLP.

Many nationalists would have liked Sinn Féin to be included in
the talks, but the Government understandably held this to be
unthinkable unless the party first renounced violence. Today the
Sinn Féin leadership is believed to be split on this issue. Its
moderates consider that an IRA cease-fire could open the way for
a negotiated British withdrawal, so political pressure might now
be the best strategy. But the hard-liners argue that the IRA's
violence is still bringing political dividends, for it weakens British
resolve.

Of the several possible scenarios for Northern Ireland's political
future, three might in theory find some favour on the loyalist side:
(1) *Full integration into the United Kingdom, as with Scotland and
Wales.* This would please many loyalists, but would be unaccept-
able to most British and Irish opinion and is not a serious option.
(2) *Full sovereign independence from both Ireland and Britain.* This is
not a realistic option either, for even within an EU confederal
framework it would make little sense either economically or
politically. Some loyalists promote the idea – illogically, for it is
the negation of 'unionism'. (3) *The option of devolution.* The North

would remain within the United Kingdom, but with its own elected assembly and government, i.e. a kind of return to the pre-1972 Stormont days, but with fairer power-sharing and different institutions. This would be the choice of most Protestants. In fact, in 1993 the Unionist parties were pressing London to grant an immediate degree of devolution, at least as an interim phase, for they were chafing under the 'colonization' of direct rule; they wanted greater powers restored to local councils. John Major's Government was in some ways sympathetic, but did not want to alienate Dublin.

The nationalists, and most Irish in the Republic too, reject devolution within the UK as a final solution, but might accept some form of it as a transitional arrangement. They have their sights set on the ultimate goal of a United Ireland, but the SDLP knows that this can be achieved only gradually. A great many Catholics realize, as Father Faul said, that in economic terms they are better off staying within the UK, for the time being. Vincent Currie, the SDLP leader in Dungannon, spelt it out further: 'If we are in no hurry for unity, it is not just for economic reasons. We are ready to wait some years, for the situation here to settle down, for terrorism to end, for the South to evolve too, bringing in divorce and improving its economy, so that finally the Protestants here will have less fear of joining the Republic, and the Irish in the South will be less fearful of having to absorb these tough loyalists.'

For the longer term, the SDLP and Irish politicians have been putting forward various ideas. Some of them were formulated by Dick Spring after he became foreign minister early in 1993. He made a good impression on Unionists as someone who understood their anxieties and would try to help, but they doubted how far he could persuade the tougher men of Fianna Fáil to accept his own moderate stance. One of the suggestions put forward by him and others was for a measure of Anglo-Irish shared sovereignty in the North (some British Labour leaders favour this, too); or else for EU involvement in a kind of confederation, linking Belfast, Dublin and London with Brussels. Earlier, in 1991, Charles Haughey when Taioseach had declared: 'It is in the context of the new European union that we will find a solution. In effect the people of Ireland will be united in a united Europe . . . We are the new Unionists!' Since then, the waning of the Maastricht Utopia has somewhat dimmed this vision, and there are many today who see a Euro-federal solution for the North as a mere liberal pipedream. But the '1992' single market is operating, removing cross-border trade barriers; and I have even met Unionists who believe that European economic union will inevitably help to shape Ireland's future, bringing North and South closer to the point where old issues of sovereignty lose much of their meaning.

Down in the South, views on the Northern problem have been evolving. The Republic no longer sees itself as in conflict with Britain over Ulster's future, as it did twenty years ago. Since then, the two Governments' interests have grown steadily closer; and today, though they may not see eye to eye on all points, they feel a sense of partnership in facing an issue that is thorny and hazardous for both of them. This new mutual trust was born of the Anglo-Irish Agreement of 1985, which alarmed and angered the Protestants but has pleased Dublin, for London now formally recognizes its right to be involved in British policy-making for the North. However, though the Republic is eager to be consulted, its attitudes towards Irish unity are just as ambivalent as those of Northern Catholics – and this applies alike to politicians and to public opinion. Here again, it is a question of 'Lord, make us united but not yet', plus a reluctance to get too embroiled in the drama of the North so long as the violence persists.

On the one hand, a majority of older conservative voters in the South still subscribe to the ideal of a free and united Ireland for which the patriots fought and died. It all goes back to the civil war, once again. Parading their hatred of partition, these worthies make up a sizeable part of the Fianna Fáil vote, especially in rural areas, so the Haughey and Reynolds Governments have felt the need to take account of this. Hence their wariness about modifying the crucial Articles 2 and 3 in the 1937 Constitution, which assert Dublin's right to rule the whole of Ireland and commit it to seeking 'the reintegration of the national territory'. Speaking in the Dáil in 1993, Reynolds even drew a parallel with the old West

German Constitution's pre-1989 claim to sovereignty over the former East Germany – but the Taoiseach studiously overlooked the fact that over 75 per cent of East Germans did then vote for unification in 1990, which would hardly be the figure in Northern Ireland. So his parallel was false. And loyalists are infuriated by the 'presumptuous' claims in Articles 2 and 3, which are clearly an obstacle to a settlement: when Mary Robinson visits Belfast and Derry, DUP leaders there have refused to meet her, because she is 'the president of a foreign country making illegal claims to our territory'. Maybe they do have a point. Yet the irony is that Mary Robinson herself is one of a growing number of Irish Catholic leaders – Cardinal Daly, Des O'Malley and Dick Spring are others – who want to see Articles 2 and 3 modified. They would like the ideal of unity to become merely an aspiration, to be achieved only by majority consent. Fianna Fáil and the SDLP agree that the Articles could be changed, but only as part of a wider final settlement.

Fianna Fáil and its voters may pay tribute to the ideal of Irish unity. Yet in practice few Dublin politicians would welcome having to take charge of a province still racked by violence and extremism. In fact, Irish Governments have built up a certain aversion to the North and its problems, and privately they are glad to be able to leave Britain to take the main responsibility. That is the central paradox, which again reflects public opinion. In border areas such as Donegal and Cavan there may be a good deal of North/South contact, as I have shown; but viewed from Cork or Limerick the North seems a far-off, almost alien place, and Dubliners go far more often to London than to Belfast. Southerners do not seek out the North for their holidays; and if the Dublin–Belfast main road remains so antiquated along its southern stretch, it is because it does not get used much and is thus a low priority. Southerners may feel a vague empathy with Northern Catholics, and a sense of shame at the violence in their island, but the ignorance and sense of lassitude about the North's real problems are almost as great as in Britain. People are worried, but they avoid talking about it, so I found.

An opinion poll for the *Irish Times* in 1993 produced some interesting results. Of those questioned, 82 per cent felt that Irish unity was 'something to hope for', but an equal 82 per cent were prepared to postpone this unity 'if it helped bring about an internal settlement in the North': in other words, they tacitly veered closer to the official British line than to Sinn Féin's. However, 58 per cent wanted Articles 2 and 3 kept and only 25 per cent wished them to go. Yet when asked, 'When will Ireland be united?', only 20 per cent thought it would be within the next ten years, and 21 per cent within the next twenty-five years, while 30 per cent answered, 'Never'. These replies seemed another classic example of the Irish desire to retain their old ideals without having to apply them too strictly in practice. Realism, or hypocrisy?

In October 1993 John Hume announced that he had been holding talks with Gerry Adams of Sinn Féin; and he indicated that a 'war-weary' IRA might be ready to accept a cease-fire, so long as Sinn Féin were then to be included in the talks on a political future. As if to disprove him, the IRA promptly let off a bomb in the Shankill Road of Protestant West Belfast, killing ten; and the loyalists replied with an attack on a pub near Derry, killing eight. It was evident that Sinn Féin and the IRA were as divided as ever between hawks and doves, and few of the IRA hard-liners backed the Adams peace moves. But public feeling in both islands ran very high after these killings; it was revealed that the British Government too had been holding secret talks with the IRA; and the impetus of this chain of events led prime ministers Major and Reynolds to issue a joint declaration in December, outlining a compromise in their positions on Irish unity.

The statement notably contained the sentence: 'The British Government agrees that it is for the people of the island of Ireland alone, by agreement between the two parts respectively, to exercise their right of self-determination on the basis of consent, freely and concurrently given, North and South, to bring about a united Ireland, if that is their wish.' For the first time, London was now publicly recognizing that Irish unity was a possible goal, and that the people of all Ireland had the right to decide on it. This alarmed the loyalists, even though the statement also made it clear that majority consent in *each* part of Ireland would be needed – i.e. the

Unionists could still veto Irish unity if they chose, so long as they remained the larger community in the North.

For some months, Sinn Féin/IRA prevaricated in their response to the joint declaration, and the violence continued, including a mortar attack on Heathrow Airport in March 1994. Some critics, notably the ever-abrasive Conor Cruise O'Brien, argued that the IRA had no real interest in peace at present, and London and Dublin were simply falling into their trap in trying to 'appease' and woo them into a cease-fire. Britain, however, went ahead with its peace feelers. It insisted that the IRA must first lay down its arms: but if it did so, then Sinn Féin would be invited to play its part in negotiating a solution for the North, and its proposals would be taken seriously.

As this book went to press in June 1994, it seemed clear that much depended on the great debate going on within Sinn Féin and the IRA: could the more moderate voices, led by Adams, convince the hard-line gunmen that the time had come to drop the armed struggle and turn instead to politics? It was by no means certain: yet despite all the delays, prospects for a cease-fire were still looking brighter than for some years. The problem remained, however, of including the loyalists in any such deal. For the future, too, if the Catholic social advance continues, and if political talks seem to be veering away from unionism, there will remain the serious danger of a sudden, bloody, loyalist explosion.

Since the Troubles began in 1969, this has been an absurd conflict for Western Europe in the late twentieth century, an archaic hangover from an earlier age. Yet it has proved to be liveable with, and in terms of violence and lives lost it has been a tiny conflict compared with several others in the world today, even within Europe (i.e. Bosnia). If a political settlement can be reached between the two Governments and the main parties, including Sinn Féin, in the shorter term it could well involve some kind of devolution within the United Kingdom, maybe confederal, with joint sovereignty. But for the longer term the logic is surely towards a united Ireland. If the violence ends and Britain begins to pull out and reduce its special aid, then the nationalists in the North would be likely to drop their Augustinian disdain for unity.

And if the South continues to evolve towards a more pluralist and secular society, with the introduction of divorce, then Protestant fears of being subsumed into a 'papist' State will also wane. This process has already begun.

Far from being pushed out, as happened to Protestants in the South after 1921, the one million of them in the North might find themselves in positions of some dominance within a united Ireland – 'They'll be running *us*, and why not? We could do with their energy,' was the comment of one Dublin cabinet minister. Then finally the North would begin to make its due impact on the easygoing South.

The Irish Republic has changed hugely in the past forty years. It has moved into Europe, done much to broaden and modernize its economy and society, and chosen a radical President who stands as flag-bearer of the new order. The transformation is far from complete ('We are in an exciting state of flux,' says Dermot Bolger): the political system, though democratic, still awaits a proper overhaul, and the Irish psyche has still not quite healed its bruises from the long centuries of colonial injustice. Many Irish are still unsure how to adapt their old cherished values to a modern world, without losing something that is precious and Irish; and often they seem to be still too self-preoccupied with their own uniqueness. They look down on the North, with some reason, as politically archaic, locked in a tribal past. Yet, paradoxically, it is the North that has much of the zest and creativity.

The Irish are a great people, with special talents: but in today's Europe they can no longer afford the luxury and hubris of regarding themselves as somehow unique. The ending of the last absurdity from the past, partition, could allow all Irish together to work on becoming at last a normal, uncomplexed European nation. Or will the wayward demons of the Irish spirit make this never quite possible?

BIBLIOGRAPHY

POLITICS, GENERAL

Bruce Arnold, *What Kind of Country? – Modern Irish Politics, 1968–83*, London, Cape, 1984.

Bruce Arnold, *Haughey: His Life and Unlucky Deeds*, HarperCollins, 1993.

Dermot Bolger (ed.), *Letters from the New Island*, Dublin, Raven Arts Press, 1991.

Richard Breen, Damian F. Hannan, David B. Rottman, Christopher T. Whelan, *Understanding Contemporary Ireland*, Dublin, Gill, 1990.

Noel Browne, *Against the Tide*, Dublin, Gill & Macmillan, 1986.

Tim Pat Coogan, *Disillusioned Decades: Ireland 1966–87*, Dublin, Gill & Macmillan, 1987.

Department of Foreign Affairs, *Facts about Ireland*, Dublin, DFA, 1985.

Garret FitzGerald, *All in a Life, an Autobiography*, London, Macmillan, 1991.

Gemma Hussey, *Ireland Today: Anatomy of a Changing State*, Dublin, Town House and Country House, 1993/London, Viking, 1994.

Joe Joyce and Peter Murtach, *The Boss: Charles J. Haughey in Government*, Dublin, Poolbeg Press, 1983.

Richard Kearney (ed.), *Across the Frontiers: Ireland in the 1990s*, Dublin, Wolfhound Press, 1988.

Thomas Keneally, *Ireland and the Irish*, London, Ryan, 1991.

Conor Cruise O'Brien, *States of Ireland*, London, 1972.

Seán O'Faoláin, *The Irish*, Harmondsworth, Penguin, 1969.

Fintan O'Toole, *A Mass for Jesse James: A Journey through 1980s Ireland*, Dublin, Raven Arts Press, 1990.

Anne Simpson, *Blooming Dublin*, Edinburgh, Mainstream, 1991.

Colm Tóibín, *The Trial of the Generals*, Dublin, Raven Arts Press, 1990.

John Waters, *Jiving at the Crossroads*, Belfast, Blackstaff Press, 1991.

Bibliography

HISTORY

Terence Brown, *Ireland: A Social and Cultural History, 1922–85*, London, Fontana, 1985.

T. P. Coogan, *De Valera*, London, Hutchinson, 1993.

Liam de Paor, *The People of Ireland: From Prehistoric to Modern Times*, London, Hutchinson, 1986.

Roy Foster, *Modern Ireland, 1600–1972*, Harmondsworth, Penguin, 1989.

Robert Kee, *The Green Flag*, London, Weidenfeld & Nicolson, 1972; Harmondsworth, Penguin, 1989.

Robert Kee, *The Laurel and the Ivy*, London, Hamish Hamilton, 1993.

Joseph Lee, *Ireland, 1912–85, Politics and Society*, Cambridge University Press, 1989.

Patrick Loughrey (ed.), *The People of Ireland*, Belfast, Appletree Press, Belfast, 1988.

F. S. L. Lyons, *Ireland since the Famine*, 1971.

Cecil Woodham-Smith, *The Great Hunger: Ireland 1845–49*, London, Hamish Hamilton, London, 1962; Harmondsworth, Penguin, 1991.

ECONOMY, AGRICULTURE, DUBLIN, REGIONS, SOCIETY

Mark Bence-Jones, *Twilight of the Ascendancy*, London, Constable, 1987.

Dermot Bolger (ed.), *Invisible Dublin*, Dublin, Raven Arts Press, 1991.

Hugh Brody, *Inishkillane: Change and Decline in the West of Ireland*, London, Allen Lane, 1973.

Raymond Crotty, *Farming Collapse: National Opportunity*, Dublin, Amarach-Ireland, 1990.

John Healy, *The Death of an Irish Town: No One Shouted STOP!*, Achill, House of Healy, 1988.

Frank McDonald, *The Destruction of Dublin*, Dublin, Gill & Macmillan, 1985.

Frank McDonald, *Saving the City: How to Halt the Destruction of Dublin*, Dublin, Tomar, 1989.

John McKenna and Sally McKenna, *The Bridgestone Irish Food Guide*, Dublin, Estragon Press, 1991.

Ann Morrow, *Picnic in a Foreign Land: The Eccentric Lives of the Anglo-Irish*, London, Grafton Books, 1990.

Andrew Sanger, *Exploring Rural Ireland*, London, Helm, 1989.

Paul Tansey, *Making the Irish Labour Market Work*, Dublin, Gill & Macmillan, 1991.

Bibliography

LITERATURE, CULTURE AND TRADITIONS (WORKS OF FICTION NOT LISTED)

Gay Byrne, *The Time of My Life: An Autobiography*, Dublin, Gill & Macmillan, 1989.

Seamus Deane (ed.), *The Field Day Anthology of Irish Literature*, London, Faber & Faber, 1991.

Reginald Hindley, *Death of the Irish Language*, London, Routledge.

Herbert A. Kenny, *Literary Dublin, A History*, Dublin, Gill & Macmillan, 1991.

Edna Longley (ed.), *Culture in Ireland: Division or Diversity?*, Belfast, Institute of Irish Studies, 1991.

Ferdia Mac Anna, *Bald Head*, Dublin, Raven Arts Press, 1988.

Nuala O'Connor, *Bringing It All Back Home*, London, BBC Books, 1991.

Brian Ó Cuiv (ed.), *A View of the Irish Language*, Dublin, Stationery Office, 1969.

IRELAND AND THE WORLD

Heinrich Böll, *Irisches Tagebuch*, Cologne, Kiepenheuer & Witsch, 1961.

Dermot Keogh, *Ireland and Europe, 1919–89: A Diplomatic and Political History*, Cork and Dublin, Hibernian University Press, 1990.

Dermot Keogh (ed.), *Ireland and the Challenge of European Integration*, Cork and Dublin, Hibernian University Press, 1989.

National Economic and Social Council (ed.), *The Economic and Social Implications of Emigration*, Dublin, NESC, 1991.

National Economic and Social Council, *Ireland in the European Community*, NESC, 1989.

Patrick O'Farrell, *The Irish in Australia*, New South Wales University Press, NSW, 1987.

Roger Swift and Sheridan Gilley (eds.), *The Irish in Britain, 1815–1939*, London, Pinter, 1989.

NORTHERN IRELAND

Paul Arthur and Keith Jeffrey, *Northern Ireland since 1968*, Oxford, Basil Blackwell, 1988.

Jonathan Bardon, *A History of Ulster*, Belfast, Blackstaff Press, 1993.

Steve Bruce, *The Red Hand: Protestant Paramilitaries in Northern Ireland*, Oxford University Press, 1992.

Gerry Conlon, *Proved Innocent*, London, Hamish Hamilton, 1990.

T. P. Coogan, *The IRA*, London, HarperCollins, 1971, 1993.

Roy Foster and others, *Varieties of Irishness*, Belfast, Institute of Irish Studies, 1989.

Bibliography

Carlo Gebler, *The Glass Curtain: Inside an Ulster Community*, London, Hamish Hamilton/Abacus, 1991.

Eamonn McCann, *Bloody Sunday in Derry*, Dingle, Brandon, 1992.

Dervla Murphy, *A Place Apart*, London, John Murray, 1978; Harmondsworth, Penguin, 1979.

Tony Parker, *May the Lord in His Mercy be Kind to Belfast*, London, Cape, 1993.

Con Short, *The Crossmaglen GAA Story*, Crossmaglen, Raonaithe na Croise, 1987.

A. T. Q. Stewart, *The Narrow Ground: The Roots of Conflict in Ulster*, London, Faber & Faber, 1977, 1989.

Peter Stringer and Gillian Robinson (eds.), *Social Attitudes in Northern Ireland*, Belfast, Blackstaff Press, 1992.

Colm Tóibín, *Walking Along the Border*, London, Macdonald, 1987.

ACKNOWLEDGEMENTS

Hundreds of people gave up their time to help me with my field research. They are too many to be mentioned all by name. But first I want to thank some individuals and organizations that were especially helpful: Conor Brady and his colleagues on the *Irish Times*, notably the staff of its library; Ambassador Joseph Small and his colleagues at the Irish Embassy in London; John Lahiffe and his colleagues at Bord Fáilte; Professor Joseph Lee, Professor John Coolahan, Ruth Dudley-Edwards, Ronald Long and Breandan Ó Caollai, who read some draft chapters and made useful comments. Cahal and Patsy O'Shannon, Brendan Halligan, Maeve Lynch, Gerry Watson, Myrtle and Ivan Allen, Richard Wood, Tom Barrington, Constance Short and Richard and Susan Lynn were all most kind and hospitable.

Amongst others, my special thanks go to the following (for brevity's sake, I do not give titles – except for bishops and a few others):

In Dublin:
Politics and general: Mary Robinson, Garret FitzGerald, Albert Reynolds, Desmond O'Malley, Bertie Ahern, Mary O'Rourke, Máire Geoghegan-Quinn, Mary Harney, Gemma Hussey, Alan Dukes, Bride Rosney, P. J. Mara, Martin Mansergh, Bart Cronin, Conor O'Riordan, Michael FitzGerald, Jeremy Thorp, T. K. Whitaker, Brian Farrell, Tom Garvin, Brendan Walsh, Richard Kearney, Terence Brown, Tim Pat Coogan, Bruce Arnold, Dick Walsh, Tom McGurk, Maureen Cairnduff.

Dublin planning, environment: Frank McDonald, Carmencita Hederman, Deirdre Kelly, Sam Stephenson, Lewis Clohessy, Maurice Craig, Anngret and David Simms. *Economy and industry*: Michael Smurfit, Michael Tutty, Tom Rochford, Gerard O'Flynn, John FitzGerald, Paul Tansey. *Tourist development*: Matt McNulty, Tim Magennis, John Tunney. *Agriculture*: Joe Walsh, Tom Arnold, Jarlath Coleman, Con Lucey, the late Raymond Crotty. *Education*: Thomas Mitchell, Trevor West, Stella Mew, Hugh Clifford, Tim Macey, Pat Collings, Christine Murphy.

The Churches: Tom Stack, Bishop Desmond Williams, Jim Cantwell, Seán

Acknowledgements

Healy, Liam Ryan, Desmond Forrestal, Peter McVerry. *Moral issues, women's rights, social issues, lifestyles*: David Norris, Moira Woods, Carmel Foley, Frances FitzGerald, Sylvia Meehan, Mary Maher, Damian Hannan, Gerard O'Neill, Jack Jones, Sally and John McKenna, Elsie O'Donoghue, Ann Fitzpatrick.

Literature, arts, media: John Banville, Dermot Bolger, Ferdia Mac Anna, Roddy Doyle, Val Mulkerns, Brendan Kennelly, Séamus Deane, Lar Cassidy, Michael Colgan, Gary Hynes, Peter Sheridan, Neil Jordan, Jim Sheridan, Gay Byrne, Joe Mulholland, Bob Collins, Seán Mac Réamoinn, Kenneth Churchill.

Irish music, language and traditions: Labhras and Una Ó Murchú, Paddy Moloney, Paul McGuinness, Dermot McLoughlin, Proinsias Mac Aonghusa, Nuala Ní Dhomhnaill.

Near Dublin: Desmond Guinness, Kieran and Vivienne Guinness, Vincent Poklewski-Koziell, Garech Browne, Paddy and Jane Falloon, Brenda and Tommy O'Brien.

Waterford and the south-east: Bishop Brendan Comiskey, Julian Walton, T. V. Honan, Sheila Fitzgerald, Pat Nolan.

Cork and the south-west: Peter and Esther Langley, Peter Finke, Bishop Michael Murphy, John Murphy, Barry Murphy, Eileen Keane, Pat Dineen, Gerry Wrixon, Barry Condron, Piaras Mac Einri, Angela Ryan, Martin Fitzgerald.

Limerick and county: Bishop Jeremiah Newman, Jim Kemmy, Edward Walsh, Noel Mulcahy, Desmond Fitz-Gerald, Knight of Glin, and his wife Olda, Frances and Seamus O'Donnell, Margaret and Tom Kearney.

Clare and Shannon: Colman Garrihy, Nandi O'Sullivan, Harry Bohan, Michael Neylon, Michael Lee, Liam and Maureen Meehan.

Galway and county: Archbishop Joseph Cassidy, former bishop Éamonn Casey, Michael D. Higgins, Colm Ó hEocha, Gearoid Ó Tuathaigh, Peader Mac an Oimaire, Emer Colleran, Leila Doolan, Macliosa Stafford, Carmel Reynolds, Jim Doolan, Mary Bennett, Tom Hyland, Donal Ó Donoghue, Bob Quinn, Martine Goggins, Padraig Ó Healai, Joe Ó Cuig, John and Anne Darbe, Paddy and Theresa Coleman.

Mayo: Aubrey Bourke, Susan Kellett, Myles Staunton, Seán Smith, Seán Clarke, Denis Michael, John Higgins, Dominic Greally, Michael and Eithne Viney, Peter and Jane Mantle, Peter and Hildegard Peltz.

Sligo area: Sandy and Deb Perceval, Seamus Monaghan, Wendy Lyons, the Keohane family.

Leitrim, Cavan, Monaghan, Louth: John McGahern, Patrick Gallagher, Dick Hinchy, the McGowan family of Dromahair, Frank and Eileen McGuinness, Raymond Maguire, Phyllis and Maeve MacAdam, Michael Cropp, John Madden, Eugene McCabe, Dermot Ahern.

Northern Ireland:
Janet McIver and Anne Moore, of the Northern Ireland Tourist Board, were

especially helpful; so were Irene Orr of Stormont, and Mick Cox and Fiona Stephen.

Belfast: Joe Hendron, Mark Durkin, Cecil Walker, Ian Paisley, Rhonda Paisley, Sammy Wilson, George Patton, Tony McCusker, Derek Black, John Ledlie, Sir Kenneth Bloomfield, Maurice Hayes, John McGuckian, Robert Cooper, Graham Gudgin, Charles Brett.

Paul and Margaret Arthur, Paul Bew, David Harkness, Jonathan Bardon, David Gallagher, Adrian Guelke, Myles Kavanagh, Seán Nellis, Matt Wallace, Desmond Wilson, Bishop Samuel Poyntz, John Dunlop, Jackie Redpath, Edna and Michael Longley, David Hammond, Robert McLiam Wilson, Tony McAuley, Austin Hunter, Martin Cowley.

Derry: John Hume, Paddy Doherty, Will Hay, Gregory Campbell, Glen Barr, Tony Crowe, John Keanie, Mitchell McLaughlin, Bishop James Mehaffey, Bishop Francis Lagan, Jennifer Johnston, David Gilliland, Joe Cowan, Jim Foster, Colm Cavanagh, Anne Murray, Andy McCarter.

Co. Londonderry and Co. Tyrone: Lord Moyola, Denis Faul, Vincent Currie, Jim Hamilton, Jim Canning, Donald Frazer. *Co. Fermanagh*: Seán Quinn, Raymond Ferguson, Aideen McGinley, Eddie McGovern, Anita Gallagher, Ethne O'Connor, Joan Trimble. *Co. Armagh*: Harry Tipping, Patricia and Steve Smith, Jim McAllister.

In England:
Gerald Clark, George Huxley, Marigold Johnson, Tony Duff, Thomas Pakenham, Seán Hutton, Des Balmer, Kenelm Digby-Jones, Sir Alan Goodison, Sir Robert Chichester-Clark, the Marchioness of Dufferin and Ava, William Trevor, Edna O'Brien, Shane and Anne Connaughton, Patricia Kerr, Sheila Clifford, the late Bob Forster, the late Finn O'Shannon, Máire Nic Suibhne, Seamus McCormack, Tom Beisty, Bobby Gilmore, Paul Murray, Colin Wrafter, Brendan McMahon, Patrick Lennon, Alan Percival, Graham Archer, Chris Laming.

Lastly, my thanks go to my publishers, to Andrew Franklin and his colleagues at Hamish Hamilton, and to Peter Carson at Penguin Books; and to my wife Katinka, who was endlessly patient, wise and encouraging.

INDEX

Principal references are in **bold** type. Some minor references are not indexed, especially of non-Irish people and places. Book, play and film references are mostly not indexed: see under name of author or director. Many general themes are indexed – e.g. 'unemployment', 'divorce' – but not always when the subject's location is evident from the Contents list on pp. vii–ix (e.g. agriculture, literature).

Index

310; in NI, 352, 353, 355, 373, 401
Unionists in NI, 23, 57, 59, 345–445
passim, notably 351, 387, 399, 400,
407, 412, 422, 426, 431, 432, 438–9,
440, 441, 443
united Ireland, goal of, 424, 436, **440–
44**
United Nations, 305, 340, 341, 343
United States, 59, 100, 143, 343, 403;
Irish emigrants in, 278, 279, 284,
305, 306, 307–8, **317–19**; US
investment, **74–5**, 145; in NI, 354,
403; and GATT, 103; *see also*
Anglo–US cultural threat
universities, 216–17, **217–21**, 333; in
NI, 427–9
University College, Cork, 136,
217, 218, 220, 280, 294, **333**
University College, Dublin, 33, 61,
217, **219–20**, 294, 309
University College, Galway, 140,
217, 218, 220, 294, 302
University of Limerick, 217, **220**, 294,
332
University of Ulster, 427, 428–9
U2 rock group, 11, 183, 235, **285–6**

VAT, 34, 66, 389
Vatican, 12, 55, 157, 158, 162, 169,
176, 177, 179, 418; Vatican Council
Two, 172, 211
vegetables, 110–12, 224
Vernon, Máire, 194
Virgin Megastore, 183

Walker, Cecil, 377
Walsh, Dick, 274
Walsh, Professor Edward, 139, 220,
294–5, 309

Walsh, Jo, 101
Walton, Julian, 320
Waterford city, 90, 135, **137**, 232, 281;
Red Kettle theatre, 261; Waterford,
Co., xii, 320; Waterford Crystal,
77, 137
Waters, John, 36, 62
Welsh language, 290, 303
Western European Union, 343
Westmeath, Co., 322
West of Ireland, 2, 52, 76, 90, 98,
102–3, **104–20**, **141–8**, 215, 260,
295–8
Wexford, Co., 197
Wexford town, 149, 260; opera
festival, 263
Whelehan, Harry, 190
Whitaker, Kenneth, 31, 52, **70**, 92
Whitelaw, William, 349
Wicklow, Co., 45, 150; Wicklow
mountains, 114, 151, 154, 324
Wilde Oscar, 186, 218, 235, 249
William of Orange, 21, 426
Williams, Bishop Desmond, 185, 233,
234
Williams, Tennessee, 239
Wilson, Fr Desmond, 378
Wilson, Robert McLiam, 253
Wilson, Sammy, 355, 430
Wogan, Terry, 314
women, position of, 5, 59, **204–6**; *see
also* marriage
Woodham-Smith, Cecil, 22, 23, 307
Workers' Party, 43; in NI, 358
World Cup (football), 287, 288
World War Two, **30**, 312, 343, 432

Yeats, W. B., 25, 149, 176, 177, 257,
325, 430; influence today, 250; and
Gaelic revival, 23, 235, 241, 258